The Southern
Junior League Cookbook

THE PARTICIPATING JUNIOR LEAGUES INCLUDE:

The Junior League of Atlanta, Georgia
The Junior League of Charleston, South Carolina
The Junior League of Charleston, West Virginia
The Junior League of Charlotte, North Carolina
The Junior League of Corpus Christi, Texas
The Junior League of Dallas, Texas
The Junior League of Durham, North Carolina
The Junior League of El Paso, Texas
The Junior League of Gainesville, Florida
The Junior League of Greenville, South Carolina
The Junior League of High Point, North Carolina
The Junior League of Huntsville, Alabama
The Junior League of Jackson, Mississippi
The Junior League of Lafayette, Louisiana
The Junior League of Greater Lakeland, Florida
The Junior League of Little Rock, Arkansas
The Junior League of Memphis, Tennessee
The Junior League of Mobile, Alabama
The Junior League of Nashville, Tennessee
The Junior League of Odessa, Texas
The Junior League of Pine Bluff, Arkansas
The Junior League of Roanoke Valley, Virginia
The Junior League of Shreveport, Louisiana
The Junior League of Spartanburg, South Carolina
The Junior League of Tampa, Florida
The Junior League of Tyler, Texas
The Junior League of Wichita Falls, Texas
The Junior League of Wilmington, North Carolina
The Junior League of Winston-Salem, North Carolina

Illustrations by Lauren Jarrett

The Southern Junior League Cookbook

· · · · · · · · · · · · · · · · · · · ·

Edited by Ann Seranne

· · · · · · · · · · · · · · · · · · · ·

BALLANTINE BOOKS · NEW YORK

Published in the United States by
Ballantine Books, a division of Random House, Inc., New York,
and simultaneously in Canada by Random House of Canada,
Limited, Toronto, Canada.

Library of Congress Catalog Card Number: 77-4370
ISBN 0-345-33899-5
This edition published by arrangement with David McKay
Company, Inc.

Designed by The Etheredges

Manufactured in the United States of America

First Ballantine Books Edition: April 1981

10 9 8 7 6

. . . .

Preface

. . . .

The purpose of the Junior League is exclusively educational and charitable and is to promote voluntarism; to develop the potential of its members for voluntary participation in community affairs; and to demonstrate the effectiveness of trained volunteers.

Proceeds from the sale of Junior League cookbooks go into the Community Trust Funds, which finance the League's community programs.

To find out how to obtain a particular Junior League's own book of recipes, turn to pages 601–607.

. . . .

Contents

. . . .

Metric Equivalent Chart

LENGTH

1 inch (in)	=	2.5 centimeters (cm)
1 foot (ft)	=	30 centimeters (cm)
1 millimeter (mm)	=	.04 inches (in)
1 centimeter (cm)	=	.4 inches (in)
1 meter (m)	=	3.3 feet (ft)

MASS WEIGHT

1 ounce (oz)	=	28 grams (g)
1 pound (lb)	=	450 grams (g)
1 gram (g)	=	.035 ounces (oz)
1 kilogram (kg) or 1000 g	=	2.2 pounds (lbs)

LIQUID VOLUME

1 fluid ounce (fl. oz)	=	30 milliliters (ml)
1 fluid cup (c)	=	240 milliliters (ml)
1 pint (pt)	=	470 milliliters (ml)
1 quart (qt)	=	950 milliliters (ml)
1 gallon (gal)	=	3.8 liters (l)
1 milliliter (ml)	=	.03 fluid ounces (fl. oz)
1 liter (l) or 1000 ml	=	2.1 fluid pints or 1.06 fluid quarts
1 liter (l)	=	.26 gallons (gal)

Appetizers

Benne (Sesame) Seed "Cocktailers"

This is the original benne seed biscuit which the *New York Times* has called "a cocktail biscuit that should revolutionize cocktail parties."

2 cups unsifted flour
1 teaspoon salt
Dash cayenne
¾ cup shortening or margarine
Ice water
1 cup roasted sesame seeds
Additional salt

Mix flour, 1 teaspoon salt, and cayenne; cut in shortening; add enough ice water (about ¼ cup) to make a dough the consistency of pie crust; add seeds which have been roasted in shallow pan at 350° for about 20 minutes. Roll thin, cut into small round wafers.

Place in biscuit pan and cook in slow oven (about 300°) for 20 or 30 minutes. Before removing from pan and while hot, sprinkle with additional salt.

These may be kept in a covered tin or cracker jar and, before serving, put into a slow oven to crisp.

YIELD: SEVERAL DOZEN

Charleston Receipts
THE JUNIOR LEAGUE OF CHARLESTON, SOUTH CAROLINA

. . . .

Audrey's Cheese Straws

1 stick butter
2 cups sifted flour
½ teaspoon red pepper
1 teaspoon salt
1 pound New York State Cheddar cheese, shredded

Cream butter well. Sift dry ingredients together, add to butter, then add cheese. Press through cookie press onto greased tin and bake at 400° for 10 minutes.

The dough may be rolled on floured board and cut in strips for cheese straws, or rolled out in round thin biscuits with a nut in center of each one.

YIELD: 36 STRAWS

The Memphis Cook Book
THE JUNIOR LEAGUE OF MEMPHIS, TENNESSEE

Sesame Cheese Biscuits

¼ cup soft butter or margarine
¼ pound sharp cheddar cheese, shredded
(or 1 cup club cheddar, crumbled)
½ cup unsifted flour
½ teaspoon salt
Dash cayenne
Lightly toasted sesame seeds

Combine all ingredients except sesame seeds and shape into rolls approximately 1½ inches in diameter. Slice ⅜ inch thick and drop in sesame seeds. Bake at 375° for 12–15 minutes on cookie sheet.

Dough may be prepared ahead and wrapped and frozen. Delightful with cocktails.

YIELD: 24–30 BISCUITS

Winston-Salem's Heritage of Hospitality
THE JUNIOR LEAGUE OF WINSTON-SALEM, NORTH CAROLINA

Parmesan Sticks

1 loaf salt-rising bread
1 pound butter
8 ounces grated Parmesan cheese
Paprika

Remove crusts and cut bread into strips.

Melt butter, a stick at a time, in small saucepan. Soak bread sticks in butter, roll in Parmesan cheese, and place on cookie sheet. Sprinkle sticks with paprika.

Bake about 10 minutes at 400° until toasted.

YIELD: 10 SERVINGS

Little Rock Cooks
THE JUNIOR LEAGUE OF LITTLE ROCK, ARKANSAS

. . . .

Hot Peanuts

3–4 tablespoons crushed red pepper
3 tablespoons olive oil
4 cloves garlic
1 12-ounce can cocktail peanuts
1 12-ounce can Spanish peanuts
1 teaspoon salt
1 teaspoon chili powder

Heat red pepper in oil for 1 minute. Crush garlic and add to oil. Add peanuts. Cook over medium heat for 5 minutes. Remove from heat; add salt and chili powder.

Drain on paper towels.

YIELD: 1½ POUNDS

Southern Accent
THE JUNIOR LEAGUE OF PINE BLUFF, ARKANSAS

. . . .

Curried Olives

1 9-ounce can ripe olives
½ teaspoon curry powder
1 teaspoon Worcestershire sauce

Pour liquid from olives into saucepan. Add seasonings and boil. Pour over olives.

Refrigerate for 24 hours or more before serving.

YIELD: 4–6 SERVINGS

Fun Foods
THE JUNIOR LEAGUE OF GREATER LAKELAND, FLORIDA

· ·

Belle Fontaine Crab Dip

2 3-ounce packages cream cheese
1 very small onion, grated fine
Few dashes Worcestershire sauce
1–2 dashes Louisiana hot sauce
Salt and pepper to taste
4 tablespoons mayonnaise
1 pound crabmeat

Mix cream cheese and seasonings. Add crabmeat.

Serve as hors d'oeuvres or in stuffed tomato.

YIELD: ABOUT 3 CUPS

Recipe Jubilee
THE JUNIOR LEAGUE OF MOBILE, ALABAMA

· ·

Curry Dip

1 cup mayonnaise, plus
½ cup sour cream if desired
3 tablespoons catsup
3 teaspoons curry powder
1 tablespoon Worcestershire sauce
1 teaspoon onion juice
Salt, pepper, and garlic

Mix first six ingredients until well blended. Add salt, pepper, and crushed garlic in small amounts (about ½ teaspoon each) until properly seasoned for your taste.

This is wonderful with shrimp. Put small bowl of dip in center of large bowl filled with cracked ice. Place shrimp, raw cauliflower, celery, carrots, and green and ripe olives on surface of ice.

YIELD: APPROXIMATELY 1½ CUPS

That Something Special
THE JUNIOR LEAGUE OF DURHAM, NORTH CAROLINA

. . . .

Guacamole

1 medium tomato, peeled
2 ripe avocados, peeled
3 tablespoons finely chopped canned green chili peppers
½ cup finely chopped onion
1½ teaspoons white vinegar
1 teaspoon salt
½ teaspoon pepper

Mash tomato, then add sliced avocados and crush with tomato until well blended.

Add peppers, onion, vinegar, salt, and pepper. Mix well, refrigerate, and serve on lettuce leaf.

YIELD: 4 SERVINGS

Fun Foods
THE JUNIOR LEAGUE OF GREATER LAKELAND, FLORIDA

. . . .

Oriental Dip

½ cup minced green onions
½ teaspoon ground coriander
¼ cup chopped parsley
2 tablespoons chopped ginger root
1 tablespoon soy sauce
2 tablespoons minced canned water chestnuts
1 cup sour cream
2 tablespoons mayonnaise

Blend all ingredients, chill, and use as a dip for bite-size pieces of raw mushrooms, cauliflower, carrots, and other vegetables.

YIELD: ABOUT 2 CUPS

Fun Foods
THE JUNIOR LEAGUE OF GREATER LAKELAND, FLORIDA

. . . .

Miss Katie's Shrimp Dip

2 tablespoons lemon juice
2 tablespoons onion juice
2 tablespoons horseradish
1 teaspoon Worcestershire sauce
1 teaspoon hot sauce
½ cup catsup
½ cup chili sauce
1 cup sour cream
2 cups cooked shrimp, cut into small pieces

Mix ingredients until blended. Chill until ready to serve.

YIELD: 12 SERVINGS

Seafood Sorcery
THE JUNIOR LEAGUE OF WILMINGTON, NORTH CAROLINA

· · · · · · · · · · · · · · · ·

Cocktail Shrimp Spread or Dip

1 8-ounce package cream cheese
Juice of 1 lemon
1 small onion, grated
1 stalk celery, finely chopped
½ cup mayonnaise
¼ cup catsup
Salt to taste
1 pound cooked shrimp, broken into bits

Mash cream cheese well with lemon juice; add onion, celery, mayonnaise, catsup, and salt and blend well.

Add shrimp. Let stand about 1 hour. Serve with crackers.

YIELD: 25 SERVINGS

Seafood Sorcery
THE JUNIOR LEAGUE OF WILMINGTON, NORTH CAROLINA

Chili con Queso

2 tablespoons butter
2 tablespoons flour
1 cup light cream or evaporated milk
1 1-pound can Italian-style tomatoes, chopped fine
½ teaspoon finely chopped garlic
½ teaspoon salt
1 4-ounce can green chilies, drained and chopped
½ pound Monterey Jack cheese, shredded

Melt butter in heavy medium-size pan over moderate heat.

Add flour and mix well, stirring constantly with wire whisk.

Pour cream in slow stream and cook, stirring, until sauce comes to a boil, thickens heavily, and is smooth. Reduce heat to low and simmer 2–3 minutes. Set aside.

Combine tomatoes, garlic, and salt in heavy skillet, stirring frequently. Cook briskly, uncovered, until mixture thickens. Reduce heat and stir in cream sauce and chilies. (Try hot green chilies if you really like this dish spicy. But handle chilies carefully. They can cause burns to skin and eyes.) Without letting mixture boil, stir in cheese a handful at a time.

Serve with corn chips or tortilla chips.

YIELD: ABOUT 1 QUART

Fun Foods
THE JUNIOR LEAGUE OF GREATER LAKELAND, FLORIDA

Watercress Dip

6 ounces cream cheese
4 tablespoons milk
½ teaspoon grated onion
½ pound bacon, fried and crumbled
½ cup chopped watercress

Blend ingredients. Refrigerate until ready to serve.

YIELD: 2½ CUPS

Huntsville Heritage Cookbook
THE JUNIOR LEAGUE OF HUNTSVILLE, ALABAMA

· · · · · · · · · · · · · · · · · · ·

Hot Artichoke Spread

1 14-ounce can artichoke hearts, drained and chopped
1 cup mayonnaise
1 cup grated Parmesan cheese
Garlic powder to taste

Mix all ingredients and put into ramekin. Heat at 350° for 20 minutes or until mixture bubbles.

Serve with crackers for spreading or for dipping.

YIELD: 6 SERVINGS

Southern Accent
THE JUNIOR LEAGUE OF PINE BLUFF, ARKANSAS

· · · · · · · · · · · · · · · · · · ·

Clam–Cream Cheese Dip

1 7½-ounce can minced clams, drained
1 tablespoon lemon juice
1 teaspoon Worcestershire sauce
⅛ teaspoon pepper
1 tablespoon mayonnaise
½ tablespoon chopped parsley
¼ teaspoon prepared mustard
½ tablespoon chopped chives or onions
1 8-ounce package cream cheese, softened

Mix all ingredients with softened cream cheese. Heat through before serving. Good with club crackers or potato chips. May be served cold, but delicious hot.

YIELD: 6–8 SERVINGS

Mountain Measures
THE JUNIOR LEAGUE OF CHARLESTON, WEST VIRGINIA

. . . .

Crabmeat Dip

1 8-ounce package cream cheese
1 stick butter
1 pound white crabmeat
1 small onion, finely chopped
Dash Tabasco
Dash minced garlic
Red pepper

In a double boiler, melt the cream cheese and butter. Add crabmeat and seasonings.

Serve in a chafing dish with corn chips or crackers, or in small patty shells.

Recipe continues . . .

This is quick and very good.

YIELD: ABOUT 3 CUPS

Talk About Good!
THE JUNIOR LEAGUE OF LAFAYETTE, LOUISIANA

Crab Mornay

1 stick butter
1 bunch green onions, chopped with some tops
Small amount dry parsley flakes
2 tablespoons flour
1 pint light cream
½ pound Swiss cheese, shredded
1 pound crabmeat
1 tablespoon sherry
Dash salt
Red pepper

Melt butter in heavy pan. Add onions and parsley, then blend in flour. Stir in cream slowly to make cream sauce. Add cheese.

After cheese has melted, add crabmeat and sherry with salt and red pepper to taste.

Serve in chafing dish with Melba toast or crackers.

YIELD: 20 SERVINGS

Fun Foods
THE JUNIOR LEAGUE OF GREATER LAKELAND, FLORIDA

Spinach Crabmeat Dip

1 10-ounce package frozen chopped spinach
1 bunch green onions and tops, chopped
4 tablespoons butter
2 7-ounce cans crabmeat
⅓ cup grated Parmesan cheese

Cook spinach and drain. Sauté green onions in butter.

Mix all ingredients together, heat, and serve in chafing dish with crackers or large corn chips.

YIELD: 15 SERVINGS

VARIATION:

Omit 1 can crabmeat and add another package spinach, another bunch green onions, 2 tablespoons butter, Tabasco, and garlic powder.

Little Rock Cooks
THE JUNIOR LEAGUE OF LITTLE ROCK, ARKANSAS

. . . .

Piccalilli

2½ pounds ground round
1 pound lean ground pork
3 large onions, chopped fine
5–6 cloves garlic, chopped fine
5–6 extra large ripe tomatoes, skinned and diced
1 5-ounce package almonds, chopped
1 cup seedless raisins
1 small jar jalapeño peppers, diced
3 teaspoons oregano
Salt to taste
Cracked pepper to taste
½ cup flour

Recipe continues . . .

Cook meat until brown.

Sauté onions with meat but do not let them brown. Add garlic, tomatoes, almonds, raisins, jalapeño peppers, oregano, salt, and pepper. Simmer until tomatoes are done.

Sprinkle with flour and stir until thick enough to dip. Do not use any water.

Serve hot in a chafing dish and dip with corn chips.

YIELD: ABOUT 1 QUART

Of Pots and Pipkins
THE JUNIOR LEAGUE OF ROANOKE VALLEY, VIRGINIA

Prairie Fire

1 1-pound can ranch-style beans, sieved
½ tablespoon butter or margarine
⅓ pound sharp cheddar cheese, shredded
2 jalapeño peppers, chopped, with a little juice
1 medium onion, grated fine
1 clove garlic, grated

Heat all ingredients in double boiler until cheese is melted.

Serve in a chafing dish with tray of taco-flavored corn chips.

YIELD: ABOUT 2 CUPS

Fun Foods
THE JUNIOR LEAGUE OF GREATER LAKELAND, FLORIDA

Beer Puffs

1 cup beer
¼ pound butter
1 cup sifted flour
½ teaspoon salt
4 eggs
1 7-ounce can crabmeat

Bring beer and butter to boil. When butter melts, add flour and salt all at once. Cook over low heat, stirring until mixture leaves sides of pan.

Remove from heat; beat in 1 egg at a time until dough is shiny.

Drop by teaspoonfuls 1 inch apart on buttered baking sheet. Bake 10 minutes at 450°. Reduce to 350°; bake 10 minutes longer, until browned and free from moisture.

Cool, split, and fill with crabmeat or other desired filling.

YIELD: 60–80 SMALL PUFFS

Huntsville Heritage Cookbook
THE JUNIOR LEAGUE OF HUNTSVILLE, ALABAMA

Cheese Ball Pick-Me-Ups

1 8-ounce package cream cheese
1 4-ounce package blue cheese
1 5-ounce jar Old English cheddar cheese
1 6-ounce roll smoked cheese
1 teaspoon monosodium glutamate
1 clove garlic, crushed
1 tablespoon Worcestershire sauce
⅛ teaspoon Tabasco
1 cup parsley, finely snipped
1 cup pecans, finely chopped
Pretzel sticks

Recipe continues . . .

Have cheeses at room temperature. Blend well with monosodium glutamate, garlic, and sauces.

Add ⅓ cup parsley and ½ cup chopped pecans; blend.

Chill cheese mixture until it is easy to handle.

Mix remaining parsley and nuts together.

Form cheese into tiny balls about 1 inch in diameter and roll in reserved parsley-nut mixture. Refrigerate.

Cheese balls will keep for several days.

Insert a pretzel stick in each cheese ball just before serving.

YIELD: 7½ DOZEN

Fun Foods
THE JUNIOR LEAGUE OF GREATER LAKELAND, FLORIDA

. . . .

Marinated Mushrooms

2 cups button mushrooms
Water
Salt
2 tablespoons lemon juice
1 cup white vinegar
½ cup olive oil
2 cloves garlic, crushed
Pinch thyme
Few coriander seeds
Few leaves fennel
1 bay leaf

Cover mushrooms with water; add salt and lemon juice. Bring to boil for 2–3 minutes. Drain mushrooms.

Combine rest of ingredients for marinade and boil 8–10 minutes. Pour over mushrooms. Let stand in jar in refrigerator at least 12 hours.

Serve with picks for snacks or for a party.
These mushrooms will keep in refrigerator for a month.

YIELD: 6 SERVINGS

That Something Special
THE JUNIOR LEAGUE OF DURHAM, NORTH CAROLINA

· · · · · · · · · · · · ·

Cheese-Stuffed Mushrooms

¼ pound Roquefort cheese
1 3-ounce package cream cheese, softened
2 tablespoons butter, softened
1 tablespoon grated onion
1 teaspoon Worcestershire sauce
36 medium-size fresh mushroom caps
(remove stems and save for other use)
Parsley or paprika for garnish

Cream cheeses and butter until smooth. Stir in onion and Worcestershire.
Pipe cheese into mushroom caps with pastry bag fitted with large star tube
or mound with spoon. Garnish with parsley or paprika.

If you don't like raw mushroom taste, poach mushrooms in boiling
lemon water for 5 minutes. Drain and chill before stuffing.

YIELD: 36 APPETIZERS

Fun Foods
THE JUNIOR LEAGUE OF GREATER LAKELAND, FLORIDA

· · · · · · · · · · · · ·

Pickled Okra

2 pounds tender, small, fresh okra
5 pods hot red or green pepper
5 cloves garlic, peeled
1 quart white vinegar
½ cup water
6 tablespoons salt
1 tablespoon celery seed or mustard seed

Wash okra and pack in 5 hot, sterilized pint jars. Put 1 pepper pod and 1 garlic clove in each jar. Bring remaining ingredients to boil. Pour over okra and seal. Let stand 8 weeks before using.

Serve chilled, with cocktail picks, as appetizer.

NOTE: If pepper pods are not available, use ¼ teaspoon crushed, dried, hot red pepper for each jar.

YIELD: 5 PINTS

Fun Foods
THE JUNIOR LEAGUE OF GREATER LAKELAND, FLORIDA

. . . .

Cocktail Tomatoes

½ pound crabmeat
½ cup finely diced celery
¼ cup grated onion
Salt and pepper to taste
Mayonnaise
40 cherry tomatoes
Parsley for garnish

Thoroughly mix crabmeat, celery, onion, salt, and pepper. Add enough mayonnaise to make mixture a thick paste.

Wash and cap tomatoes. Cut out inside of each tomato, leaving a shell, and fill with mixture. Arrange on tray and garnish with parsley.

Using a cake decorator makes filling the tomatoes easier.

YIELD: 40 APPETIZERS

Fun Foods
THE JUNIOR LEAGUE OF GREATER LAKELAND, FLORIDA

Marinated Shrimp

2½ pounds raw cleaned shrimp
3½ teaspoons salt
½ cup celery tops
¼ cup pickling spice
7 or 8 bay leaves
¾ cup white vinegar
2½ teaspoons celery seed
1¼ cups salad oil
1½ teaspoons salt
2½ tablespoons capers and juice
Dash Tabasco
1 pint sliced sweet onions

Cook shrimp in boiling water with 3½ teaspoons salt, celery tops, pickling spice, and bay leaves for 8–10 minutes. Peel and devein.

Mix together remaining ingredients except onions. Add shrimp and onions. Refrigerate for 24 hours.

YIELD: 10 SERVINGS

Spartanburg Secrets II
THE JUNIOR LEAGUE OF SPARTANBURG, SOUTH CAROLINA

Salami Roll-Ups

1 2½–3-inch slice liverwurst
1 8-ounce package cream cheese
1–2 tablespoons catsup
2–3 shakes Worcestershire sauce
2–3 shakes Tabasco
1 cup broken pecan pieces
3 dozen thin slices Genoa salami

Cream liverwurst and cheese together at room temperature. Add enough catsup to blend easily. Blend in sauces and pecans with a fork. This filling can be stored in the refrigerator for a week.

Cut slices of Genoa salami in half. Place ½ teaspoon of filling on each piece, roll up lengthwise, and secure with a pick.

YIELD: 6 DOZEN APPETIZERS

Fun Foods
THE JUNIOR LEAGUE OF GREATER LAKELAND, FLORIDA

. . . .

Pickled Shrimp

1 cup salad oil
Juice of 3 lemons
5 bay leaves
1 teaspoon dill seed
1 teaspoon celery salt
Dash cayenne
1 cup vinegar
2 tablespoons sugar
1 teaspoon crushed peppercorns
½ teaspoon tarragon leaves
1 teaspoon dry mustard
3 pounds cleaned and cooked shrimp
6 medium onions, sliced

Combine all ingredients except shrimp and onions and simmer for 10 minutes. Add shrimp and simmer for 3 more minutes.

Choose a large casserole with a lid. Make a layer of sliced onions, then a layer of shrimp, until all are used. Pour the hot marinade over and be very sure that all shrimp and onions are covered. When cold, cover and place in refrigerator to "age."

Chill at least 48 hours before serving with cocktail picks.

YIELD: 12 SERVINGS

Fun Foods
THE JUNIOR LEAGUE OF GREATER LAKELAND, FLORIDA

. . . .

Hidden Treasures

2 cups mayonnaise
½ cup horseradish, drained
½ teaspoon monosodium glutamate
2 teaspoons dry mustard
2 teaspoons lemon juice
½ teaspoon salt
1 pound medium-size shrimp, cleaned and cooked
1 basket small cherry tomatoes
1 6-ounce can pitted black olives
1 8-ounce can water chestnuts
1 6-ounce can whole mushrooms
½ head cauliflower, cut into bite-size pieces

Mix mayonnaise with seasonings and add other ingredients except cauliflower. Best made early in the day or night before.

Add cauliflower just before serving.

Serve in a shallow bowl with cocktail picks.

YIELD: 10 SERVINGS

Nashville Seasons Encore
THE JUNIOR LEAGUE OF NASHVILLE, TENNESSEE

. . . .

Millie's Marinated Vegetables

2 heads cauliflower
3 green peppers
2 bags raw carrots
1 bunch celery
1 pound mushrooms
3 squash
1 head broccoli
2 cucumbers
½ cup salad oil
½ cup olive oil
3 cups tarragon vinegar
½–¾ cup sugar
3 cloves garlic, minced
1 tablespoon prepared mustard
1 tablespoon salt
2 teaspoons tarragon leaves
Pepper to taste

Cut up all vegetables. Combine other ingredients and pour over vegetables. Cover and chill at least 12 hours. Vegetables should be turned occasionally.

Serve with cocktail picks.

Any fresh vegetable that is good raw can be used.

YIELD: 30 SERVINGS

Winston-Salem's Heritage of Hospitality
THE JUNIOR LEAGUE OF WINSTON-SALEM, NORTH CAROLINA

Sesame Seed Cheese Spread

¾ cup sesame seeds
½ pound blue cheese
½ pound cream cheese
1 cup butter
1 cup chopped pimento-stuffed green olives
1 tablespoon chopped chives
1 tablespoon chopped parsley
½ teaspoon garlic salt
3 tablespoons cognac

Roast sesame seeds in shallow pan at 350° about 20 minutes. Watch carefully so they do not burn.

Cream cheeses and butter. Add all ingredients except sesame seeds and blend.

Divide cheese mixture and place in six 4-ounce crocks. Sprinkle sesame seeds on top. Serve with crackers.

YIELD: 6 CROCKS

Home Cookin'
THE JUNIOR LEAGUE OF WICHITA FALLS, TEXAS

·　·　·　·　·　·　·　·　·　·　·　·　·　·　·　·

Liptoi Cheese

½ pound cream cheese
¼ cup sour cream
¼ cup soft butter
2 teaspoons anchovy paste
2 teaspoons capers, drained
2 green onions, chopped
1 tablespoon paprika
2 teaspoons caraway seeds
½ teaspoon dry mustard
1 ounce dry white wine

Recipe continues ...

Place all ingredients in blender and blend until smooth. You will have to stop blender a few times and stir with a spatula.

Chill and serve with thin slices of pumpernickel.

YIELD: ABOUT 2 CUPS

Gator Country Cooks
THE JUNIOR LEAGUE OF GAINESVILLE, FLORIDA

Sherry Cheese Pâté

2 3-ounce packages cream cheese, softened
1 cup shredded sharp cheddar cheese
4 teaspoons cocktail sherry
½ teaspoon curry powder
¼ teaspoon salt
1 8-ounce jar mango chutney, finely chopped
Finely sliced green onions with tops
Sesame or wheat wafers

Beat together thoroughly the cream cheese, cheddar cheese, sherry, curry powder, and salt. Spread on a serving platter, shaping a layer about ½ inch thick. Chill until firm. At serving time, spread with chutney and sprinkle with green onions.

Serve pâté with wafers.

YIELD: APPETIZERS FOR ABOUT 8

Gator Country Cooks
THE JUNIOR LEAGUE OF GAINESVILLE, FLORIDA

Quickie Cream Cheese Hors D'oeuvres

Cover an 8-ounce block of cream cheese with *one* of the following:

Small jar of red or black caviar
Layer of hot pepper jelly
Chutney

Surround with crackers of your choice and serve.

Fun Foods
THE JUNIOR LEAGUE OF GREATER LAKELAND, FLORIDA

· · · · · · · · · · · · · · · · · · ·

Atlanta Chicken Liver Pâté

½ pound chicken livers
2 tablespoons finely minced onion
Pinch cayenne
¼ teaspoon nutmeg
1 teaspoon dry mustard
⅛ teaspoon ground cloves
1 teaspoon salt
½ cup rendered chicken fat or soft, sweet butter

Cover chicken livers with water and bring to a boil. Simmer, covered, for 15–20 minutes, until just done.

Drain the chicken livers and put in blender with onion, spices, and fat or butter. Blend until smooth.

Place in crock and refrigerate.

YIELD: ABOUT 1 CUP

The Cotton Blossom Cookbook
THE JUNIOR LEAGUE OF ATLANTA, GEORGIA

· · · · · · · · · · · · · · · · · · ·

Lakeland Chicken Liver Pâté

1 cup chopped onion
¾ cup butter (no substitute)
1 clove garlic, mashed
1 pound chicken livers
1 tablespoon flour
1 teaspoon salt
1 teaspoon white pepper
1 bay leaf
⅛ teaspoon oregano
3 tablespoons brandy

Sauté onion until soft and transparent in ½ cup butter with garlic. Sauté livers separately in ¼ cup butter until tender. Add flour and spices. Cover and simmer 2 minutes.

Remove bay leaf. Add livers to onion. Add brandy and purée in blender or put through a meat grinder 3 times.

Pack in crocks, cover, and refrigerate or freeze. Serve on crackers or party rye.

YIELD: ABOUT 3 CUPS

Fun Foods
THE JUNIOR LEAGUE OF GREATER LAKELAND, FLORIDA

Pâté of Chicken Livers in Aspic

1 pound chicken livers
3 coarsely chopped shallots or green onions
½ cup butter or margarine
1½ tablespoons brandy
1½ tablespoons sherry
2 teaspoons salt
¼ teaspoon nutmeg
¼ teaspoon pepper
Pinch thyme
Pinch basil
Pinch marjoram
Aspic
Bits of pimento

Sauté chicken livers with shallots or green onions in butter or margarine for 3–4 minutes or until livers are browned on outside but are still pink inside. Stir in brandy and sherry. Season with salt, nutmeg, pepper, thyme, basil, and marjoram.

Combine mixture well and purée about one-third at a time in electric blender until smooth.

Spoon into an earthenware bowl and chill.

Very good without a covering of aspic, but the aspic prevents the pâté from drying out. If you wish, cover surface with a thin layer of aspic, garnish with bits of pimento, then add another thin layer of aspic. Chill until aspic is firm. Serve with cocktail toast.

YIELD: ABOUT 2 CUPS

ASPIC:
2½ cups chicken stock
1 sliced onion
Salt and pepper to taste
Crushed shell and slightly beaten white of 1 egg
1 tablespoon unflavored gelatin
½ cup cold stock

Recipe continues . . .

Simmer chicken stock, onion, salt and pepper, crushed shell, and slightly beaten white of egg for 10 minutes.

Let mixture stand for 20 minutes, then gently strain through several thicknesses of cheesecloth to clarify.

Soften gelatin in ½ cup cold stock, dissolve over boiling water, and stir into clarified stock.

That Something Special
THE JUNIOR LEAGUE OF DURHAM, NORTH CAROLINA

· · · · · · · · · · · · · · · ·

Hot Crab Canapé

2 cups frozen crabmeat
1 pint mayonnaise
½ jar capers, drained
2 tablespoons prepared horseradish
Dash Tabasco
Salt and pepper to taste
½ cup shredded sharp cheddar cheese
Dash paprika

Mix all ingredients except cheese and paprika well and pour into casserole. Sprinkle with cheese and dash of paprika.

Bake in 350° oven for 20 minutes. Serve on crackers or melba toast rounds.

YIELD: ABOUT 20 SERVINGS

Spartanburg Secrets II
THE JUNIOR LEAGUE OF SPARTANBURG, SOUTH CAROLINA

· · · · · · · · · · · · · · · ·

Oriental Crab Spread

1 cup sour cream
1 teaspoon curry
½ teaspoon onion powder
⅛ teaspoon white pepper
¼ teaspoon salt
½ cup shredded coconut
¼ pound flaked crabmeat

Mix all ingredients together. Chill. Spread on crackers or bread, or use as a stuffing for celery.

YIELD: ABOUT 2 CUPS

Fun Foods
THE JUNIOR LEAGUE OF GREATER LAKELAND, FLORIDA

·   ·   ·   ·   ·   ·   ·   ·   ·   ·   ·   ·   ·   ·

Oyster Roll

2–3 tablespoons mayonnaise
2 8-ounce packages cream cheese
2 teaspoons Worcestershire sauce
1 large or 2 small cloves garlic, pressed
½ small onion, pressed
2 cans smoked oysters
At least ⅛ teaspoon salt

Cream enough mayonnaise into cheese to hold it together. Add Worcestershire sauce, garlic, and onion. Combine well. Spread about ½ inch thick on wax paper.

Recipe continues . . .

Chop oysters and spread them on top of cheese mixture. Sprinkle with salt. Roll as for jelly roll, using a knife to start it. Chill for 24 hours. Serve with toast rounds or crackers.

YIELD: A 1-POUND ROLL

A Cook's Tour of Shreveport
THE JUNIOR LEAGUE OF SHREVEPORT, LOUISIANA

· · · · · · · · · · · · ·

Tuna Puff Sandwich

1 7-ounce can tuna, drained and flaked
1½ teaspoons prepared mustard
¼ teaspoon Worcestershire sauce
¼ cup mayonnaise
1½ teaspoons grated onion
2 tablespoons chopped green pepper or green chilies
3 hamburger buns or split English muffins
½ cup mayonnaise
¼ cup finely shredded American cheese
6 tomato slices

Blend first six ingredients; pile onto bun or muffin halves. Top each with tomato slice.

Blend ½ cup mayonnaise with cheese; spread on tomato slice.

Broil 4 inches from heat until topping puffs and browns.

YIELD: 6 SERVINGS

VARIATIONS:

5-ounce can lobster, 7½-ounce can crabmeat, or 2 5-ounce cans shrimp may be used instead of tuna.

Seasoned with Sun: Recipes from the Southwest
THE JUNIOR LEAGUE OF EL PASO, TEXAS

· · · · · · · · · · · ·

Barbecued Brisket Sandwiches

3 pounds brisket
1 cup catsup
1 teaspoon salt
2 cups water
⅓ cup Worcestershire sauce
2 dashes Tabasco
1 teaspoon chili powder
1 teaspoon liquid smoke
1 small onion, chopped

Cook brisket uncovered in a 350° oven for 2 hours.

Mix remaining ingredients; pour over meat. Cover; cook 2 more hours at 300°. Remove meat from sauce; refrigerate both overnight.

Slice meat paper-thin; lay slices in a flat pan. Cover with sauce; heat in a 300° oven. Serve on buns.

YIELD: 12–16 SANDWICHES

The Blue Denim Gourmet
THE JUNIOR LEAGUE OF ODESSA, TEXAS

·　·　·　·　·　·　·　·　·　·　·

Baked Crabmeat Sandwich

20 slices sandwich bread
2 7½-ounce cans crabmeat
1 small can mushrooms, drained and sliced
⅔ cup mayonnaise
2 5-ounce jars Old English cheddar cheese
1 cup butter
2 raw eggs

Trim crusts from bread and put slices together with mixture of crabmeat, mushrooms, and mayonnaise.

Recipe continues ...

Cream together cheese, butter, and eggs in mixer until fluffy. Frost sides and tops of sandwiches generously. Place, not too close together, on cookie sheet and refrigerate for 12 hours.

Bake at 400° for 12–15 minutes. May be frozen; let thaw 2 hours before baking.

YIELD: 10 SANDWICHES

Little Rock Cooks
THE JUNIOR LEAGUE OF LITTLE ROCK, ARKANSAS

. . . .

English Muffin Sandwich

1 cup ripe olives, sliced
1 cup shredded cheddar cheese
½ cup chopped onion
½ cup mayonnaise
Cayenne to taste
3 English muffins

Combine above ingredients with exception of muffins.

Split muffins in half and spread generously with mixture. Bake at 350° for 5–10 minutes until puffy and hot.

Marvelous for lunch with gazpacho and mixed green salad.

YIELD: 6 SERVINGS

Nashville Seasons Encore
THE JUNIOR LEAGUE OF NASHVILLE, TENNESSEE

. . . .

Josefinas

8 Mexican hard rolls
1 4-ounce can green chilies
1 cup butter
1 clove garlic, minced
1 cup mayonnaise
8 ounces Monterey Jack cheese, shredded

Slice rolls into ½-inch slices; toast on one side.

Rinse seeds off chilies and chop; mix with butter, garlic, mayonnaise, and cheese.

Spread the mixture on untoasted sides of bread slices.

Broil until cheese is brown and puffy. Serve at once.

One thin loaf of French bread may be substituted for the rolls.

Chili mixture will keep indefinitely in refrigerator.

YIELD: ABOUT 30 SLICES

Fiesta: Favorite Recipes of South Texas
THE JUNIOR LEAGUE OF CORPUS CHRISTI, TEXAS

· · · · · · · · · · · · · ·

Luncheon Sandwich

1 stick margarine, melted
1 tablespoon poppy seeds
1 tablespoon minced onion
1 tablespoon prepared mustard
6 hamburger buns
6 slices Swiss cheese
6 slices pressed ham

Combine margarine, poppy seeds, onion, and mustard. Spread on open hamburger buns.

Recipe continues ...

Add a slice of cheese and a slice of ham. Place on baking sheet and cover with foil.

Bake at 350° for 15 minutes or until cheese melts.

YIELD: 6 SERVINGS

Winston-Salem's Heritage of Hospitality
THE JUNIOR LEAGUE OF WINSTON-SALEM, NORTH CAROLINA

Artichoke Squares

2 6-ounce jars marinated artichokes
1 onion, chopped
1 clove garlic, minced
4 eggs
¼ cup bread crumbs
Dash Tabasco
½ teaspoon oregano
Salt and pepper
2 cups shredded cheddar cheese

Drain the juice from 1 jar of artichokes into a skillet. Sauté the onion and garlic in the juice.

Drain the other jar and chop all artichokes. In a bowl, beat the eggs, then add the bread crumbs, Tabasco, oregano, salt, and pepper. Stir in the onion, garlic, cheese, and artichokes. Mix well.

Bake in a 9 × 13-inch pan for ½ hour at 325°. Cut into squares and serve hot.

These squares can be made in advance and then rewarmed on a cookie sheet.

YIELD: ABOUT 30 SQUARES

Southern Sideboards
THE JUNIOR LEAGUE OF JACKSON, MISSISSIPPI

Artichokes à la Roquefort

¼ pound butter
¼ pound Roquefort cheese
2 cans artichokes, drained

Melt butter and cheese, mixing well. Add artichokes (cut them into halves or quarters if large) and heat. Serve in chafing dish as hors d'oeuvres.

YIELD: 6 SERVINGS

300 Years of Carolina Cooking
THE JUNIOR LEAGUE OF GREENVILLE, SOUTH CAROLINA

· · · · · · · · · · · · · · · · ·

Bacon Bites Flambé

2 pounds shelled raw shrimp
½ pound sliced bacon
½ cup warm rum

Wrap each shrimp in a narrow strip of bacon. Fasten with toothpick. Spread in shallow pan and bake in 450° oven, turning frequently until bacon is crisp. Drain.

Put in chafing dish. Pour rum over shrimp and bacon. Ignite and serve immediately.

YIELD: 6 SERVINGS

Fun Foods
THE JUNIOR LEAGUE OF GREATER LAKELAND, FLORIDA

· · · · · · · · · · · · · · · · ·

Chili Quiche

2 sticks pie crust mix
2 4-ounce cans green chilies, chopped
4 tablespoons flour
1 pound Swiss cheese, shredded
Salt and pepper to taste
2 tablespoons onion flakes
6 eggs
2 cups milk, heated

Prepare crust and fit into a 12 × 15-inch cookie sheet with sides.

Drain chilies; spread over crust.

Mix flour with shredded cheese; add salt, pepper, and onion flakes. Beat eggs with milk; add to cheese mixture. Pour over crust and bake in 325° oven for 30–40 minutes. Quiche is done when knife is inserted in center and comes out clean.

Cut into 2-inch squares.

YIELD: 40 SQUARES

Seasoned with Sun: Recipes from the Southwest
THE JUNIOR LEAGUE OF EL PASO, TEXAS

· · · · · · · · · · · · · · · · ·

Crab-Swiss Bites

½ pound fresh crabmeat
1 tablespoon sliced green onion
4 ounces Swiss cheese, shredded
½ cup mayonnaise
1 teaspoon lemon juice
¼ teaspoon curry powder
1 package flaky-style rolls
Salt to taste

Combine crabmeat, green onion, Swiss cheese, mayonnaise, lemon juice, and curry powder. Mix well. Separate rolls each in three layers. Place on ungreased baking sheet. Sprinkle with salt. Spoon on crabmeat mixture. Bake at 400° for 9–12 minutes or until golden brown.

The crab mixture may be made 2–3 hours in advance. One hour before serving, the rolls may be spread with the mixture and refrigerated until baking time.

YIELD: 36

The Dallas Jr. League Cookbook
THE JUNIOR LEAGUE OF DALLAS, TEXAS

·   ·   ·   ·   ·   ·   ·   ·   ·   ·   ·   ·   ·   ·   ·   ·   ·   ·   ·

Nachos

6 tortillas
Drippings
6 tablespoons refried beans
6 tablespoons shredded cheddar or longhorn cheese
3 pickled jalapeño peppers, cut into thirds

Slice tortillas into quarters. Fry in hot drippings until crisp. Spread with refried beans; sprinkle with cheese and top each with a slice of jalapeño pepper.

Broil until cheese melts. Serve hot.

YIELD: 24 NACHOS

Seasoned with Sun: Recipes from the Southwest
THE JUNIOR LEAGUE OF EL PASO, TEXAS

·   ·   ·   ·   ·   ·   ·   ·   ·   ·   ·   ·   ·   ·   ·   ·   ·   ·   ·

Cheese Puffs

2 cups mayonnaise
½ cup finely grated Parmesan cheese
2 tablespoons finely grated onion
2 teaspoons prepared hot mustard
40 toast rounds

Mix together first four ingredients and spread on packaged toast rounds (or make your own). Use 1 heaping teaspoon per round, carefully spreading to very edge.

Just before serving, broil 6 inches from heat for 2 minutes or until golden brown.

YIELD: 40 PUFFS

Fun Foods
THE JUNIOR LEAGUE OF GREATER LAKELAND, FLORIDA

. . . .

Chestnut Chicken Livers

⅓ pound chicken livers, cut into halves or thirds
1 8-ounce can water chestnuts
8 slices bacon, cut into halves
½ cup soy sauce
¼ teaspoon ground ginger
¼ teaspoon curry powder

Wrap each piece chicken liver around chestnut, then wrap chestnut and liver with bacon. Fasten with pick. Marinate one hour in soy sauce, ginger, and curry powder.

Preheat broiler. Broil 7 minutes on each side.

YIELD: 16 PIECES

Fun Foods
THE JUNIOR LEAGUE OF GREATER LAKELAND, FLORIDA

. . . .

Hot Olive Cheese Puffs

2 cups grated Parmesan or Romano cheese
6 tablespoons soft butter
1 cup flour, sifted
½ teaspoon salt
1 teaspoon paprika
48 large stuffed olives, drained and dried

Blend cheese with butter; stir in flour, salt, and paprika and mix well.

Wrap small amount of cheese dough around each olive. Make sure each olive is covered well.

Place on ungreased cookie sheet and bake in 400° oven for 10 or 15 minutes, until golden brown.

These may be frozen before cooking.

YIELD: 48 PUFFS

The Charlotte Cookbook
THE JUNIOR LEAGUE OF CHARLOTTE, NORTH CAROLINA

·   ·   ·   ·   ·   ·   ·   ·   ·   ·   ·   ·   ·   ·   ·

Chicken with Lemon and Mustard

3 whole chicken breasts
3 tablespoons butter
1 tablespoon flour
¾ teaspoon monosodium glutamate
¼ teaspoon salt
1 teaspoon dried tarragon
1 chicken bouillon cube
½ cup hot water
1 tablespoon Dijon mustard
3 thin lemon slices, halved
1 teaspoon finely chopped parsley

Recipe continues . . .

Bone chicken breasts; remove skin and cut breasts in half. Cut each half into 6–8 bite-size squares.

Melt butter in a large skillet over high heat. Add chicken and sprinkle with flour, monosodium glutamate, salt, and tarragon. Cook 5 minutes, stirring constantly.

Dissolve bouillon cube in hot water and add to chicken along with mustard and lemon slices. Stir to loosen any browned particles. Cover and cook 2 or 3 minutes. Sprinkle with chopped parsley.

Serve with cocktail picks.

YIELD: 36 APPETIZERS

Southern Sideboards
THE JUNIOR LEAGUE OF JACKSON, MISSISSIPPI

.   .   .   .

Clam Filling for Puff Shells

1 7½-ounce can minced clams, drained
½ pound cooked ham, chopped
½ cup sour cream
½ cup mayonnaise
½ cup grated Parmesan cheese
2 tablespoons finely chopped onion
1 teaspoon anchovy paste
¼ teaspoon pepper
40–50 miniature puff shells (see following recipe)

Combine all ingredients except puff shells and set aside.

Split puffs in seam and fill with clam filling. Refrigerate until serving time.

Heat in 350° oven until warm.

YIELD: FILLING FOR 40–50 SHELLS

Southern Accent
THE JUNIOR LEAGUE OF PINE BLUFF, ARKANSAS

.   .   .   .

Puff Shells Filled with Crabmeat

PUFF PASTE:
¼ cup shortening
½ cup boiling water
½ cup flour
¼ teaspoon salt
2 eggs

FILLING:
1 cup crabmeat
¼ cup lime juice
3 ounces cream cheese
¼ cup heavy cream
2 tablespoons mayonnaise
Pinch salt
1 tablespoon minced onion
1 clove minced garlic
1 teaspoon finely chopped chives
2 dashes Tabasco
1 teaspoon Worcestershire sauce

To make puffs, melt shortening in boiling water. Add flour and salt, stirring constantly. Cook until mixture leaves sides of pan in a smooth ball. Remove from heat. Cool 1 minute. Add eggs, one at a time, beating after each until mixture is smooth again. Drop by ½ teaspoonfuls on greased baking tin. Bake at 400° for 10 minutes.

To make filling, marinate crabmeat in lime juice for 1 hour. Whip cream cheese and heavy cream until smooth. Add remaining ingredients, folding crabmeat in last. Fill puffs. Wrap tightly and freeze.

When ready to use, remove from freezer, place on baking sheets, and bake in 375° oven for 10 minutes. Serve warm.

YIELD: 40–50 PUFFS

Gator Country Cooks
THE JUNIOR LEAGUE OF GAINESVILLE, FLORIDA

Clam Puffs

1 8-ounce package cream cheese
1 7½-ounce can minced clams, drained
¼ teaspoon salt
2 teaspoons lemon juice
1 tablespoon grated onion
1 tablespoon Worcestershire sauce
1 egg white, stiffly beaten
Bread rounds

Beat cheese until smooth. Combine remaining ingredients except bread. Pile on toasted bread rounds and bake at 450° for 3 minutes.

YIELD: 36 PUFFS

Fun Foods
THE JUNIOR LEAGUE OF GREATER LAKELAND, FLORIDA

. . . .

Chafing Dish Meat Balls

2 pounds ground chuck
1 teaspoon salt
½ cup fine, dry bread crumbs
1 egg
¼ teaspoon pepper
½ cup milk
¼ cup vegetable oil
2 tablespoons flour
2 cups tomato juice
¾ cup bottled barbecue sauce
¼ cup water
1 1-pound can pineapple chunks, drained

Mix together ground chuck, salt, bread crumbs, egg, pepper, and milk. Form into small, round balls. Place in bottom of broiler pan, add oil, and cook in 350° oven for 30 minutes.

Meanwhile, in a saucepan, mix flour with tomato juice and cook, stirring, until smooth. Add barbecue sauce, water, and pineapple chunks. Pour over browned meat balls, return to oven, and cook an additional 45 minutes.

YIELD: ABOUT 50 BALLS

Of Pots and Pipkins
THE JUNIOR LEAGUE OF ROANOKE VALLEY, VIRGINIA

· · · · · · · · · · · · · · · · · · ·

Mushroom Turnovers

CREAM CHEESE PASTRY:
½ cup butter
3 3-ounce packages cream cheese at room temperature
1½ cups flour

Mix butter and cream cheese. Add flour and work dough until smooth. Chill.

MUSHROOM FILLING:
1 large onion, chopped fine
3 tablespoons butter
½ pound mushrooms, chopped fine
¼ teaspoon thyme
½ teaspoon salt
Freshly ground pepper
2 tablespoons flour
¼ cup sour cream

Recipe continues . . .

Sauté onion in butter. Add mushrooms and cook 3 minutes. Add seasonings and sprinkle with flour. Stir in sour cream. Cook until thick.

Roll pastry out ⅛ inch thick. Cut into 3-inch rounds. Drop onto rounds about ¼–½ teaspoon mushroom filling. Fold over rounds as for turnovers and press down edges with fork. Be sure to prick tops with a fork.

Bake on ungreased cookie sheet at 425° for 15 minutes.

These turnovers can be made in advance and frozen before cooking.

YIELD: ABOUT 4 DOZEN

That Something Special
THE JUNIOR LEAGUE OF DURHAM, NORTH CAROLINA

· · · · · · · · · · · · · · · ·

Spinach-Stuffed Mushrooms

*1 10-ounce package frozen spinach, cooked according to
package directions and drained
½ cup sour cream
¼ cup tomato sauce
Dash wine vinegar
1 cup grated Parmesan cheese
1 pound fresh mushrooms
4 tablespoons butter*

Combine all ingredients except mushrooms and butter. This may be done a day ahead.

Wash mushrooms, dry on paper towels, and remove stems. Melt butter and dip each mushroom in butter before putting on cookie sheet. Spoon about a teaspoon of spinach mixture into each mushroom cap, or pipe mixture on with large pastry tube.

Bake at 350° for 15 minutes. If possible, serve on a tray set over a warmer.

YIELD: 30 STUFFED MUSHROOMS

Southern Sideboards
THE JUNIOR LEAGUE OF JACKSON, MISSISSIPPI

· · · · · · · · · · · · · · · ·

Clark's Famous Mushrooms

4 pounds fresh mushrooms, cleaned
1 pound butter
1 quart Burgundy
1½ tablespoons Worcestershire sauce
1 teaspoon dill seed
1 teaspoon ground pepper
1 tablespoon monosodium glutamate
1 teaspoon garlic powder
2 cups boiling water
4 beef bouillon cubes
4 chicken bouillon cubes
2 teaspoons salt, if needed

Combine all ingredients except salt in large pan. Bring to slow boil on medium heat; reduce to simmer. Cook 5–6 hours with pot covered. Remove lid. Cook another 3–5 hours until liquid barely covers mushrooms. Season to taste with salt. Allow to cool.

Serve hot in chafing dish with picks.

May be refrigerated; freezes beautifully.

YIELD: 12–16 SERVINGS

Winston-Salem's Heritage of Hospitality
THE JUNIOR LEAGUE OF WINSTON-SALEM, NORTH CAROLINA

·   ·   ·   ·   ·   ·   ·   ·   ·   ·   ·   ·   ·   ·   ·   ·

Cheese-Stuffed Mushrooms

½ cup shredded processed Swiss cheese
1 hard-boiled egg, finely chopped
3 tablespoons fine, dry bread crumbs
½ clove garlic, minced
2 tablespoons butter or margarine, softened
1 pound fresh mushrooms, each about 1–1½ inches in diameter
4 tablespoons butter or margarine, melted

Recipe continues . . .

In mixing bowl, combine cheese, egg, crumbs, garlic, and the softened butter or margarine. Blend thoroughly.

Remove stems from mushrooms; place unfilled mushrooms rounded side up on baking sheet. Brush tops with the melted butter or margarine. Broil 3–4 inches from heat for 2–3 minutes, until lightly browned.

Remove from broiler. Turn mushrooms; fill each with cheese mixture. Return the filled mushrooms to broiler; broil 1–2 minutes more. Keep warm on electric serving tray.

YIELD: ABOUT 3 DOZEN

Fun Foods
THE JUNIOR LEAGUE OF GREATER LAKELAND, FLORIDA

Two-Bite Pizza

1 pound pork sausage meat
1 cup chopped onions
1½ cups shredded sharp cheddar cheese
½ cup grated Parmesan cheese
1½ teaspoons oregano
1 teaspoon garlic salt
1 6-ounce can tomato paste
1 8-ounce can tomato sauce
2 cans flaky-style biscuits
Mozzarella cheese, shredded

Simmer sausage until half done. Add onions and cook until both are done. Drain. Add sharp cheddar and Parmesan cheeses, oregano, garlic salt, tomato paste, and sauce. Simmer 20 minutes. Cool.

Take 12 biscuits from 1 can and separate each biscuit into 4 layers. Place on cookie sheet. Add 1 teaspoon of pizza mixture to top of each layer. Repeat process on second can of biscuits.

Freeze on cookie sheet. Remove when frozen and store in plastic bag in freezer.

When ready to serve, take from freezer and top with mozzarella cheese. Bake at 400° for 10 minutes.

YIELD: 100 PIZZA BITES

Winston-Salem's Heritage of Hospitality
THE JUNIOR LEAGUE OF WINSTON-SALEM, NORTH CAROLINA

· · · · · · · · · · · ·

Spicy Sausage Balls

2 pounds hot bulk sausage
2 eggs, well beaten
⅔ cup seasoned bread crumbs
4 teaspoons curry powder
½ teaspoon chili powder
⅓ cup catsup
2 8-ounce cans tomato sauce with mushrooms
2 tablespoons soy sauce
2 tablespoons Worcestershire sauce
1 3-ounce can mushroom crowns (optional)

Break up sausage; add eggs, bread crumbs, curry powder, and chili powder and mix well. Shape into ¾-inch balls and brown over low heat on all sides, draining off fat as it accumulates.

Put sausage balls on paper towels to drain.

Combine remaining ingredients in sauce pan. Add sausage balls. Simmer, covered, 15 minutes. Serve in chafing dish.

This freezes well. Thaw completely before removing from freezer container to keep from breaking meat balls. Add 1 8-ounce can tomato sauce to pan when reheating.

YIELD: 100 BALLS

Fiesta: Favorite Recipes of South Texas
THE JUNIOR LEAGUE OF CORPUS CHRISTI, TEXAS

· · · · · · · · · · · ·

Garnelen Bollen (Shrimp Puffs)

1 pound bread
Milk
2 pounds cleaned shrimp, finely ground
1 pound potatoes, cooked and mashed
2 teaspoons salt
Pepper

Soak bread in milk; squeeze dry.

Mix all ingredients together, kneading mixture with hands until smooth. Form into 1-inch balls and fry until brown in deep fat heated to 370°. Drain on paper towels.

Reheat in a 350° oven before serving.

YIELD: 100 PUFFS

Fiesta: Favorite Recipes of South Texas
THE JUNIOR LEAGUE OF CORPUS CHRISTI, TEXAS

. . . .

Tamale Balls

1 pound beef
1 pound pork
1½ cups corn meal
¾ cup tomato juice
¼ cup flour
Garlic to taste
1 tablespoon chili powder
2 teaspoons salt

SAUCE:
3 1-pound 4-ounce cans tomatoes
2 teaspoons salt
1 tablespoon chili powder

Grind beef and pork together twice. Add all other ingredients and form small balls.

Combine sauce ingredients. Drop meat balls into sauce and simmer 2 hours.

Keep hot in chafing dish and serve on cocktail picks.

YIELD: 150 BALLS

The Blue Denim Gourmet
THE JUNIOR LEAGUE OF ODESSA, TEXAS

· · · · · · · · · · · · · · ·

Whole Beef Tenderloin for Hors d'Oeuvres

Bacon
1 whole beef tenderloin
1 5-ounce bottle steak sauce
¼ pound butter
1 7-ounce can mushroom buttons, undrained
1 loaf Cuban or French bread (Cuban preferred)

Preheat oven to 400°. Lay several strips of bacon over the tenderloin; place on rack in roasting pan and bake uncovered for 15–25 minutes total time (15 minutes for rare to 25 minutes for well done, or use meat thermometer).

While meat is cooking, heat to boiling the steak sauce, butter, and mushrooms with juice.

Cut bread into bite-size pieces.

To serve, place meat while hot on platter. Have bread on separate tray beside chafing dish containing sauce. Slice bite-size pieces of meat very thin, dip in sauce, place on piece of bread, and eat as small open-faced sandwich.

YIELD: 10–12 SERVINGS (4 tenderloins will serve about 50 with double the sauce)

The Gasparilla Cookbook
THE JUNIOR LEAGUE OF TAMPA, FLORIDA

· · · · · · · · · · · · · · ·

Stuffed Clams, Piedmont Club

12 empty clam shells
1 pound shucked clams, chopped fine
Reserved clam liquid
¼ cup shallots or onion chopped
1 clove garlic, chopped
3 ounces cooked ham, chopped
2 tablespoons chopped green pepper
2 tablespoons olive oil
2 tablespoons flour
2 eggs, beaten
2 tablespoons grated Parmesan cheese
Pinch thyme
Pinch chopped parsley
2 tablespoons chopped pimento
Paprika

Drain clams and reserve the liquid.

Brown shallots or onion, garlic, ham, and green pepper in olive oil. Add flour and cook 5 minutes. Add drained, chopped clams and boiling clam juice. Cook 10 minutes. Add beaten eggs, cheese, thyme, parsley, and pimento.

Cool and stuff shells. Sprinkle with paprika.

Bake at 350° for 20 minutes.

Freezes well.

YIELD: 6 SERVINGS

Of Pots and Pipkins
THE JUNIOR LEAGUE OF ROANOKE VALLEY, VIRGINIA

. . . .

Minced Oysters

1 quart oysters
1 medium onion, chopped
Chopped parsley
¼ pound butter
Worcestershire sauce
Juice of 1 large lemon
4 or 5 eggs
3 cups dry bread crumbs
Additional crumbs for topping

Strain oysters, reserving liquid. Grind oysters.

Lightly brown onion and parsley in butter, add reserved oyster liquid and remaining ingredients except topping crumbs, and stir until thickened.

Place in greased shells, cover with additional crumbs, and bake until brown.

YIELD: 6 SERVINGS

Spartanburg Secrets II
THE JUNIOR LEAGUE OF SPARTANBURG, SOUTH CAROLINA

·   ·   ·   ·   ·   ·   ·   ·   ·   ·   ·   ·   ·   ·   ·   ·

Crabmeat Imperial

1 green pepper, finely diced
2 pimentos, finely diced
1 tablespoon English mustard
1 teaspoon salt
½ teaspoon white pepper
2 eggs, beaten
1 cup mayonnaise
3 pounds lump crabmeat
Paprika

Recipe continues . . .

Mix green pepper and pimentos. Add mustard, salt, white pepper, eggs, and mayonnaise. Mix well. Add crabmeat and mix with fingers so lumps are not broken.

Divide mixture into 8 crab shells or ramekins, heaping lightly. Top with a little additional mayonnaise and sprinkle with a little paprika.

Bake at 350° for 15 minutes.

Serve hot or cold.

YIELD: 8 SERVINGS

Talk About Good!
THE JUNIOR LEAGUE OF LAFAYETTE, LOUISIANA

. . . .

Escargots in Ramekins

½ cup finely chopped onion
½ cup finely chopped celery
1 clove garlic, minced
4 tablespoons butter
1 pound mushrooms, sliced
1 cup heavy cream
1 egg, beaten
2 tablespoons minced parsley
¼ cup sherry
36–48 large snails, halved
Salt and pepper

Sauté onion, celery, and garlic in butter about 5 minutes. Add mushrooms and cook 10–15 minutes. Remove from heat and add cream, egg, parsley, sherry, snails, salt, and pepper.

Put into ramekins. Bake at 350° for 15–20 minutes.

YIELD: 10 SERVINGS

The Dallas Jr. League Cookbook
THE JUNIOR LEAGUE OF DALLAS, TEXAS

. . . .

Cantonese Egg Rolls

1½ cups bean sprouts
1 cup diced cooked shrimp
1 cup minced cooked beef or ground raw beef
1 cup minced celery
1 cup finely chopped green onion
1 6½-ounce can water chestnuts, drained and diced
1 tablespoon oil
1 tablespoon smooth peanut butter
1 teaspoon salt
1 teaspoon sugar
1 teaspoon monosodium glutamate
⅛ teaspoon ground black pepper
⅛ teaspoon Chinese 5 spices powder
20–21 egg roll wrappers
Oil for frying

Mix all ingredients together except egg roll wrappers and frying oil. Place 2–3 teaspoonfuls mixture in center of egg roll wrappers. Wrap 2 sides over and roll.

Fry in lots of oil until golden.

Serve with hot mustard and sweet and sour sauce.

YIELD: 10 SERVINGS

Home Cookin'
THE JUNIOR LEAGUE OF WICHITA FALLS, TEXAS

Oysters Rockefeller

Rock salt
Oysters and oyster shells

ROCKEFELLER SAUCE:
3 bags fresh spinach
Tops only from 2 bunches green onions
2 bunches parsley
1 10-ounce bottle Worcestershire sauce
1 or 2 cloves garlic, grated
2 pounds soft butter, creamed
1 10-ounce box bread crumbs
1 14-ounce bottle catsup
1 tube anchovy paste
Salt and pepper to taste
Dash red pepper
Dash Tabasco

Purée spinach, onions, and parsley in blender or food processor, adding enough Worcestershire sauce to allow blender to work easily. Add puréed mixture to remaining ingredients in large mixing bowl and beat until smooth.

Cover a large cookie sheet with foil and spread with a layer of rock salt. Place drained oysters on oyster shells, then on bed of salt. Top oysters with Rockefeller Sauce (about 1 or 2 tablespoons on each).

Bake at 400° for 15 minutes.

This sauce may be stored in jars in the refrigerator for several months or in the freezer for a year. Spoon out as needed.

YIELD: 6 PINTS SAUCE

Southern Sideboards
THE JUNIOR LEAGUE OF JACKSON, MISSISSIPPI

. . . .

Smoked Salmon Rolls with Horseradish Cream

1 cup cream cheese
1 cup sour cream
1 cup freshly grated horseradish
Salt
12 slices Nova Scotia smoked salmon, cut thin and long
Capers
Chopped parsley
Lemon wedges

Beat cream cheese and sour cream to a smooth paste and add horseradish, reserving a little for garnish. Add salt to taste. Spread slices of salmon with mixture and roll them loosely.

To serve, arrange rolls on individual serving plates and garnish with capers, parsley, lemon wedges, and reserved horseradish.

Pass thin rye bread and butter sandwiches cut into tiny fingers.

YIELD: 6 SERVINGS

The Dallas Jr. League Cookbook
THE JUNIOR LEAGUE OF DALLAS, TEXAS

Spiced Shrimp

½ gallon water
1 tablespoon caraway seeds
1 tablespoon black pepper
1 tablespoon pickling spice
1 teaspoon cayenne
1 bay leaf
1 teaspoon dry mustard
4 teaspoons salt
Top leaves of 1 bunch celery
6 pounds shrimp, washed well and not peeled
½ pound butter
Juice of 2 large lemons
1 tablespoon tarragon vinegar
1 tablespoon Worcestershire sauce
2 tablespoons soy sauce
7 or 8 dashes Tabasco
1 teaspoon salt

Boil water and caraway seeds, black pepper, pickling spice, cayenne, bay leaf, mustard, salt, and celery leaves for 20 minutes before putting in shrimp. Shrimp must be put in the boiling spicy water and cooked 10 minutes after water starts to boil again.

To make sauce, melt butter and put in rest of ingredients and mix well. Do not boil.

Use brown wrapping paper for a table cloth.

Each person peels his or her own shrimp, putting shells on paper.

YIELD: 6 SERVINGS

Gator Country Cooks
THE JUNIOR LEAGUE OF GAINESVILLE, FLORIDA

Quiche Lorraine (Cheese Custard Pie)

Pastry for 9-inch pie
6 slices bacon
12 slices Swiss or Gruyère cheese
4 eggs
1 tablespoon flour
Nutmeg
Cayenne
2 cups light cream
1½ tablespoons butter, melted

Line 9-inch pie plate with pie crust.

Broil and drain 6 slices of bacon (Canadian bacon or ham may be used instead, or combination of all three).

Arrange thick slices of cheese and meat in overlapping layers in pie crust.

Beat eggs with flour, generous grating of nutmeg, and cayenne to taste. Add cream and melted butter.

Pour this mixture over meat and cheese and bake in 350° oven until custard is set and lightly browned, about 40 minutes.

This recipe enlarges beautifully. In fact, it seems better for 9 or 12. Naturally it must cook longer when made in larger quantity.

YIELD: 6–8 SERVINGS

VARIATION AND EVEN BETTER:

Add 1 clove mashed garlic and a wine glass of brandy to custard before pouring into pie crust.

The Memphis Cook Book
THE JUNIOR LEAGUE OF MEMPHIS, TENNESSEE

. . . .

Savannah Quiche

1 unbaked 9-inch pie shell
2 fresh tomatoes
Salt and pepper
Flour
2 tablespoons oil
1 cup chopped onions
3 slices provolone cheese, broken into bite-size bits
¾ cup heavy cream
2 eggs, beaten
1 cup shredded Swiss cheese

Brown pie shell in 350° oven for 5 minutes.

Peel and slice tomatoes. Salt and pepper and dip in flour. Sauté in oil. Remove and drain.

Place tomatoes and onions in bottom of pie crust, then top with provolone cheese. Mix cream and eggs together. Pour into pie shell. Sprinkle Swiss cheese on top. Bake at 375° for 35–40 minutes.

YIELD: 6–8 SERVINGS

300 Years of Carolina Cooking
THE JUNIOR LEAGUE OF GREENVILLE, SOUTH CAROLINA

Soups

Avocado Soup

1 ripe avocado
1 cup light cream
Juice of 1 lime
2 cups chicken broth
½ teaspoon salt
2 tablespoons white rum
½ teaspoon curry powder
Freshly ground pepper to taste
Chopped chives

Put all ingredients into blender; cream. Chill thoroughly.

Serve with finely chopped chives on top. Cannot be prepared ahead or frozen.

YIELD: 6 SERVINGS

Seasoned with Sun: Recipes from the Southwest
THE JUNIOR LEAGUE OF EL PASO, TEXAS

· · · · · · · · · · · · · · · ·

Cold Curry Soup

2 tablespoons butter
2 tablespoons curry powder
1 quart chicken broth
6 egg yolks
½ pint heavy cream
Chopped parsley

Put butter in large saucepan, add curry powder, mix, and let simmer 5 minutes. Add chicken broth and bring to a boil. Mix egg yolks and cream well, and add to the broth. Stir over low heat until thickened. *Do not boil.* Chill and serve ice cold with garnish of chopped parsley.

YIELD: 4 SERVINGS

Nashville Seasons
THE JUNIOR LEAGUE OF NASHVILLE, TENNESSEE

·   ·   ·   ·   ·   ·   ·   ·   ·   ·   ·   ·   ·   ·   ·   ·

Chilled Cucumber Soup

2 medium cucumbers, peeled and sliced
1 cup buttermilk
½ cup light cream
1 small green onion, including 3 inches of top
A few sprigs parsley
¼ teaspoon garlic salt
½ teaspoon salt
Dash white pepper
½ teaspoon white wine tarragon vinegar
½ cup sour cream
Cucumber slice or chopped parsley for garnish

Purée cucumbers in blender with ½ cup of buttermilk, cream, green onion, and parsley. Add garlic salt, salt, white pepper, ½ cup of buttermilk, and vinegar. Blend a few seconds. Add sour cream and blend only long enough to mix.

Refrigerate several hours or overnight to develop flavor.

Serve this refreshing soup thoroughly chilled, and garnish with a thin slice of cucumber or chopped parsley.

YIELD: 6 SERVINGS

Winston-Salem's Heritage of Hospitality
THE JUNIOR LEAGUE OF WINSTON-SALEM, NORTH CAROLINA

·   ·   ·   ·   ·   ·   ·   ·   ·   ·   ·   ·   ·   ·   ·   ·

Gazpacho with Sour Cream

1 cucumber
½ onion or 3–4 scallions
1 avocado
1 tomato
1 green pepper
6 tablespoons salad oil
4 tablespoons wine vinegar
8 cups tomato juice
Juice of 4 limes
3–4 dashes Tabasco
1 teaspoon salt
½ pint sour cream
Celery
Croutons
Bacon bits

Chop first five ingredients. Mix with next six ingredients. Refrigerate.

Serve with sour cream and pass bowls of chopped celery, croutons, and bacon bits.

YIELD: 8–10 SERVINGS

Seasoned with Sun: Recipes from the Southwest
THE JUNIOR LEAGUE OF EL PASO, TEXAS

. . . .

Watercress Soup

2 pounds potatoes, peeled and sliced
2 pounds leeks or yellow onions, sliced
2 quarts chicken stock
1 cup watercress, packed
1 cup heavy cream
Salt and pepper to taste
Minced chives

Simmer potatoes and leeks in stock, covered, for 45 minutes. Add watercress; cook 5 minutes. Purée in blender. Add cream, salt, and pepper. Chill.

Serve cold and garnish with minced chives.

YIELD: 8 SERVINGS

VARIATIONS:

Substitute 1 cup spinach or 2 cups asparagus cooked until tender and cut in pieces in place of watercress. Serve hot or cold.

Little Rock Cooks
THE JUNIOR LEAGUE OF LITTLE ROCK, ARKANSAS

. . . .

Glorious Gazpacho

¼ cup olive oil
2 tablespoons lemon juice
3 cups tomato juice
1 cup beef broth
¼ cup minced onion
1 tomato, cubed
1 cup minced celery
Dash Tabasco
1 teaspoon salt
⅛ teaspoon freshly ground pepper
1 green or red pepper, minced
1 cucumber, diced
Croutons

Beat together the oil and lemon juice. Stir in the tomato juice, broth, onion, tomato, celery, Tabasco, salt, and pepper.

Recipe continues . . .

Chill 3 hours. Serve peppers, cucumber, and croutons as garnishes. Keeps several weeks in refrigerator.

YIELD: 4 SERVINGS

Fiesta: Favorite Recipes of South Texas
THE JUNIOR LEAGUE OF CORPUS CHRISTI, TEXAS

. . . .

Crème Vichyssoise

4 leeks or 3 peeled medium onions
2½ cups diced peeled potatoes
2 cups canned chicken broth
1 tablespoon butter
2 cups milk
1 cup heavy cream
2 teaspoons salt
¼ teaspoon pepper
2 tablespoons minced chives
¼ teaspoon paprika

Cut the leeks and about 3 inches of their green tops into fine pieces. (If using onions, chop them fine.) Cook with the potatoes in about 3 cups boiling water until very tender. Drain, then press through a fine strainer into a saucepan.

Add the broth, butter, milk, cream, salt, and pepper and mix thoroughly. Reheat to blend.

Serve hot or very cold, garnished with chopped chives and paprika.

YIELD: 6 SERVINGS

The Cotton Blossom Cookbook
THE JUNIOR LEAGUE OF ATLANTA, GEORGIA

. . . .

Artichoke Soup

4 large or 6 medium artichokes
½ cup finely chopped onion
½ cup finely chopped celery
6 tablespoons butter
6 tablespoons flour
6 cups clear chicken broth
¼ cup lemon juice
1 bay leaf
1 teaspoon salt
¼ teaspoon ground pepper
¼ teaspoon thyme
2 cups light cream
2 egg yolks, beaten
Lemon slices
Parsley

Boil artichokes for 1 hour. Scrape soft vegetable from leaves and finely chop bottoms.

In saucepan sauté onion and celery in butter until soft, not brown. Add flour and cook 1 minute, stirring constantly. Add stock and lemon juice and stir until blended. Add bay leaf, salt, pepper, thyme, and artichoke scrapings and bottoms. Cover and simmer 20 minutes or until slightly thickened.

When ready to serve, heat to boiling point and remove from heat. Stir in cream and egg yolks which have been beaten together. Keep heated over hot water. Serve garnished with lemon slices and parsley.

YIELD: 12 SERVINGS

The Dallas Jr. League Cookbook
THE JUNIOR LEAGUE OF DALLAS, TEXAS

Black Bean Soup

2 cups black beans
2 quarts cold water
4 tablespoons butter
½ cup chopped celery leaves
2 stalks celery, cut up
½ cup chopped onion
2 medium-size carrots, chopped
4 whole cloves
10 peppercorns, gently bruised
2 bay leaves
8 grains mustard seed
2 teaspoons salt
2 small cloves garlic
Large ham bone
Dash cayenne
⅓ cup Marsala or sherry
Thin lemon slices
Hard-boiled egg, sliced

Wash and pick over beans. Put them in soup kettle with water and bring to a boil.

Meanwhile, sauté in butter the celery leaves, celery, onion, and carrots, until they just begin to brown. Add these to beans, as well as cloves, peppercorns gently bruised, bay leaves, mustard seed, salt, garlic and large ham bone. Let simmer until beans are tender, about 4 hours. Add a little more water if it cooks away too much.

At end of cooking time, remove ham bone and purée soup in blender.

Reheat to boiling point; taste for seasoning; add cayenne, and stir in Marsala or sherry.

When serving, place a thin slice of lemon and a slice of hard-boiled egg in each soup plate or bowl and pour hot soup over them.

YIELD: 12 SERVINGS

Home Cookin'
THE JUNIOR LEAGUE OF WICHITA FALLS, TEXAS

Cauliflower Soup

2 tablespoons shortening
½ cup chopped onion
1 small carrot, cut up
1 cup chopped celery
1 head firm white cauliflower (about 1 quart cut up)
2 tablespoons chopped parsley
2 quarts chicken broth
1 tablespoon salt
½ teaspoon peppercorns, ½ bay leaf, 1 teaspoon tarragon,
tied in a cheesecloth bag
4 tablespoons butter
6 tablespoons flour
2 cups milk
1 cup half and half
1 cup sour cream at room temperature

In large pot, melt shortening, add onion; stir constantly over medium heat until onions start to turn yellow. Continue stirring, add carrot and celery, and cook 2 minutes. Add cauliflower and 1 tablespoon parsley. Cover pot and turn heat very low, stirring occasionally to prevent sticking. After 15 minutes, add chicken broth, salt, and cheesecloth bag of herbs. Bring to a boil over medium heat. Reduce heat and let simmer.

In a small pan, melt butter. Mix flour into milk with wire whisk and slowly, using wire whisk, add to butter. Cook to medium consistency. Remove from heat; dilute with half and half and pour into simmering soup. Stir gently with wooden spoon and simmer for 15–20 minutes.

Just before serving, place sour cream in a soup tureen and mix in remaining tablespoon of parsley. Put 2 or 3 ladles hot soup in tureen and

Recipe continues . . .

stir into sour cream. Remove cheesecloth bag from soup and pour all of soup into tureen. Serve immediately.

NOTE: If you make your own chicken broth, put leaves, hard white core, and stalks from cauliflower in to cook with soup bones. This gives the broth a stronger cauliflower flavor.

YIELD: 8 SERVINGS

Southern Accent
THE JUNIOR LEAGUE OF PINE BLUFF, ARKANSAS

. . . .

Canadian Cheese Soup

½ cup butter
¾ cup finely diced onion
½ cup finely diced carrot
½ cup finely diced celery
½ cup flour
2 tablespoons cornstarch
1 quart chicken stock
1 quart milk
⅛ teaspoon baking soda
1 cup shredded cheddar cheese
Salt and pepper to taste
2 tablespoons finely chopped parsley

Melt butter in large pot. Add onion, carrot, and celery and sauté until soft. Add flour and cornstarch and stir well. Add chicken stock and milk. Cook, stirring constantly, until mixture has smooth velvet texture and thickens. Add soda and cheese and stir until blended. Season with salt and pepper.

Add parsley a few minutes before serving.

YIELD: 10–12 SERVINGS

The Dallas Jr. League Cookbook
THE JUNIOR LEAGUE OF DALLAS, TEXAS

. . . .

Hearty Lentil Soup

1¼ cups dry lentils
5 cups water
4 slices bacon, cut into small pieces
1 onion, chopped fine
1 clove garlic, crushed
1 carrot, sliced thin
1 green pepper, chopped
1 tomato, chopped
3 tablespoons butter
3 tablespoons flour
1 10½-ounce can consommé or stock
2 teaspoons salt
2 teaspoons vinegar

Soak lentils overnight; cook for 1 hour in the water in which they soaked.

Cook bacon pieces in large skillet until almost crisp. Sauté vegetables with bacon and fat until they are limp (about 5 minutes). Drain off the bacon drippings. Add vegetables and bacon to cooked lentils.

In same skillet, melt butter and stir in flour to make a smooth paste. Add consommé, season with salt and vinegar, and cook until smooth and slightly thickened. Add this sauce to lentil mixture; stir, cook over low heat for another 30 minutes or longer.

May be mixed in blender for smoother consistency.

Serve with crisp French bread and green salad. For variety, try slicing Vienna sausage into soup before serving.

YIELD: 8 SERVINGS

Cooking Through Rose Colored Glasses
THE JUNIOR LEAGUE OF TYLER, TEXAS

Hot Madrilène

¼ cup butter
¼ cup chopped onion
2 18-ounce cans tomato juice
1 bay leaf
2 10½-ounce cans beef broth or bouillon
Grated Parmesan cheese
Parsley

In a 3-quart saucepan, melt butter and sauté onion. Add tomato juice, bay leaf, and broth. Heat just to boiling point; reduce heat and simmer for 5 minutes. Serve in cups, garnished with cheese and parsley.

YIELD: 10–12 SERVINGS

Cooking Through Rose Colored Glasses
THE JUNIOR LEAGUE OF TYLER, TEXAS

· · · · · · · · · · · · · · · · ·

Summer Squash Soup

2 medium yellow squash
2 small zucchini
1½ cups celery leaves
3 tablespoons butter
4 cups chicken stock
Salt and pepper to taste
Celery salt
2 tablespoons finely chopped parsley

Chop unpeeled squash and zucchini into small pieces.

In a covered pan, cook squash, zucchini, and celery leaves with butter over very low heat until tender (about 20 minutes). Purée mixture in blender, adding 1 cup of stock.

Mix purée with rest of stock. Correct seasoning with salt, pepper, and celery salt. Bring back to boil. Serve hot or cold, garnished with parsley.

YIELD: 6 SERVINGS

Southern Accent
THE JUNIOR LEAGUE OF PINE BLUFF, ARKANSAS

· · · · · · · · · · · · · · · · ·

Cream of Cucumber Soup

2 8-inch cucumbers (1 pound)
2 tablespoons butter
¼ cup chopped shallots or scallions
4 cups clear chicken broth
1 teaspoon wine vinegar
½ teaspoon dried dill weed or tarragon
3 tablespoons quick-cooking farina cereal
Salt and white pepper
1 cup sour cream
1 tablespoon dill weed or parsley for garnish

Peel cucumbers. Cut 12–14 paper-thin slices and reserve in a bowl for decoration later. Chop rest into ½-inch chunks—about 3 cups in all.

Melt butter in a heavy 3-quart saucepan, stir in shallots or scallions, and cook over moderate heat for 1 minute. Add cucumber, chicken broth, vinegar, and either dill weed or tarragon. Bring to a boil and stir in farina gradually. Boil slowly, uncovered, for 20 minutes, until farina is very tender.

Purée through food mill (medium disk) or coarse sieve and return soup to pan. Mixture should be consistency of vichyssoise; thin with milk if necessary. Season to taste with salt and white pepper.

To serve cold, add extra salt and beat in sour cream. Top with cucumber slices and dill or parsley.

Recipe continues . . .

To serve hot, bring soup to simmer and beat in sour cream just before serving. Top with cucumber slices and dill or parsley.

May be frozen before adding sour cream.

YIELD: 6 SERVINGS

Cooking Through Rose Colored Glasses
THE JUNIOR LEAGUE OF TYLER, TEXAS

Whole Tomato Soup

2 beef bouillon cubes
½ cup boiling water
1 tablespoon butter
1 fresh tomato, peeled
2 stalks celery with leaves, cut to convenient lengths
Salt and pepper
Cayenne
Marjoram or basil

Combine bouillon cubes and water to make bouillon.

Melt butter in saucepan. Add whole tomato, bouillon, and celery. Sprinkle with salt, pepper, cayenne, and marjoram or basil, to taste. Cover and simmer 30 minutes.

Remove celery.

Serve in large soup plate.

YIELD: 1 SERVING

Mountain Measures
THE JUNIOR LEAGUE OF CHARLESTON, WEST VIRGINIA

Tortilla Soup

1 small onion, chopped
1 4-ounce can chopped green chilies
2 cloves garlic, crushed
2 tablespoons oil
1 cup tomatoes, peeled and chopped
1 10½-ounce can condensed beef bouillon
1 10¾-ounce can condensed chicken broth
1½ cups water
1½ cups tomato juice
1 teaspoon ground cumin
1 teaspoon chili powder
1 teaspoon salt
⅛ teaspoon pepper
2 teaspoons Worcestershire sauce
1 tablespoon steak sauce
3 tortillas, cut into ½-inch strips
¼ cup shredded cheddar cheese

Sauté onion, chilies, and garlic in oil until soft. Add tomatoes, bouillon, chicken broth, water, tomato juice, cumin, chili powder, salt, pepper, and Worcestershire and steak sauces.

Bring soup to a boil; lower heat, simmer covered for 1 hour.

Add tortillas and cheese and simmer 10 minutes longer.

YIELD: 6 SERVINGS

Seasoned with Sun: Recipes from the Southwest
THE JUNIOR LEAGUE OF EL PASO, TEXAS

Cream of Zucchini Soup

1 pound young zucchini
2 tablespoons butter
2 tablespoons finely chopped shallots
1 clove garlic, minced
1 teaspoon curry powder
½ teaspoon salt
½ cup heavy cream
1¾ cups chicken broth
Croutons or chopped chives

Scrub zucchini and slice thin.

Heat butter and add zucchini, shallots, and garlic. Cover tight and simmer 10 minutes. Shake occasionally; do not let mixture brown. Spoon mixture into blender; add curry powder, salt, cream, and broth and blend for 30 seconds.

Serve hot with croutons or cold with chopped chives.

YIELD: 4 SERVINGS

Home Cookin'
THE JUNIOR LEAGUE OF WICHITA FALLS, TEXAS

.   .   .   .

Carolina or She-Crab Soup

1 pint milk
4 blades whole mace
2 pieces lemon peel
1 pound white crabmeat
½ stick butter
1 pint light cream
¼ cup cracker crumbs
Salt and pepper to taste
2 tablespoons sherry

Put milk in top of double boiler with mace and lemon peel and allow to simmer for a few minutes. Then add crab, butter, and cream and cook for 15 minutes.

Thicken with cracker crumbs; season with salt and pepper and allow to stand on back of stove for a few minutes to bring out the flavor.

Just before serving, add sherry.

YIELD: 6 SERVINGS

VARIATION:

This same soup can be made with ground shrimp instead of crab.

Charleston Receipts
THE JUNIOR LEAGUE OF CHARLESTON, SOUTH CAROLINA

·   ·   ·   ·   ·   ·   ·   ·   ·   ·   ·   ·   ·   ·   ·   ·

Neely's Oyster Bisque

1 quart oysters, minced
1 bunch shallots, minced
1 clove garlic, minced
½ cup butter
2 tablespoons flour
1 pint heavy cream
1 pint half and half
Salt and pepper
Dry sherry

Heat oysters, shallots, and garlic in hot butter until oysters curl. Stir in flour.

In a double boiler, heat cream and half and half, and add oyster mixture. Add salt, pepper, and sherry to taste.

YIELD: 8–12 SERVINGS

Fiesta: Favorite Recipes of South Texas
THE JUNIOR LEAGUE OF CORPUS CHRISTI, TEXAS

·   ·   ·   ·   ·   ·   ·   ·   ·   ·   ·   ·   ·   ·   ·   ·

Cioppino

The name of this stew comes from the fishermen at the San Francisco wharf who used to "chip in" everything they had caught that day that had not been sold. They would make this marvelous stew, open a bottle of wine, put out some French bread, and have themselves a feast!

2 large onions, cut into wedges
2 bunches green onions, diced
2 green peppers, seeded and diced
4 large cloves garlic, crushed
½ cup olive oil
2 cups red wine
1 8-ounce can tomato purée
4 cups water
1 bay leaf
1 teaspoon oregano
1 teaspoon basil
½ pound lump crabmeat or crab claws
2 dozen clams in shell
2 dozen large shrimp
2 pounds firm-fleshed fish
1 whole lobster (optional)
1 teaspoon hot-pepper sauce
Salt and pepper

Sauté onion, green onions, green peppers, and garlic in oil for 5 minutes. Add wine and simmer briskly. Add purée, water, and herbs. Cover and simmer 1 hour.

Place crabmeat, clams in shells, shrimp, fish, and lobster, cut into good-sized chunks, into a large kettle. Add hot sauce and simmer 20–30 minutes or until clams open. Salt and pepper to taste.

YIELD: 6–8 SERVINGS

The Dallas Jr. League Cookbook
THE JUNIOR LEAGUE OF DALLAS, TEXAS

Crab Bisque

½ cup butter
½ cup chopped onion
1 cup chopped green onion
4 cups chicken stock
4 carrots, cut in small bits
1 cup chopped parsley
2 cups chopped celery
3 teaspoons salt
½ teaspoon white pepper
½ teaspoon powdered mace
½ teaspoon thyme
3 bay leaves
¼ teaspoon Tabasco
3 pounds redfish, scamp, or similar fish
4 cups milk
⅓ cup flour
4 cups heavy cream
1 pound cleaned, cooked, and chopped shrimp
1 pound lump crabmeat
½ teaspoon paprika

Melt butter in large pot. Add onion and green onion and cook slowly until tender. Add chicken stock, carrots, parsley, celery, salt, pepper, mace, thyme, bay leaves, Tabasco, and fish. Simmer for 45 minutes, adding additional stock or water if necessary.

Slowly add 1 cup of milk to the flour, mixing until smooth. Add this milk-and-flour mixture to the pot. Stirring constantly, slowly add remaining milk and the cream to the pot. Continue stirring over medium heat until smooth and thick.

Reserve 3 tablespoons shrimp. Add remaining shrimp and crabmeat. Continue stirring and cook for 10 minutes more. Serve in large ramekins or soup bowls. Garnish with chopped shrimp and paprika.

YIELD: 14 SERVINGS

The Gasparilla Cookbook
THE JUNIOR LEAGUE OF TAMPA, FLORIDA

.   .   .   .

Artichoke Oyster Soup

½ cup butter
1½ cups chopped green onions, including 2 onion tops
2 garlic cloves, minced
3 tablespoons flour
3 14-ounce cans artichoke hearts, drained, rinsed, and quartered
6 cups chicken stock
½ teaspoon crushed red pepper
¼ teaspoon anise seed
1 teaspoon salt
1 quart oysters, cut in half if large

Melt butter in a large heavy pot, add green onions and garlic, and sauté for 3–5 minutes. Add flour and cook 5 minutes, stirring constantly. Stir in artichokes; add stock and seasonings and cook 20 minutes. Add oysters and their liquor and simmer 10 minutes. *Do not boil* and *do not overcook.*

This soup is most delicious if made the day before serving, allowing flavors to blend. If you want to drink the soup from mugs, purée in blender and top with a lemon slice.

YIELD: 12–14 SERVINGS

Southern Accent
THE JUNIOR LEAGUE OF PINE BLUFF, ARKANSAS

· · · · · · · · · · · · · · · ·

Adair McKoy Graham's Oyster Stew

1 quart milk
½–¾ stick butter
1 pint oysters
Salt and pepper

Heat milk and butter to just below boiling point (stir to avoid scalding milk). In a separate saucepan, heat oysters in their juice until edges of oysters curl. Pour contents into milk. Salt and pepper to taste.

Serve hot with saltine crackers.

YIELD: 4 SERVINGS

Seafood Sorcery
THE JUNIOR LEAGUE OF WILMINGTON, NORTH CAROLINA

·　·　·　·　·　·　·　·　·　·　·　·　·　·　·　·

Oyster Stew

1 pint fresh oysters and liquor
½ stick butter
1 medium green onion, chopped
1 teaspoon dry parsley flakes
½ teaspoon Worcestershire sauce
¼ teaspoon Tabasco
Salt and pepper to taste
2 cups milk, cream, or half and half
Paprika

In a saucepan, combine all ingredients except milk. Heat and simmer until edges of oysters curl (about 10 minutes). In another saucepan, scald milk, cream, or half and half. Add to other ingredients and serve. Sprinkle paprika over each serving.

YIELD: 4 SMALL SERVINGS

Recipe Jubilee
THE JUNIOR LEAGUE OF MOBILE, ALABAMA

·　·　·　·　·　·　·　·　·　·　·　·　·　·　·　·

Louisiana Oyster Bisque

1 pint oysters
1 chicken bouillon cube
1 teaspoon grated onion
1 large sprig parsley
1 bay leaf
3 tablespoons butter
4 tablespoons flour
1 quart half and half
¾ teaspoon salt
Dash pepper
½ pint heavy cream

Chop oysters fine (this releases all the flavor and makes a strongly flavored bisque) and pour oysters and liquor in a saucepan. Add bouillon cube, onion, parsley, and bay leaf. Cook gently for about 3 minutes.

Melt butter in top of large double boiler, add flour, and stir until blended. Add half and half gradually and cook until thickened. Stir constantly.

Add oyster mixture, salt, and pepper, and then stir in cream. Reheat and serve after removing parsley and bay leaf.

This may be made ahead, as it keeps nicely for two days.

YIELD: 6 SERVINGS

A Cook's Tour of Shreveport
THE JUNIOR LEAGUE OF SHREVEPORT, LOUISIANA

Florida Fish Chowder

1 cup diced potatoes
1 cup sliced carrots
½ cup diced celery
½ teaspoon salt
2 tablespoons butter (or more)
1 medium onion, sliced thin
1–2 pounds snapper, grouper, snook, or other firm-meat fish,
skinned, boned, and cut into 1-inch pieces
1 teaspoon Worcestershire sauce
1 teaspoon salt
¼ teaspoon pepper
2–3 cups milk
Paprika

Cook potatoes, carrots, celery, and salt in water to cover until vegetables are almost tender.

Melt butter in large saucepan. Add onion and cook over low heat until limp but not brown. Add fish and Worcestershire sauce and cook 1 minute, stirring gently.

Add vegetables and water and cook this mixture 10 minutes. Add salt, pepper, and milk; heat slowly to boiling.

Sprinkle paprika on each bowlful of chowder.

YIELD: 6–8 SERVINGS

The Gasparilla Cookbook
THE JUNIOR LEAGUE OF TAMPA, FLORIDA

Sausage-Bean Chowder

1 pound bulk pork sausage
2 16-ounce cans kidney beans
1 1-pound 13-ounce can tomatoes, broken up
1 quart water
1 large onion, chopped
1 bay leaf
1½ teaspoons seasoned salt
½ teaspoon garlic salt
½ teaspoon thyme
⅛ teaspoon pepper
1 cup diced potatoes
½ green pepper, chopped

In a skillet, cook sausage until brown. Pour off drippings.

In a large kettle, combine beans, tomatoes, water, onion, bay leaf, seasoned salt, garlic salt, thyme, and pepper. Add sausage and simmer, covered, for 1 hour.

Add potatoes and green pepper. Cook covered for 15–20 minutes, until potatoes are tender. Remove bay leaf.

YIELD: 8 GENEROUS SERVINGS

The Charlotte Cookbook
THE JUNIOR LEAGUE OF CHARLOTTE, NORTH CAROLINA

· · · · · · · · · · · · · · · · · ·

Shrimp Bisque

4 tablespoons flour
4 tablespoons butter
2 cups hot milk
Salt and cayenne
½ pound cooked shrimp
Large spoonful sherry

Put flour and butter in double boiler and cook, stirring, until blended. Add hot milk. Stir until smooth.

Season with salt and cayenne. Add shrimp, cut into small pieces. Flavor with sherry.

YIELD: 4 SERVINGS

Spartanburg Secrets II
THE JUNIOR LEAGUE OF SPARTANBURG, SOUTH CAROLINA

. . . .

Court Bouillon

1 cup oil
1 cup flour
3 large onions, chopped
1 cup chopped celery
3 cloves garlic, chopped
1 large can tomatoes
2 6-ounce cans tomato paste
2½ quarts water
4 pounds firm fish (catfish, goo, large sac-a-lait, redfish)
Salt and pepper to taste
2 tablespoons chopped green onion tops
2 tablespoons chopped parsley

Make brown roux of oil and flour. Add onions, celery, and garlic; let cook until soft. Add tomatoes and tomato paste. Cook slowly, stirring, for 5 minutes. Add water and simmer 1 hour. Add 4 pounds fish, cut into pieces. Cook about 15 minutes. Do not overcook. Season to taste and add onion tops and parsley about 5 minutes before serving.

Serve over rice in soup plates.

YIELD: 6–8 SERVINGS

Talk About Good!
THE JUNIOR LEAGUE OF LAFAYETTE, LOUISIANA

. . . .

Crabmeat Bisque

1 10¾-ounce can condensed pea soup
1 10¾-ounce can condensed tomato soup
¾ cup chicken broth (optional)
1½ pints light cream
½ pound crabmeat
1 wineglass sherry

Combine and heat soups (and chicken broth if used). When just under the boiling point, add cream, crabmeat, and sherry.

YIELD: 4 SERVINGS

The Memphis Cook Book
THE JUNIOR LEAGUE OF MEMPHIS, TENNESSEE

·   ·   ·   ·   ·   ·   ·   ·   ·   ·   ·   ·   ·   ·

Duck Gumbo Original

3 ducks
3 quarts hot chicken stock
1 cup flour
½ cup bacon drippings
3 yellow onions, chopped
4 stalks celery, chopped, with leaves
¼ cup chopped parsley
2 green peppers, chopped
8 large cloves garlic, pressed
2 10-ounce packages frozen okra or 3 cups chopped fresh
½ bunch green onions, chopped (set tops aside)

Boil ducks in chicken stock until tender; cool and pull meat off bones. Cut into small pieces and place back in stock to keep moist.

In heavy black skillet, make dark brown roux with flour and drippings over medium high heat. Stir constantly with wooden paddle to keep from sticking until roux is dark and glossy like chocolate.

Add chopped vegetables to roux and cook until okra stops stringing. Add hot stock (1 pint at first) and incorporate into roux. Add duck meat and cover. Simmer slowly 2 hours.

Serve over a scoop of cooked rice in bowl. Sprinkle with green onion tops.

Cajuns never serve a salad with gumbo, just French bread!

NOTE: Never add anything cold to a hot roux, even if it means placing chopped ingredients in a warm oven.

YIELD: 2 GALLONS

Southern Sideboards
THE JUNIOR LEAGUE OF JACKSON, MISSISSIPPI

. . . .

Smoked Duck and Oyster Gumbo

3 wild ducks
½ cup butter
½ cup flour
1 medium green pepper, chopped
1 large onion, chopped
1 large clove garlic, minced
¼ cup fresh parsley, chopped
1 10-ounce package frozen cut okra or ½ pound fresh, cut
1 16-ounce can tomatoes or 4–6 fresh tomatoes
Salt, pepper, paprika, and red pepper to taste
1 pint fresh oysters
Cooked rice

Recipe continues . . .

Smoke the ducks, away from the flame, on a charcoal smoker with hickory chips on the charcoal for flavor. Keep smoker closed throughout cooking period, about 4 hours.

Next stew the ducks in a covered Dutch oven, in water halfway up the depth of the ducks, for 2–3 hours or until meat almost falls away from bones. Debone and cut meat into bite-size chunks. (Use as much meat as possible, but take care to remove any shot!) Strain and reserve duck broth.

Melt butter in a large iron skillet; add flour and brown until roux is dark golden. Add green pepper and onion, continuing to brown slowly; add garlic toward the end.

Pour reserved broth into a large Dutch oven and whisk in roux mixture. Add duck meat and cook, covered, at low temperature for 30 minutes. Stir in parsley, okra, tomatoes, and seasonings. Cook slowly until okra is tender.

Can be chilled at this point.

When ready to serve, heat to boiling and add oysters (which you have picked over carefully), cooking until *just* done. Check seasonings and ladle large amount of gumbo over rice in large soup bowls.

YIELD: 8 SERVINGS

Southern Accent
THE JUNIOR LEAGUE OF PINE BLUFF, ARKANSAS

· · · · · · · · · · · · · · ·

Chicken or Seafood Okra Gumbo

10 pounds okra, sliced
3 onions, chopped
½ stalk celery, chopped
2 cloves garlic, minced
2 15-ounce cans tomatoes
1 6-ounce can tomato paste

Put all ingredients in heavy Dutch oven in 250° oven. Let cook about 3 hours, removing cover last half hour. Stir once or twice while cooking.

You can cook okra mixture in advance, freeze it, and have it ready to use.

If for *Chicken Gumbo:* Brown 1 large chicken cut into pieces; add 1 gallon water; cook chicken until tender. Add okra mixture; season. Heat for about 20 minutes. Serve over rice in soup plates.

If for *Seafood Gumbo:* Add 1 gallon of water to okra mixture; heat; add 2 pounds raw, peeled, deveined shrimp, or 1 dozen cleaned crabs. Cook for 15–20 minutes; season; serve in same way as chicken gumbo.

YIELD: 12–16 SERVINGS

Talk About Good!
THE JUNIOR LEAGUE OF LAFAYETTE, LOUISIANA

· · · · · · · · · · · · · · · · ·

Okra Gumbo

4 tablespoons lard or oil
2 tablespoons flour
3 large onions, chopped
3 pounds okra, sliced thin
Salt and pepper
1 tablespoon vinegar
3 large tomatoes, peeled and chopped
1 quart water
3 pounds shrimp or 2 pounds shrimp and ½ pound crabmeat
Gumbo filé (optional)

Make a roux by blending 2 tablespoons of the oil or lard and the flour in a stew pan over low heat. Stir with a wooden cooking spoon until it begins to brown lightly. Add 2 more tablespoons oil or lard, and in this, smother onions and okra. Increase heat and cook until vegetables are soft and aroma is good.

Add salt, pepper, and vinegar, stir briefly, and then add tomatoes and water.

Recipe continues . . .

After boiling gently for about 20 minutes, add raw shrimp or shrimp plus crabmeat. Boil gently until shrimp are cooked and gumbo flavor is at its peak (up to a half hour).

Gumbo filé adds flavor when sprinkled on individual servings at the table, but do not add earlier. Filé thickens and becomes bitter when heated.

Serve with steamed rice and hot buttered French bread.

YIELD: 6 SERVINGS

Seafood Sorcery
THE JUNIOR LEAGUE OF WILMINGTON, NORTH CAROLINA

· · · · · · · · · · · · · · · · ·

Spinach Soup

2 packages frozen chopped spinach
2 quarts chicken stock
2 eggs
Salt
Grated Parmesan cheese

Cook spinach in stock. Just before spinach is done and while stock is still boiling, drop slightly beaten eggs into pot. Stir 1 minute. Add salt to taste.

Serve topped with grated Parmesan cheese.

YIELD: 8 SERVINGS

That Something Special
THE JUNIOR LEAGUE OF DURHAM, NORTH CAROLINA

· · · · · · · · · · · · · · ·

Spicy Seafood Gumbo

3 cups bacon drippings
1 cup flour
4 pounds okra, sliced
1 tablespoon paprika
3 cups chopped onion
2 cups chopped green pepper
2 cups chopped celery
2 cups chopped parsley
4 8-ounce cans tomato sauce
4 10-ounce cans tomatoes with green chilies
2 gallons chicken stock
4 bay leaves
4 teaspoons thyme
¼ cup pepper
¼ cup Worcestershire sauce
¼ cup salt
2 tablespoons oregano
Tabasco
Dry white wine (optional)
4–5 pounds peeled cleaned shrimp
2–3 pounds crabmeat
6–8 pints oysters
Cooked rice (optional)
Gumbo filé (optional)

Make a roux in a 12- to 14-quart kettle by heating 2 cups bacon drippings and adding flour. Cook over low heat, stirring constantly, until roux is brown. Add okra and paprika and cook over low heat, stirring constantly, until okra is brown and ropy.

In a large skillet, heat remaining cup of drippings and sauté onion, green pepper, celery, and parsley until onion is clear. Add the mixture to the roux. Add tomato sauce, tomatoes with chilies, stock, and seasonings and simmer for 5 hours. Maintain the liquid level by adding wine or water as needed.

Recipe continues . . .

About 30 minutes before serving, add seafood. Serve in deep soup bowls, over rice if desired.

Gumbo filé may be sprinkled lightly in the gumbo.

YIELD: 3 GALLONS

VARIATION:

For a chicken gumbo, omit seafood and add the cooked meat from a 3- to 4-pound hen and 2–3 pounds cooked ham.

Fiesta: Favorite Recipes of South Texas
THE JUNIOR LEAGUE OF CORPUS CHRISTI, TEXAS

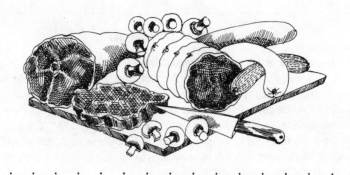

Meats

Standing Rib Roast

Foolproof with delicious texture and flavor.

This recipe is for a standing rib roast of any size. Meat should be at room temperature. Preheat oven to 375°. Cook roast, seasoned to taste, in shallow pan, fat side up, for 1 hour. NEVER OPEN OVEN DOOR. Turn oven off. Before serving, turn on oven again for 40 minutes at 375°. Cook in the morning the first time or at least 3 hours before the second cooking (If the roast is small, cook only 35 minutes for the second cooking.) This makes a rare to medium-rare roast.

YIELD: 2 SERVINGS PER RIB

Party Potpourri
THE JUNIOR LEAGUE OF MEMPHIS, TENNESSEE

·   ·   ·   ·   ·   ·   ·   ·   ·   ·   ·   ·   ·   ·   ·   ·   ·

Marinated Roast

5 pounds eye of round or sirloin tip roast
1 clove garlic, cut into 8 slivers
1 teaspoon salt
½ teaspoon pepper
1 teaspoon thyme

MARINADE:
½ cup Italian dressing
1 cup red wine
1 bay leaf, crumbled

SAUCE:
2 tablespoons flour
1 cup red wine
¼ teaspoon salt
Dash pepper

The day before cooking, make 8 slits, 1-inch deep, across top of roast; insert a sliver of garlic into each. Rub entire surface of meat with seasonings. Place in a plastic bag and cover with combined marinade ingredients; refrigerate overnight.

Next day, preheat oven to 450°. Place roast in shallow, open roasting pan. Insert meat thermometer into thickest part. Roast 25 minutes; pour marinade over and roast 25 minutes longer or until thermometer registers 140° for rare or 160° for medium. Remove to a platter and keep warm. Let stand 15 minutes for easier carving.

Pour fat from roasting pan; reserve 2 tablespoons of drippings in pan. Stir in flour to make a smooth paste. Add remaining ingredients; bring to a boil, stirring well. Simmer until thickened.

Cut meat into thin diagonal slices. Serve with sauce.

YIELD: 8–10 SERVINGS

Southern Accent
THE JUNIOR LEAGUE OF PINE BLUFF, ARKANSAS

.   .   .   .

Filet of Beef with Green Peppercorns

4 pounds filet, trimmed and tied
2 tablespoons oil
3 tablespoons cognac
1½ cups brown stock or bouillon
1 cup heavy cream
3 tablespoons green peppercorns, well drained
Lemon juice, salt, and pepper to taste
3 tablespoons butter, softened

In a large, heavy skillet, brown the filet well on all sides in the oil over moderately high heat. Transfer the meat to an oval gratin dish and roast uncovered 20–25 minutes in a 450° oven for rare (140° on a meat thermometer). Transfer the meat to a serving platter and let it rest for 10 minutes.

Recipe continues . . .

Meanwhile, make the sauce. Pour off fat from the skillet, add cognac, and flame, shaking the pan until the flames go out and stirring in the brown bits. Add the stock and cream. Reduce over moderately high heat to 2 cups. Add the peppercorns and lemon juice, salt, and pepper to taste. Remove pan from heat and swirl in butter, softened and cut into bits.

Slice meat and re-form into filet. Pour some of the sauce over, then serve remaining in a sauce boat. The sauce may also be served with sautéed steak, such as steak Diane or steak au poivre.

YIELD: 6 SERVINGS

The Dallas Jr. League Cookbook
THE JUNIOR LEAGUE OF DALLAS, TEXAS

Roast Peppered Rib Eye of Beef

½ cup coarsely cracked pepper
½ teaspoon ground cardamom seed
5 or 6 pounds boneless rib eye beef roast
1 tablespoon tomato paste
½ teaspoon garlic powder
1 cup soy sauce
¾ cup vinegar
1½ tablespoons cornstarch mixed with ¼ cup cold water (optional)

Rub pepper and cardamom all over meat.

Marinate meat in refrigerator for 24 hours in sauce made by mixing tomato paste, garlic powder, soy sauce, and vinegar.

One hour before cooking, spoon marinade over meat several times, and let stand at room temperature.

Wrap meat in foil. Place in shallow pan and roast at 300° for 2 hours for medium rare. Open foil. Ladle out and reserve drippings. Brown roast uncovered at 350° while making gravy.

Strain pan drippings and skim off fat. To each cup meat juice, add 1 cup water. Bring to boil. Taste. If desired, add a little marinade.

Serve the roast au jus or thicken gravy with cornstarch mixed with cold water.

YIELD: 8–10 SERVINGS

Of Pots and Pipkins
THE JUNIOR LEAGUE OF ROANOKE VALLEY, VIRGINIA

.   .   .   .

Eye of the Round

Eye of the round roast (1½ pounds per person)
Red wine vinegar
Olive oil
Salt and freshly ground pepper
1 clove garlic, mashed

Marinate roast overnight in mixture of 3 parts red wine vinegar to 1 part olive oil, using enough marinade to cover one-half of the meat, and adding a great deal of freshly ground pepper, salt, and mashed garlic clove. Turn occasionally. Place in roasting pan and bake in oven at 400° for about 20 minutes per pound if you want it rare—longer for well-done meat.

It may also be cooked out on the grill (use hickory chips) and turned once. This takes longer but tastes better. Serve on cooked artichoke bottoms, and cover with Béarnaise Sauce (see page 321).

Nashville Seasons
THE JUNIOR LEAGUE OF NASHVILLE, TENNESSEE

.   .   .   .

Beef in Nutmeg

5 pounds sirloin tip roast
Garlic
Ground nutmeg
Butter
Parsley

SAUCE PIQUANTE:
1½ cans (2 cups) beef consommé
1 can beef gravy
All of juice from roast
½ cup dry red wine
1 cup sliced pitted ripe olives
2 tablespoons catsup
Salt and pepper to taste
1 tablespoon flour

Rub roast with garlic and nutmeg. Bake at 250° for 18 minutes per pound. Cut off oven and leave until cool. Slice thin with electric knife when cooled, sauté in butter, and sprinkle each piece with parsley

Combine sauce ingredients and bring to a simmer. Add meat slices and simmer for half day. Serve with rice pilaf and green salad.

YIELD: 4–6 SERVINGS

The Blue Denim Gourmet
THE JUNIOR LEAGUE OF ODESSA, TEXAS

· · · · · · · · · · · · · · · · · · ·

Miss Neida's Marinated Beef Tenderloin

3½–4 pounds beef tenderloin roast

MARINADE:
1 stick butter
½ cup olive oil
¼ cup vinegar
Juice of 2 lemons
2 heaping tablespoons sugar
Salt and garlic powder
Crushed red pepper
3 tablespoons dried parsley flakes
2 tablespoons Worcestershire sauce

Combine marinade ingredients in saucepan and bring to boil. Pour over tenderloin and marinate at least 2 hours or overnight if possible.

Broil whole tenderloin about 10 minutes per side or cook over charcoal.

YIELD: 6–8 SERVINGS

Huntsville Heritage Cookbook
THE JUNIOR LEAGUE OF HUNTSVILLE, ALABAMA

. . . .

Marinated Chuck Roast

3–5 pounds chuck roast
Tenderizer
1 tablespoon sesame seeds, browned in butter
½ cup strong coffee
½ cup soy sauce
1 tablespoon Worcestershire sauce
1 tablespoon vinegar
1 large onion, chopped

Recipe continues . . .

Sprinkle meat with tenderizer. Add sesame seeds and other ingredients and pour over roast. Let stand, turning every few hours, at room temperature all day (or even overnight).

Then charcoal broil until medium rare, about 45 minutes. Test for doneness with meat thermometer.

This is as good as a charcoaled sirloin!

YIELD: 4–6 SERVINGS DEPENDING ON SIZE OF ROAST

Nashville Seasons
THE JUNIOR LEAGUE OF NASHVILLE, TENNESSEE

· · · · · · · · · · · · · · · ·

Barbecued Beef Tenderloin

½ cup margarine
2 tablespoons Worcestershire sauce
½ teaspoon Tabasco
2 tablespoons vinegar
Juice of ½ lime
3–4 cloves garlic, pressed
2 tablespoons olive oil
Dash cayenne
1 teaspoon sugar
¼ cup catsup
2 tablespoons dry wine or beer
Salt to taste
3- to 5-pound beef tenderloin

Melt margarine in saucepan. Add remaining ingredients, except meat.

Take meat out of refrigerator, wipe, baste with sauce, and let stand about 30 minutes.

Sear over hot fire on grill. Move away from flame and hottest coals. Smoke with cover on grill for about 30 minutes. Serve with favorite sauce.

YIELD: 6–10 SERVINGS

Fiesta: Favorite Recipes of South Texas
THE JUNIOR LEAGUE OF CORPUS CHRISTI, TEXAS

·   ·   ·   ·   ·   ·   ·   ·   ·   ·   ·   ·   ·   ·   ·

Oven-Barbecued Beef

3 ounces liquid smoke
6 or 7 pounds beef brisket
Celery salt
Onion salt
Garlic salt
Salt and pepper
Worcestershire sauce
6 ounces barbecue sauce (or more)
2 tablespoons flour
½ cup water

Barbecuing beef in a kitchen oven takes all day, but you don't have to watch the meat once it starts to cook. Smoking it the night before is the secret to the smoky flavor.

Pour liquid smoke over brisket placed in a roasting pan. Generously sprinkle meat on both sides with celery, onion, and garlic salts; this tenderizes it. Place beef in refrigerator overnight.

Next morning, allow 5 hours for cooking, plus another hour to bake the meat with the barbecue sauce and a final cooling period of 1 hour.

When ready to bake in a 275° oven, sprinkle both sides of meat with salt, pepper, and Worcestershire sauce. To cover, put foil on top of meat and secure around edges of pan, not around meat. If pan has lid, use that. After 5 hours, uncover meat and pour barbecue sauce over it. Continue baking 1 more hour. Remove meat to a platter and let sauce cool. Remove fat.

Recipe continues . . .

Add flour and water to meat sauce. Add more barbecue sauce to taste. Serve sauce piping hot. The meat will slice nicely after cooling at least 1 hour. It can be served hot, but it may crumble.

YIELD: 10–12 SERVINGS

The Blue Denim Gourmet
THE JUNIOR LEAGUE OF ODESSA, TEXAS

Bolichi (Stuffed Eye of the Round of Beef)

3–4 pounds eye of the round
1 chorizo sausage, chopped
1 medium slice cured ham, chopped
1 clove garlic, minced
1 medium Spanish onion, chopped
½ green pepper, chopped
Salt and pepper
Paprika
3 tablespoons bacon drippings
¾ cup hot water
Piece of suet
1 bay leaf
4 whole cloves
Potato balls (optional)

Ask butcher to cut lengthwise pocket in center of beef, leaving opposite end closed.

Mix sausage, ham, garlic, onion, and green pepper and stuff roast, packing well but not too tightly. Secure open end with skewers or wire. Salt and pepper all over and sprinkle generously with paprika.

Brown well in bacon drippings over medium heat. Turn often to get an even browning because the better the browning, the more delicious the sauce.

When browned, add hot water, scraping pan well. Lay suet on top of meat. Add bay leaf and cloves to liquid.

Cover and place in 325° oven. Baste occasionally and cook about 3 hours or until meat is fork tender.

Potato balls may be added during the last 30 minutes. Serve Bolichi cut into round slices and pass gravy separately.

YIELD: 8–10 SERVINGS

The Gasparilla Cookbook
THE JUNIOR LEAGUE OF TAMPA, FLORIDA

·   ·   ·   ·   ·   ·   ·   ·   ·   ·   ·   ·   ·   ·   ·   ·

Roast Beef with Coffee

3–5 pounds roast beef (any cut)
Garlic or onion slivers
1 cup vinegar
2 tablespoons salad oil
2 cups black coffee
2 cups water
Salt and pepper

Use a large knife to cut slits completely through the meat. Insert slivers of garlic or onion down into the slits. Pour vinegar over meat, making sure it runs down into the slits. Marinate in refrigerator 24–48 hours.

When ready to cook, place in a big heavy pot and brown well on all sides in oil. Cover with coffee and water. Simmer covered on top of stove 2 to 4 hours.

Season with salt and pepper 20 minutes before serving.

YIELD: 6 SERVINGS

Little Rock Cooks
THE JUNIOR LEAGUE OF LITTLE ROCK, ARKANSAS

·   ·   ·   ·   ·   ·   ·   ·   ·   ·   ·   ·   ·   ·   ·   ·

Brisket Roast with Beer

4–5 pounds brisket roast
2 medium onions, sliced
12-ounce bottle chili sauce
Seasoned salt
Freshly ground pepper
12-ounce can beer
Dash Worcestershire sauce

Place brisket in roaster, fat side up. Cover with sliced onions, then add chili sauce. Fill empty chili sauce bottle with water and pour over roast. Add salt and pepper.

Cook uncovered in 225° oven for 3 hours. Baste every 30 minutes, adding small amounts of water if needed. Pour beer over meat and cook covered 1½ hours more.

For sauce or gravy, skim grease off liquid in pan and add dash of Worcestershire sauce. Slice roast and serve hot with parsleyed new potatoes and a tossed salad.

To serve cold, cook the day before, chill overnight, then have butcher slice roast thin as bacon. Cut long slices in half to serve as cocktail food, and serve with slices of thinly sliced rye or French bread. Serve with cold or hot sauce, mayonnaise, and mustard.

YIELD: 6–8 SERVINGS (HOT), 12–20 SERVINGS (COLD)

Little Rock Cooks
THE JUNIOR LEAGUE OF LITTLE ROCK, ARKANSAS

Beef à la Mode

6 pounds beef off the round or a haunch of venison
1 pound bacon, cut up
3 large onions, chopped
Ground cloves
Freshly ground black peppercorns
2 teaspoons whole allspice, ground
Bay leaf
1 quart cider vinegar
Red pepper
Salt and pepper
About 1 cup shortening
Flour

Use a very carefully selected cut of beef off the round, without bones—which costs now about one million dollars. (Less expensive chuck meat may be used instead. Stuff it with bacon, onions, spices, and a bit of bay leaf—no salt. It is stuffed by piercing meat with sharp knife and ramming down the mixed seasonings. These gashes are cut in the top of the beef as well as both sides. When the beef is fairly bursting and as swollen as a pouter pigeon, then all is well. Bind cord around the meat to keep seasonings in. Put in an earthenware bowl with vinegar and enough water to cover.

Next morning lift the meat out, rub with salt and pepper, cover heavily with shortening, and coat with flour. Sear on top of the stove until a rich brown. Pour off all the liquid except 1 cup, adding 1 cup of water to this. Cook in a covered roaster in a 300° oven for 20 minutes to the pound.

The gravy can be thickened after the meat is taken out. It is good eaten hot with rice or Hopping John (see page 374). Sliced cold, it will keep well for weeks (but it will not last that long).

YIELD: 25 SERVINGS

Charleston Receipts
THE JUNIOR LEAGUE OF CHARLESTON, SOUTH CAROLINA

· · · · · · · · · · · · · · · · ·

Brown's Roast

A delicious way to "spice up" everyday roast.

5 pounds boneless rump roast
1 teaspoon salt
½ teaspoon black pepper
½ teaspoon garlic salt
½ teaspoon herb seasoning
Flour
Small amount of fat
1 8-ounce can tomato purée
4 whole cloves
1½ cups water
2 green peppers, sliced
2 onions, quartered
3 tablespoons brown sugar

Roll roast in salt, pepper, garlic salt, and herb seasoning and coat with flour. Sear roast in small amount of fat. Add tomato purée, cloves, and water. Bring to a fast boil. Turn to simmer. Add green peppers and onions and cook 3½–4 hours on simmer.

One hour before serving add brown sugar. Slice and serve with sauce that has been made in cooking.

YIELD: 6 SERVINGS

The Blue Denim Gourmet
THE JUNIOR LEAGUE OF ODESSA, TEXAS

Short Ribs with Herbs

6 short ribs of beef
3 tablespoons beef suet or shortening
1 clove garlic, peeled and chopped
3 leeks, sliced thin
1 8-ounce can tomato sauce
1 teaspoon salt
¼ teaspoon pepper
¼ teaspoon chili powder
¼ teaspoon rosemary
¼ teaspoon basil

In large skillet, brown ribs in shortening.

Push meat to one side and sauté garlic and leeks for 5 minutes.

Mix tomato sauce and seasonings (not herbs) and stir into mixture in pan. Heat for 2 minutes. Place browned ribs in casserole. Spoon sauce over and around meat. Cover casserole. Bake at 325° for 1½ hours.

Add herbs. Cover and bake 30 minutes longer.

Skim off excess fat and serve.

YIELD: 6 SERVINGS

Of Pots and Pipkins
THE JUNIOR LEAGUE OF ROANOKE VALLEY, VIRGINIA

· · · · · · · · · · · · · ·

Corned Beef in Foil

3–4 pounds corned beef
¼ cup water
2 tablespoons pickling spice
1 small orange, sliced
1 onion, sliced
1 stalk celery with leaves
1 carrot, sliced

Recipe continues . . .

This recipe calls for beef already corned, just as it comes from the market.

Soak beef in cold water to cover for ½ hour, or longer if more deeply corned.

Place large sheet of heavy-duty foil in a shallow pan. Pat meat dry and place in center of foil. Pour ¼ cup water over it. Sprinkle with the spice and arrange orange slices and vegetables over and around meat. Bring long ends of foil up over meat and seal with a tight double fold. Seal other ends, turning them so liquid cannot run out.

Bake 4 hours in 300° oven. Drain and cool. Slice paper-thin. (A time-saver: Return your cooked meat to your friendly neighborhood butcher and have him slice it for you!) Serve for sandwiches with hot mustard.

YIELD: 6–8 SANDWICHES

Party Potpourri
THE JUNIOR LEAGUE OF MEMPHIS, TENNESSEE

. . . .

Spiced Round

10–12 pounds round of beef (5 or more inches thick)
¼ teaspoon salt
¼ teaspoon pepper
2 cups brown sugar
2 cups salt
1 tablespoon each ground nutmeg, ground cinnamon,
ground ginger, ground allspice, and black pepper
1½ teaspoons cayenne
3 pounds beef suet

Rub each side of beef with ¼ teaspoon salt and pepper. Let stand in cool place all night after covering with brown sugar and salt.

Mix ground spices and cayenne. Cover the round with these spices and let stand 2 weeks, turning each day. This should be kept cool but not allowed to freeze.

Grind beef suet and mix with the remaining spices and the juice which has run from the meat. Make holes through the meat and stuff with the suet, adding more spices in proportion if needed. Special emphasis might be put on black pepper and allspice.

Tie meat in heavy pudding bag and boil 15 minutes to the pound.

This dish is better the second day, served cold as a buffet along with country ham and turkey. It is a rich meat and therefore goes a long way.

Nashville Seasons
THE JUNIOR LEAGUE OF NASHVILLE, TENNESSEE

Peppered Steak

6 filets of beef, 1–2 inches thick
Freshly ground pepper
Salt
¼ cup butter
¼ cup olive oil
1 chicken bouillon cube
3 ounces water
3 ounces dry white wine
2 ounces brandy

Press freshly ground pepper into both sides of filets. (Use a mortar and pestle to grind pepper coarsely.) Salt the beef to taste.

Heat butter and olive oil in a large skillet. Dissolve bouillon cube in water. When butter and oil are at frying temperature, sear filets on both sides; then cook for about 5 minutes on each side. Put meat on heated platter. Add the wine and bouillon to skillet. Stir and scrape to deglaze the pan. Add brandy.

Pour sauce over filets and serve immediately.

YIELD: 6 SERVINGS

Mountain Measures
THE JUNIOR LEAGUE OF CHARLESTON, WEST VIRGINIA

Steak Diane

4 sirloin steaks, ½ inch thick, 4 inches in diameter
Salt and pepper
2 tablespoons butter
½ cup good cognac, warmed

SAUCE:
4 tablespoons melted butter
4 tablespoons chopped green onions (include tops)
2 tablespoons finely chopped parsley
2 tablespoons steak sauce
4 tablespoons good sherry or Madeira
2 tablespoons Worcestershire sauce

Combine sauce ingredients and heat gently for 30–45 seconds.

Season steaks with salt and pepper. Melt 1 tablespoon butter in a carefully controlled skillet. Cook two steaks at a time, 1½ minutes on each side. Pour half the sauce over two steaks; cook until bubbly. Prepare remaining two steaks in the same way.

Add the warmed cognac, light it, and spoon the mixture over the steaks. Serve immediately.

YIELD: 4 SERVINGS

Southern Accent
THE JUNIOR LEAGUE OF PINE BLUFF, ARKANSAS

. . . .

Barbecued Flank Steak

2 pounds flank steak
1 clove garlic
2–3 tablespoons soy sauce
1 tablespoon tomato paste
1 tablespoon oil
¼ teaspoon pepper
½ teaspoon oregano

Score flank steak diagonally on both sides.

Combine remaining ingredients in blender until smooth. Pour sauce over steak and marinate overnight. Broil 4–7 minutes on each side over hot coals.

YIELD: 4 SERVINGS

VARIATION:

Combine the following and mix well. Use as a marinade over flank steak and cook as above.

¾ cup oil
½ cup soy sauce
2 tablespoons vinegar
2 tablespoons honey
1½ teaspoons ginger
1 teaspoon garlic powder
1 scallion with tops, finely chopped

Seasoned with Sun: Recipes from the Southwest
THE JUNIOR LEAGUE OF EL PASO, TEXAS

Grilled Flank Steak with Wine Sauce

1½–2 pounds flank steak
1 teaspoon salt
1 teaspoon pepper
1 teaspoon crushed thyme
Soy sauce

WINE SAUCE:
1 cup chopped shallots or ¾ cup chopped green
onion, including tops
1¼ cups red wine
1 stick butter
2 tablespoons chopped parsley

Lightly score steak and rub in salt, pepper, and thyme. Brush on soy sauce with pastry brush until lightly coated on one side. Allow to stand at room temperature for 30 to 45 minutes.

Cook over charcoal to desired degree of doneness. Slice in thin diagonal strips, arrange on platter, and serve with Wine Sauce.

To make sauce, mix shallots and wine. Bring to boil, then add butter and parsley. Heat until butter melts.

YIELD: 4 SERVINGS

Winston-Salem's Heritage of Hospitality
THE JUNIOR LEAGUE OF WINSTON-SALEM, NORTH CAROLINA

London Broil with Mushroom Sauce

2 pounds prime flank steak
1 tablespoon salad oil
1 teaspoon lemon juice
1 teaspoon salt
⅛ teaspoon pepper
1 clove garlic, crushed
2 teaspoons chopped parsley

Wipe steak with damp paper. Combine oil, lemon juice, salt, pepper, garlic, and parsley. Use half of mixture to brush top of steak.

Arrange on lightly greased rack in broiler pan. Broil 4 inches from heat for 5 minutes. Turn. Brush with remaining liquid. Broil 3–5 minutes longer.

Slice thin across grain. Serve with Mushroom Sauce.

YIELD: 4–6 SERVINGS

MUSHROOM SAUCE:
3 tablespoons butter
1 shallot, chopped
1 clove garlic, chopped
1 slice onion
2 carrot slices
Sprig parsley
6 whole black peppercorns
1 whole clove
1 bay leaf
2 tablespoons flour
1 cup canned beef bouillon
1 cup thickly sliced mushrooms
¼ teaspoon salt
⅛ teaspoon pepper
⅓ cup Burgundy
2 tablespoons parsley

Recipe continues . . .

Heat butter. Add shallot, garlic, onion and carrot slices, parsley, pepper-corns, clove, and bay leaf. Sauté about 3 minutes.

Remove from heat. Add flour and stir until smooth. Cook, stirring, until flour is lightly browned, about 5 minutes.

Remove from heat; gradually stir in the bouillon. Over medium heat, bring to boiling point, stirring constantly. Reduce heat. Simmer gently 10 minutes.

Sauté mushrooms in separate skillet about 5 minutes. Strain bouillon mixture, discarding vegetables. Add salt, pepper, Burgundy, parsley, and mushrooms.

This can be made ahead and reheated.

YIELD: 1⅓ CUPS

Of Pots and Pipkins
THE JUNIOR LEAGUE OF ROANOKE VALLEY, VIRGINIA

Chinese Pepper Steak

1½ pounds lean round steak
1 tablespoon paprika
3 tablespoons butter
1 teaspoon minced garlic
1½ cups beef broth
½ pound mushrooms
1 large green pepper
1 medium zucchini
1 bunch green onions
2 stalks celery
2 tablespoons cornstarch
¼ cup water
¼ cup soy sauce
2 large fresh tomatoes, cut into eighths (optional)
1 6-ounce can water chestnuts, sliced
4 cups hot cooked rice

Slice steak in ¼-inch wide strips and pound thin. Sprinkle with paprika. In a large skillet or wok, brown meat in butter. Add garlic and broth. Cover and simmer 30 minutes.

While meat is simmering, slice mushrooms, pepper, zucchini, green onions, and celery and start the rice.

After meat has cooked for 30 minutes, stir in the sliced vegetables. Cover and cook 5 minutes. Blend cornstarch, water, and soy sauce. Stir into meat mixture. Cook, stirring, until clear and thickened—about 2 minutes. Add tomatoes, if desired, and water chestnuts and stir.

Serve over fluffy rice with extra soy sauce.

YIELD: 6 SERVINGS

The Dallas Jr. League Cookbook
THE JUNIOR LEAGUE OF DALLAS, TEXAS

.   .   .   .

Southwestern Pepper Steak

4 teaspoons cornstarch
5 tablespoons soy sauce
¾ cup beef broth or bouillon
⅓ cup chopped chilies
1 pound flank steak
4 tablespoons salad oil
2 stalks celery
1 onion
2 green peppers
1 16-ounce can bean sprouts, drained
Salt and pepper
4 cups hot cooked rice

Prepare broth mixture of cornstarch and soy sauce; stir in beef broth and add chopped chilies.

Cut steak in half lengthwise; slice the halves diagonally across the grain into ⅛-inch-thick slices.

Recipe continues . . .

Heat 1 tablespoon of oil in frying pan until very hot. Cook half the meat at a time until lightly browned, adding more oil if necessary. Remove meat to dish.

Add 1 tablespoon oil to pan.

Cut celery, onion, and peppers into 1-inch pieces. Cook celery and onion about 2 minutes or until onion is tender-crisp. Add pepper and cook and stir 1 minute longer, adding more oil if necessary. Place on dish with meat.

Add broth mixture to pan. Stir until thickened and boiling. Return meat and vegetables to pan; add bean sprouts and cook until hot. Season with salt and pepper.

Serve with rice.

YIELD: 6 SERVINGS

Seasoned with Sun: Recipes from the Southwest
THE JUNIOR LEAGUE OF EL PASO, TEXAS

·   ·   ·   ·   ·   ·   ·   ·   ·   ·   ·   ·   ·   ·   ·   ·

Tahitian Beef

1½ pounds sirloin steak, cut into 1-inch cubes
1½ teaspoons monosodium glutamate
¼ cup oil
1 onion, chopped
2 tablespoons steak sauce
Dash Kitchen Bouquet browning and seasoning sauce
(2 teaspoons soy sauce can substitute for the 3 previous ingredients)
1 13½-ounce can pineapple chunks, drained (reserve syrup)
2 tablespoons wine vinegar
1 cup chopped celery
1 cucumber, chopped or sliced
1 tomato, cut into small wedges
1 green pepper, cut into thin slices
Salt and pepper
Chopped almonds (optional)
Hot cooked rice

Sprinkle cubes of sirloin with monosodium glutamate and brown quickly in hot oil. Add onion and brown lightly.

Mix together Sauce Robert, steak sauce, and Kitchen Bouquet (or substitute 2 teaspoons soy sauce).

Add sauces, pineapple syrup, and vinegar to meat. Simmer 20 minutes.

About 10 minutes before serving, add pineapple chunks, celery, cucumber, tomato, and green pepper. Simmer 10 minutes. Salt and pepper to taste.

Add chopped almonds if you wish. Serve with rice.

YIELD: 3–4 SERVINGS

Gator Country Cooks
THE JUNIOR LEAGUE OF GAINESVILLE, FLORIDA

Memphis Beef Stroganoff

1½ pounds beef (filet or sirloin)
3 tablespoons prepared mustard
1 cup thinly sliced onions
Butter
1 6-ounce can tomato paste, mixed with equal amount water
1 tablespoon Worcestershire sauce
1 tablespoon paprika
1 4-ounce can mushrooms
1 cup sour cream
Red Rice or French fried potatoes

Cut meat into finger strips. Spread mustard over meat and let stand 1 hour in refrigerator.

Fry onions in butter. Sear meat in hot skillet, add tomato paste and water, Worcestershire sauce, and paprika. Simmer beef 1 hour if top of round, ½ hour if filet.

Recipe continues . . .

Add mushrooms and sour cream. Stir until well heated. Serve with cooked rice or Red Rice (see page 370) or French fried potatoes.

YIELD: 6–8 SERVINGS

The Memphis Cook Book
THE JUNIOR LEAGUE OF MEMPHIS, TENNESSEE

· · · · · · · · · · · · · · · ·

Dallas Beef Stroganoff

1½ pounds round steak or beef tenderloin
3 tablespoons butter
2 tablespoons flour
½ teaspoon salt
1 teaspoon pepper
1 heaping tablespoon paprika
½ teaspoon nutmeg
1 teaspoon sugar
1 cup sour cream
½–¾ cup mushrooms, sliced (may use reconstituted dried mushrooms)
White rice, brown rice, or noodles

Brown steak in 1 tablespoon butter. Remove from skillet. Let cool and then slice or cut with scissors into 2 × ½-inch pieces. In the same skillet, melt 2 tablespoons butter and add flour. Make a light roux. Then add salt, pepper, paprika, nutmeg, and sugar. Stir until combined, then turn off heat and add sour cream.

In another skillet, brown mushrooms in additional butter. Then add mushrooms and meat to sour cream mixture. Heat through.

Serve over white or brown rice or noodles.

YIELD: 4 SERVINGS

The Dallas Jr. League Cookbook
THE JUNIOR LEAGUE OF DALLAS, TEXAS

· · · · · · · · · · · · · · · ·

Boeuf au Sec

2 large yellow onions, sliced thin
3 tablespoons butter
2 pounds round steak, cut into 1-inch cubes
Flour
Salt
Coarsely ground pepper
Paprika
1 cup rosé wine
1 pound mushrooms, sliced
4 tablespoons butter
Buttered rice or noodles

In a large skillet or Dutch oven, sauté onions in 3 tablespoons butter until they are limp and golden. Remove onions and reserve butter. Dredge beef cubes lightly with flour, salt, pepper, and enough paprika to make a nice color. Brown the meat well in the reserved butter, adding more butter if necessary. Add the onions and wine and simmer the meat, covered, for about 30 minutes, or until tender. Remove cover, increase the heat, and simmer the mixture until the liquid is reduced and the meat is almost dry.

In another skillet, sauté mushrooms in 4 tablespoons butter until lightly browned. Arrange mushrooms over beef on platter and serve with buttered rice or noodles.

YIELD: 4–6 SERVINGS

Furniture City Feasts
THE JUNIOR LEAGUE OF HIGH POINT, NORTH CAROLINA

Rouladen

4 slices beef sirloin tip
Salt and pepper to taste
Prepared mustard (optional)
4 slices bacon
2 small carrots, sliced thin
2 medium onions (1 chopped, 1 sliced thin)
1 dill pickle, sliced (optional)
Parsley
1 tablespoon butter
1 tablespoon flour
1 cup water

Have butcher slice steak about ¼ inch thick and about size of dessert plate.

Sprinkle meat with salt and pepper; spread with mustard if desired. Place bacon strips an inch apart on meat slice; place carrots between bacon strips. Cover with chopped onion, pickles, and parsley.

Roll like jelly roll; fasten with toothpicks.

Heat butter in skillet; brown meat rolls on all sides. Add sliced onion and lightly brown. Remove meat and onion. Stir flour in skillet. Replace meat and onion; add water. Cover tight; cook 45 minutes.

YIELD: 2 SERVINGS

Huntsville Heritage Cookbook
THE JUNIOR LEAGUE OF HUNTSVILLE, ALABAMA

Braised Sirloin Tips and Almond Rice

1½ pounds mushrooms, sliced
¼ cup melted butter
1 tablespoon salad oil
3 pounds sirloin, cubed
¾ cup bouillon
¾ cup red wine
2 tablespoons soy sauce
2 cloves garlic, minced
½ onion, grated
2 tablespoons cornstarch
½ 10¾-ounce can condensed cream of mushroom soup
Salt and pepper

Sauté mushrooms in 2 tablespoons of the butter. Place in 3-quart casserole.

Add remaining butter and oil to skillet. Brown meat. Pour over mushrooms.

Combine ½ cup of the bouillon, wine, soy sauce, garlic, and onion in skillet. Blend cornstarch with remaining ¼ cup bouillon. Stir into wine mixture. Cook until thick. Spoon over meat and mix.

Cover and bake at 275° for 1 hour. Add mushroom soup and salt and pepper to taste and stir until smooth. Bake 10–15 minutes more and serve over or with Almond Rice.

YIELD: 8 SERVINGS

ALMOND RICE:
½ cup slivered almonds
3 tablespoons melted butter
1½ cups raw rice
4½ cups water
Salt

Recipe continues . . .

Sauté almonds in butter until golden. Add rice and stir. Add water and salt. Stir and boil until water barely disappears from surface. Lower heat, cover, and cook for 20–30 minutes.

Home Cookin'
THE JUNIOR LEAGUE OF WICHITA FALLS, TEXAS

· · · · · · · · · · · · · · · · · ·

Beef Tips Creole

3 pounds beef sirloin tips
3 tablespoons shortening
½ cup chopped onion
¼ cup chopped celery
¼ cup chopped green pepper
¼ teaspoon salt
1 teaspoon chopped parsley
½ teaspoon oregano
¼ teaspoon garlic powder
½ teaspoon sweet basil
¼ teaspoon chili powder
Dash nutmeg
1 16-ounce can tomatoes
1 cup water
2 teaspoons gumbo filé
Hot cooked rice

Cut beef tips into 1-inch cubes.

Sauté beef in shortening until it becomes a rich brown color. Add onion, celery, and green pepper.

Cook over medium heat for 20 minutes; stir. Add remaining seasonings except gumbo filé; cook 15 minutes more over low heat. Then add tomatoes and water and simmer about 1 hour or until meat is tender. Serve over rice. Season with gumbo filé.

Freezes well.

YIELD: 8 SERVINGS

Fiesta: Favorite Recipes of South Texas
THE JUNIOR LEAGUE OF CORPUS CHRISTI, TEXAS

. . . .

Cadillac Stew

6 pounds beef chuck roast, cut into 1½–2-inch cubes
(about 5 pounds meat)
1 pound salt pork, cut into very small pieces (size of lima bean)
4 16-ounce cans or glass jars small white boiled onions, drained

GRAVY:
3 tablespoons flour
¼ teaspoon freshly ground black pepper
3 cloves garlic, chopped
3 teaspoons grated fresh or dried orange peel
3 bay leaves
⅛ teaspoon thyme
⅛ teaspoon nutmeg
3 teaspoons dry parsley flakes
Dash cayenne
1½ or 2 bottles dry red cooking wine
(2 quarts Chianti may be used)
3 large cans mushrooms

Cut beef into cubes. Chop salt pork as directed and fry until brown and crisp. Remove salt pork and reserve fat. Brown onions in fat from salt pork. Remove onions and reserve fat. Next brown beef cubes in same fat. (Do not flour beef.) Remove beef from fat and reserve.

Recipe continues . . .

Make gravy of remaining fat and juices in roaster. Add flour first and cook briefly before adding other ingredients, except mushrooms. Use wine as liquid for gravy, being sure to heat wine before adding. Now add beef and salt pork to gravy and cook 3 hours, covered, in heavy roaster at 325°. Add more wine if needed.

Add the browned onions and the mushrooms and cook for 20 more minutes.

YIELD: 12 SERVINGS

Cooking Through Rose Colored Glasses
THE JUNIOR LEAGUE OF TYLER, TEXAS

. . . .

Caldillo (Mexican Stew)

3 pounds cubed beef
1½ cups diced onion
Bacon drippings
3 cups diced tomatoes
1½ cups sliced green chilies
½ cup beef stock
½ cup chicken stock
2 teaspoons salt
2 teaspoons pepper
2 teaspoons garlic salt
2 teaspoons cumin
2 pounds potatoes, cubed

Sauté beef and onion in bacon drippings. Add tomatoes, sliced green chilies, stocks, and seasonings. Cook over low heat until meat is tender.

Add cubed potatoes during last 30 minutes.

Caldillo may be frozen after preparation.

YIELD: 1 GALLON

Seasoned with Sun: Recipes from the Southwest
THE JUNIOR LEAGUE OF EL PASO, TEXAS

. . . .

Our Town Stew

This is a stew for the purist. When it is well made, the result should be beautifully brown gravy containing tender pieces of meat, whole small onions, and mushrooms.

Salt and pepper
3 pounds good beef stew meat, cut into chunks or cubes
Flour
Shortening (or half olive oil and half butter)
2 cloves garlic, sliced (or more)
12 ounces beer
Cayenne
30–35 small pearl onions, peeled
30–35 fresh mushroom caps

Salt and pepper meat well. Dredge in flour, making sure that all sides are well coated.

Brown meat well in the shortening in a heavy pot, along with 1 sliced clove of garlic. When the meat is richly brown, pour the beer over it. Then add water to cover the meat. (More beer may be used if desired, but too much will give the stew a slightly bitter taste. This can be remedied by the judicious addition of a small amount of sugar.)

Add the second clove of garlic—or more if you desire—and a small amount of cayenne (careful!). Bring to a boil, reduce heat, and simmer 1½–2 hours.

Correct seasoning and add pearl onions, cooking until the onions are tender but still whole. During the last 10 minutes stir in mushroom caps from which the stems have been removed. (The removal of stems is purely for visual effect. Leave them on if you want.)

A little water may be added at this point or during cooking to increase the liquid volume slightly. The rich brown gravy is imperative.

The stew should be served with potatoes, preferably mashed with a

Recipe continues ...

hand masher and enriched with milk, butter, salt, and pepper. It can also be served with noodles. Serve beer with it, or wine. This stew, incidentally, can be made with red wine instead of beer as a variation.

It freezes well and its flavor improves if made one day and served the next.

YIELD: 8 SERVINGS

Little Rock Cooks
THE JUNIOR LEAGUE OF LITTLE ROCK, ARKANSAS

. . . .

Boeuf en Daube 85th Street

3 pounds round of beef, cut into 1½-inch cubes
½ cup flour
1 teaspoon salt
¼ teaspoon pepper
¼ cup butter
2 cloves garlic, finely chopped
2 ounces brandy
1 10½-ounce can condensed beef bouillon
1½ cups Burgundy
About 1 dozen small onions
1 can button mushrooms
About 1 dozen small carrots
4 whole cloves
2 bay leaves
¼ teaspoon marjoram (more or less)
¼ teaspoon thyme (more or less)
3 tablespoons chopped parsley
Pie crust or biscuit dough
Parsley

Roll beef in flour seasoned with salt and pepper. Melt butter in heavy skillet, add garlic, and add floured beef and brown on all sides. Pour in brandy and remove from heat.

Place beef in casserole with tight cover. Heat bouillon and wine in skillet, stirring from bottom to loosen all brown that may adhere. Pour liquid into casserole and add onions, mushrooms, carrots, and seasonings. To hold in aroma, seal casserole with pie crust or biscuit dough.

Bake at 300° for 3 hours. Sprinkle each serving generously with parsley.

YIELD: 8 SERVINGS

Recipe Jubilee
THE JUNIOR LEAGUE OF MOBILE, ALABAMA

. . . .

Boeuf à la Provençale

3 pounds beef, cut into ½-inch cubes
¼ pound salt pork
½ cup white wine
2 cups beef stock
½ teaspoon salt
½ teaspoon thyme
¼ teaspoon rosemary
2 cloves garlic, minced
12 small onions
12 small carrots
1½ tablespoons arrowroot
¾ cup green olives, pitted
¾ cup black olives, pitted
24 cherry tomatoes, peeled
Salt and pepper

Recipe continues . . .

Add beef to marinade (it's not necessary to cool marinade before adding beef). *Refrigerate overnight.*

The next day, pat beef dry. Cook salt pork and brown beef in the fat. Remove salt pork. Strain marinade and add to beef, about 1 cup. Add white wine, beef stock, and seasonings.

Bake at 325° for 1½ hours. Remove from oven and add onions and carrots. Stir in arrowroot. Bake at 325° for 1 hour.

Refrigerate or let stand long enough to remove excess fat.

Add olives and tomatoes. Sprinkle with salt and pepper. Heat but do not cook. Serve in bowls with juice and crusty French bread.

YIELD: 8–10 SERVINGS

RED WINE MARINADE:
2 onions, sliced
1 stalk celery, diced
1 carrot, diced
3 cloves garlic, minced
¼ cup olive oil
1 teaspoon salt
½ teaspoon rosemary
½ teaspoon thyme
12 peppercorns
1½ cups red wine

Cook onions, celery, carrots, and garlic in olive oil until onions are transparent and other vegetables tender. Add remaining ingredients and simmer 15 minutes.

Home Cookin'
THE JUNIOR LEAGUE OF WICHITA FALLS, TEXAS

Beef Bourguignonne

2 pounds sirloin tip or top round steak, cut into 1½–2-inch cubes
4 tablespoons butter
2 tablespoons brandy
2 tablespoons flour
1 teaspoon tomato paste
1 teaspoon Kitchen Bouquet browning and seasoning sauce
¾ cup beef broth
¾ cup dry red wine
½ teaspoon pepper
Parsley, bay leaf, thyme tied in a cheesecloth bag
12 small white onions
16 mushroom caps
Buttered noodles

Brown meat in 2 tablespoons butter.

Pour brandy over meat and ignite. Sprinkle flour over meat, then stir in tomato paste and Kitchen Bouquet. Slowly blend in beef broth and wine, stirring until liquid boils. Add seasonings. Reduce heat, cover, and simmer 1 hour.

In another pan, lightly brown onions in remaining butter and sauté mushroom caps 3 minutes. Add to meat and cook 30 minutes. Remove parsley, bay leaf, and thyme.

Serve over buttered noodles.

YIELD: 4 SERVINGS

Huntsville Heritage Cookbook
THE JUNIOR LEAGUE OF HUNTSVILLE, ALABAMA

Bengal Curry and Pineapple Rice

CURRY:

¼ cup shortening

4 pounds chuck, cut into 1-inch cubes

1 cup sliced onion

2 tablespoons curry powder

2 teaspoons salt

¼ teaspoon pepper

¼ teaspoon ground cloves

¼ cup slivered crystallized ginger

2 tablespoons chopped fresh mint leaves or 1 teaspoon dried mint leaves

¼ cup unsifted flour

3 10½-ounce cans beef bouillon, undiluted

1 cup canned flaked coconut

¼ cup lime juice

1 cup half and half

CURRY ACCOMPANIMENTS:

Cashew nuts, chopped

Cucumber, chopped

Chutney or preserved kumquats

The day before serving, make the curry.

In hot shortening, in large Dutch oven, sauté beef cubes, turning until browned all over—about 20 minutes. Remove the beef cubes as they brown. Add 2 tablespoons drippings and sauté onion, curry powder, salt, pepper, cloves, ginger, and mint about 5 minutes.

Remove from heat and add flour, stirring until well combined. Gradually stir in bouillon. Return beef to Dutch oven and bring to boil. Reduce heat; simmer, covered, 1½ hours or until beef is tender. Remove from heat, let cool; refrigerate, covered, overnight.

About 40 minutes before serving, let curry stand at room temperature 15 minutes. Prepare curry accompaniments and put each into a small serving bowl. Over medium heat, gently reheat curry for about 20 minutes, stirring occasionally. Stir in coconut, lime juice, and half and half. Heat gently about 5 minutes.

Turn into chafing dish. Serve with Pineapple Rice surrounded by curry accompaniments.

PINEAPPLE RICE:

2½ cups raw, long-grain white rice
2½ teaspoons salt
2½ tablespoons butter
1 8½-ounce can crushed pineapple, drained

The day before serving, cook the rice.

In 3-quart heavy saucepan, combine rice with 1 quart cold water and the salt. Over high heat, bring just to boil, stirring several times with a fork. Reduce heat; simmer covered 12–14 minutes or until liquid is absorbed and rice is tender. If necessary, drain rice. Refrigerate covered overnight.

About 40 minutes before serving, preheat oven to 300°. Turn rice into a 15½ × 10½ × 1-inch pan; fluff it with a fork. Sprinkle with ¼ cup water. Heat, covered with foil, 30 minutes, stirring several times with a fork. Add butter and pineapple; toss with a fork to mix well.

YIELD: 8 SERVINGS

Southern Accent
THE JUNIOR LEAGUE OF PINE BLUFF, ARKANSAS

. . . .

Steak Tartare

3 tablespoons olive oil
1 tablespoon red wine vinegar
1 teaspoon Dijon mustard
2 egg yolks
¼ cup finely minced onion
Salt and pepper to taste
1 pound ground round or other lean beef
Capers and/or parsley

Recipe continues . . .

Mix oil, vinegar, mustard, and egg yolks into thick sauce. Add onion and salt and pepper and blend with the beef. Chill thoroughly before serving.

Serve garnished with capers and/or parsley.

YIELD: 2–4 SERVINGS

The Cotton Blossom Cookbook
THE JUNIOR LEAGUE OF ATLANTA, GEORGIA

· · · · · · · · · · · · · · · ·

Swedish Meat Balls

2 eggs, slightly beaten
1 cup milk
½ cup dry bread crumbs
3 tablespoons butter or margarine
½ cup finely chopped onion
1¼ pounds ground round
1¾ teaspoons salt
¾ teaspoon dill weed
¼ teaspoon allspice
⅛ teaspoon nutmeg
⅛ teaspoon cardamom
3 tablespoons flour
⅛ teaspoon pepper
1 10½-ounce can beef broth
½ cup light cream

In a large bowl, combine eggs, milk, and dry bread crumbs.

In large skillet, heat 1 tablespoon butter. Sauté chopped onion until soft, about 5 minutes. Lift out with slotted spoon. Add to bread crumb mixture, along with ground round, 1½ teaspoons salt, ¼ teaspoon dill weed, allspice, nutmeg, and cardamom. With a wooden spoon or your hands mix well to combine. Refrigerate covered for 1 hour.

Shape meat mixture into balls, each about 1 inch in diameter.

In remaining hot butter, sauté meat balls, about half at a time, until browned all over. Remove meat balls to a 2-quart casserole as they are browned. Remove skillet from heat. Pour off drippings.

Measure 2 tablespoons drippings, adding more butter if necessary. Pour back into skillet; add flour, the remaining ¼ teaspoon salt, and the pepper, stirring together to make a smooth mixture. Gradually stir in beef broth. Bring mixture to boil, stirring constantly. Add cream and remaining ½ teaspoon dill weed. Pour over meat balls in casserole.

Bake covered at 325° for 30 minutes.

YIELD: 6 SERVINGS

Gator Country Cooks
THE JUNIOR LEAGUE OF GAINESVILLE, FLORIDA

.   .   .   .

Swedish Meat Balls in Sour Cream

1 pound ground beef
½ pound ground fresh pork
½ pound salt pork
1 cup fine, dry bread crumbs
1 egg
1 medium onion, minced
Dash marjoram
Dash basil
1½ teaspoons salt
1½ teaspoons pepper
1–1¼ cups half and half
3 tablespoons butter
3 tablespoons flour
2 beef bouillon cubes
1½ cups hot water
¾ cup sour cream

Have butcher grind meat twice. Combine meat, bread crumbs, egg, onion, spices, salt, and pepper. Add half and half until you can shape into balls

Recipe continues . . .

or until not dry. Mix well and shape into small cocktail meat balls or larger ones (slightly larger than golf ball) for dinner.

Brown in butter and place in casserole dish. Add flour to butter in pan. Stir well and add bouillon cubes dissolved in hot water. Mix and boil 3 minutes. Remove from heat and stir in sour cream. Pour over meat balls.

If making for dinner, serve on hot buttered noodles.

Can make and freeze meat balls; when ready to use, prepare sauce.

YIELD: 120 COCKTAIL MEAT BALLS OR 30–36 MEAT BALLS FOR DINNER
Winston-Salem's Heritage of Hospitality
THE JUNIOR LEAGUE OF WINSTON-SALEM, NORTH CAROLINA

Curry Beef in Pastry

3 tablespoons oil
½ cup chopped onion
1 pound ground round
2 cups chopped mushrooms
2 teaspoons salt
½ teaspoon pepper
1 tablespoon curry powder
1 cup thick cream sauce (see page 355)
1 cup sour cream
¼ cup chopped chutney

Heat oil in skillet. Sauté onion, beef, and mushrooms 10 minutes. Add salt, pepper, curry powder, and cream sauce. Mix well and set aside to cool.

Roll out dough into a rectangle ⅓ inch thick. Spread beef mixture down center. Bring edges together on top and seal. Brush with beaten egg yolk. Bake at 400° about 35 minutes or until browned.

Serve with sour cream mixed with chopped chutney.

PASTRY:
2 cups sifted flour
2 teaspoons baking powder
½ teaspoon salt
4 tablespoons butter
½ (scant) cup white wine
1 egg yolk, beaten

Sift flour, baking powder, and salt into bowl. Cut in butter; stir in wine gradually till ball of dough is formed.

YIELD: 8 SERVINGS

Party Potpourri
THE JUNIOR LEAGUE OF MEMPHIS, TENNESSEE

. . . .

Aunt Sue's Stuffed Cabbage Rolls

1 medium cabbage
1 pound ground chuck
¾ cup raw rice
1 medium onion, chopped
Salt and pepper
1 1-pound can tomatoes
3 tablespoons lemon juice (or more)
2 tablespoons brown sugar
Garlic (optional)

Core cabbage and separate all leaves. Put in pan of hot water to wilt. Set aside.

Mix ground chuck, rice, onion, salt, and pepper.

When leaves are well wilted, remove hard stems. Place about 2 teaspoons of meat and rice mixture in cabbage leaf and roll. Place in pot or baking dish, rolled side down. Crush and add canned tomatoes. Add ¼ cup water and about 3 tablespoons lemon juice and the sugar. Garlic may

Recipe continues . . .

be added. If you wish, use more lemon juice and more brown sugar for the sweet and sour sauce. Pour sauce over cabbage rolls.

Cook on top of stove, covered, for 3–4 hours, just simmering. Or place covered casserole in preheated 400° oven; reduce heat to 350° and bake for 3 hours.

YIELD: 6 SERVINGS

Gator Country Cooks
THE JUNIOR LEAGUE OF GAINESVILLE, FLORIDA

. . . .

Mama's Chili con Carne

1 pound coarsely ground pork
2 pounds coarsely ground beef
1 large onion, cut up
1 3-ounce container chili powder
¼ cup chili molido (ground chili)
2–3 tablespoons cumin
1 teaspoon oregano
1 large clove garlic, minced
1 16-ounce can small tomatoes
1 10½-ounce can beef broth
2 cups cooked beans

Brown pork, beef, and onion at same time; drain. Add chili powder and chili molido, cumin, oregano, and garlic; continue to cook.

Add tomatoes and break them as they stew. Add beef broth as needed, cooking at least 30 minutes.

This may be served in bowls with or without beans, but is much better if beans are added during last 15 minutes of cooking time.

Chili con Carne is even better warmed the next day.

YIELD: 4 SERVINGS WITHOUT BEANS, 6 WITH BEANS

Seasoned with Sun: Recipes from the Southwest
THE JUNIOR LEAGUE OF EL PASO, TEXAS

. . . .

Enchiladas

1 pound ground round
1 8-ounce can red chili sauce
Garlic salt
Cheddar or longhorn cheese
10 tortillas
1 onion, finely chopped
Oil

Brown meat; drain off grease. Mix in red chili sauce (if too soupy, add a little flour). Add garlic salt to taste. Shred cheese.

Fry tortillas in oil (at about 250°) until soft. Drain on paper towel. Fill each tortilla with cheese and onions, reserving some for topping; roll and place in greased casserole dish. Pour chili sauce over enchiladas. Sprinkle with cheese and onions. Bake at 325° until cheese bubbles. Serve piping hot. May be frozen before baking.

YIELD: 5 SERVINGS

The Blue Denim Gourmet
THE JUNIOR LEAGUE OF ODESSA, TEXAS

· · · · · · · · · · · · · · · · ·

Chilies Rellenos Casserole

16 green chilies, peeled (or 4 4-ounce cans)
1 pound ground round
1 package taco seasoning
¾–1 pound sliced cheddar cheese
3 eggs, separated
¼ teaspoon flour
1 10-ounce can tomatoes with green chilies
Garlic
¾–1 pound cheddar cheese, shredded

Recipe continues ...

Line loaf pan with half of the green chilies, making a single layer. Brown meat and add taco seasoning. Sprinkle meat over the chilies. Top the meat with the sliced cheese. Cover the cheese with the other half of the green chilies.

Beat 3 egg whites until stiff. Fold in egg yolks and flour and pour over chilies. Bake 50–60 minutes at 325°.

Make chili con queso by bringing the tomatoes with green chilies to boil. Season with garlic and add the shredded cheese. Take off heat and stir. Pour over casserole before serving.

YIELD: 6 SERVINGS

The Blue Denim Gourmet
THE JUNIOR LEAGUE OF ODESSA, TEXAS

. . . .

Moussaka

4 pounds eggplant
Salt
2 pounds lean ground beef
1½ cups chopped onion
1 stick butter or margarine
2 teaspoons salt
¼ teaspoon freshly ground pepper
1½ teaspoons oregano or thyme
1 tablespoon chopped parsley
½ cup Burgundy
2 eggs, beaten
1 cup shredded sharp cheddar cheese
½ cup dry bread crumbs
Olive oil
2 1-pound cans plum tomatoes, drained
⅓ cup flour
4 egg yolks, lightly beaten
Salt, pepper, and nutmeg to taste
3 cups milk

Peel eggplant and slice crosswise thinly. Sprinkle with salt; place in colander and weight with a plate to drain (to remove bitterness). Let stand ½ hour.

Sauté beef and onion until browned and cooked. Drain to remove excess fat, and add 2 tablespoons butter or margarine, seasonings, and wine. Stir to melt butter and blend in seasonings. Simmer until no liquid remains. Stir in 2 eggs, ¾ cup of the cheese, and half the bread crumbs.

Lightly dip eggplant in oil; place on cookie sheets and broil until brown on both sides.

Grease a 4-quart casserole well and sprinkle with remaining crumbs. Fill with layers of eggplant, meat, tomatoes—ending with eggplant and leaving room for expansion at the top.

Melt rest of butter; blend in flour, egg yolks, and remainder of seasonings mixed with milk. Cook until thickened, stirring constantly. Pour sauce over casserole; sprinkle with remaining cheese.

Bake at 350° for 45–60 minutes, until top is golden.

May be frozen before adding the sauce and finished at serving time.

YIELD: 10–12 SERVINGS

Mountain Measures
THE JUNIOR LEAGUE OF CHARLESTON, WEST VIRGINIA

· · · · · · · · · · · · · · · ·

Corned Beef Loaf

1 envelope unflavored gelatin
3 beef bouillon cubes
1½ cups water
1 1-pound can corned beef, chopped
4 hard-boiled eggs, chopped
1 cup mayonnaise
1 teaspoon prepared mustard
1 teaspoon lemon juice
1 cup chopped celery

Recipe continues . . .

Soften gelatin in ½ cup cold water. Dissolve gelatin and bouillon cubes in 1 cup hot water. Add remaining ingredients. Poor into 6-cup mold and chill until set.

YIELD: 6 SERVINGS

Spartanburg Secrets II
THE JUNIOR LEAGUE OF SPARTANBURG, SOUTH CAROLINA

. . . .

Picadillo

2 medium onions
1 large green pepper (optional)
Olive oil
6 small tomatoes (or 2 small cans)
2 teaspoons salt
1 teaspoon garlic powder
Pepper to taste
1 pound ground beef
1 pound ground pork
1 tablespoon brown sugar
¼ cup vinegar
¼ cup stuffed green olives, chopped
½ cup raisins
1 tablespoon capers
½ cup red wine or tomato juice or bouillon

Chop onions and green pepper very fine and brown in the olive oil. Add chopped tomatoes, salt, garlic, pepper, and meat, stirring constantly to break into small bits.

Add remaining ingredients and cook slowly until meat is tender, about 1 hour.

Serve over rice, mashed potatoes, or split buttered and toasted hamburger buns.

YIELD: 10 SERVINGS

The Gasparilla Cookbook
THE JUNIOR LEAGUE OF TAMPA, FLORIDA

·   ·   ·   ·   ·   ·   ·   ·   ·   ·   ·   ·   ·

Hungarian Veal Roast

Veal roast
Salt and pepper to taste
1 1-pound can tomatoes
3 stalks celery, cut up
1 medium onion, sliced
Several sprigs parsley
1 lemon, sliced
Flour
Kitchen Bouquet browning and seasoning sauce (optional)

Brown roast first at 450°; lower oven heat to 350° and salt and pepper the roast. Place tomatoes, celery, onion, parsley, and lemon slices around meat. Cover tightly with foil and roast 40 minutes per pound. Add water throughout baking, if necessary, to depth of 1–2 inches in pan.

When roast is done, run all liquid and vegetables through food mill. Thicken liquid with small amount of flour for gravy. Add Kitchen Bouquet to darken, if necessary. Add salt and pepper to taste.

Serve gravy over sliced roast.

YIELD: 2 SERVINGS PER POUND

Of Pots and Pipkins
THE JUNIOR LEAGUE OF ROANOKE VALLEY, VIRGINIA

·   ·   ·   ·   ·   ·   ·   ·   ·   ·   ·   ·   ·

Chouchoukft

This unusual dish comes from North Africa.

2 tablespoons bacon drippings
1 small onion
3 medium green peppers
3 medium tomatoes (or 1 cup canned)
1 medium eggplant
1 cup diced cooked meat
Hot cooked rice

Heat drippings in heavy iron pot or deep frying pan.

Slice onion into small pieces into it. Cut peppers, tomatoes, and eggplant into small pieces and mix well before adding to drippings and onion. Cover and let simmer slowly for 2 hours.

When almost ready to serve, add diced meat (leftover meat can be used). Heat. Serve with rice.

YIELD: 4 SERVINGS

The Cotton Blossom Cookbook
THE JUNIOR LEAGUE OF ATLANTA, GEORGIA

. . . .

Cordon Bleu

Salt and pepper
4 large, thin veal steaks
4 slices ham
4 slices Swiss cheese
1 egg white
Flour
Milk
1 egg yolk
Dry bread crumbs
Fat for frying

Salt and pepper veal steaks. Cover half of each steak with thin slice of ham and slice of Swiss cheese. Leave edges of meat free and brush them with egg white. Fold each slice in half and press edges of meat together. You may use toothpicks to help hold meat envelopes together.

Put each envelope of meat in flour, then dip into a mixture of small amount of milk and egg yolk, and then roll in dry bread crumbs.

Fry in hot fat until golden brown and serve at once.

YIELD: 4 SERVINGS

Gator Country Cooks
THE JUNIOR LEAGUE OF GAINESVILLE, FLORIDA

·   ·   ·   ·   ·   ·   ·   ·   ·   ·   ·   ·

Veal Bohemian

2 pounds veal steaks, cut into ¼-inch strips
Flour
2 tablespoons shortening
1 teaspoon salt
⅛ teaspoon garlic powder
⅛ teaspoon pepper
½ teaspoon paprika
1 teaspoon dry mustard
½ teaspoon Worcestershire sauce
2 tablespoons catsup
1 cup hot water
1 cup sour cream
Hot cooked noodles

Roll veal in flour and brown in shortening.

Combine remaining ingredients except sour cream and pour over veal. Cover and simmer 1 hour or until tender.

Remove meat to platter and keep hot.

Recipe continues . . .

Add sour cream to drippings and heat but do not boil.
Pour over meat and serve over noodles.

YIELD: 6 SERVINGS

Huntsville Heritage Cookbook
THE JUNIOR LEAGUE OF HUNTSVILLE, ALABAMA

· · · · · · · · · · · · · · · ·

Veal Parmigiana

1½–2 pounds veal cutlet, cut into serving-size pieces (3 or 4)
1 egg, beaten
Salt and pepper
Dry bread crumbs
Grated Parmesan cheese
Olive oil
1 onion, chopped
½ green pepper, chopped
1 1-pound can tomatoes
Dash each oregano, marjoram, basil, bay leaf
1 clove garlic, mashed
Mozzarella cheese
Buttered noodles

Dip veal into egg seasoned with salt and pepper and then into a mixture of
¾ part bread crumbs and ¼ part Parmesan cheese. Allow to stand at
least ½ hour. Sauté in olive oil, browning on both sides.

To make sauce, brown the onion and green pepper in olive oil until
clear. Add tomatoes, spices, and garlic. Simmer for 1 hour.

Arrange veal in bottom of casserole, pour sauce over meat, top with
thin slices of mozzarella cheese, and sprinkle with a little grated Parmesan.

Bake at 350° for about 15 minutes or until cheese is melted.
Serve with buttered noodles.

YIELD: 3 OR 4 SERVINGS

Nashville Seasons
THE JUNIOR LEAGUE OF NASHVILLE, TENNESSEE

· · · · · · · · · · · · · · · ·

Veal Sabrosa

¼ cup flour
½ cup grated Parmesan cheese
1 teaspoon salt
⅛ teaspoon pepper
1½ pounds veal cutlets, sliced ¼ inch thick in 2-inch strips
2 tablespoons olive oil
1 clove garlic
½ cup dry white wine
½ cup consommé
1 tablespoon lemon juice
Chopped parsley

Mix flour, cheese, salt, and pepper together.

Wipe meat dry; sprinkle with flour mixture and pound it into meat.

Heat olive oil with garlic and brown meat lightly on both sides. Remove garlic; add wine, consommé, and lemon juice. Cover and simmer slowly for about 30 minutes.

Sprinkle with chopped parsley and serve from hot platter.

YIELD: 6 SERVINGS

Seasoned with Sun: Recipes from the Southwest
THE JUNIOR LEAGUE OF EL PASO, TEXAS

* * * * * * * * * * * * *

Veal Cutlet Niçoise

½ cup flour
½ teaspoon salt
¼ teaspoon pepper
1 pound veal cutlet, cut sliver-thin
3 tablespoons olive oil
1 clove garlic, finely chopped
1 4-ounce can sliced mushrooms, drained
¼ cup port wine

Recipe continues . . .

Combine flour, salt, and pepper. Dredge cutlets with flour mixture. Heat oil in large heavy skillet. Add cutlets and garlic. Cook over brisk flame for 10 minutes on each side or until well browned. Remove meat to heated serving dish and keep warm.

Add mushrooms to pan and cook 5 minutes. Remove mushrooms to serving dish. Raise heat under frying pan. Add port wine and heat, stirring until brown parts which stick to bottom of pan dissolve. Do not allow to boil. Pour over meat. Serve hot.

YIELD: 4 SERVINGS

The Charlotte Cookbook
THE JUNIOR LEAGUE OF CHARLOTTE, NORTH CAROLINA

. . . .

Baked Sesame Veal Cutlets

6 veal cutlets
1 egg, beaten
½ pint sour cream
1 cup flour
1 teaspoon baking powder
2 teaspoons salt
¼ teaspoon pepper
2 teaspoons paprika
¼ cup chopped pecans
2 tablespoons sesame seeds
½ cup butter

Dip veal into egg mixed with sour cream, then into mixture of flour, baking powder, salt, pepper, paprika, pecans, and sesame seeds.

Melt butter in shallow pan in hot oven (400°). Remove from oven. As coated pieces of veal are placed in pan, turn to coat with butter. Bake in single layer for 30 minutes. Turn and bake 30 minutes more.

If meat cannot be served immediately, reduce heat and baste with melted butter.

YIELD: 6 SERVINGS

The Gasparilla Cookbook
THE JUNIOR LEAGUE OF TAMPA, FLORIDA

. . . .

Veal Birds

2 veal cutlets, cut thin
½ pound ground veal
1 slice uncooked bacon, cut fine
Dry bread crumbs
1 egg, slightly beaten
Boiling water
Flour
Salt
Pepper
Butter
1 10½-ounce can condensed beef bouillon

Cut cutlets into neat pieces about 2 × 4 inches. Place between two pieces of wax paper and pound thin.

To make a stuffing: Combine ground veal and bacon and measure. Add half this amount bread crumbs. Add the egg and moisten with boiling water.

Let stuffing stand 5 minutes. Then spread a small amount on each piece of meat, roll up, fasten with picks, roll in flour, season with salt and pepper, brown in butter. Then add bouillon and simmer until tender.

YIELD: 6 SERVINGS

Of Pots and Pipkins
THE JUNIOR LEAGUE OF ROANOKE VALLEY, VIRGINIA

. . . .

Italian Veal and Peppers

1 pound veal, sliced thin and pounded
Olive oil
1 onion, minced
2–3 green peppers, sliced (long, light green Italian banana
peppers, if possible)
1 small clove garlic, minced
⅛ teaspoon pepper
1 teaspoon salt
1 8-ounce can tomato sauce

Cut veal into 1½-inch pieces. Start to brown in pan. Veal will "water," so pour this liquid off several times. Continue to brown and add a small amount of olive oil.

Add onion and brown along with veal. Add large, wide slices of green pepper and brown a little. Add garlic, pepper, salt, and tomato sauce.

Cover and continue to cook slowly for 1 hour. Stir occasionally.

YIELD: 4–6 SERVINGS

Of Pots and Pipkins
THE JUNIOR LEAGUE OF ROANOKE VALLEY, VIRGINIA

. . . .

Veal in Sherry Sauce

Salt
Pepper
4 veal cutlets
Flour
4 tablespoons butter

Salt and pepper cutlets and flour lightly. Sauté in butter until brown. Place in shallow baking dish and cover with Sherry Sauce. Bake in 350° oven for 30 minutes.

Good served with wild rice.

May be prepared ahead of time and reheated before serving.

YIELD: 4 SERVINGS

SHERRY SAUCE:

1 green onion, chopped
1 4-ounce can sliced mushrooms in butter
4 tablespoons butter
⅓ cup sherry
1 can prepared brown gravy

Sauté onion and mushrooms in butter. Add sherry and brown gravy. Bring to a low boil and cook slowly for 3–5 minutes. For a thinner sauce, add consommé.

A Cook's Tour of Shreveport
THE JUNIOR LEAGUE OF SHREVEPORT, LOUISIANA

.   .   .   .

Vagliette alla Perugina (Little Veal Suitcases)

12 thin slices prosciutto or ham
12 slices mozzarella or fontina cheese
12 small veal scallops
Salt and pepper
Flour
2 tablespoons butter
2 tablespoons olive oil
½ cup Marsala (dry) wine (more if needed or desired)
1 tablespoon lemon juice
1–2 tablespoons finely chopped parsley

Place one ham slice and one cheese slice on each veal scallop. Fold them and close them with picks on all open sides. Season with salt and pepper and dip in flour, shaking off excess flour.

Recipe continues . . .

Brown in butter and olive oil, removing them to a plate as browned. Add wine to remaining juices and replace veal in skillet. Simmer until tender. Add lemon juice and parsley. Continue simmering 1–2 minutes. Serve sauce over veal.

YIELD: 6 SERVINGS

The Dallas Jr. League Cookbook
THE JUNIOR LEAGUE OF DALLAS, TEXAS

. . . .

Braised Sweetbreads

2 pairs sweetbreads
Juice of ½ lemon
2 tablespoons butter
1 onion, sliced
1 carrot, sliced
1 bay leaf
2 sprigs parsley
Pinch thyme
2 teaspoons flour
Salt and pepper
1 cup chicken stock
2 tablespoons dry white wine

Wash and soak sweetbreads in ice water for 1 hour. Put in saucepan, cover with fresh water, and add lemon juice and a little salt. Bring to a boil and simmer gently for 15 minutes.

Drain and chill in ice water. Remove tough sinews and outside membrane. Flatten sweetbreads between two plates, weighted down. Keep cold.

Melt butter in flameproof and ovenproof casserole. Add onion, carrot, bay leaf, parsley, and thyme. When vegetables begin to brown, blend in flour. Season sweetbreads with salt and pepper, arrange on top of vegetables (do not overlap), and add chicken stock.

Bake uncovered, basting occasionally, at 400° for 45 minutes, or until brown on top and liquid is half cooked away.

Stir in white wine and serve.

YIELD: 4 SERVINGS

Of Pots and Pipkins
THE JUNIOR LEAGUE OF ROANOKE VALLEY, VIRGINIA

· · · · · · · · · · · · · · ·

Herbed Roast Leg of Lamb

1 clove garlic, crushed
1 teaspoon salt
2 tablespoons corn oil
1 6-pound leg of lamb
1 teaspoon minced marjoram
1 teaspoon minced thyme
1 teaspoon minced rosemary
2 tablespoons flour
1 cup dry white wine
1 cup water

Crush garlic with salt and mix with oil. Spread on lamb. Sprinkle lamb with marjoram, thyme, rosemary, and flour.

Pour wine and water in roasting pan with lamb. Roast in slow oven (325°) for 2½ hours, basting frequently.

YIELD: 6–8 SERVINGS

Spartanburg Secrets II
THE JUNIOR LEAGUE OF SPARTANBURG, SOUTH CAROLINA

· · · · · · · · · · · · · · ·

Leg of Lamb American

1 leg of lamb
⅔ cup grape jelly
¼ cup vinegar
½ teaspoon thyme
1 clove garlic, crushed
2 tablespoons salt
½ teaspoon pepper

Place leg of lamb on rack in roasting pan. Roast uncovered at 325° for 2 hours.

Drain drippings. Combine remaining ingredients, pour over lamb, and roast 30 minutes or more until done.

YIELD: 6–8 SERVINGS

Seasoned with Sun: Recipes from the Southwest
THE JUNIOR LEAGUE OF EL PASO, TEXAS

. . . .

Leg of Lamb with Mint Sauce

1 6-pound leg of lamb
1 tablespoon melted butter
1 tablespoon oil
1 tablespoon salt
1 cup water
½ cup sugar
½ teaspoon ground black pepper
1 scant cup white vinegar
1 teaspoon Worcestershire sauce
2 tablespoons strained mint sauce

Wipe lamb with damp paper towel. Dry with paper towel.

Combine butter and oil and brush mixture over the meat. Preheat oven to 450°. Place lamb in a roasting pan which has sides for holding sauce. Roast lamb for about 20–25 minutes, turning often, until meat is brown on all sides.

Remove pan from oven and reduce heat to 325°. Place a meat thermometer in thickest part of lamb. Sprinkle the salt in the side of the pan. Add water and stir.

Sprinkle sugar and pepper over the meat. Pour vinegar over the meat. Baste. Return to oven and roast about 1½ hours, or until thermometer reaches 160°, basting often during the cooking.

When lamb is done, remove from pan and place on platter. Cover lightly with foil to keep warm.

Skim all fat from the liquid. Add the Worcestershire and mint sauces. Reheat and serve with lamb. Sauce will be very thin and a rich dark brown.

YIELD: 8 SERVINGS

Southern Accent
THE JUNIOR LEAGUE OF PINE BLUFF, ARKANSAS

. . . .

Mrs. Frank Stahlman's Lamb Roast

Leg of lamb (1 pound per person)
Salt
Cayenne
Black pepper
Sugar
Onions
Worcestershire sauce
Bacon drippings
Sifted flour
½ cup mild vinegar
½ cup water
Carrots
Celery

Recipe continues . . .

Wipe lamb clean with cold water and make small slashes at several places on top. Rub in salt, cayenne, black pepper, and sugar on both top and bottom of lamb. Put small pieces of onion in slashes and any crevice you can find, along with a drop of Worcestershire sauce. Now rub with bacon drippings and sprinkle lightly with sifted flour.

Place on rack in roasting pan, bottom up. Put in 450° oven and brown slightly. Remove from oven and turn the leg over. Sprinkle with flour again and return to oven and brown the top.

Pour vinegar and water in bottom of pan. Lower heat and place thin slices of carrots and celery across the top. Bake in 325° oven until tender (about 2 hours), basting frequently.

The celery and carrots are good served in the gravy. They make a delightful flavor, but are not necessary. The rubbing is a messy chore, but should be done thoroughly with freshly scrubbed hands.

Nashville Seasons
THE JUNIOR LEAGUE OF NASHVILLE, TENNESSEE

· · · · · · · · · · · · · · · · ·

Bobbie's Butterflied Leg of Lamb

½ teaspoon freshly ground pepper
½ cup red wine vinegar
1½ cups oil
2 cloves garlic, minced
1 teaspoon rosemary
½ teaspoon salt
2 bay leaves, crumbled
1 6-pound leg of lamb, boned and butterflied

Combine all ingredients except lamb and marinate lamb overnight or longer, covered and refrigerated.

One hour before serving, remove. Put on grill, fat side up. Cook 40–50 minutes, basting often with marinade.

Cut across grain.

YIELD: 6–8 SERVINGS

The Dallas Jr. League Cookbook
THE JUNIOR LEAGUE OF DALLAS, TEXAS

. . . .

Lamb Curry

5 tablespoons butter
1 teaspoon mild, fresh curry powder (or to taste)
1 cup sliced onions
2 medium-size apples, cored, peeled, and sliced
2 cups diced cooked lamb
2 tablespoons flour
2 chicken bouillon cubes mixed with 2 cups hot water
1 tablespoon lemon juice
Salt and pepper to taste

Melt 3 tablespoons butter in large frying pan. Add curry powder. Sauté onions and apples until onions are tender. Remove from pan. Brown lamb in pan. Remove lamb from pan.

In same pan, melt remaining 2 tablespoons butter and stir in 2 table-spoons flour. Let this bubble for a minute but do not brown. Add bouillon—must be hot—all at once. Stir until sauce is smooth and thick. Add onions, apples, and meat. Stir in lemon juice, and add salt and pepper to taste.

This can and should be made ahead of time. Reheat when ready to serve, but do not overcook, as apples will become too mushy.

YIELD: 4 SERVINGS

The Charlotte Cookbook
THE JUNIOR LEAGUE OF CHARLOTTE, NORTH CAROLINA

. . . .

No-Peek Stew

2 pounds stew meat
1 package dry onion soup mix
1 10¾-ounce can condensed cream of mushroom soup
1 2½-ounce can mushrooms, drained
1 cup ginger ale

Throw all ingredients into a pot with a tight-fitting lid and bake at 350° for 2½–3 hours. Do not peek!

This is a great dish that smells and tastes as if you've been in the kitchen all afternoon, when you were actually home for fifteen minutes at four o'clock!

YIELD: **6 SERVINGS**

The Blue Denim Gourmet
THE JUNIOR LEAGUE OF ODESSA, TEXAS

· · · · · · · · · · · · · ·

Curried Lamb and Eggplant

4 pounds boneless lamb stew meat, cut into 1-inch cubes
¼ cup flour
2 teaspoons salt
½ teaspoon black pepper
3–4 tablespoons olive oil
1 large eggplant, peeled and diced
2 large onions, sliced
2 tart apples, diced
4 stalks celery, diced
3 teaspoons curry powder (or to taste)
2 beef bouillon cubes
½ cup dry white wine
½ cup water
2 large tomatoes, peeled and cut into wedges
½ cup pine nuts

Shake lamb cubes in paper bag with mixture of flour, salt, and pepper until nicely coated. Heat oil in large pot and brown floured meat on all sides. Add eggplant, onions, apples, and celery and stir. Sprinkle with curry powder, tuck bouillon cubes in, and pour wine and water over all. Bring to a slow boil, then reduce heat and let simmer 1 hour, covered.

Add tomatoes and pine nuts and simmer another 15 minutes or until meat is tender.

YIELD: 8 SERVINGS

Winston-Salem's Heritage of Hospitality
THE JUNIOR LEAGUE OF WINSTON-SALEM, NORTH CAROLINA

· · · · · · · · · · · · · · ·

Baked Lamb Shanks

6 lamb shanks
1 cup flour
2 teaspoons salt
½ teaspoon black pepper
¼ cup salad oil
1 cup finely chopped onion
2 cloves garlic, crushed
3 cups water
3 beef bouillon cubes
1 bay leaf, crushed
Brown gravy sauce (optional)
1 cup finely chopped carrots
1 cup finely chopped celery

Remove excess fat from lamb shanks. Shake the shanks in a bag with flour, salt, and pepper.

Sauté the shanks in salad oil until well browned on all sides. Remove to 4-quart casserole. Drain off all but 2 tablespoons fat. Sauté the onion and garlic until tender in the lamb drippings. Stir in the remaining seasoned

Recipe continues . . .

flour; add water, beef bouillon cubes, and bay leaf. Heat and stir until thickened. Add brown gravy sauce, if desired.

Pour sauce over meat in casserole. Scatter the carrots and celery over the meat. Cover and bake at 375° for 2 hours, until meat is very tender. Skim off any excess fat. Season to taste with salt and pepper.

YIELD: 6 SERVINGS

Of Pots and Pipkins
THE JUNIOR LEAGUE OF ROANOKE VALLEY, VIRGINIA

· · · · · · · · · · · · · · · · · · ·

Dolmades (Greek Stuffed Grape Leaves)
WITH AVGOLEMONO SAUCE

1 pound ground lamb or chuck
⅓ cup raw rice
1 egg
2 tablespoons chopped parsley
2 tablespoons chopped mint leaves
1 large onion, finely chopped
½ cup chopped celery
¼ cup butter
3 cups chicken broth
Salt and pepper to taste
1 10-ounce jar grape leaves
Additional chicken broth

Mix first five ingredients in a large bowl.

Sauté onion and celery in butter until golden brown; add to meat mixture. Add ½ cup chicken broth and season to taste with salt and pepper.

Carefully unroll grape leaves, rinse, and boil in water for 5 minutes; drain well. (Fresh grape leaves may be used instead of canned and should be parboiled also. Fresh leaves may be frozen for future use.)

Place 1 tablespoon meat mixture on the longest point of each grape leaf; fold over once; fold edges toward center and roll again to complete each little package.

Place in layers in a large pan; cover with remaining 2½ cups chicken broth, cover if desired, and simmer for 1 hour.

YIELD: ABOUT 40

AVGOLEMONO SAUCE:
3 eggs
Juice of 1 lemon
Additional chicken broth if needed
2 teaspoons flour, mixed to a paste with water

This sauce should be prepared just before serving.

Beat eggs well, adding lemon juice gradually.

Remove dolmades from pan; add enough chicken broth to liquid to make 2 cups. (You may not need to add any.) Stir flour paste into broth and then gradually add hot broth to eggs, stirring constantly. Return to heat and cook until thickened, stirring constantly.

Pour over dolmades and serve immediately.

Little Rock Cooks
THE JUNIOR LEAGUE OF LITTLE ROCK, ARKANSAS

·   ·   ·   ·   ·   ·   ·   ·   ·   ·   ·   ·   ·   ·   ·   ·

Pork Roast in Mustard

Pork roast
Prepared mustard
Salt
Pepper
Flour

Recipe continues . . .

Coat roast with mustard until well covered. Sprinkle with salt and pepper to taste. Sift a thin layer of flour over entire roast. Place in open pan in preheated 450° oven for 30 minutes.

Turn down to 300° until done, about 30 minutes per pound.

This is also a good way to prepare lamb roast.

Fiesta: Favorite Recipes of South Texas
THE JUNIOR LEAGUE OF CORPUS CHRISTI, TEXAS

Fresh Pork Ham

1 5–8-pound fresh pork ham
Salt
Red and black pepper
Slivers of garlic
1 small onion, slivered
1 green pepper, slivered
Flour

Cut excess fat from ham and remove thick skin. With sharp knife, cut 5 or 6 deep slits in meat and fill each with salt, peppers, and a sliver each of garlic, onion, and green pepper. Season entire outside. Place in shallow pan, fat side up, and roast in 325° oven for 30–35 minutes per pound.

When done, remove roast but do not carve for at least 15 minutes.

Pour off some of the drippings. Over low heat stir in a little flour and add water to make gravy.

Good served with rice and a spinach casserole.

YIELD: 8–12 SERVINGS

Talk About Good!
THE JUNIOR LEAGUE OF LAFAYETTE, LOUISIANA

Sesame-Stuffed Tenderloin

2 pork tenderloins
¼ cup sesame seeds
¼ cup chopped celery
2 tablespoons chopped onion
¼ cup butter
2 cups toasted bread cubes
1 teaspoon Worcestershire sauce
1 teaspoon salt
½ teaspoon poultry seasoning
⅛ teaspoon pepper
1 egg, slightly beaten
1 tablespoon lemon juice

Cut each tenderloin almost through lengthwise; flatten.

Sauté sesame seeds, celery, and onion in butter in skillet until lightly browned. Add bread cubes, seasonings, egg, and lemon juice. Toss lightly.

Spread stuffing on cut surface of 1 tenderloin. Place remaining tenderloin on top. Fasten with string or skewers.

Place on rack in open roasting pan. Roast at 325° for 1½–2 hours or until well done.

YIELD: 6 SERVINGS

Furniture City Feasts
THE JUNIOR LEAGUE OF HIGH POINT, NORTH CAROLINA

Pork Chop Casserole

5 or 6 center-cut pork chops
2 bouillon cubes
2 cups boiling water
1 cup raw rice
1 sliced onion
1 tomato, sliced
1 green pepper, sliced
Salt and pepper to taste

Brown pork chops in skillet and then remove from skillet. Add bouillon cubes dissolved in boiling water. Stir in rice and place pork chops back in skillet.

Cover each chop with a slice of onion, a slice of tomato, and a slice of pepper and season. Cover and simmer until done, about 30 minutes.

YIELD: 5–6 SERVINGS

Cooking Through Rose Colored Glasses
THE JUNIOR LEAGUE OF TYLER, TEXAS

· · · · · · · · · · · · · · · · · ·

Stuffed Pork Chops

2 eggs
¼ cup milk
5 tablespoons flour
½ teaspoon baking powder
Salt and pepper
4 double loin pork chops (about 1 inch thick) with pockets
¾ cup seedless raisins
1 cup chopped celery
½ cup crushed pineapple
Fat for frying
½ cup pineapple juice

Beat eggs. Add milk mixed with flour and baking powder. Mix well to make a smooth batter.

Sprinkle chops with salt and pepper. Fill pocket with mixture of raisins, celery, and pineapple and pin slits together with picks.

Dip pork chops in batter and fry immediately in deep, hot fat until golden brown.

Drain and place in baking casserole. Add pineapple juice. Cover and bake at 350° for 1 hour.

Chops may be prepared and placed in baking dish and put in refrigerator until time for baking. Remove from refrigerator 1 hour before baking time.

YIELD: 4 SERVINGS

The Cotton Blossom Cookbook

THE JUNIOR LEAGUE OF ATLANTA, GEORGIA

. . . .

Apple Brandy Pork Chops

6 thick center-cut pork chops, about 8 ounces each
3 tablespoons minced shallots or onion
¼ cup very finely minced green pepper
¼ cup butter
6 tablespoons (3 ounces) apple brandy
Dry bread crumbs
12–15 large fresh basil leaves, finely minced, or
2 teaspoons dried basil
Salt and pepper
Flour
2 eggs
4 teaspoons oil
Cooking oil

Preheat oven to 350°. Cut a lateral pocket in each pork chop 2 inches long and 1 inch deep.

Recipe continues ...

Sauté shallots or onion and green pepper in butter until vegetables are merely tender. Add apple brandy and set ablaze. When flames disappear, add ½ cup bread crumbs and basil. Mix well. Add salt and pepper to taste.

Stuff pork chops with bread crumb mixture. Dip chops in flour. Beat eggs with 4 teaspoons oil. Dip chops in beaten eggs, coating thoroughly. Dip chops in bread crumbs; pat crumbs on chops to make firm coating. Close pockets shut with several toothpicks (cut ends of picks with scissors). Heat ¼ inch oil in skillet. Sauté chops until medium brown on both sides. Place chops in a shallow baking pan, stacking them upright. Bake at 325° for 1 hour.

YIELD: 6 SERVINGS

The Dallas Jr. League Cookbook
THE JUNIOR LEAGUE OF DALLAS, TEXAS

· · · · · · · · · · · · · · ·

Stuffed Pork Chops Baked in Apple Juice

6 double pork chops
Salt and pepper
½ cup chopped onion
½ cup chopped celery
Margarine
¾ cup water
Green pepper and chopped mushrooms (optional)
2 cups herb dressing mix
2 cups apple juice

Ask butcher to cut large pockets in chops, leaving a small opening for stuffing. Salt and pepper chops, brown in frying pan, and set aside.

Cook onion and celery in a little margarine until soft and then pour water into pan. (Optional ingredients for dressing mix are green pepper and chopped mushrooms.) Combine this mixture with dressing mix to get a dressing consistency. You may add more water if necessary.

Stuff the dressing mixture into chops and place in a flat baking pan. Pour apple juice over all and cover pan.

Bake in a slow oven, about 325°, for 2 hours.

YIELD: 6 SERVINGS

300 Years of Carolina Cooking
THE JUNIOR LEAGUE OF GREENVILLE, SOUTH CAROLINA

Pork Chops St. John

4 lean pork chops
3 tablespoons Madeira wine
⅓ cup sour cream
Salt and pepper to taste

Brown chops over high heat and cook, turning frequently, until tender.

Remove from pan and pour off excess fat. Add wine and sour cream to pan, stirring frequently to scrape off brown bits in pan. Return chops to pan, season, and simmer 5–10 minutes, basting frequently.

YIELD: 4 SERVINGS

The Charlotte Cookbook
THE JUNIOR LEAGUE OF CHARLOTTE, NORTH CAROLINA

Quick Barbecued Pork Chops

4–6 center-cut pork chops
¾ cup water
¼ cup vinegar
1 tablespoon sugar
2 tablespoons Worcestershire sauce
½ cup catsup
1 teaspoon salt
Dash pepper

Place pork chops evenly in baking dish. Combine remaining ingredients and pour over chops.

Bake uncovered at 350° for 1 hour.

YIELD: 4–6 SERVINGS

Huntsville Heritage Cookbook
THE JUNIOR LEAGUE OF HUNTSVILLE, ALABAMA

. . . .

Grilled Pork Chops in Honey and Soy Sauce

1 cup honey
1 tablespoon soy sauce
4 pork chops, cut thick
Ground ginger to taste
Garlic salt to taste

Mix honey and soy sauce. Sprinkle chops with ginger and garlic salt. Marinate at least overnight in honey and soy sauce mixture. Stab the meat with a fork to be sure the flavor penetrates the meat. Turn the chops several times.

The outdoor fire is the secret to this recipe. Make sure the fire is hot enough to cook the pork thoroughly but won't flame up and burn the outside. The chops should be cooked about 45 minutes with constant attention.

YIELD: 4 SERVINGS

Of Pots and Pipkins
THE JUNIOR LEAGUE OF ROANOKE VALLEY, VIRGINIA

Pork Chops and Sauerkraut

½ pound sliced bacon, diced
1 19-ounce can sauerkraut, drained and rinsed
1 15-ounce jar applesauce
1 tablespoon brown sugar
½ teaspoon dry mustard
¼ cup dry white wine (optional)
Dash pepper
¼ teaspoon paprika
6 medium shoulder pork chops
Bacon drippings

Sauté bacon until crisp; drain.

To sauerkraut, add bacon, applesauce, brown sugar, mustard, white wine, and pepper. Turn into a shallow casserole. Sprinkle with paprika.

Sauté chops in bacon drippings until golden on both sides. Place on top of sauerkraut. Cover and bake at 350° for about 1 hour or until chops are tender.

YIELD: 4–6 SERVINGS

Seasoned with Sun: Recipes from the Southwest
THE JUNIOR LEAGUE OF EL PASO, TEXAS

Barbecued Ribs

3 pounds spareribs, lean and cut into strips between bones
½ cup onion slices
1 cup chili sauce
2 cups catsup
2 tablespoons Worcestershire sauce
1 tablespoon soy sauce
2 tablespoons lemon juice
Juice of 1 lime
¼ cup vinegar
2 tablespoons brown sugar
2 tablespoons honey
Seasoned salt
2 cloves garlic, minced
Salt and pepper

Place ribs in shallow pan.

Mix remaining ingredients and cook together 30 minutes to thicken. Pour sauce over ribs. Cook covered in oven at 325° for 1½ hours.

Remove ribs and cool enough to skim off fat from sauce. Turn oven to 450° and brown ribs or brown on outdoor charcoaler.

YIELD: 6 SERVINGS

Home Cookin'
THE JUNIOR LEAGUE OF WICHITA FALLS, TEXAS

"Cheaper by the Dozen" Spareribs

3 or 4 pounds spareribs
Salt and pepper
2 onions, sliced
2 teaspoons vinegar
2 teaspoons Worcestershire sauce
1 teaspoon salt
1 teaspoon paprika
½ teaspoon red pepper
½ teaspoon black pepper
1 teaspoon chili powder
¾ cup catsup
¾ cup water

Select meaty spareribs. Cut into servings or leave uncut. Sprinkle with salt and pepper. Place in roaster and cover with onions.

Combine remaining ingredients and pour over meat. Cover and bake in moderate oven (350°) about 1½ hours. Baste occasionally, turning spareribs once or twice. Remove cover last 15 minutes to brown ribs.

YIELD: 6 SERVINGS

Charleston Receipts
THE JUNIOR LEAGUE OF CHARLESTON, SOUTH CAROLINA

Sweet and Sour Pork

1½ pounds lean pork shoulder, cut into strips
2 tablespoons fat
¼ cup water
¼ cup brown sugar
2 tablespoons cornstarch
½ teaspoon soy sauce
½ teaspoon salt
¼ cup vinegar
Juice from pineapple
1 1-pound 4-ounce can pineapple chunks, drained
¾ cup green pepper strips
¼ cup thinly sliced onion
2 cans Chinese noodles

Brown pork slowly in hot fat. Add water, cover, and simmer until tender (about 1 hour).

In saucepan, combine brown sugar, cornstarch, soy sauce, salt, vinegar, and pineapple juice. Cook over low heat, stirring constantly until thick. Pour this sauce over hot cooked pork and let stand 10 minutes or longer.

Add pineapple chunks, pepper strips, and sliced onion. Cook 2 or 3 minutes.

Serve over noodles.

YIELD: 4–6 SERVINGS

A Cook's Tour of Shreveport
THE JUNIOR LEAGUE OF SHREVEPORT, LOUISIANA

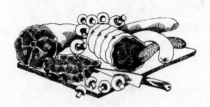

Chalupas

This is great for a party and no trouble.

4 pounds pork roast (minus fat)
2 jalapeño peppers
1½ teaspoons oregano
2 tablespoons chili powder
2 cloves garlic
2 pounds pinto beans, soaked overnight
1½ teaspoons each salt and pepper

GARNISHES:
Corn chips
Hot sauce
Shredded cheese
Chopped onion
Shredded lettuce
Chopped tomato
Chopped avocado

Combine all ingredients in *large* container with water to cover. Cook 6–8 hours, stirring frequently. When ready to serve, have bowls in following order: corn chips, meat and bean mixture, hot sauce, shredded cheese, chopped onion, shredded lettuce, chopped tomato, chopped avocado. Guests serve themselves from the bowls and have as much or as little as they like. Serve pralines for dessert.

YIELD: 20–24 SERVINGS

The Blue Denim Gourmet
THE JUNIOR LEAGUE OF ODESSA, TEXAS

· · · · · · · · · · · · · · · · ·

Sausage-Apple Ring

2 pounds bulk sausage
1½ cups cracker crumbs
2 eggs, slightly beaten
½ cup milk
¼ cup minced onion
1 cup finely chopped apple
8–10 eggs
Grated cheese
Parsley flakes
Paprika

Combine first six ingredients and mix thoroughly with fork.

Press lightly into greased ring mold, then turn out into shallow baking pan. Bake at 350° about 1 hour. (May be partially baked 30 minutes, then finished when ready to serve.)

Fill center with eggs scrambled with cheese and parsley. Sprinkle with paprika. Good for brunch or midnight supper.

YIELD: 10–12 SERVINGS

Huntsville Heritage Cookbook
THE JUNIOR LEAGUE OF HUNTSVILLE, ALABAMA

How to Cook a Country Ham

1 20–22-pound ham
1 cup pickle juice or ½ cup cider vinegar
1 red pepper pod (seeds removed)
1 lemon, quartered
1 onion, halved
2 bay leaves

HAM COATING:
Prepared mustard
Brown sugar
Fine, dry bread crumbs
½ cup sherry
Whole cloves

Scrub ham in cold water with stiff brush; soak overnight in cold water, making certain that the ham is completely covered.

Remove ham and place it in a covered ham boiler, skin side down. Barely cover with fresh water and add pickle juice or vinegar, pepper, lemon, onion, and bay leaves.

Let come to a boil and cut heat to medium. Ham is done when large flat bone can be removed with your fingers—this takes less than 15 minutes per pound. When done, remove lid and cool ham in the liquid in which it was cooked.

When ham is cool, skin off the rind and lightly pierce the fat side. Rub ham with mustard. Then pat on brown sugar. Sprinkle with sifted bread crumbs and pour sherry over entire top of ham. Stick with whole cloves and brown lightly in 350° oven.

Let cool for at least 12 hours before slicing.

YIELD: 2 SERVINGS PER POUND

Nashville Seasons
THE JUNIOR LEAGUE OF NASHVILLE, TENNESSEE

· · · · · · · · · · · · · · · · ·

Sherried Virginia Ham

1 ham
½ pound brown sugar
1 cup sherry

Select a Smithfield ham of about 14 pounds for best results. Scrub ham, and place in pan skin down and cover with cold water. Soak 48 hours, changing water once.

Place in roaster and cover with cold water. Simmer 25 minutes to the pound. Let cool in water. Remove skin.

Place ham in baking pan and cook in 350° oven until heated through.

Dissolve brown sugar in sherry. When ham is heated, take a skewer and stick into ham all over side where skin was removed. Pour into openings a little of the wine and sugar mixture. Put back into oven, and after a few minutes repeat until all mixture is used. Cool.

YIELD: 2 SERVINGS PER POUND

Spartanburg Secrets II
THE JUNIOR LEAGUE OF SPARTANBURG, SOUTH CAROLINA

· · · · · · · · · · · · · · · · · · ·

Gingered Ham Slice

1 fully cooked center cut ham slice, 1 inch thick
½ cup ginger ale
½ cup orange juice
¼ cup brown sugar
1 tablespoon salad oil
1½ teaspoons wine vinegar
1 teaspoon dry mustard
¼ teaspoon ground ginger
⅛ teaspoon ground cloves

Slash fat edge of ham. Thoroughly combine remaining ingredients and pour over ham in shallow dish.

Refrigerate overnight or let stand at room temperature 2 hours. Spoon marinade over ham several times.

Brown over coals of a charcoal fire about 15 minutes on each side, brushing frequently with marinade.

YIELD: 2 SERVINGS PER POUND

Southern Accent
THE JUNIOR LEAGUE OF PINE BLUFF, ARKANSAS

· · · · · · · · · · · · · · · ·

Calico Ham Casserole

4 10-ounce packages frozen mixed vegetables
3 cups ½-inch fresh bread cubes
¼ cup melted butter
1 cup flour
1 teaspoon salt
¼ teaspoon pepper
2 teaspoons dry mustard
2 teaspoons Worcestershire sauce
6 cups milk
¾ cup butter or margarine
1 medium onion, grated
2–3 cups shredded sharp American cheese
2 pounds fully cooked ham, cut into 1½ × ¼-inch strips

The day before serving: Cook vegetables as label directs. Coat bread cubes with melted butter and refrigerate. In bowl, mix flour, salt, pepper, mustard, and Worcestershire sauce and slowly stir in 2 cups milk. Heat remainder of milk in a large pan; stir in flour mixture and ¾ cup butter or

Recipe continues . . .

margarine; cook over low heat, stirring often. When sauce thickens, add onion and cheese, and stir until cheese melts. Add vegetables and ham. Pour into 2 baking dishes (12 × 8 × 2 inches) and refrigerate.

The following day, 1 hour before serving, sprinkle buttered cubes over casserole. Bake uncovered at 350° for 40 minutes. This recipe halves nicely.

YIELD: 25 SERVINGS

Home Cookin'
THE JUNIOR LEAGUE OF WICHITA FALLS, TEXAS

Poultry

Baked Stuffed Broilers

Broilers
Salt
Pepper
Paprika
Ground ginger
Dressing
Onions
Chicken fat or butter

Clean and dress broilers, and rub inside and out with salt, pepper, paprika, and a few grains of ginger. Stuff each broiler with dressing and place in a roasting pan with a sliced onion and 2 tablespoons chicken fat or butter over each chicken.

Bake in a hot oven (400°) until tender, basting frequently. This should be about 1 hour. Arrange broilers on serving platter and keep warm.

GRAVY:
4 tablespoons flour
2½ cups hot chicken stock or water
Salt and pepper
2 tablespoons sour cream

To make gravy: Pour off all but 4 tablespoons fat in roasting pan. Stir in flour and brown. Pour hot chicken stock or boiling water in gradually. Cook until smooth and thick. Season and add sour cream.

When ready to serve cut chickens in half.

YIELD: ONE BROILER SERVES 2

The Cotton Blossom Cookbook
THE JUNIOR LEAGUE OF ATLANTA, GEORGIA

Poulet Roulade

2 3-pound roasting chickens
Salt and pepper
Melted butter
⅓ teaspoon each ground thyme, oregano, savory

Debone the chickens. Leave in the drumsticks, if desired. Place the chickens skin side down. Salt, pepper, and baste with melted butter. Sprinkle with the thyme, oregano, and savory. The chickens are now ready for stuffing.

POACHING STOCK:
Chicken bones, necks, and giblets
2 carrots, coarsely chopped
1 large onion, coarsely chopped
2 stalks celery, coarsely chopped
1 bouquet garni: ¼ teaspoon thyme leaves, 4 sprigs parsley,
1 bay leaf, tied in cheesecloth

Place the chicken bones, necks, and giblets (but not the livers) in a large pan and add the vegetables and the bouquet garni. Cover with water and simmer for 2 hours or more. Strain.

ZUCCHINI STUFFING:
1 pound small, firm zucchini
2 teaspoons salt
6 tablespoons butter
1 medium onion, finely chopped
½ cup ricotta cheese
Salt and pepper
Large pinch of fresh marjoram, finely chopped
1 egg, slightly beaten
½ cup freshly grated Parmesan cheese

Finely grate the zucchini; add salt and let sit for ½ hour. Squeeze out the

Recipe continues . . .

zucchini, then put it in a sieve and mash it well to release all water. Sauté the zucchini in 2 tablespoons butter for 7 minutes or until dry. Cool.

Sauté the onion in 2 tablespoons butter for 15 minutes without letting it color. Cool. Mash the ricotta cheese and the remaining 2 tablespoons butter with the seasonings. Add the egg, onion, zucchini, and Parmesan cheese.

TO ASSEMBLE:

Divide the stuffing between the two chickens. Leave a ½-inch border around the edge of the chicken so the stuffing will not escape when it is rolled. Fold up the edges of the chicken, then fold the chicken in half to fully encase the stuffing. Roll the chicken tightly in a large length of cheesecloth. Twist and tie the ends with string; tie the entire roll at 1-inch intervals.

Place the chickens in the poaching stock and simmer for 1 hour. Remove from the liquid and let stand for 10 minutes before taking off the cheesecloth.

Degrease the chicken stock and serve a little stock over each slice of chicken.

YIELD: 8–10 SERVINGS

Southern Sideboards
THE JUNIOR LEAGUE OF JACKSON, MISSISSIPPI

. . . .

Aunt Clara's Chicken and Dumplings

1 3–5-pound stewing chicken
3 sprigs parsley
3 stalks celery with leaves
1 carrot, sliced
1 onion, sliced
2 teaspoons salt
½ teaspoon pepper

Place chicken in Dutch oven, cover with water, and add parsley, celery, carrot, onion, salt, and pepper. Bring to boil and boil 5 minutes; simmer 2 hours or until tender. Add more water if necessary. Remove chicken and vegetables from broth. Bone chicken or cut into serving pieces.

YIELD: 8 SERVINGS

DUMPLINGS:
1 cup milk
1 egg, beaten
1½ cups flour
2 heaping teaspoons baking powder
1 teaspoon salt
1 teaspoon sugar
3 tablespoons minced parsley or chives (optional)

Mix milk and egg. Sift together flour, baking powder, salt, and sugar.

Combine milk and egg mixture with dry ingredients. Drop by table-spoonfuls into boiling broth.

Cover tightly and cook 15 minutes. *Do not peek!* Add chicken and garnish of parsley or chives before serving.

YIELD: 20 DUMPLINGS

Home Cookin'
THE JUNIOR LEAGUE OF WICHITA FALLS, TEXAS

· · · · · · · · · · · · · · · ·

Picnic Cornish Hens

8 Cornish hens
Salt and pepper
½ cup Dijon mustard
⅔ cup fine, dry white bread crumbs
3 tablespoons minced shallots or green onions
½ cup butter
White wine

Recipe continues . . .

Rub each bird with salt, pepper, and 1 tablespoon of the mustard. Sprinkle with bread crumbs. Place in square of foil and fold foil to center. Add 1 teaspoon shallots or green onions, 1 tablespoon butter, and 3 tablespoons white wine to each package. Fold over the foil tightly and bake at 400° for 45 minutes. Open foil, baste hens, and bake about 15 minutes more, until browned. Reseal and carry to picnic in foil. If you are serving at home, remove from foil, stuff cavity with fresh parsley, and serve juices separately. Good cold, too!

YIELD: 8 SERVINGS

Southern Accent
THE JUNIOR LEAGUE OF PINE BLUFF, ARKANSAS

· · · · · · · · · · · · · · ·

Faber's Pilaf

1 6–7-pound hen or rooster
Neck, giblets, and liver
1 large onion, chopped fine
2 tablespoons salt
2 or 3 twigs thyme
2 1-pound 4-ounce cans tomatoes
1 tablespoon whole black peppercorns
¼ pound margarine
3 cups raw rice
3 tablespoons flour

Wash hen or rooster and put in roasting pan on top of stove. Cover two-thirds with hot water. Put neck, giblets, and liver in water also. Add onion, salt, thyme, and tomatoes put through a colander. Cover and boil hard.

After 1 hour, add peppercorns and margarine. Turn down to simmer. Baste and turn fowl occasionally.

After 2½ hours of cooking, take out 2½ cups of liquid. Put in separate pot, bring to boil, then into that put washed, unsalted rice, and cook.

After 3½ hours of cooking, remove fowl from roasting pan and thicken liquid in pan with flour. After flour is thoroughly mixed, return fowl to roasting pan for thorough heating before serving.

Serve with rice spread on big platter and rooster in nest of rice.

When using hens for this pilaf, cut down cooking time and do not put in margarine if hens are fat.

YIELD: 10 SERVINGS

Charleston Receipts
THE JUNIOR LEAGUE OF CHARLESTON, SOUTH CAROLINA

· · · · · · · · · · · ·

Clyde's Barbecued Chicken

4 broilers, halved
Salt and pepper

BARBECUE SAUCE:
1 pound margarine
1 cup lemon juice
2 tablespoons Worcestershire sauce
2 teaspoons salt
½ teaspoon black pepper
6 drops Tabasco
½ cup sherry

Combine all sauce ingredients in saucepan and heat slowly, stirring occasionally, until margarine is melted.

Salt and pepper chicken, then paint with barbecue sauce.

Grill over low charcoal fire to which 2 or 3 hickory chips, presoaked in water, have been added. Cook until tender (about 1½ hours or until meat leaves bone on drumstick). Turn and baste often.

YIELD: 8 SERVINGS

Southern Sideboards
THE JUNIOR LEAGUE OF JACKSON, MISSISSIPPI

· · · · · · · · · · · · ·

Fried Chicken and Cream Gravy

Ladies who have fried chicken for years tested this method and rated it Platonic.

Chicken pieces
Eggs
Cooking oil
Flour

Read the *Rules for Frying Chicken* (see below) and apply throughout this recipe.

In medium-size bowl combine 1 egg and 1 tablespoon water per chicken. Beat slightly. Place pieces of chicken in egg mixture to sit while you are heating skillet. Use just enough oil (*always* cooking oil) so that when chicken is placed in skillet, oil does not come up over halfway on the pieces. Make certain oil is *very hot* before frying. (A good test is to drop a little of the egg mixture in skillet to see if it sizzles.)

Put a generous amount of flour into a brown paper bag. Place chicken pieces in sack and shake vigorously. (Hold top securely or you'll have a mess!) Starting with dark pieces, place them in the middle of skillet. Then place the rest of chicken to outside. Allow pieces to brown at least 1 minute, then turn and brown on other side. (Use tongs to turn—do not pierce with a fork.) Place lid on skillet and reduce heat to medium. Let chicken cook 10 minutes on one side; turn and cook 10 minutes more. Remove lid and turn heat on high again. Cook about 1 more minute. Remove chicken and drain.

CREAM GRAVY:
2 tablespoons oil from fried chicken
2 tablespoons butter
5 tablespoons flour
Salt and pepper
1½ cups milk
½ cup heavy cream
2 tablespoons butter
Paprika
Red pepper (optional)

Pour off all but 2 tablespoons of oil from the chicken, keeping the brown crispy bits in the skillet. Add butter and stir over medium high heat. Add about 5 tablespoons flour. (This varies, depending on how thick or thin you prefer gravy.) Stir and reduce heat. Continue to stir at least 3 minutes. Add salt and pepper. Pour in milk and cream. Reduce heat again and let gravy bubble 2–3 minutes. Add remaining 2 tablespoons butter and a generous amount of paprika. Stir well and remove from heat.

If gravy is too thick, add more milk and cream; if too thin, put flour in a glass with a small amount of milk and stir vigorously before adding to gravy and cook, stirring for 5 minutes. (This avoids lumps.) Sprinkle red pepper over gravy if desired.

YIELD: 6 SERVINGS

RULES FOR FRYING CHICKEN

1. Cut up chicken yourself. Precut chickens lose a great deal of flavor and moistness.

2. Buy small chickens. Larger ones just do not have the flavor of the smaller.

3. After cutting the chickens, be certain to remove outside skin. They fry crisper when skin is removed.

4. Always place dark meat in center of skillet because it takes a little longer to cook.

5. Never salt and pepper chicken before frying, but generously season immediately after removing from skillet.

6. Chicken should be allowed to drain on paper towels at least 1 minute before being placed on a serving platter.

Southern Accent
THE JUNIOR LEAGUE OF PINE BLUFF, ARKANSAS

· · · · · · · · · · · · · · · · ·

Oven-Barbecued Chicken

Flour
Salt and pepper
2 3-pound chickens, cut into quarters or halves
¾–1 cup melted butter
Paprika

You can use half recipe; use less chicken, but all of sauce.

Sift flour, salt, and pepper together, or place in paper bag, and coat chicken thoroughly. Place floured chicken in oblong buttered baking dish and pour melted butter over it. Sprinkle generously with paprika. Bake in 350° oven for 1 hour. (This may be done ahead.) At end of hour remove from oven.

Combine sauce ingredients. Turn chicken pieces and pour sauce over all.

BARBECUE SAUCE:
1 cup catsup
1 cup water
2 teaspoons prepared mustard
¼ teaspoon red pepper (optional)
1 tablespoon Worcestershire sauce
1 tablespoon vinegar
1 tablespoon chopped garlic

Bake chickens ½–1 hour longer, basting occasionally.

Splendid for company. Bake chicken first, and pour on sauce when you want to eat in 30 or 45 minutes.

YIELD: 6 SERVINGS

Spartanburg Secrets II
THE JUNIOR LEAGUE OF SPARTANBURG, SOUTH CAROLINA

Barbecued Chicken Wings

1 cup soy sauce
3 teaspoons sugar or ¼ cup pineapple syrup
¼ cup white wine
2 cloves garlic, mashed (or sprinkle wings generously with garlic powder)
¼ cup cooking oil
1 teaspoon monosodium glutamate
1 level teaspoon ground ginger
2–3 pounds chicken wings, cut up (throw away the tips)

Combine all sauce ingredients.
   Marinate wings in the sauce for 16 hours.
   Bake at 325° for 1½–2 hours.
   Sauce may be saved in refrigerator and used again.

YIELD: 4–6 SERVINGS

The Charlotte Cookbook
THE JUNIOR LEAGUE OF CHARLOTTE, NORTH CAROLINA

.   .   .   .

Chicken Bordelaise

1 stick butter
1 large sweet onion, chopped fine
1 2½-pound fryer, quartered
1 cup light cream
2 tablespoons chopped parsley
1 bay leaf
½ cup sherry

Melt butter (do not brown). (It is best to use heavy cooking utensil, such as a Dutch oven with close-fitting lid.) Add onion and cook until clear. Scoop off onion and set aside to use later.

Recipe continues . . .

Brown chicken in butter. Turn heat low. Add cream, onion, parsley, and bay leaf.

Heat sherry until warm and add to mixture. Cover well and cook at low heat about 40 minutes.

YIELD: 4 SERVINGS

The Cotton Blossom Cookbook
THE JUNIOR LEAGUE OF ATLANTA, GEORGIA

· · · · · · · · · · · · · · · · · · · ·

Coq au Vin

4 slices bacon, diced
2½ to 3 pounds chicken pieces
2 tablespoons butter
Salt and pepper
1 1-pound jar whole onions
1 4-ounce can mushrooms
½ cup sliced onion
2 cloves garlic, minced
2 tablespoons flour
2 ounces brandy
14 ounces Burgundy
3 sprigs parsley, chopped
½ bay leaf
⅛ teaspoon thyme
Minced parsley for garnish

Brown bacon and set aside. Add chicken pieces and 2 tablespoons butter to fat in skillet and season with salt and pepper.

Place chicken in a good-size casserole after it is browned. Add and brown in skillet: whole onions, mushrooms, sliced onion, and garlic. Remove to casserole.

Add flour to skillet. Stir in brandy and Burgundy. Pour into casserole. Sprinkle with parsley, bay leaf, and thyme. Add bacon.

Bake uncovered at 400° for 1½ hours. Serve with minced parsley.

YIELD: 4 SERVINGS

The Charlotte Cookbook
THE JUNIOR LEAGUE OF CHARLOTTE, NORTH CAROLINA

·   ·   ·   ·   ·   ·   ·   ·   ·   ·   ·   ·   ·   ·   ·   ·

Chicken with Sauce Piquant

⅔ cup flour
About ¾ cup oil
2 cups chopped onions
1 6-ounce can tomato paste
1 1-pound can whole tomatoes
1 hen (about 5 pounds), cut up
Salt, red pepper, and black pepper
2 stalks celery, chopped
½ cup chopped green pepper
1 large can mushrooms
1 teaspoon sugar
Parsley and garlic, chopped fine (optional)

Brown flour in oil or melted chicken fat in heavy pot (black iron pot, if possible), stirring constantly. Add onions and cook until wilted. Add tomato paste and tomatoes and cook over slow fire stirring often until fat comes over the tomatoes, about 45 minutes. (Cook longer if recipe is doubled or tripled.)

Season chicken well with salt, red pepper, and black pepper. (The more red pepper the more "piquant" the gravy will be.)

Put chicken and all other ingredients in the pot, then add water to cover the chicken. Add more water later if gravy is too thick.

Cover and cook slowly, stirring often until chicken is tender. Add more salt, pepper, garlic, and parsley, if desired.

Recipe continues . . .

Serve over rice with a green salad and French bread for a special company treat.

May be prepared ahead of time and frozen. Gravy must be completely cooled before freezing large quantities.

YIELD: 6 SERVINGS

Talk About Good!

THE JUNIOR LEAGUE OF LAFAYETTE, LOUISIANA

· · · · · · · · · · · · · · · · · · · ·

Golden Brown Chicken Casserole

1 stick butter
Salt and pepper
1 chicken, cut into serving pieces
1 4-ounce can mushrooms
1 tablespoon flour
2 tablespoons Worcestershire sauce
1 bay leaf
Lemon juice
1 10½-ounce can condensed beef bouillon

Melt butter in skillet. Salt and pepper chicken and brown well in melted butter. Transfer chicken to large casserole dish. Brown mushrooms in same butter, take out, and place with chicken. Add flour to the butter and mix well. Add Worcestershire sauce, bay leaf, lemon juice, and beef bouillon. Pour over chicken and mushrooms, and cook for 1 hour in oven.

The chicken and mushrooms get brown and the gravy thickens. This gravy is excellent for rice or mashed potatoes.

May be prepared a day ahead. Prepare and place in casserole. Next day, cook in oven until hot and bubbly.

YIELD: 4 SERVINGS

A Cook's Tour of Shreveport

THE JUNIOR LEAGUE OF SHREVEPORT, LOUISIANA

· · · · · · · · · · · · · · · · · · · ·

Chicken Enchiladas

1 medium onion, chopped
3 tablespoons butter
1 10¾-ounce can condensed cream of chicken soup
1 10¾-ounce can condensed cream of mushroom soup
1 cup chicken broth
1 4-ounce can chopped green chilies
1 2–3-pound chicken, cooked and boned
1 package corn tortillas
1 pound longhorn cheese, shredded

Sauté onion in butter. Combine with soups, broth, and green chilies. Add pieces of chicken and mix well.

In large baking dish, place a layer of corn tortillas, a layer of sauced chicken, and a layer of cheese. Repeat until casserole is filled.

Bake at 350° for 30 minutes.

YIELD: 8 SERVINGS

Cooking Through Rose Colored Glasses
THE JUNIOR LEAGUE OF TYLER, TEXAS

· · · · · · · · · · · · · · · · · ·

Chicken Ambassador

6–8 large chicken breasts (1 per person if large)
1 tablespoon salt
1 teaspoon poultry seasoning (more if desired)
Paprika
½ cup melted butter
1 10½-ounce can condensed beef consommé
½ cup sherry
½ pound mushrooms (must be fresh), sliced
2 10-ounce cans artichoke hearts

Recipe continues . . .

Season chicken breasts with salt and poultry seasoning, and sprinkle with paprika to give them a good color. Spread out in roasting pan, skin side up. Baste with combined melted butter and consommé. Bake in 325° oven for at least 1 hour, basting every 20 minutes.

Add sherry to pan drippings and keep on baking and basting for ½ hour longer.

Sauté the sliced fresh mushrooms in butter. When ready to serve, remove chicken breasts to heated platter and combine drippings in pan with mushrooms and artichoke hearts. Heat thoroughly and pour sauce over the chicken. Serve at once.

YIELD: 6–8 SERVINGS

Nashville Seasons
THE JUNIOR LEAGUE OF NASHVILLE, TENNESSEE

· · · · · · · · · · · · · · · · · · · ·

Tiny Chicken Wings

3 pounds chicken wings
½ cup strong chicken broth
⅓ cup soy sauce
3 tablespoons sugar
3 tablespoons brown sugar
3 tablespoons vinegar
1 teaspoon ground ginger
Garlic powder
Monosodium glutamate
Pepper

Cut off tips of chicken wings and boil for broth.

Mix chicken broth, soy sauce, sugars, vinegar, ginger, and garlic powder. Spread over wings in baking pan. Sprinkle with monosodium glutamate and ground pepper. Marinate 2 hours, turning often.

Bake at 325° for 1½–2 hours, until juice is almost gone.
Also good as a meal with larger pieces of chicken.

YIELD: 6 SERVINGS

The Cotton Blossom Cookbook
THE JUNIOR LEAGUE OF ATLANTA, GEORGIA

·   ·   ·   ·   ·   ·   ·   ·   ·   ·   ·   ·   ·   ·

Cheesy Chicken Wings

4 pounds chicken wings, disjointed
1 cup grated Parmesan cheese
2 tablespoons chopped parsley
2 teaspoons paprika
1 tablespoon oregano
2 teaspoons salt
½ teaspoon pepper
½ cup melted butter

Discard tips of chicken wings.

Mix together cheese and seasonings. Dip pieces in butter, then roll in cheese mixture.

Place on a foil-lined cookie sheet, forming a lip with foil, and bake at 350° for 1 hour and 15 minutes.

YIELD: 8–10 SERVINGS

Little Rock Cooks
THE JUNIOR LEAGUE OF LITTLE ROCK, ARKANSAS

·   ·   ·   ·   ·   ·   ·   ·   ·   ·   ·   ·   ·

Chicken Kiev

4 whole chicken breasts
Salt
½ cup chopped green onion
½ cup chopped parsley
¼ pound chilled butter
Flour
2 eggs, beaten
1 cup dry bread crumbs
Fat for frying
Lemon wedges

Cut chicken breasts lengthwise in half. Remove skin and bone (try not to tear meat) and place each piece between two pieces of waxed paper. With wooden mallet, pound until ¼ inch thick. Peel off paper and sprinkle each breast half with salt and 1 tablespoon each of green onion and parsley.

Cut butter into 8 pieces. Place at end of each cutlet and roll like jellyroll, tucking in sides. Press to seal well. Dust with flour and dip in beaten eggs, then roll in dry bread crumbs. Chill at least 1 hour.

Fry in deep, hot fat (340°) for about 5 minutes or until golden brown. Serve with lemon wedges.

YIELD: 4–6 SERVINGS

Little Rock Cooks
THE JUNIOR LEAGUE OF LITTLE ROCK, ARKANSAS

. . . .

Foolproof Chicken Breasts

1 10¾-ounce can condensed cream of celery soup
1 10¾-ounce can condensed cream of chicken soup
1 package dry onion soup mix
1 soup can dry white wine
1 cup raw wild rice or brown rice
3 whole chicken breasts, boned, skinned, and split

Mix soups, wine, and raw rice and let stand several hours. Spread rice in baking dish and arrange chicken on top of mixture. Cover. Bake at 350° for 1 hour, then remove cover, stir gravy, and cook another 20–30 minutes.

YIELD: 6 SERVINGS

Cooking Through Rose Colored Glasses
THE JUNIOR LEAGUE OF TYLER, TEXAS

. . . .

King Ranch Chicken

1 dozen corn tortillas
Chicken stock
1 large hen, stewed, boned, and cut into bite-size pieces
1 large green pepper, chopped
1 large onion, chopped
2–4 tablespoons cooking oil
1 pound cheddar cheese, shredded
1 teaspoon chili powder
Garlic powder to taste
Salt to taste
1 10¾-ounce can condensed cream of chicken soup
1 10¾-ounce can condensed cream of mushroom soup
1 10-ounce can tomatoes with green chilies, crushed

Recipe continues . . .

Soak tortillas in boiling chicken stock; place in bottom of 3-quart casserole. Top with chicken pieces.

Sauté green pepper and onion in oil until tender and layer over chicken. Add cheese to casserole, sprinkle with chili powder, garlic powder, and salt; spoon undiluted soups over and top with crushed tomatoes and chilies.

Bake at 375° for 30 minutes, or freeze and bake after thawing.

YIELD: 6–8 GENEROUS SERVINGS

Cooking Through Rose Colored Glasses
THE JUNIOR LEAGUE OF TYLER, TEXAS

· · · · · · · · · · · · · · · ·

Chicken Suzanne

4–6 half chicken breasts
Salt and pepper
1 stick margarine
½ cup sour cream
½ cup sherry
1 10¾-ounce can condensed cream of mushroom soup

Season chicken with salt and pepper; brown in melted margarine. Remove to greased shallow casserole. Add sour cream, sherry, and mushroom soup to melted margarine. Mix well and pour over chicken.

Cover and bake at 350° for 1½ hours or until done.

YIELD: 4–6 SERVINGS

The Blue Denim Gourmet
THE JUNIOR LEAGUE OF ODESSA, TEXAS

· · · · · · · · · · · · · · · ·

Green Enchiladas

3 medium green tomatoes
1 4-ounce can green chilies
1 clove garlic
Salt to taste
1 cup chicken broth
3 tablespoons oil
Small piece of onion
1 small package tortillas
1 chicken, boiled with garlic and boned
1 cup sour cream
1 8-ounce package Monterey Jack cheese, shredded

Boil tomatoes for 15 minutes, peel, then add to blender along with green chilies, garlic, salt to taste, and chicken broth. Blend.

Heat oil in skillet, fry onion until brown, then remove and add mixture from blender. Heat a few minutes. Fry tortillas in some oil to soften, then dip through mixture in skillet.

Place some chicken inside each tortilla and roll up. Place side by side in an oblong casserole dish. Spread sour cream over top and pile the shredded Monterey Jack cheese on top. Cover and heat for about 20–30 minutes at 350°. Heat the remainder of tomato and chili mixture and serve, to be poured over enchiladas.

YIELD: 4 SERVINGS

The Blue Denim Gourmet
THE JUNIOR LEAGUE OF ODESSA, TEXAS

. . . .

Chicken Divan

The original Chicken Divan recipe, from an old New York restaurant by the same name, called for cheese sauce, Hollandaise sauce, and whipped

Recipe continues . . .

cream mixed together. This is a deceitfully easy and surprisingly superb substitute.

3 whole chicken breasts
2 10-ounce packages frozen broccoli
2 10¾-ounce cans condensed cream of chicken soup
½ pint sour cream
1 cup mayonnaise
1 cup shredded sharp cheddar cheese
1 tablespoon lemon juice
1 teaspoon curry (or less to taste)
Salt and pepper to taste
Grated Parmesan cheese
Paprika
Butter

Cook chicken breasts. (Can simmer in water with onion, celery, carrot, bay leaf, peppercorns, salt, etc.) Cook broccoli. Mix soup, sour cream, mayonnaise, grated cheddar cheese, lemon juice, and seasonings.

Drain broccoli and arrange in bottom of flat greased 3-quart casserole. Sprinkle generously with Parmesan cheese. Remove skin from chicken and take chicken from bone, pulling apart into pieces, and spread over broccoli. Sprinkle again with Parmesan cheese. Pour sauce over all. Sprinkle with Parmesan and paprika. Dot with butter. Bake 30–40 minutes at 350° or until bubbly and hot through.

This can be made ahead and refrigerated or frozen and cooked later. Good with tomato aspic for luncheon or buffet supper or with baked stuffed tomatoes and green salad.

YIELD: 6–8 SERVINGS

300 Years of Carolina Cooking
THE JUNIOR LEAGUE OF GREENVILLE, SOUTH CAROLINA

Hot Chicken Salad

2 cups chopped cooked chicken or turkey
2 hard-boiled eggs, chopped or sliced
1 cup chopped celery
½ cup mayonnaise
1 tablespoon lemon juice
1 10¾-ounce can condensed cream of mushroom soup
½ cup sliced water chestnuts
Salt and pepper to taste
Crushed potato chips

Mix all ingredients except potato chips. Put in greased 1½-quart casserole and top with potato chips.

Bake at 375° for 30 minutes or until it bubbles.

YIELD: 6 SERVINGS

The Charlotte Cookbook
THE JUNIOR LEAGUE OF CHARLOTTE, NORTH CAROLINA

. . . .

Chicken Casserole

1 6-ounce box long-grain and wild rice
2 2½-pound fryers, cooked and boned
1 10¾-ounce can condensed cream of celery soup
1 onion, minced
1 2-ounce jar pimentos
2 cups mayonnaise
1 8-ounce can water chestnuts, sliced thin
2 16-ounce cans French-style green beans, drained
Paprika
Grated Parmesan cheese

Recipe continues . . .

Cook rice as directed on box. Add all ingredients except paprika and cheese and mix thoroughly. Pour into greased shallow 3-quart baking dish. Sprinkle with paprika and Parmesan cheese. Bake at 350° until bubbly, about 30–40 minutes.

Freezes well. When frozen, remove from freezer at least 4 hours before heating.

Serve with mixed green salad and hot rolls or corn bread.

YIELD: 12 SERVINGS

Fiesta: Favorite Recipes of South Texas
THE JUNIOR LEAGUE OF CORPUS CHRISTI, TEXAS

. . . .

Coq avec les Perlettes et les Oranges (Fruity Chicken)

¾ cup flour
2 teaspoons salt
½ teaspoon pepper
1 teaspoon tarragon
8 half chicken breasts, boned
6 tablespoons butter
1 clove garlic, pressed
1 pound fresh mushrooms, sliced
3 cups chicken stock
1 chicken bouillon cube
2 tablespoons Curaçao or Cointreau (or more)
2 11-ounce cans mandarin oranges
½ pound green seedless grapes or 1 16-ounce can

Mix flour, salt, pepper, and tarragon. Dredge clean, wiped chicken breasts with the flour mixture, reserving leftover mixture. Let stand a short while. Then melt 4 tablespoons butter in skillet and add garlic. Brown the chicken just until golden brown; it does not have to be cooked.

Lay in baking dish. Add 2 tablespoons butter to skillet, brown the mushrooms, and put them on the chicken. If necessary, add more butter to skillet and make a roux with the remaining flour mix, about ¼ cup. Add the stock slowly, then the bouillon cube and Curaçao or Cointreau.

Pour sauce over the chicken. (May be frozen at this point.) Cover tightly with foil and bake 1 hour at 325°, 15 minutes longer if it has been frozen and thawed, or refrigerated.

Before serving, heat the oranges and grapes in their own juice and drain. Arrange chicken on platter and place fruit over it.

YIELD: 8 SERVINGS

Of Pots and Pipkins
THE JUNIOR LEAGUE OF ROANOKE VALLEY, VIRGINIA

. . . .

Walnut Chicken with Lime Sauce

6 large half chicken breasts, boned and skinned
Salt and pepper
2 egg whites
1 cup finely chopped walnuts

LIME SAUCE:
2 tablespoons butter
2 tablespoons flour
1 cup chicken broth
¼ teaspoon salt
Dash white pepper
2 egg yolks
2 whole eggs
½ teaspoon grated lime peel
2 tablespoons fresh lime juice

Season chicken with salt and pepper. Beat 2 egg whites lightly. Dip chicken in egg whites, turning to coat. Drain well, then roll in walnuts. Place in buttered baking pan and bake at 350° for 20–25 minutes, just until chicken is cooked through.

Recipe continues . . .

To make Lime Sauce, melt butter and stir in flour. Add chicken broth, salt, and white pepper. Cook, stirring, until mixture boils thoroughly. Beat egg yolks and whole eggs. Stir hot sauce into eggs, stirring quickly. Return mixture to lowest possible heat and stir constantly until thickened. Remove from heat and blend in grated lime peel and juice.

Serve chicken with Lime Sauce.

YIELD: 6 SERVINGS

Gator Country Cooks
THE JUNIOR LEAGUE OF GAINESVILLE, FLORIDA

· · · · · · · · · · · · · · ·

Breast of Chicken Véronique

9 tablespoons butter
3 large whole chicken breasts, split
18 medium mushroom caps, quartered
3 tablespoons flour
1½ cups light cream
¾ cup white wine
1 cup diced ham
Salt and pepper to taste
1½ cups seedless grapes

Melt 6 tablespoons butter in large heavy pan and brown chicken breasts over medium heat. Remove to a casserole.

Melt 3 tablespoons butter in same pan. Sauté mushrooms over high heat for 3 minutes. Remove with a slotted spoon and scatter over chicken. Reduce heat and stir flour into skillet. Cook the roux 1 minute. Gradually add cream and wine, stirring constantly. Cook until sauce is thick. Add diced ham and season with salt and pepper. Pour sauce over chicken.

Bake covered in a 350° oven 35–40 minutes. Uncover and scatter grapes over chicken and bake another 10 minutes.

This can be prepared ahead and refrigerated until baking time, but grapes should not be added until last 10 minutes of cooking.

YIELD: 6 SERVINGS

Party Potpourri
THE JUNIOR LEAGUE OF MEMPHIS, TENNESSEE

·   ·   ·   ·   ·   ·   ·   ·   ·   ·   ·   ·   ·   ·   ·   ·

Chicken Chasseur

Salt
8–10 half chicken breasts
½ cup flour
6 tablespoons butter
6 tablespoons olive oil
1 medium onion, chopped fine
1 pound mushrooms, sliced thin
1 cup white wine
1 jigger brandy
1 cup tomato sauce
½ cup canned chicken broth
1 tablespoon Kitchen Bouquet browning and seasoning sauce
Juice of 1 lemon
4 tablespoons chopped fresh parsley

Salt chicken and dredge in flour. Brown in mixture of butter and olive oil. Transfer to casserole and sauté onions until transparent. Add mushrooms to onions, sauté for a few minutes, then add remaining ingredients except parsley. Bring sauce to a quick boil, stirring all the while; pour over chicken.

Cover casserole and set aside in a cool place.

Before serving, bake uncovered in 325° oven for 1½ hours or until tender. Sprinkle with freshly chopped parsley.

Recipe continues ...

With this chicken, serve rice prepared in the following way:

3 cups rice
¼ pound butter
3 cups canned chicken broth

Wash rice and drain until dry. In a heavy 3-quart pan, sauté rice in butter until butter is absorbed. Add chicken broth and stir thoroughly. Cover tight and bring to a quick boil. Turn heat as low as possible and let rice cook for 30 minutes. Do not remove cover until ready to serve.

This dish may seem complicated to prepare but is well worth the effort. The chicken can be made the day before, refrigerated, and baked just before serving. The rice can be prepared just before guests arrive. You can keep it warm as long as needed.

A marinated green bean salad is good with this.

YIELD: 8 SERVINGS

The Charlotte Cookbook
THE JUNIOR LEAGUE OF CHARLOTTE, NORTH CAROLINA

· · · · · · · · · · · · · ·

Turkey or Chicken Sopa

1 pint sour cream
3 10-ounce cans tomatoes with green chilies
1 onion, finely chopped
4 cups diced cooked turkey, or 3 chicken breasts,
cooked, halved, and cut in pieces
8–10 tortillas, softened in hot oil and cut in half
1 cup shredded Monterey Jack cheese

Lightly grease a 3-quart casserole. Mix sour cream, tomatoes with chilies, onion, and turkey or chicken. Line casserole with tortillas, slightly overlapping. Cover with chicken mixture. Add another layer of tortillas and chicken and top with cheese. Bake at 325° for 1 hour.

May be prepared ahead and frozen. Allow the uncooked casserole to defrost at room temperature for 2 hours and proceed to bake for 1 hour.

YIELD: 8 SERVINGS

Seasoned with Sun: Recipes from the Southwest
THE JUNIOR LEAGUE OF EL PASO, TEXAS

.   .   .   .

Chicken Country Captain

16–18 half chicken breasts, preferably boned
Salt and pepper
Paprika
Flour
Cooking oil
6 green peppers, chopped
3 large onions, chopped
1 large bunch parsley, chopped
2 1-pound 4-ounce cans tomatoes (about 5 cups)
1½ teaspoons ground mace
3 teaspoons curry powder
¼ teaspoon garlic powder
1 cup currants
¾ pound blanched, shredded almonds
Steamed rice (3 cups raw rice for 12 servings, or
4 cups to have extra for seconds)

In brown paper bag, shake chicken with salt, pepper, paprika, and flour. Fry in hot oil until brown. Put aside.

In large frying pan, heat more oil. Slowly cook the peppers, onions, and parsley for approximately 15 minutes. Put this mixture in large casserole or roaster. Add tomatoes, spices, and garlic powder. Simmer for 15 minutes. Taste and adjust salt and pepper.

Lay chicken in the sauce. Cover casserole or roaster. Place in 275° oven for 1½ to 2 hours. Stir in currants ½ hour before serving.

Recipe continues . . .

Toast almonds in slow oven. Serve chicken with cooked rice and toasted almonds.

Chicken should be served in casserole or deep platter with sauce poured over it. Each guest should serve himself first to rice, then place chicken and sauce on rice; sprinkle almonds on top.

YIELD: 12 SERVINGS

The Charlotte Cookbook
THE JUNIOR LEAGUE OF CHARLOTTE, NORTH CAROLINA

. . . .

Hawaiian Luau Chicken

1 5-pound stewing hen
2 cups water
⅓ cup chopped onion
⅓ cup chopped green pepper
2 cups slivered celery
1 8-ounce can water chestnuts, sliced
½ cup chicken fat
¼ cup flour
1 tablespoon salt
2 cups reserved chicken broth
1 3-ounce package slivered almonds
2 tablespoons butter
1½ cups pitted ripe olives, sliced
1 6-ounce can bamboo shoots, sliced
1 4-ounce jar pimentos, sliced
2 cups shredded cheddar cheese
Shredded coconut
Diced green pepper
Chopped peanuts
Chutney

Simmer hen in water until tender; cool in broth; remove skin and bones from chicken; reserve broth and fat.

Sauté onion, pepper, celery, and water chestnuts in ¼ cup chicken fat until wilted and clear.

In a Dutch oven, melt ¼ cup chicken fat, stir in flour to make a roux, add salt and reserved broth, and cook until thick. Add chicken pieces and sautéed vegetables. Heat until steaming. (You may do this ahead of time; simply reheat and complete at serving time.)

Brown almonds in butter. Just before serving, stir almonds, olives, bamboo shoots, pimentos, and cheese into hot chicken mixture and heat until cheese melts.

Serve over rice with side dishes of shredded coconut, diced green pepper, chopped peanuts, and chutney.

YIELD: 12 SERVINGS

Fiesta: Favorite Recipes of South Texas
THE JUNIOR LEAGUE OF CORPUS CHRISTI, TEXAS

·   ·   ·   ·   ·   ·   ·   ·   ·   ·   ·   ·   ·   ·   ·   ·

Almond Chicken

2 chickens, boned and skinned
3 tablespoons oil
½ cup thinly sliced onion
1 cup thinly sliced celery
1 8-ounce can water chestnuts, sliced
1 6-ounce can bamboo shoots, sliced
2 cups chicken broth
2 tablespoons soy sauce
2 teaspoons monosodium glutamate
1 8-ounce package frozen snow pea pods
2–3 tablespoons cornstarch
2 tablespoons water
Salt
½ cup toasted, shredded almonds
Hot, cooked rice

Recipe continues . . .

Cut chicken into ¼-inch slices. Sauté in hot oil 3 minutes. Add onion and celery. Cook 5 minutes. Add water chestnuts, bamboo shoots, chicken broth, soy sauce, and monosodium glutamate.

Cover and simmer 3 minutes. Add pea pods and simmer 2 minutes.

Blend cornstarch and water; add and cook until thickened. Salt to taste and sprinkle with toasted almonds. Serve with rice.

Ingredients can be assembled ahead of time and the chicken cooked in front of guests in a chafing dish. Do not use water pan for sautéeing chicken, onion, and celery.

YIELD: 6 SERVINGS

Fiesta: Favorite Recipes of South Texas
THE JUNIOR LEAGUE OF CORPUS CHRISTI, TEXAS

· · · · · · · · · · · · · · · · ·

Mock Turtle Doves (Stuffed Chicken Breasts in Mushroom Sauce)

Great at holiday time instead of turkey for a small family.

2 cups corn bread stuffing
4 whole boned chicken breasts with skin
Salt and pepper
Melted butter or margarine

Mix dressing as directed on package or make your own. Put ⅓–½ cup dressing in center of each breast. Skewer breasts together with picks. (They will resemble little doves.) Sprinkle with salt and pepper.

Pour melted butter or margarine over each breast and bake uncovered at 325° for 1½ hours, basting once or twice. Serve with Mushroom Sauce.

YIELD: 4 SERVINGS

MUSHROOM SAUCE:
½ pound fresh mushrooms, sliced
¼ cup minced onion
2 tablespoons butter
2 tablespoons flour
½ cup half and half
½ teaspoon salt
Dash pepper
Dash Tabasco or Worcestershire sauce
½ cup sour cream

Sauté mushrooms and onion in butter until tender but not brown. In double boiler combine flour, half and half, seasonings, and sour cream. Cook over simmering water, stirring occasionally, until thick.

Nashville Seasons Encore
THE JUNIOR LEAGUE OF NASHVILLE, TENNESSEE

· · · · · · · · · · · · · ·

Boer Chicken Pie

2 3-pound stewing chickens, quartered
1 tablespoon salt
1 teaspoon whole allspice
1 teaspoon peppercorns
3 bay leaves
3 medium carrots, halved
3 stalks celery, halved
3 medium onions, quartered
About 10 sprigs parsley
¼ pound cooked ham, sliced, then quartered
4 hard-boiled eggs, sliced
¼ cup butter or margarine
¼ cup flour
2 cups reserved chicken broth
⅓ cup sherry
2 tablespoons lemon juice
¼ teaspoon mace
¼ teaspoon pepper
Salt to taste
2 egg yolks
1 package pie crust mix
1 egg, beaten

Start preparing early in the day or on the day before serving.

In a large kettle, bring chickens to a boil in 1 quart water with salt, allspice, peppercorns, and bay leaves. Add carrots, celery, onions, and parsley; simmer, covered, for ½ hour or until vegetables are tender-crisp.

Remove vegetables and chicken from kettle; strain broth. Slice carrots and celery diagonally ½ inch thick. Carefully cut chicken from bones in chunks, removing skin. In 12 × 8 × 2-inch baking dish, arrange chicken, vegetables, ham, and eggs. (If making half the recipe, use a 10 × 6 × 2-inch baking dish.)

In saucepan, melt butter or margarine; stir in flour, then gradually add 2 cups chicken broth, sherry, lemon juice, mace, and pepper and salt to taste. Cook, stirring, until thickened.

Beat egg yolks, then slowly stir into sauce; heat, stirring, until thickened, but do *not* boil. Pour over chicken. Prepare pie crust mix as label directs, then roll into 14 × 10-inch rectangle. Fold in half crosswise; unfold, as top crust, over chicken. Turn overhang under, press firmly to edge of dish, then make scalloped edge.

In center of top crust, with knife, cut out a rectangle 7 × 3 inches. At each corner of rectangle make a ½-inch diagonal slit, then turn its pie crust edges up to form a scalloped edge. With remaining dough and small cookie cutter, cut out small designs; arrange over top of pie crust; then refrigerate.

About 45 minutes before serving, start heating oven to 425°. Brush pie with beaten egg. Bake 30 minutes or until golden and hot.

YIELD: 8 SERVINGS

Furniture City Feasts
THE JUNIOR LEAGUE OF HIGH POINT, NORTH CAROLINA

·　·　·　·　·　·　·　·　·　·　·　·　·　·　·　·

Chicken Bombay

8–10 whole chicken breasts, deboned, with skin

FILLING:
¼ cup butter
¼ cup chopped onion
1 small apple, peeled and chopped
½ cup raisins
⅛ teaspoon ground ginger
1–2 teaspoons curry powder
¼ teaspoon salt
⅓ cup slivered almonds, toasted
1½ cups cooked rice
Melted butter
Salt and pepper
Paprika (optional)

Recipe continues . . .

GRAVY:

1 10¾-ounce can condensed cream of chicken soup
1 teaspoon curry powder
¼ cup chutney

To make filling, melt butter in saucepan; add onion and apple and simmer until tender. Remove from fire, add raisins, spices, salt, almonds, and rice, and blend well.

Fill breasts with filling and fold ends of breast so filling will not fall out. Place in baking pan and brush tops well with melted butter. Sprinkle with small amount of salt and pepper and, if desired, a bit of paprika.

Bake covered at 350° for 1 hour, then ½ hour more uncovered.

Serve with gravy made by heating together the chicken soup, curry powder, and chutney.

YIELD: 8–10 SERVINGS

Nashville Seasons Encore
THE JUNIOR LEAGUE OF NASHVILLE, TENNESSEE

. . . .

Chicken Dijon

4 chicken breasts, split, skinned, and boned by butcher
3 tablespoons butter or margarine
2 tablespoons flour
1 cup chicken broth
½ cup light cream
2 tablespoons Dijon mustard
Tomato wedges and parsley for garnish

Brown chicken in butter or margarine for about 20 minutes. Remove to warm serving platter.

Stir flour into skillet drippings. Add chicken broth and light cream. Cook and stir over moderate heat for 10 minutes. Stir in mustard. Garnish with tomato wedges and parsley.

Serve with rice and asparagus spears.

YIELD: 4 SERVINGS

A Taste of Tampa

THE JUNIOR LEAGUE OF TAMPA, FLORIDA

· · · · · · · · · · · · · · · ·

Poulet à la Vallée d'Auge (Chicken with Celery and Apple)

12 half chicken breasts
8 tablespoons butter
6 tablespoons hot brandy
2 onions, sliced
6 small stalks celery, sliced
6 apples, sliced
8–9 level tablespoons flour
3–4 beef bouillon cubes
4½ cups chicken stock
Salt and pepper
Bouquet of herbs
3 cups sour cream, thinned to 4 cups with milk
A little grated Parmesan cheese
1 apple, cored and cut into rings
Additional butter
Additional celery
1½ cups sherry

Brown chicken all over in hot butter; pour the brandy over the chicken and ignite. Remove the chicken.

Place in the pan the onions, celery, and sliced apples; cook slowly until vegetables are soft and nearly cooked. Remove from flame and care-

Recipe continues . . .

fully stir in the flour and meat glaze. Pour in the stock. Stir over flame until mixture comes to a boil.

Put back chicken with salt, pepper, and herbs. Cover and cook very slowly until tender (approximately 40 minutes). Remove the chicken and arrange in casserole. (Dish can be prepared ahead to this point.)

Strain liquid in which chicken has been cooked and pour over the vegetables in the pan. Bring slowly to a boil. When bubbling, stir in the sour cream and grated cheese. Simmer for 4–5 minutes. Pour over the chicken and garnish top with apple rings, which have been. fried until golden in butter, and little bundles of celery, which have been cooked in sherry.

YIELD: 12 SERVINGS

The Dallas Jr. League Cookbook
THE JUNIOR LEAGUE OF DALLAS, TEXAS

.   .   .   .   *l*   .   .   .   .

Brandied Chicken

1 frying chicken, cut up (or use cut-up parts, enough for 4 people)
Flour
Cooking oil
1 6-ounce frozen orange juice concentrate, thawed
¾ teaspoon garlic powder
1 teaspoon onion powder
1 teaspoon ground ginger
¼ cup brandy

Dip chicken in flour and brown slowly in skillet in small amount of oil.

Place melted orange juice concentrate in bowl and add spices mixing thoroughly. Pour over chicken. Add brandy and simmer slowly until chicken is tender. Add a little water if needed while cooking. Serve over rice.

YIELD: 4 SERVINGS

Talk About Good!
THE JUNIOR LEAGUE OF LAFAYETTE, LOUISIANA

Sautéed Chicken Suprême

8 half chicken breasts
½ cup butter
2 tablespoons brandy
1 teaspoon tomato paste
2 tablespoons flour
1 cup chicken stock
1 pint sour cream
2 tablespoons Parmesan cheese
1 tablespoon grated lemon rind

Sauté chicken in butter in skillet until brown. Pour brandy over chicken. Remove breasts; add tomato paste and flour to the butter. Gradually add stock and cook until thickened. Add sour cream, Parmesan cheese, and lemon rind. Do not boil.

Place chicken back in skillet with sauce and simmer, covered, for 45 minutes. Serve with rice.

YIELD: 8 SERVINGS

Little Rock Cooks
THE JUNIOR LEAGUE OF LITTLE ROCK, ARKANSAS

Brunswick Stew

1 4-pound hen
1½ pounds beef without fat
1 pound lean pork backbone
2 quarts cold water
2 tablespoons salt
½ teaspoon whole black peppercorns
2 tablespoons dried red pepper
1 cup diced potatoes
1 cup snap beans
1 cup peas
1½ cups chopped onion
2 cups sliced okra
2 cups lima beans
2 cups corn kernels cut from cob
2½ quarts fresh tomatoes
1 teaspoon black pepper
⅓ cup margarine
Tabasco to taste

Put chicken, beef, and pork into *large* kettle with water, salt, peppercorns, and red pepper. Cover and cook slowly for 2 hours or until meat falls from bones. Discard bones.

Cut meat into cubes and return to stock. Add remaining ingredients. Cover and cook gently several hours, stirring frequently to prevent scorching.

YIELD: 1½ GALLONS

Spartanburg Secrets II
THE JUNIOR LEAGUE OF SPARTANBURG, SOUTH CAROLINA

Chicken Crepes

CREPES:
1 cup flour
Dash salt
3 eggs
¾ cup milk
3 tablespoons heavy cream
1 tablespoon melted butter
Cooking oil

Mix all ingredients except oil well with beater. To make crepes, heat a 5- or 6-inch frying pan or crepe pan. Oil lightly. Pour in just enough batter to form a very thin layer, tilting pan so batter spreads evenly. Cook on one side, turn, and brown on the other side. Repeat until all batter is finished; stack finished crepes with a layer of wax paper between them.

FILLING FOR CREPES:
5 tablespoons butter
1 cup fresh mushrooms
6 tablespoons flour
1 cup chicken broth
1½ cups half and half
Dash salt
Dash hot pepper sauce
¼ cup sherry
Yellow food coloring (optional)
2 cups diced cooked chicken
1 tablespoon grated onion
Grated Parmesan cheese
Sliced almonds

Melt 1 tablespoon butter. Add mushrooms and sauté. Set aside. Melt 4 tablespoons butter, stir in flour, and cook 5 minutes. Add *hot* chicken broth. Stir well. Add *hot* half and half. Cook until thick. Season with hot sauce and stir in sherry and food coloring if desired.

Mix the sauce with the chicken, onion, and sautéed mushrooms.

Recipe continues . . .

Place a spoonful of filling in each crepe. (Reserve some sauce to put on top of each filled crepe.) Sprinkle with Parmesan cheese. Broil until brown. Sprinkle with almonds.

May be made ahead and reheated. Freezes well. Recipe may be doubled or tripled.

YIELD: 4–6 SERVINGS

Winston-Salem's Heritage of Hospitality
THE JUNIOR LEAGUE OF WINSTON-SALEM, NORTH CAROLINA

. . . .

Crepas de Pollo

CREPES:
1 cup flour
4 tablespoons butter
2 eggs
1 cup milk

Mix ingredients and make very thin pancakes in an 8-inch pan. Add more milk to batter if necessary and tilt pan to make as thin as possible. Turn pancakes once and cook until done but not brown.

FILLING:
1 large chicken
2 mild jalapeño peppers, chopped
1 teaspoon salt
1 pound shredded Swiss cheese
1 cup heavy cream

Boil chicken until done in water to cover. Bone. Add the chopped peppers, salt, and ⅔ of the cheese. Mix well.

Place a spoonful of chicken mixture on each pancake, roll into a cone, and place in a pan. When all pancakes have been placed, sprinkle with remaining cheese and pour cream over them.

Bake until cheese melts and they are thoroughly heated. Serve 2 crepes per person. Can be frozen.

YIELD: 8 8-INCH CREPES

That Something Special
THE JUNIOR LEAGUE OF DURHAM, NORTH CAROLINA

.   .   .   .

Poulet à la Crème

Flour for dredging
1 chicken, quartered
3 tablespoons butter
1 onion, sliced thin
½ pound mushrooms, sliced
Juice of ½ lemon
Pinch salt
1 shallot, minced fine
½ cup dry white wine
½ cup heavy cream
Salt and pepper
2 tablespoons cognac

Flour chicken, then brown it in hot butter. Add onion and reduce heat. Cover and cook 25 minutes, basting from time to time.

Put mushrooms in buttered saucepan, add lemon juice and pinch salt, and cover with wax paper. Bring to a boil and cook 2 minutes. Set aside.

When chicken is cooked, arrange it in serving dish. Discard fat and onion from frying pan. Add shallot and wine. Boil. Add broth from mushrooms and bring to boil. Add cream and bring again to boil. Add salt, pepper, mushrooms, and cognac. Heat for 2–3 minutes and pour over chicken. Serve immediately.

YIELD: 4 SERVINGS

The Cotton Blossom Cookbook
THE JUNIOR LEAGUE OF ATLANTA, GEORGIA

.   .   .   .

Chicken Croquettes

CROQUETTE MIXTURE:
½ small onion, finely chopped
½ pound fresh mushrooms, diced very fine
8 tablespoons butter
½ teaspoon salt
½ teaspoon freshly ground pepper
2 tablespoons dry sherry
4 tablespoons flour
1 cup milk, scalded
2 eggs, lightly beaten
½ teaspoon salt
¼ teaspoon black pepper
¼ teaspoon red pepper
2 cups diced cooked chicken
1 egg, beaten
4 tablespoons milk
1 tablespoon salad oil
½ teaspoon salt
Flour
Fine, dry bread crumbs
Deep fat for frying

Sauté onion and mushrooms in half the butter with ½ teaspoon salt, pepper, and half the sherry until moisture is absorbed. Set aside. Melt remaining butter in saucepan, add flour, and cook, stirring constantly, over medium-low heat until roux begins to turn golden.

Gradually add hot milk, stirring with wire whisk; add 2 beaten eggs and cook until very thick. Season with salt, peppers, and remaining sherry. Add chicken and mushrooms and cook, stirring constantly, until mixture cleans sides of pan. Correct seasoning with salt; cool in refrigerator.

Shape croquettes into cones. Beat together 1 egg, milk, salad oil, and salt. Dip croquettes in flour, then egg mixture; drain and roll in bread crumbs. Fry in deep, hot fat until golden brown. Serve with Velouté Sauce.

YIELD: 4 SERVINGS

VELOUTÉ SAUCE:
4 tablespoons butter
4 tablespoons flour
2 cups hot chicken broth
½ teaspoon salt
¼ teaspoon red pepper

Melt butter, add flour, and cook slowly, stirring constantly for about 5 minutes. Gradually add chicken broth, stirring constantly with wire whisk. Simmer, stirring constantly, until thick as heavy cream. Add salt and red pepper.

This sauce can be made ahead and heated just before serving over croquettes.

Southern Accent
THE JUNIOR LEAGUE OF PINE BLUFF, ARKANSAS

. . . .

Lilly Ferrell's Chicken Cutlets

HEN:
1 5-pound hen
2 quarts water
4 stalks celery, with some leaves
2 carrots
1 turnip
1 onion
4 or 5 bay leaves
6 or 8 whole black peppercorns

The day before serving, place the hen in a large pot; add the water, vegetables, and seasonings. Cover and bring to a boil. Reduce and simmer until tender, about 3 hours. Let cool a while in the broth. Strain and reserve the broth.

Recipe continues . . .

CREAM SAUCE:
½ pound butter
¼ cup plus 1 teaspoon flour
1 quart milk
1 teaspoon salt

Melt butter in double boiler (or in saucepan over low heat). Add flour gradually and stir until smooth. Add milk and salt and cook until thickened. This takes quite a while, so be patient!

CUTLET MIXTURE:
Meat from hen
½ onion, grated
Juice of 1 lemon
2 3-ounce cans chopped mushrooms, drained (save the broth)
2 teaspoons chopped fresh parsley

Remove the chicken meat from the carcass and grind in a meat grinder. Add the grated onion, lemon juice, chopped mushrooms, and parsley. Combine with the cream sauce and let stand overnight in the refrigerator.

TO FRY THE CUTLETS:
4 eggs, beaten
6 teaspoons water
Bread crumbs (about 10 slices of bread, dried in oven,
crushed fine, and sifted)
Vegetable oil to fill fry pot about ⅔ deep

Mix eggs and water. Shape about ½ cup of the chicken mixture into the traditional flat oval cutlet shape—about 1½ inches thick. There should be 18–20 cutlets. Dip in beaten egg and lightly crumb. Place on waxed paper to stand over the morning (about 4 hours).

Then, handling with care, one at a time, dip each cutlet in egg again and then in crumbs. Fry in oil that has been thoroughly heated on medium-high heat. (A deep-fat thermometer reading at this point would be helpful.) Drain cutlets on paper towels.

At this point cutlets may be placed on a cookie sheet and heated in a 350° oven until they puff up a little and the "skin" wiggles from the steam inside (about 15 minutes or so). They may be frozen at this point, or served at once with Mushroom Sauce.

MUSHROOM SAUCE:
½ stick butter
4 tablespoons flour
1 cup mushroom broth
1½ cups chicken stock
2 3-ounce cans mushrooms, chopped
2 teaspoons Kitchen Bouquet browning and seasoning sauce
Salt and pepper

Melt butter in double boiler (or saucepan over low heat) and add flour. Stir for a few minutes and let it brown. Add liquids and stir until thickened. (This doesn't happen quickly, either!) Add mushrooms and Kitchen Bouquet and check for seasoning. Add salt and pepper to taste.

YIELD: 20 ½-CUP SERVINGS

Winston-Salem's Heritage of Hospitality
THE JUNIOR LEAGUE OF WINSTON-SALEM, NORTH CAROLINA

· · · · · · · · · · · · · · · · · ·

Chicken Loaf

LOAF:
2 eggs
1 cup milk
2 cups chopped cooked chicken
1 cup dry bread crumbs
2 tablespoons chopped green pepper
2 tablespoons chopped pimento
2 tablespoons chopped celery
½ teaspoon salt
¼ teaspoon paprika

Recipe continues . . .

Beat eggs and add the milk. Add remaining ingredients and pour into a buttered loaf pan. Bake in moderate oven 30 minutes. Unmold and serve sliced with mushroom sauce.

YIELD: 8 SMALL SERVINGS

MUSHROOM SAUCE:
1 cup fresh or canned sliced mushrooms
2 tablespoons butter
3 tablespoons flour
1½ cups milk or stock or combination
½ teaspoon salt
⅛ teaspoon nutmeg
Pepper to taste
2 teaspoons lemon juice
2 beaten egg yolks

Brown mushrooms in butter, add flour, and blend. Add milk, salt, nutmeg, and pepper. Cook until thick. Add lemon juice to beaten egg yolks. Slowly stir egg mixture into sauce. Cook 2 minutes.

The Gasparilla Cookbook
THE JUNIOR LEAGUE OF TAMPA, FLORIDA

. . . .

Chicken Livers with Mushrooms Douglass

2 cups sliced fresh mushrooms
2–3 tablespoons butter
1½ cups diced chicken livers
2 tablespoons flour
1½ cups light cream
Salt and pepper
4 tablespoons sherry

Sauté mushrooms in hot butter; then add livers a few at a time and sauté briskly. Sprinkle with flour. Add cream and seasonings to taste. Simmer 5 minutes. Add sherry. Heat through and serve on buttered toast.

YIELD: 4 SERVINGS

Furniture City Feasts
THE JUNIOR LEAGUE OF HIGH POINT, NORTH CAROLINA

·   ·   ·   ·   ·   ·   ·   ·   ·   ·   ·   ·   ·   ·   ·   ·   ·   ·

Breast of Chicken Perigourdine

8 whole chicken breasts
Salt
1 13¾-ounce can chicken broth
¼ cup dried mushrooms
½ cup water
Butter or margarine
8 large fresh mushrooms, sliced
⅓ cup all-purpose flour
¼ teaspoon salt
2 tablespoons light cream
3 tablespoons sherry
1–1¼ cups Hollandaise Sauce (see Index)

Have butcher bone chicken breasts, reserving bones. About 1½ hours before serving: Salt chicken breasts lightly and let sit for about 1 hour.

Simmer chicken bones in chicken broth, covered, about 1 hour; discard bones; reserve broth.

Let dried mushrooms stand in water 1 hour. If you can't buy dried mushrooms, you may use 4 extra fresh mushrooms and increase the chicken broth to 1½ cups.

In small amount of hot butter, in large, metal-handled skillet, gently brown chicken breasts on both sides, adding more butter as needed; remove. In more butter in same skillet, sauté sliced fresh mushrooms until golden;

Recipe continues . . .

remove. Into drippings in same skillet, stir flour, salt, dried mushrooms plus their liquid, 1 cup chicken broth (add water if necessary to make 1 cup), and light cream. Cook, stirring, over medium heat until thickened and smooth. Place chicken breasts in sauce; simmer gently, covered, about 20 minutes, or until chicken is tender.

Meanwhile, preheat broiler 10 minutes. When chicken is tender, add sherry and fresh mushrooms. Then spread Hollandaise over chicken; run under broiler 1 minute or until just golden. Serve at once.

YIELD: 8 SERVINGS

Spartanburg Secrets II
THE JUNIOR LEAGUE OF SPARTANBURG, SOUTH CAROLINA

· · · · · · · · · · · · · · · · ·

Chicken Livers

1 pound chicken livers, floured
Salt
Pepper
Cooking oil
¼ cup butter
1 large onion, chopped
½ cup sliced mushrooms
1 tablespoon sherry

Flour chicken livers. Salt and pepper them. Sauté a few at a time in oil until good and brown.

In another pan, heat butter. Cook chopped onion until clear. Add mushrooms and cook a few minutes. Add the livers and sherry to pan and simmer about 5 minutes.

YIELD: 4 SERVINGS

That Something Special
THE JUNIOR LEAGUE OF DURHAM, NORTH CAROLINA

· · · · · · · · · · · · · · · · ·

Kingdom-Come Duck

4 ducks
2 apples
Celery
2 10½-ounce cans consommé, undiluted
1 can water
Cooked, crumbled bacon

Stuff ducks with apple and celery. Place breast down in consommé and water. Cover tightly and bake for 3 hours at 350°. Duck should be very tender. Slice breast away. Place duck breast in greased, shallow casserole. Pour sauce over duck, cover, and bake at 350° *just until hot*. Place breast on mound of rice and sprinkle with bacon. Pass sauce as gravy. This is a must!

KINGDOM-COME SAUCE:
1½ cups butter
⅔ cup sherry
½ cup bourbon
1 5-ounce jar currant jelly
4 tablespoons Worcestershire sauce

In a saucepan, slowly heat all ingredients. If too thin, thicken with a little flour.

YIELD: 6–8 SERVINGS

Little Rock Cooks
THE JUNIOR LEAGUE OF LITTLE ROCK, ARKANSAS

Grilled Duck

Duck
Bacon
Italian salad dressing

Remove breast from duck. Wrap breast with bacon and secure with picks as for filet. Marinate in commercial Italian salad dressing (may use low-calorie dressing) about 6 hours.

Cook over hot charcoal fire at least 8 minutes on each side.

Huntsville Heritage Cookbook
THE JUNIOR LEAGUE OF HUNTSVILLE, ALABAMA

Fish and Seafood

Easy Elegant Baked Fish

1 3–4-pound fish
Butter
Salt
Cayenne
Lemon wedges
Parsley
Shrimp (optional)
Capers (optional)

Clean, scale, wash, and dry fish. You may cut off head if desired.

Put generous amount of butter in cavity; spread more butter on outside. Sprinkle with a little salt and cayenne.

Place in generously buttered shallow casserole and cover with well-buttered brown paper cut in the shape of the casserole. Bake at 400° about 10 minutes per pound, or about 20 minutes for fillets.

To serve, garnish with lemon wedges and parsley.

To be really elegant, surround fish with hot boiled shrimp and a sprinkling of capers.

Sheepshead is especially good prepared this way, but redfish or snapper is fine. You may also use several small whole trout instead, or even fillets, but one big fish is prettier.

YIELD: 4 SERVINGS

Fiesta: Favorite Recipes of South Texas
THE JUNIOR LEAGUE OF CORPUS CHRISTI, TEXAS

· · · · · · · · · · · · ·

Stuffed Flounder

1 4-pound flounder, ready to cook
½ package stuffing mix
½ pound crabmeat or raw peeled shrimp
Juice of ½ lemon
4 strips bacon
Parsley

Cut a pocket on each side of the backbone. Mix together the stuffing, crab or shrimp, and lemon juice. Stuff the pockets and lay the bacon across the stuffed pockets.

Bake for 1 hour at 400° in a well-greased pan.

Garnish with parsley before serving.

YIELD: 6 SERVINGS

Seafood Sorcery
THE JUNIOR LEAGUE OF WILMINGTON, NORTH CAROLINA

·   ·   ·   ·   ·   ·   ·   ·   ·   ·   ·   ·   ·   ·   ·   ·   ·   ·   ·

Baked Trout

Trout
Lemon juice
Salt
Cracked pepper
Lemon slices
Butter
Onion slices (optional)
Dry parsley flakes
Fresh parsley

Clean fish thoroughly. (Leave on head and tail if desired.) Squeeze lemon juice over fish. Place salt, pepper, lemon slices, and pats of butter on fish. Raw onion slices may be used, too. Sprinkle with parsley flakes.

Bake a small fish (1–1½ pounds) at 325° for 30–40 minutes. A larger fish (2½ pounds and over) takes 1 hour to 1 hour and 15 minutes. Serve with more lemon and fresh parsley.

A natural brook trout is far preferable to a stocked fish. Bass or salmon may also be used.

Serve with chilled Chablis.

YIELD: 1 SERVING PER POUND

300 Years of Carolina Cooking
THE JUNIOR LEAGUE OF GREENVILLE, SOUTH CAROLINA

·   ·   ·   ·   ·   ·   ·   ·   ·   ·   ·   ·   ·   ·   ·   ·   ·   ·   ·

Chilled Smoked Fish with Horseradish Sauce

Whole redfish
Garlic salt
Lemon pepper
Juice of 3 lemons
1 stick butter, melted
2 tablespoons Worcestershire sauce
Dash Tabasco
1 teaspoon chopped parsley

Sprinkle fish with garlic salt and lemon pepper.

Combine next five ingredients to make basting sauce. Place aluminum foil over tail and head of fish and smoke on covered grill over low fire for about 1 hour. Baste every 15 minutes. Don't overcook. Fish should flake easily.

Cool and refrigerate, and serve with Horseradish Sauce. As an appetizer, serve a piece of smoked fish on a Melba round with a dab of sauce on top. The fish also makes an excellent buffet dish.

YIELD: ABOUT 1 SERVING PER POUND

HORSERADISH SAUCE:
2 cups sour cream
1 tablespoon horseradish
2 teaspoons lemon juice
Salt to taste
¼ teaspoon lemon pepper
1 tablespoon chives or 1 teaspoon dill seed or fresh dill

Mix together all ingredients and spoon into bowl. Sprinkle with paprika.

Southern Sideboards
THE JUNIOR LEAGUE OF JACKSON, MISSISSIPPI

Baked Snapper

3 pounds snapper or other large whole fish
Salt
Pepper
Flour
1 stick butter
1 onion, chopped fine
2 cups chopped celery
¼ cup chopped green pepper
3 cups canned tomatoes
1 tablespoon Worcestershire sauce
1 tablespoon catsup
1 teaspoon chili powder
Juice of ½ lemon
1 clove garlic, minced
1 teaspoon salt
Cayenne

Dredge fish inside and out with salt, pepper, and flour. Melt butter; add onion, celery, and green pepper and simmer until tender.

Add tomatoes, Worcestershire sauce, catsup, chili powder, lemon juice, garlic, salt, and cayenne. Simmer for about 45 minutes, then pour over fish. Bake at 350° for 1 hour or longer, basting frequently.

YIELD: 3–4 SERVINGS

Recipe Jubilee
THE JUNIOR LEAGUE OF MOBILE, ALABAMA

. . . .

Fred's Charcoaled Fish

1 stick margarine
1 8-ounce bottle unsweetened lime juice
Worcestershire sauce
Fillets of mackerel or bluefish (½–¾ pound per person)

Recipe continues . . .

Melt margarine. Add lime juice and enough Worcestershire to make the sauce dark.

Marinate fillets in this sauce for a minimum of 2 hours (more if possible).

Punch numerous holes (about every 3 inches) in aluminum foil and lay over grill. This allows smoke through. Be sure fire is medium to low (not hot), as they must cook slowly.

Place fillets on fire, skin down. Baste frequently with remaining sauce to keep moist. Do not turn. Cook 20–25 minutes. Remove from grill with spatula to keep fish from falling apart.

> *Seafood Sorcery*
> THE JUNIOR LEAGUE OF WILMINGTON, NORTH CAROLINA

. . . .

Channel Bass

1 2- or 3-pound bass
Salt and pepper
¼ pound butter
Lemon juice
1 tablespoon dry white wine
Grated Parmesan cheese
Paprika

Fillet fish and salt and pepper. Put butter in shallow baking dish in hot oven (400°–500°) until it is browned. This gives the dish its distinctive flavor.

Place fillets flesh side down in sizzling hot butter and return to oven for 10 or 15 minutes. Turn with spatula and baste with juice. Sprinkle each piece with lemon juice and wine, Parmesan cheese and paprika. Return to oven until done—approximately 5 minutes.

Run under broiler and broil quickly. Baste fish with sauce and serve in the sauce.

This recipe is good for any filleted white fish.

YIELD: 4 SERVINGS

Charleston Receipts
THE JUNIOR LEAGUE OF CHARLESTON, SOUTH CAROLINA

.   .   .   .

Southern-Fried Catfish

3 pounds catfish fillets
Salt and pepper
2 cups yellow corn meal
3 inches cooking oil for deep frying

Wash and drain fillets. Salt and pepper them.

Place corn meal and fish in a large plastic bag and shake until fish is well coated.

Fill a deep-fat fryer with cooking oil to a depth of 3 inches. Preheat oil and cook fish at 350° until brown on both sides, turning only once.

YIELD: 6–8 SERVINGS

Little Rock Cooks
THE JUNIOR LEAGUE OF LITTLE ROCK, ARKANSAS

.   .   .   .

Cove Hollow Fish

Fish fillets cut into pieces (about 2 inches)
Condensed milk
Flour
Salt
Black pepper

Recipe continues . . .

Dip each piece of fish in condensed milk, then into plain flour that has been salted and peppered well. Cook in deep fat until light brown.

Nashville Seasons
THE JUNIOR LEAGUE OF NASHVILLE, TENNESSEE

. . . .

Migg's Fish

¾ pound fresh mushrooms, sliced
2 tablespoons butter
Salt and pepper
2 tablespoons minced shallots or green onions
2½ pounds sole, flounder, or redfish fillets
1½ tablespoons butter, cut into bits
1 cup white wine mixed with ½ cup water
2½ tablespoons flour blended to a paste with
3 tablespoons softened butter
¾–1 cup heavy cream
Salt and pepper
Lemon juice
¼ cup shredded Swiss cheese
1 tablespoon butter, cut into bits

Sauté mushrooms in 2 tablespoons butter with salt and pepper without browning and set aside. Put half the onions in the bottom of a baking dish. Season fillets with salt and pepper. Arrange them in one slightly over-lapping layer. Sprinkle fillets with remaining onions and all of the mush-rooms. Dot with 1½ tablespoons butter. Pour in the liquid, enough so that fish are barely covered—you may need to add more water. Bring almost to a simmer on top of the stove. Lay waxed paper over the fish and put in a preheated oven of 350° for 8–12 minutes, until fish is done.

Drain poaching liquid into a saucepan and preheat broiler. Boil down liquid until it is reduced to about 1¼ cups. Off the heat, beat flour paste into hot liquid and add ½ cup cream. Bring to a boil and thin out the sauce with tablespoons of cream until it coats the spoon. Season sauce with salt, pepper, and drops of lemon juice. Spoon over the fish. Sprinkle the cheese over and dot with butter. Run under the broiler for 2–3 minutes.

This dish may be done several hours ahead and reheated. After adding the cheese and butter, just set aside. Before serving, reheat to simmer on top of the stove and then run under the broiler to lightly brown the sauce.

YIELD: 6 SERVINGS

The Dallas Jr. League Cookbook
THE JUNIOR LEAGUE OF DALLAS, TEXAS

· · · · · · · · · · · · · · ·

Baked Stuffed Flounder

6 flounder fillets
Paprika
Butter
Lemon juice and melted butter

At a seafood market pick out pieces of white fillet of flounder that, when folded in half, will be the correct size on a dinner plate. Place a portion of the stuffing on one half of the fillet and fold the other side over. Cover generously with paprika and wrap immediately in waxed paper, tying well at both ends with string. Freeze this a day ahead of serving.

When ready to bake, remove string and paper. Place on well-buttered baking tray and place in preheated 375° oven for approximately 25 minutes, basting often with lemon juice and butter mixture.

YIELD: 6 SERVINGS

Recipe continues . . .

FISH STUFFING:
1 medium onion, chopped
¾ cup butter
1½ cups cooked shrimp
1½ cups picked-over chunk crabmeat
1 egg, well beaten
1 tablespoon water
1 teaspoon chopped parsley
3 tablespoons sherry
Salt and pepper to taste
Toasted bread crumbs

Sauté onion in butter until transparent. Remove from heat and cool. Add shrimp and crabmeat. Stir into this the egg, water, parsley, sherry, salt, pepper, and enough toasted bread crumbs to make dressing consistency.

The Charlotte Cookbook
THE JUNIOR LEAGUE OF CHARLOTTE, NORTH CAROLINA

. . . .

Filets Farcis à la Crème

6 fillets of sole or flounder
Salt and pepper
2 small onions, chopped
½ pound mushrooms, sliced
2 tablespoons butter
2 tablespoons snipped parsley
2 cans tiny shrimp or 2½ cups fresh crabmeat
2 tablespoons flour
1 cup light cream
½ cup dry white wine
2 tablespoons cognac (optional)
½ cup shredded Swiss cheese

Sprinkle fillets with salt and pepper. Sauté onions and mushrooms in butter until golden. Stir in parsley and shrimp or crabmeat and heat thoroughly.

Place part of this mixture by teaspoonfuls on large end of each fillet. Roll up and place side by side in shallow baking dish.

Into remaining onion-shrimp mixture, stir flour, then cream, wine, and cognac if desired. Season with salt and pepper. Bring to boil while stirring and pour over fillets. Sprinkle with cheese.

Bake at 400° about 25 minutes or until golden.

YIELD: 3–4 SERVINGS

Mountain Measures
THE JUNIOR LEAGUE OF CHARLESTON, WEST VIRGINIA

. . . .

This is a Norwegian recipe.

Gratin of Fish

1 pound flounder fillets
2½ tablespoons margarine
4 tablespoons flour
1 cup milk
⅛ teaspoon nutmeg
1 teaspoon salt
3 eggs, separated
Cracker crumbs
Melted butter

Cut fish into small pieces (about ½ inch square or less).

Melt margarine, stir in flour, and gradually add milk. Let thicken, add seasonings, and cool. Add beaten egg yolks and fish and finally fold in stiffly beaten egg whites.

Turn into buttered casserole. Sprinkle cracker crumbs on top and bake 45 minutes to 1 hour at 350°.

Recipe continues . . .

Serve with melted butter.

YIELD: 4 SERVINGS

300 Years of Carolina Cooking
THE JUNIOR LEAGUE OF GREENVILLE, SOUTH CAROLINA

Trout Meunière

6 ¾-pound fillets brook trout or speckled trout
(can use frozen trout fillets or other fresh or frozen fillets)
Flour
1–2 teaspoons salt
¼ teaspoon pepper
6 tablespoons butter
2 tablespoons minced fresh or dried parsley
Juice of 1 lemon

Wipe fillets and roll lightly in flour seasoned with 1 teaspoon salt and the pepper. Sauté in hot butter. After 5 minutes, when brown, turn and sauté on other side for about 3 minutes more.

Put trout in a warm serving dish. Sprinkle with parsley. Add sprinkling of salt and pepper.

Put lemon juice into the brown butter in the pan; when it is foamy, pour over the fish.

YIELD: 6 SERVINGS

Talk About Good!
THE JUNIOR LEAGUE OF LAFAYETTE, LOUISIANA

Fish Fillets

8 fillets of snapper or trout
1½ cups milk
Flour seasoned with salt
½ stick butter
1 teaspoon paprika
1 tablespoon lemon juice

Soak fillets in milk for 30 minutes. Dust with salted flour. Melt butter in skillet and heat until bubbly. Sauté fillets 10–20 minutes depending on thickness. Turn once.

Remove fillets from pan and sprinkle with paprika. Add lemon juice to butter remaining in skillet and pour over fish before serving.

YIELD: 8 SERVINGS

Recipe Jubilee
THE JUNIOR LEAGUE OF MOBILE, ALABAMA

. . . .

Charlie's Turban of Sole

TURBAN:
1 cup raw rice or 1 8-ounce box long-grain and wild rice
3 pounds fillet of sole (flounder or trout may be substituted)
Salt
Butter

Cook rice. Flatten fillets slightly with a moistened wooden mallet. Season with salt.

Butter a 6-cup ring mold generously. Lay fillets in mold, overlapping them and with tail ends over inner edge of mold. Line mold completely with fillets. Fill with rice, pressing down gently with spoon. Bring tail ends over rice to cover top side. Cover with aluminum foil. Set mold in larger

Recipe continues . . .

pan and pour in boiling water to a depth of 1 inch. Poach in 400° oven for 15 minutes.

CHARLIE'S SAUCE:
2 sticks butter
¾ cup finely chopped mushrooms
½ cup finely chopped shallots
½ cup finely chopped onion
1 cup finely chopped cooked shrimp
(reserve a few whole cooked shrimp for garnish)
1 tablespoon finely chopped garlic
4 tablespoons flour
1 teaspoon salt
½ teaspoon pepper
2 dashes red pepper
1 16-ounce jar oysters with liquid
1 cup red wine
1 teaspoon arrowroot

Lightly sauté in butter the mushrooms, shallots, onion, shrimp, and garlic. When onion is golden brown, add flour, salt, and peppers. Brown well, about 10 minutes. Blend in oyster liquid and wine and simmer 10 minutes.

Remove some of the liquid to a separate small bowl and blend in arrowroot. Add little by little to the sauce until sauce is consistency of thick gravy. Gently stir in oysters and simmer 10–15 minutes.

To serve turban, remove from oven and leave for a few minutes to set. Drain off accumulated liquids by turning upside down on a plate but *do not unmold*.

Unmold on serving platter. Fill center with sauce. Garnish top with a few whole cooked shrimp and sprinkle with paprika. Surround the turban with parsley and serve.

YIELD: 8 SERVINGS

Southern Sideboards
THE JUNIOR LEAGUE OF JACKSON, MISSISSIPPI

Cold Poached Salmon

3–4 pounds center-cut fresh salmon
1½ cups dry white wine or vermouth
1 carrot
2 small white onions, cut into pieces
1 teaspoon salt
1 bay leaf
1 cup water
2 tablespoons tarragon vinegar
4 cloves
1½ tablespoons butter
1 teaspoon peppercorns

FOR GARNISH:
Swedish Cucumbers
Cherry tomatoes
Sliced lemons
Fresh dill (optional)

Debone salmon or have fish seller prepare for stuffing. Wrap in doubled piece of cheesecloth. Make a court bouillon of the remaining ingredients except garnish. Bring to a boil and simmer for a half hour, strain, and cool. Lower salmon into cooled bouillon and simmer 6–8 minutes per pound. The fish should be just covered by liquid; if not, add more water. Cook until tender, remove, and cool.

When cool, gently remove skin. This much can be done ahead of time. For whole poached salmon, double the bouillon recipe.

Decorate the platter with Swedish Cucumbers (see page 422), cherry tomatoes, sliced lemons, and fresh dill if available. This can be the first course or main course. Also can be served as an hors d'oeuvre served with Melba toast triangles and rye bread rounds.

YIELD: 4 SERVINGS

The Dallas Jr. League Cookbook
THE JUNIOR LEAGUE OF DALLAS, TEXAS

Salmon Pie

1 cup Ritz cracker crumbs
¼ cup butter
¼ teaspoon dill seed
Butter
1 7-¾-ounce can salmon
1 cup cottage cheese
3 eggs, separated
½ cup heavy cream
2 tablespoons flour
Salt to taste
⅛ teaspoon pepper
1 tablespoon chopped chives
1 teaspoon lemon juice

Combine crackers, butter, and dill seed. Press into buttered 9-inch glass pie plate.

Mix salmon, cottage cheese, and egg yolks. Beat until well mixed. Stir in cream, flour, salt, pepper, chives, and lemon juice. Beat egg whites. Fold in. Bake in low rack at 350° for 35 minutes.

YIELD: 6 SERVINGS

Winston-Salem's Heritage of Hospitality
THE JUNIOR LEAGUE OF WINSTON-SALEM, NORTH CAROLINA

. . . .

Shad Roe

2 or 3 strips bacon
One set shad roe
Salt and pepper
Butter

Cook bacon in an iron skillet. Carefully separate one set of roe. Salt and pepper each piece and with pat of butter put into separate sheets of wax paper (just wide enough to double-fold and long enough to twist with a couple of inches to spare as handles).

Remove bacon from pan and cook roe at medium heat, turning by twisted paper to brown both sides, about 10–12 minutes. Paper will not burn, nor will roe break or split.

Serve with hominy, bacon, and sliced tomatoes.

YIELD: 2 SERVINGS

Seafood Sorcery
THE JUNIOR LEAGUE OF WILMINGTON, NORTH CAROLINA

· · · · · · · · · · · · · ·

Fish Roe Ring

3 eggs
2 cans fish roe
Salt and pepper
Cooked tiny peas
Sautéed potato balls

An inexpensive luncheon dish.

Beat eggs and add to roe. Season with salt and pepper. Empty into 6-cup ring mold, place mold in shallow pan containing 1 inch water, and bake at 350° for about 1 hour or until set.

Unmold onto serving platter and fill center with peas. Pour Quick Mushroom Sauce over mold and garnish around it with potato balls.

YIELD: 6–8 SERVINGS

Recipe continues . . .

QUICK MUSHROOM SAUCE:
½ stick butter
3 tablespoons flour
1 cup milk
1 4-ounce can mushrooms
Salt and pepper

Brown butter in saucepan. Stir in flour. Gradually stir in milk and cook, stirring, until sauce is smooth and slightly thickened. Stir in mushrooms and correct seasoning with salt and pepper.

The Cotton Blossom Cookbook
THE JUNIOR LEAGUE OF ATLANTA, GEORGIA

· · · · · · · · · · · · · ·

Creamed Crabmeat with Mushrooms

1 pound mushrooms (or 1 large can, sliced)
2½ sticks butter
½ onion, chopped
5 tablespoons chopped chives
5 tablespoons chopped parsley
10 tablespoons flour
2½ pints sour cream
Salt and pepper to taste
4 pounds crabmeat
Sherry to taste
Truffles (optional)

Wash and slice mushrooms. Cook stems in water to cover and set stock aside.

Heat butter. Add mushrooms, onion, chives, and parsley. Cook 3 or 4 minutes. Stir in flour gradually. Add sour cream mixed with mushroom stock. Season with salt and pepper. Add crabmeat and cook 5 minutes. Add sherry and serve in chafing dish with toast rounds. Garnish with truffles if desired.

YIELD: 16–20 SERVINGS

Seafood Sorcery
THE JUNIOR LEAGUE OF WILMINGTON, NORTH CAROLINA

Crabmeat Rector

1 bunch green onions, minced
3 cloves garlic, diced
½ green pepper, diced
¼ pound butter
2 tomatoes, peeled and sliced
1 4-ounce can chopped mushrooms
½ cup white wine (Sauterne)
1 pound lump crabmeat
Salt to taste
Crushed red pepper
Grated Parmesan cheese

Sauté green onions, garlic, and green pepper in butter until golden. Add sliced tomatoes and cook until tomatoes are soft. Add mushrooms and cook 5 or 10 minutes longer. Add wine, then crabmeat, salt, and pepper (generously) to taste. Sprinkle cheese generously over all.

Cook 10 minutes longer, turning crabmeat gently to prevent breaking. Serve hot, as first course or main dish.

YIELD: 4 SERVINGS

Recipe Jubilee
THE JUNIOR LEAGUE OF MOBILE, ALABAMA

Bridge Casserole

8–12 artichoke hearts (canned or frozen)
1 pound crabmeat
6 ounces fresh mushrooms
2 tablespoons butter
1½ cups medium cream sauce (see pages 220 and 355)
1 tablespoon Worcestershire sauce
¼ cup sherry
Salt and pepper
¼ cup grated Parmesan cheese
Paprika

Arrange artichokes in a buttered shallow dish. Spread flaked crabmeat over them. Cook mushrooms in butter and add. Season cream sauce with Worcestershire sauce, sherry, salt, and pepper and pour over all. Sprinkle with cheese and paprika. Bake at 375° for 20 minutes.

YIELD: 4–6 SERVINGS

Gator Country Cooks
THE JUNIOR LEAGUE OF GAINESVILLE, FLORIDA

. . . .

Deviled Crabs

¼ pound butter, melted
12 saltine crackers, crushed
1 tablespoon mayonnaise
2 tablespoons sherry
Pinch dry mustard
Pinch minced parsley
1 teaspoon Worcestershire sauce
Salt and pepper
1 pound fresh lump crabmeat

Reserve 4 teaspoons butter to put on top of the stuffed crabs and pour the rest over cracker crumbs. Add mayonnaise and other seasonings, then mix in crabmeat with fork to keep it from breaking.

Fill 6 large back shells or ramekins generously, then sprinkle with cracker crumbs, pouring the remaining butter on top. Bake at 400° for 30 minutes. Serve piping hot.

YIELD: 4–6 SERVINGS

Charleston Receipts
THE JUNIOR LEAGUE OF CHARLESTON, SOUTH CAROLINA

·   ·   ·   ·   ·   ·   ·   ·   ·   ·   ·   ·   ·   ·   ·   ·

Crabmeat and Spinach Casserole

4 tablespoons butter or margarine
¼ cup chopped onion
2 10¾-ounce cans condensed cream of mushroom soup
1 cup sour cream
1 6-ounce can sliced mushrooms with liquid
½ cup grated Parmesan cheese
Dash Angostura bitters
½ teaspoon dry mustard
½ teaspoon monosodium glutamate
1 pound crabmeat
2 tablespoons sherry
1 tablespoon chopped chives or parsley
2 10-ounce packages frozen chopped spinach,
cooked without salt and drained

Melt butter in saucepan. Sauté onion until tender. Add soup, sour cream, mushrooms, grated cheese, and seasonings. Cook until smooth and thoroughly heated.

Recipe continues . . .

Stir in crabmeat, sherry, and chives or parsley. Place in serving dish, alternating layers of crabmeat mixture and hot cooked spinach.

YIELD: 8 SERVINGS

Recipe Jubilee
THE JUNIOR LEAGUE OF MOBILE, ALABAMA

. . . .

Hazel Efird's Deviled Crab

4 hard-boiled eggs
1 pound crabmeat
10 saltine crackers, crushed
1 stick butter
Red pepper
1½ teaspoons dry mustard
1½ teaspoons salt
3 or 4 tablespoons Worcestershire sauce
3 tablespoons vinegar

Chop egg whites fine and mix with crabmeat and cracker crumbs.

Mash egg yolks in a small pan with butter and seasonings and heat until butter is melted. Mix with crabmeat and stuff into crab shells or ramekins. Bake at 375° for 15 minutes.

YIELD: 4–8 SERVINGS

Seafood Sorcery
THE JUNIOR LEAGUE OF WILMINGTON, NORTH CAROLINA

. . . .

Crab Mornay

4 tablespoons margarine
4 tablespoons flour
2 cloves garlic, minced
2 cups milk
Salt to taste
½ pound Swiss cheese, cut up
1 pound crabmeat
Dash Tabasco
Grated Parmesan cheese

Melt margarine. Add flour and garlic. Mix well. Slowly add milk. Cook and stir until thick. Add salt. Add Swiss cheese, crabmeat, and Tabasco. Mix well.

Pour into ramekins and sprinkle with Parmesan cheese. Bake at 350° for 30 minutes.

YIELD: 4–8 SERVINGS

Recipe Jubilee
THE JUNIOR LEAGUE OF MOBILE, ALABAMA

·   ·   ·   ·   ·   ·   ·   ·   ·   ·   ·   ·   ·   ·   ·   ·

Souffléed Crabmeat

8 slices bread
2 cups Alaskan King crab
1 onion, chopped
1 green pepper, chopped
1 cup chopped celery
½ cup mayonnaise
4 eggs
3 cups milk
1 10¾-ounce can condensed cream of mushroom soup
½ cup shredded cheese
Paprika

Recipe continues . . .

Dice 4 slices of bread into bottom of greased baking dish.

Mix crabmeat, onion, green pepper, celery, and mayonnaise. Put over bread. Cut crust off remaining bread and arrange on top.

Mix eggs and milk and pour over ingredients in baking dish. Put in refrigerator overnight.

Bake at 325° for 15 minutes. Remove from oven and spoon mushroom soup over casserole. Top with shredded cheese and paprika. Then return to oven and bake 1 hour more.

YIELD: 8 SERVINGS

Gator Country Cooks
THE JUNIOR LEAGUE OF GAINESVILLE, FLORIDA

· · · · · · · · · · · · · · ·

Baked Crabmeat au Gratin

½ cup chopped green onions
½ cup chopped celery
½ cup butter
6 tablespoons flour
1 5⅓-ounce can evaporated milk
2 egg yolks, beaten
½ teaspoon salt (or less)
¼ teaspoon black pepper
¼ teaspoon cayenne
1 pound white lump crabmeat
½ cup shredded American cheese

Sauté onions and celery in butter in a heavy skillet. Add flour gradually and then add milk mixed with beaten egg yolks. Add salt, pepper, and cayenne, mix with crabmeat, and put in buttered ramekins or casserole. Top with shredded cheese and bake at 350° until brown.

YIELD: 4 SERVINGS

Fiesta: Favorite Recipes of South Texas
THE JUNIOR LEAGUE OF CORPUS CHRISTI, TEXAS

· · · · · · · · · · · · · · ·

Baked Crabmeat

1 pound crabmeat
4 tablespoons butter
2 tablespoons flour
1½ cups milk
¼ teaspoon salt
Juice of one small onion
Juice of ½ lemon
1 teaspoon Worcestershire sauce
1 teaspoon chopped parsley
Dash cayenne
¼ teaspoon celery salt
2 eggs, well beaten
Buttered bread crumbs

Pick over crabmeat carefully to remove all bits of shell. Melt butter in heavy saucepan. Blend in flour; add milk and stir constantly over low heat until thickened. Add all seasonings. Add beaten eggs and stir; do not let boil. Mix sauce with crabmeat. Pour into glass baking dish. Top with buttered crumbs. Bake at 350° for 30–40 minutes.

YIELD: 4 SERVINGS

The Gasparilla Cookbook
THE JUNIOR LEAGUE OF TAMPA, FLORIDA

. . . .

Crabmeat au Gratin

1 pound white crabmeat (claw meat may be used)
1 tablespoon butter
1 tablespoon flour
1 cup light cream or half and half
Salt and pepper to taste
½ cup sherry (or to taste)
½ pound New York sharp cheddar cheese, sliced

Recipe continues . . .

Carefully pick over crabmeat and remove all pieces of shell.

Melt butter in a double boiler. Add flour and stir until smooth. Add cream and continue stirring until mixture thickens and all lumps are dissolved. Salt and pepper to taste. Add sherry and mix thoroughly.

Add crabmeat to sauce and stir gently until crab is hot.

Place in casserole or ramekins and cover generously with slices of cheese. This much may be done ahead. Place in the refrigerator.

Before serving, warm, then place in broiler until cheese has melted and is slightly brown.

YIELD: 4–6 SERVINGS

Seafood Sorcery
THE JUNIOR LEAGUE OF WILMINGTON, NORTH CAROLINA

· · · · · · · · · · · · · · · · · ·

Crawfish Étouffée

2 large onions
1 stalk celery
2 medium green peppers
2 cloves garlic
1 stick butter
1 tablespoon flour
2 pounds crawfish tails
Fat from crawfish
Salt
Red and black pepper
1 cup water
Chopped parsley
Chopped green onion tops

Mince onions, celery, green peppers, and garlic. Cook minced vegetables in melted butter over low heat. Cook slowly for 30 minutes or until vegetables are golden brown. Stir in 1 tablespoon flour.

Add crawfish tails and crawfish fat. Season with salt and peppers to taste. Add about 1 cup hot water according to desired thickness of gravy. Let simmer in a covered pot until tails are tender. Add parsley and onion tops.

Serve hot over rice.

YIELD: 4–6 SERVINGS

Talk About Good!

THE JUNIOR LEAGUE OF LAFAYETTE, LOUISIANA

. . . .

Oysters Rockefeller

2 dozen oysters and oyster shells
Rock salt (optional)
2 10-ounce packages frozen chopped spinach
1 stick butter
½ cup chopped parsley
1 teaspoon monosodium glutamate
⅛ teaspoon cayenne
1 tablespoon lemon juice
½ teaspoon salt
1 teaspoon Worcestershire sauce (optional)
Lemon wedges

Open live oysters or use can of select fresh oysters and scrubbed oyster shells.

Place oysters on the deep side of shell, in a large baking pan or individual pie plates lined with rock salt.

Cook spinach and drain well. While spinach is still hot, place in blender with all other ingredients except lemon wedges and blend. Cover each oyster with some of the mixture and bake for 10 minutes in 400° oven.

Serve at once with lemon wedges.

YIELD: 5–6 SERVINGS

Gator Country Cooks

THE JUNIOR LEAGUE OF GAINESVILLE, FLORIDA

. . . .

Oysters Poulette

3 dozen oysters and juice
Salt and pepper
1 stick butter
4 tablespoons minced green onion
4 tablespoons minced parsley
½ cup milk
2 tablespoons butter
2 tablespoons flour
2 egg yolks
1 4-ounce can mushrooms
2 tablespoons sherry
4 slices ham
4 rusks

Drain oysters (save liquid) and dry on a cloth or paper towel. Salt and pepper them and brown in a skillet in a little hot butter until they curl, pouring off liquid and adding more butter until oysters are browned.

Sauté green onion and parsley in remaining butter, and add to the cooked oysters. Heat oyster juice and add to the oysters. Make a sauce of the milk, 2 tablespoons butter, and flour. Remove from heat and beat in the egg yolks and add mushrooms. Stir this sauce and sherry into the cooked oysters.

Heat thoroughly in a double boiler. Serve on slices of hot broiled ham on a buttered and heated rusk.

YIELD: 4 SERVINGS

Seafood Sorcery
THE JUNIOR LEAGUE OF WILMINGTON, NORTH CAROLINA

Oyster Curry

1 quart oysters
1 pint cream (heavy cream preferred)
1 teaspoon curry powder (or to taste)
1 teaspoon salt
1 tablespoon flour mixed with 1 tablespoon water
Dash black pepper
4 tablespoons cooked rice per person

Cook oysters in their juice in boiler until they curl or are partially done. Add cream, curry powder, salt, flour mixture, and black pepper and cook, stirring until sauce boils. Reduce heat and continue to cook until thick, stirring constantly. Serve on cooked rice.

With this recipe for a Sunday night supper, you can serve a mixed green salad with a good French dressing, then for dessert baked peaches— drained canned peaches with a wineglass of lemon juice baked in oven, and a wineglass of rum added just before serving.

YIELD: 5–6 SERVINGS

The Cotton Blossom Cookbook
THE JUNIOR LEAGUE OF ATLANTA, GEORGIA

· · · · · · · · · · · · · · · · ·

Scalloped Oysters

1 pint oysters with their juice
2 cups coarse cracker crumbs
½ cup melted butter or margarine
Pepper
¾ cup light cream
¼ cup oyster liquor
¼ teaspoon Worcestershire sauce
½ teaspoon salt

Recipe continues . . .

Drain oysters and reserve liquor. Combine crumbs and butter and spread ⅓ of them in a greased baking dish. Cover with half the oysters, sprinkle with pepper, add a layer of crumbs, cover with remaining oysters, and sprinkle with pepper. Combine cream, oyster liquor, Worcestershire sauce, and salt. Pour over oysters. Top with crumbs. Bake 40 minutes at 350°.

YIELD: 4 SERVINGS

Seafood Sorcery
THE JUNIOR LEAGUE OF WILMINGTON, NORTH CAROLINA

. . . .

Williamsburg Oysters

½ cup butter
½ cup flour
½ teaspoon paprika
½ teaspoon salt
½ teaspoon pepper
Dash cayenne
1 onion, finely chopped
½ green pepper, chopped
½ garlic clove, minced
1 teaspoon lemon juice
1 teaspoon Worcestershire sauce
1 quart oysters with their juice

Melt butter and stir in flour until brown. Add paprika, salt, pepper, and cayenne. Cook 3 minutes. Add onion, pepper, and garlic. Cook 5 minutes.

Remove from the fire and add lemon juice, Worcestershire sauce, and oysters which have been heated in their own juice until the edges have curled.

Place in a casserole and bake 30 minutes at 400°.

YIELD: 4–6 SERVINGS

Seafood Sorcery
THE JUNIOR LEAGUE OF WILMINGTON, NORTH CAROLINA

. . . .

Oyster Mushroom Pie

1 cup sliced mushrooms
⅓ cup butter
⅓ cup flour
2 cups milk
½ cup oyster juice
1 pint oysters
½ teaspoon salt
⅛ teaspoon pepper
Dash nutmeg
½ teaspoon celery salt
Pastry or pie dough

Cook mushrooms in butter for 3 minutes. Stir in flour. When smoothly blended, gradually add milk and oyster juice. Bring to boiling point, stirring constantly, and cook until smooth.

Add oysters and seasonings and turn into baking dish. Top with any pastry, cutting several slits to allow for escape of steam.

Bake in hot oven (450°) for 15 or 20 minutes.

YIELD: 4 SERVINGS

Talk About Good!
THE JUNIOR LEAGUE OF LAFAYETTE, LOUISIANA

.   .   .   .

Scallop Casserole

1 teaspoon onion juice
7 tablespoons sherry
1 pound scallops, steamed 3 or 4 minutes, in own juice
1 8½-ounce can water chestnuts, sliced
1 14-ounce can artichoke hearts
1 cup slivered almonds
¼ cup grated Parmesan cheese

Recipe continues . . .

Make Cheddar Cheese Sauce and stir in onion juice and sherry.

Line buttered casserole with scallops, water chestnuts, artichoke hearts, and almonds. Pour on sauce, sprinkle Parmesan cheese, and bake at 325° for 20–30 minutes.

YIELD: 4 SERVINGS

CHEDDAR CHEESE SAUCE:
4 tablespoons butter
5 tablespoons flour
1 cup light cream
½ teaspoon salt
¼ teaspoon red pepper
¾ cup shredded sharp cheddar cheese

Melt butter and add flour. Cook for a minute then add cream, salt, and red pepper. Stirring constantly, add cheddar cheese and cook until cheese melts.

Gator Country Cooks
THE JUNIOR LEAGUE OF GAINESVILLE, FLORIDA

.   .   .   .

Shrimp Tempura

2 pounds shrimp
2 cups flour
2 eggs
1½ cups milk
2 teaspoons baking powder
½ teaspoon salt
½ cup flaked coconut
Oil for frying

Shell shrimp, leaving tails on, devein, and cut open lengthwise to make a butterfly shape. Dip into batter made of flour, eggs, milk, baking powder, salt, and coconut.

Fry in hot oil until the shrimp rise to the top (about 2 minutes). Serve with Tempura Sauce.

YIELD: 6 SERVINGS

TEMPURA SAUCE:
1 cup chicken stock
¼ cup soy sauce
2 teaspoons sugar
1 tablespoon sherry

Combine all ingredients.

YIELD: 1¼ CUPS

Seafood Sorcery
THE JUNIOR LEAGUE OF WILMINGTON, NORTH CAROLINA

.   .   .   .

Scallops in Wine

¾ cup water
⅓ cup Sauterne or medium-sweet sherry
½ teaspoon salt
Few grains cayenne
1 pint fresh scallops
3 tablespoons butter
2 tablespoons flour
2 tablespoons minced onion
Dash garlic salt
1 teaspoon chopped parsley
1 egg yolk, well beaten
1 4-ounce can sliced mushrooms, drained
2 tablespoons grated Parmesan cheese
¾ cup soft bread crumbs

Recipe continues . . .

Combine water, wine, salt, cayenne, and scallops in a saucepan and simmer 5 minutes. Drain and reserve liquid.

Cut scallops into small pieces.

Melt butter in a skillet and blend in flour. Stir in reserved liquid and cook until thickened. Add onion, garlic salt, and parsley and cook 5 minutes over low heat. Quickly blend in egg yolk.

Remove from heat and add scallops, mushrooms, and additional liquid if needed. Spoon scallop mixture into five buttered 5-inch shells, and top with cheese and crumbs.

Bake at 425° for 5 minutes. Never let scallops cook more than 11 minutes or they will be tough.

YIELD: 5 SERVINGS

Seafood Sorcery
THE JUNIOR LEAGUE OF WILMINGTON, NORTH CAROLINA

. . . .

Baked Stuffed Shrimp

24 jumbo shrimp
1 medium onion, minced
1 green pepper, chopped
4 tablespoons butter
1 cup fresh crabmeat (or 1 7½-ounce can)
1 teaspoon dry mustard
1 teaspoon Worcestershire sauce
½ teaspoon salt
2 tablespoons mayonnaise
2 tablespoons butter
2 tablespoons flour
1 cup milk
1 tablespoon (or more) sherry
Grated Parmesan cheese
Paprika

Clean and remove heads and shell from shrimp, leaving tails. Split shrimp and open flat. Sauté onion and pepper in butter until soft but not brown. Add the crabmeat, dry mustard, Worcestershire sauce, salt, and mayonnaise.

Make white sauce using the 2 tablespoons butter, flour, and milk.

Add to crabmeat mixture along with the sherry. Mix well, stuff the butterflied shrimp with the crabmeat, and dot with extra butter. Sprinkle lightly with Parmesan cheese and paprika.

Arrange in shallow baking pan and bake at 350° for 25–30 minutes.

YIELD: 4–6 SERVINGS

Southern Sideboards
THE JUNIOR LEAGUE OF JACKSON, MISSISSIPPI

. . . .

Shrimp Creole

⅓ cup shortening
¼ cup flour
1 pound fully peeled, deveined raw shrimp
1 clove garlic, minced
½ cup minced onion
2 tablespoons minced parsley
½ cup chopped green pepper
1 cup water
2 teaspoons salt
2 bay leaves
½ teaspoon cayenne
1 8-ounce can tomato sauce
½ teaspoon monosodium glutamate

Melt shortening in heavy skillet over high fire. Add flour and stir until it is light brown. Lower heat, add shrimp, and cook about 3 minutes or until pink.

Add garlic, onion, parsley, and pepper and cook 2 minutes longer.

Recipe continues . . .

Raise heat; gradually add water, then remaining ingredients. Bring to boil, then simmer, covered, for 20–30 minutes.

Serve very hot over fluffy rice.

YIELD: 4 SERVINGS

Talk About Good!

THE JUNIOR LEAGUE OF LAFAYETTE, LOUISIANA

. . . .

Curried Shrimp with Wilmington Green Rice

WILMINGTON GREEN RICE:
1 cup raw rice
2 eggs, well beaten
1 cup milk
¼ cup butter
¼ cup shredded sharp cheddar cheese
½ tablespoon grated onion
⅓ cup minced parsley
⅔ cup minced raw spinach
1 teaspoon Worcestershire sauce
1¼ teaspoons salt

Prepare rice to make 3 cups fluffy cooked rice. While still warm, carefully stir in remaining ingredients. Pour into greased and floured 2-quart 8-inch casserole. Bake at 325° about 45 minutes. Serve hot with curried shrimp.

CURRIED SHRIMP:
½ cup butter
½ cup flour
1 teaspoon salt
½ teaspoon pepper
2 teaspoons curry powder (or to taste)
4 cups milk
2 teaspoons lemon juice or sherry
2 pounds cleaned, cooked shrimp

Melt butter over low heat in heavy saucepan. Blend in flour, salt, pepper, and curry powder. Stir until mixture is bubbly.

Remove from heat. Stir in milk. Bring to boil, stirring constantly. Cook until thickened.

Just before serving, blend in lemon juice or sherry and shrimp.

Serve over green rice.

YIELD: 8 SERVINGS

Seafood Sorcery
THE JUNIOR LEAGUE OF WILMINGTON, NORTH CAROLINA

. . . .

Deviled Shrimp

1½ pounds fresh or frozen shrimp
7 tablespoons margarine
2 teaspoons chopped parsley
1 canned pimento, chopped
1 teaspoon Worcestershire sauce
1½ tablespoons lemon juice
2 tablespoons flour
1 cup milk
½ pound cheddar cheese, shredded
¼ teaspoon pepper
1 teaspoon dry mustard

Shell and devein shrimp. Melt ¼ cup of the margarine in skillet. Add shrimp, parsley, pimento, Worcestershire sauce, and lemon juice. Sauté for 5 minutes.

Melt remaining margarine in saucepan. Add flour and stir until smooth. Gradually stir in milk. Add cheese, pepper, and dry mustard. Cook over low heat until sauce thickens.

Recipe continues . . .

Add shrimp mixture to cheese sauce and serve over rice.

YIELD: 4 SERVINGS

Seafood Sorcery
THE JUNIOR LEAGUE OF WILMINGTON, NORTH CAROLINA

·   ·   ·   ·   ·   ·   ·   ·   ·   ·   ·   ·   ·   ·   ·   ·

Rushie Wrenn's Shrimp Dino

1 4-ounce can mushrooms, sliced
¼ cup butter
1 clove garlic, pressed
¼ cup flour
1 teaspoon salt
½ teaspoon dry mustard
Pinch cayenne
2 cups milk
½ cup dry sherry
2 pounds shrimp, boiled and deveined
2 teaspoons chopped parsley
Grated Parmesan cheese
Mozzarella cheese, shredded

Simmer mushrooms, butter, and pressed garlic for 5 minutes. Blend in flour, salt, mustard, and cayenne, then add milk slowly. Cook, stirring constantly, on medium heat until thick. Add sherry, shrimp, and parsley.

Put into 2½-quart casserole. Sprinkle generously with Parmesan and mozzarella cheeses. Place in 300° oven for 20–30 minutes or until hot through.

YIELD: 4–6 SERVINGS

Seafood Sorcery
THE JUNIOR LEAGUE OF WILMINGTON, NORTH CAROLINA

·   ·   ·   ·   ·   ·   ·   ·   ·   ·   ·   ·   ·   ·   ·   ·

Shrimp au Gratin

1 4-ounce can mushrooms
3 tablespoons chopped onion
3 tablespoons butter
¼ cup flour
½ teaspoon salt
¼ teaspoon dry mustard
Dash pepper
1½ cups milk
1 cup shredded cheese
1 pound cooked shrimp, peeled and deveined
¼ cup dry bread crumbs
Butter

Cook mushrooms and onion in butter until tender. Blend in flour and seasonings. Add milk gradually and cook until thick, stirring constantly.

Add ¾ cup cheese and stir until melted. Stir in shrimp and pour into well-greased casserole.

Combine crumbs and remaining cheese; sprinkle over top. Dot with butter. Bake at 400° for 10 minutes.

YIELD: 4 SERVINGS

A Cook's Tour of Shreveport
THE JUNIOR LEAGUE OF SHREVEPORT, LOUISIANA

·   ·   ·   ·   ·   ·   ·   ·   ·   ·   ·   ·   ·   ·   ·

Shrimp and Artichoke Casserole

3 packages frozen artichoke hearts
2 pounds shrimp, cooked and cooled
Salt and pepper
Buttered crumbs

Recipe continues . . .

CHEESE SAUCE:
½ *stick butter*
3 *tablespoons flour*
1 *13-ounce can evaporated milk*
1 *can water*
1 *cup shredded sharp cheddar cheese*
Sherry to taste

Cook artichoke hearts according to directions on package, drain, and cool.

Make sauce as follows: Melt butter in top of double boiler and stir in flour. Add milk and equal amount of water and cook, stirring constantly over hot water until smooth. Add cheese and cool. Add sherry to taste.

In buttered casserole place half of artichoke hearts, half of shrimp, salt and pepper, and Cheese Sauce. Repeat layer and cover with buttered crumbs. Bake 25–30 minutes at 375°.

Asparagus spears may be substituted for artichokes.

YIELD: 8 SERVINGS

Spartanburg Secrets II
THE JUNIOR LEAGUE OF SPARTANBURG, SOUTH CAROLINA

. . . .

Edisto Shrimp "Pie"

2 *cups fresh bread crumbs (about 3 large slices)*
1 *cup milk*
2 *cups peeled, cooked shrimp*
2 *tablespoons melted butter*
1 *tablespoon chopped celery or parsley*
2 *tablespoons sherry*
Salt and pepper to taste
1 *teaspoon Worcestershire sauce*
Pinch nutmeg or mace (optional)

Soak bread in milk; add shrimp, butter, and remaining ingredients. Place in buttered baking dish and bake in moderate oven (375°) for 30 minutes.

YIELD: 6 SERVINGS

Charleston Receipts
THE JUNIOR LEAGUE OF CHARLESTON, SOUTH CAROLINA

.   .   .   .

Shrimp, Mushroom, and Artichoke Casserole

2½ tablespoons butter
½ pound mushrooms
1½ pounds shrimp
1 1-pound can artichoke hearts
4½ tablespoons butter
4½ tablespoons flour
¾ cup milk
¾ cup heavy cream
½ cup dry sherry
1 tablespoon Worcestershire sauce
Salt and pepper to taste
½ cup grated Parmesan cheese
Paprika

Melt 2½ tablespoons butter and sauté mushrooms. Set aside.

Boil and shell shrimp.

In a 2-quart casserole, make one layer each of artichoke hearts, shrimp, and mushrooms.

To make sauce: Melt 4½ tablespoons butter. Stirring with a wire whisk, add the flour, then the milk and cream. Stir until thick. Add sherry, Worcestershire sauce, salt, and pepper.

Pour sauce over layered ingredients. Sprinkle top with cheese; then sprinkle with paprika.

Recipe continues . . .

Bake at 375° for 20–30 minutes. Serve over rice. This is better if made the day before.

YIELD: 6 SERVINGS

Party Potpourri
THE JUNIOR LEAGUE OF MEMPHIS, TENNESSEE

· · · · · · · · · · · · · · · ·

Deluxe Deviled Seafood

Butter
Garlic
¼ cup minced onion
4 tablespoons butter
4 tablespoons flour
1½ teaspoons dry mustard
2 cups milk
Cayenne
1 teaspoon Tabasco
3 or 4 teaspoons Worcestershire sauce
3 hard-boiled eggs, sieved or grated
1½ pounds seafood (shellfish preferred), any combination of
shrimp, crab, lobster, or oysters, cooked
1 cup shredded sharp cheddar cheese
1 cup fine buttered crumbs
½ cup pecans, chopped very fine

Butter a 2-quart shallow baking dish and rub it with garlic.

Cook onion in 4 tablespoons butter until transparent. Add flour and mustard and cook 1 or 2 minutes longer. Add milk and seasonings when thickened.

Add sieved eggs, seafood, and half of cheese.

Mix crumbs, rest of cheese, and nuts.

Put half creamed mixture in dish. Sprinkle half of dry mixture. Repeat. Dot with butter and place in 325° oven for 25 minutes, or until thoroughly heated.

YIELD: 8 SERVINGS

The Charlotte Cookbook
THE JUNIOR LEAGUE OF CHARLOTTE, NORTH CAROLINA

. . . .

Seafood Newburg

2 cups seafood (shrimp, lobster, etc.)
½ cup button mushrooms (optional)
2 tablespoons butter
½ cup sherry
Paprika
2 tablespoons flour
2 egg yolks
2 cups light cream
Salt and pepper

Simmer seafood and mushrooms in butter. Add sherry and paprika. Cook 2 minutes, then sprinkle with flour and mix lightly.

Beat egg yolks and combine with cream. Add to shrimp mixture and cook until smooth and thickened. Season with salt and pepper.

Serve with rice.

YIELD: 4 SERVINGS

Spartanburg Secrets II
THE JUNIOR LEAGUE OF SPARTANBURG, SOUTH CAROLINA

. . . .

Seafood au Gratin

5 pounds lobster or lobster tails (3½ pounds after cleaning)
Handful salt
1 cup cider vinegar
5 pounds shrimp (3½ pounds after cleaning)
2 pounds crabmeat
½ cup sherry (optional)
5 cups cooked rice

If frozen lobster tails are used, plunge into large pot of boiling water to which a handful of salt and a cup of cider vinegar have been added. Cover and cook over high heat for 20 minutes. Drain and cool. Slit shell and remove meat. Remove dark vein from center of tail meat. Cut lobster into bite-size chunks.

Cook shrimp same way, but allow only 10 minutes cooking time. Shell, devein, and leave whole. Add seafood to cheese sauce and heat together. Add sherry if desired. Serve over hot rice.

YIELD: 20 SERVINGS

SEAFOOD CHEESE SAUCE:
1 cup butter
1 cup flour
7 cups milk
1 cup tomato purée
1⅔ tablespoons salt
½ teaspoon cayenne
1½ teaspoons paprika
2 cloves garlic, minced fine
2 tablespoons monosodium glutamate
5 ounces Gruyère cheese
¼ pound American cheese

Melt butter in large saucepan and add flour. Blend and cook over low heat, stirring constantly for 1 minute. Add milk, tomato purée, salt, cayenne, paprika, garlic, monosodium glutamate, and cheeses which have been cut into small pieces. Cook over low heat, stirring constantly until cheese has melted and sauce is thick and bubbling.

Home Cookin'
THE JUNIOR LEAGUE OF WICHITA FALLS, TEXAS

· · · · · · · · · · · · · · · · ·

Crab-Shrimp Pie

BÉCHAMEL SAUCE:
⅓ cup butter
⅓ cup flour
3 cups hot milk
1 teaspoon salt
¼ teaspoon pepper
¼ teaspoon nutmeg
1 cup shredded Gruyère cheese (Swiss or mozzarella may be used)

Melt butter in saucepan. Stir flour in smoothly and cook a few minutes. Gradually add milk and seasonings and stir well. Cook slowly for 25 minutes, stirring gently but steadily until sauce is thick and smooth. Add cheese and allow to melt.

PIE FILLING:
Pastry for one 9-inch crust
1½ cups frozen lump crabmeat
1½ cups cooked shrimp (fresh are best)
¾ cup fresh sliced mushrooms
3 tablespoons butter
1 tablespoon chopped parsley
1 tablespoon grated onion
1 teaspoon nutmeg
2 tablespoons dry vermouth
1 tablespoon cracked black pepper
3 cups Béchamel Sauce
Paprika

Recipe continues . . .

Line a greased 9-inch pie pan with your favorite pastry. Bake 5 minutes at 325°.

In a large bowl mix crabmeat, shrimp, and mushrooms browned in butter.

Add parsley, onion, nutmeg, vermouth, and cracked black pepper.

Mix with Béchamel Sauce and fill pie shell. Sprinkle with paprika for color. Bake covered for 20 minutes at 350°.

YIELD: 6 SERVINGS

Little Rock Cooks
THE JUNIOR LEAGUE OF LITTLE ROCK, ARKANSAS

. . . .

Bones's Frog Legs

10 pairs frog legs
1 13-ounce can evaporated milk
2 eggs, beaten
Salt and pepper
Self-rising flour
Cooking oil

Split pairs of legs to make single legs. Soak legs in mixture of milk, egg, salt, and pepper for at least 30 minutes.

Dip in flour seasoned with salt and pepper. Fry in medium-hot oil in deep-fat fryer or large pot until golden brown.

YIELD: 4–6 SERVINGS

Southern Sideboards
THE JUNIOR LEAGUE OF JACKSON, MISSISSIPPI

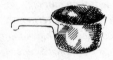

. . . .

. . . .

Game

. . . .

Roast Venison with Poivrade Sauce

4½ pounds boneless venison roast
Salt and pepper
4 tablespoons butter
½ cup cognac

Sprinkle meat with salt and pepper to taste.

Melt butter in open skillet and turn roast in the butter until coated without browning. Bake roast uncovered at 450°, basting and turning the meat frequently, for 30 minutes. Reduce heat to 400°. Continue basting and roasting 15 minutes for medium rare or longer for well done.

Remove meat and keep warm. Add cognac to skillet and ignite it. Stir.

This liquid will be added to Poivrade Sauce. Serve the meat sliced with sauce.

YIELD: 8–10 SERVINGS

POIVRADE SAUCE:
⅓ cup chopped carrots
⅓ cup chopped onion
4 tablespoons minced parsley
3 tablespoons olive oil
1 cup dry red wine
2½ cups canned beef gravy
1½ tablespoons cracked black pepper
Cognac and juices from roast

Sauté vegetables in oil for 5 minutes. Add wine and simmer until reduced by one-half. Add gravy and cook over low heat for 30 minutes. Strain. Add pan juices, dash cognac if desired, and pepper and serve with roast venison.

Little Rock Cooks
THE JUNIOR LEAGUE OF LITTLE ROCK, ARKANSAS

Marinated Roast

1 cup beer
1 cup bourbon
1 cup cooking oil
1 teaspoon salt
½ teaspoon garlic powder
½ teaspoon onion salt
1 medium onion, sliced
½ teaspoon black pepper
Wild game
2 tablespoons cornstarch

Mix above ingredients (except meat and cornstarch) and pour over your choice of meat. Cover and refrigerate for *2 weeks*. Turn meat daily to soak all sides well.

After refrigerating 2 weeks, roast the meat and mixture in a covered pan at 300° for about 5 hours. Thicken juices with cornstarch.

The Blue Denim Gourmet
THE JUNIOR LEAGUE OF ODESSA, TEXAS

. . . .

Sweet and Sour Game

Any wild game
Olive oil
1 cup water

SWEET AND SOUR SAUCE:
1½ teaspoons salt
½ cup brown sugar
2 teaspoons dry mustard
2 tablespoons vinegar
6 tablespoons olive oil

Recipe continues . . .

Brown meat in olive oil and add 1 cup water. Cover and roast at 350° for 20 minutes to each pound. Combine sauce ingredients and use to baste meat frequently. If meat is sliced or cut into steaks or chops, layer them with the sauce in between.

The Blue Denim Gourmet
THE JUNIOR LEAGUE OF ODESSA, TEXAS

. . . .

Party Venison

3 medium onions, sliced
½ cup fresh bacon drippings
2 pounds boneless venison stew meat with fat and
fibers trimmed off, cut into 1-inch cubes
4 tablespoons flour
1¾ cups California Burgundy
10½ ounces condensed beef broth (not bouillon)
Generous pinch thyme and marjoram
Salt and freshly ground pepper to taste
1 pound fresh mushrooms, sliced
Hot noodles

Sauté onions in ¼ cup of bacon drippings in a 4-quart Dutch oven until golden. Remove to a bowl. Add bacon fat to pot as needed; brown venison cubes in small portions to avoid too much liquid. When all is browned, return to the pan and stir in the flour. Add the wine and about three-quarters of the broth, thyme, marjoram, salt, and pepper. Cover and simmer gently for about 3 hours. Add onions and mushrooms and cook for another hour.

Serve over hot noodles.

Can be prepared a day or two ahead, which improves the flavor. Can also be frozen.

YIELD: 8–10 SERVINGS

The Dallas Jr. League Cookbook
THE JUNIOR LEAGUE OF DALLAS, TEXAS

. . . .

Venison Chili

½ pound dry pinto beans
2 tablespoons salt
5 cups canned tomatoes
1½ pounds onions, chopped
3 green peppers, chopped
1½ teaspoons salad oil
½ cup chopped parsley
2 cloves garlic, crushed
2½ pounds ground venison
1 pound ground pork
1½ teaspoons monosodium glutamate
½ cup butter
½ cup chili powder
1½ teaspoons pepper
1½ teaspoons cumin seeds

Wash beans thoroughly; soak overnight in water 2 inches above beans. Wash again and simmer with salt until tender (about 4 hours).

Simmer tomatoes in separate pan 5 minutes. Sauté onions and green pepper in salad oil; add to tomatoes and cook until tender. Add parsley and garlic.

Sprinkle meats with monosodium glutamate. Melt butter in large skillet and sauté meats for 15 minutes. Drain off grease; add meat to tomato and onion mixture. Stir in chili powder and cook 10 minutes; add beans, pepper, and cumin seeds. Simmer covered for 1 hour. Uncover and simmer 30 minutes more.

YIELD: 8–10 SERVINGS

Seasoned with Sun: Recipes from the Southwest
THE JUNIOR LEAGUE OF EL PASO, TEXAS

Lavington Plantation Roasted Wild Duck

Ducks
Flour
Salt and pepper
Slices of bacon or fat pork

POTATO DRESSING:
1 cup mashed potatoes
1 tablespoon finely chopped onion
2 tablespoons finely chopped celery
Salt and pepper

Prepare ducks for roasting. Combine Potato Dressing ingredients and stuff ducks (or use any other desired dressing). Dust with flour, salt, and pepper and place several strips of bacon or thin slices of fat pork over the breast. Place in roaster and add 1 cup of water. Cook uncovered in a hot oven (400°) for about 1 hour. Baste frequently.

YIELD: 2 SERVINGS PER DUCK

Charleston Receipts
THE JUNIOR LEAGUE OF CHARLESTON, SOUTH CAROLINA

.   .   .   .

Wild Duck with Cumberland Sauce

8 or 10 ducks, ready to cook
Salt and pepper
Chunks of apple, celery, onion, and potato

Wash cleaned duck in cold water and pat dry inside and out. Season each cavity with salt and pepper and stuff each bird with chunks of apple, celery, onions and potatoes.

Place ducks in roaster, close together, breast side down. Put about 2 inches of water in roaster, enough so breasts of birds are in water. Cover and bake at 350° for 3½ hours or until ducks are tender.

Remove from oven and drain off half the liquid. Turn birds breast side up and brown about 30 minutes at 400° degrees, uncovered. Watch carefully so birds do not burn or dry out. Remove all stuffing and discard.

Serve hot with Cumberland Sauce.

YIELD: 8–10 SERVINGS

CUMBERLAND SAUCE:
Juice and rind of 1 orange
Juice and rinds of 2 lemons
1 cup confectioners' sugar
1 tablespoon grated horseradish
2 tablespoons melted currant jelly

Mix together all ingredients and beat thoroughly. Heat and serve with roast duck.

Gator Country Cooks
THE JUNIOR LEAGUE OF GAINESVILLE, FLORIDA

· · · · · · · · · · · · · · · · ·

Nashville Roast Wild Duck

4 ducks
2 tablespoons baking soda
4 large apples
4 small onions
12 slices bacon
1½ cups sherry
1½ cups orange juice
1 can mushrooms
Butter
Orange slices
Currant jelly

Recipe continues . . .

Soak ducks for 2 hours in pan of water to which baking soda has been added.

Preheat oven to 500°. Stuff cavities of ducks with cut-up apples and onions (1 apple and 1 onion per duck). Apples and onions are not to be eaten; they are to absorb wild game taste.

Place 3 strips of bacon over the breast of each duck. Roast for 30 minutes at 500° with little or no water. Turn heat down to 250° and continue to cook for 30 minutes. Baste with sherry and orange juice throughout cooking.

For gravy, add mushrooms and a little butter to the juices left in the roaster.

Garnish with orange slices topped with currant jelly for an attractive tray.

YIELD: 8 SERVINGS

Nashville Seasons
THE JUNIOR LEAGUE OF NASHVILLE, TENNESSEE

·　·　·　·　·　·　·　·　·　·　·　·　·　·

Delectable Wild Duck

2 ducks, quartered
½ cup flour
1 teaspoon salt
¼ teaspoon pepper
2 tablespoons melted butter
1 10½-ounce can condensed consommé
½ cup sherry
½ medium-size onion, chopped fine and sautéed in 1 tablespoon butter
1 tablespoon chopped parsley
1 teaspoon thyme
1 teaspoon marjoram
5 stalks celery with some leaves
½ cup dry red wine
Wild rice

Place duck in bag containing flour, salt, and pepper. Shake until duck is well covered. Brown duck in butter, then arrange in a large casserole. Add consommé, sherry, onion, and herbs. Place celery stalks and leaves over top. Cover and bake at 450° for 20 minutes. Reduce heat to 300° and bake until tender (about 2½ hours). When half done, pour the dry red wine over ducks. When done, discard celery.

Serve with wild rice.

YIELD: 4 SERVINGS

The Dallas Jr. League Cookbook
THE JUNIOR LEAGUE OF DALLAS, TEXAS

. . . .

Shreveport Roast Wild Duck

1 duck
2 teaspoons baking soda
2 teaspoons salt
2 tablespoons dry mustard
1 teaspoon salt
½ teaspoon black pepper
½ raw apple, cubed
½ onion, cubed
¼ raw potato, cubed
1 clove garlic
1 stalk celery, chopped
½ cup water
1 slice orange
¼ cup sherry or red wine (optional)
Wild rice, white rice, or both
Cooked mushrooms (optional)

Wash duck thoroughly and let stand 20 minutes in pan of cold water containing baking soda and 2 teaspoons salt. Wash duck again.

Combine dry mustard, 1 teaspoon salt, and pepper in bowl. Pat each duck inside and out generously with mixture. Combine apple, onion, potato,

Recipe continues . . .

garlic, and celery and fill cavity of duck. Place duck, breast side up, in a Dutch oven or roasting pan. Pour water in pan but do not splash duck. Cover. Bake at 325° for 2 hours. Baste duck every ½ hour. After 1 hour, garnish with slice of orange and add wine.

May be prepared in advance. Use gravy over wild rice or white rice or a mixture of the two. Cooked mushrooms may be added to gravy.

YIELD: 2 SERVINGS

A Cook's Tour of Shreveport
THE JUNIOR LEAGUE OF SHREVEPORT, LOUISIANA

· · · · · · · · · · · · · ·

Duck Deluxe

2 ducks
Bacon drippings or margarine
3 cups water
2 chicken bouillon cubes
Garlic salt
1 teaspoon salt
Dash pepper
2 tablespoons Worcestershire sauce
¾–1 cup half and half
½ cup sherry
Chopped apple, onion, and celery
3–4 tablespoons flour blended with water or sherry
Juice of 2 oranges
4 tablespoons orange marmalade
½ cup brandy

In large seasoned iron skillet or Dutch oven, brown ducks on all sides in bacon drippings or margarine.

Fill a second large skillet half full with water and heat. Dissolve bouillon cubes in water and add generous sprinkling of garlic salt. Add salt, pepper, Worcestershire sauce, half and half, and sherry. Heat to boiling but *do not boil.*

Stuff ducks with apple, onion, and celery and place breast down in Dutch oven. Pour liquid mixture over ducks. Cover tightly and cook at 350° for 2–2½ hours. Baste or turn ducks in gravy every 30 minutes.

Remove ducks from gravy. Carefully stir flour mixture into gravy and add orange juice, marmalade, and brandy.

Slice duck and return to gravy. Heat thoroughly and serve.

YIELD: 4 SERVINGS

Home Cookin'
THE JUNIOR LEAGUE OF WICHITA FALLS, TEXAS

.   .   .   .

Buffet Wild Duck

5 ducks, cleaned and dried
3 red apples, cored and quartered
1 cup Burgundy
½ cup water

Stuff ducks with apples. Place in a large roasting pan. Pour Burgundy and water over ducks. Cover pan with lid or foil and bake at 325° for 2 hours or until very tender. Pour off juice and chill ducks until they are very cold so that meat slices more easily. Place ducks on carving board and remove all meat from bones. Slice meat into slivers, cover, and store in refrigerator. (This can be done a day ahead.) Prepare sauce 2 or 3 hours before serving.

YIELD: 10 SERVINGS

SAUCE:
1 cup butter
⅓ cup lemon juice
¼ cup chopped parsley
1 tablespoon Worcestershire sauce
¼ cup chopped green onions with tops
1½ teaspoons prepared mustard
Salt and pepper

Recipe continues . . .

Melt butter in a heavy saucepan and stir in half the lemon juice. Heat until very hot but not boiling. Taste sauce, which should be tart but not sour; add more lemon juice if needed. Add parsley, Worcestershire sauce, onions, and mustard and stir well.

Put one-quarter of duck meat in serving casserole. Season with salt and pepper, drizzle with lemon butter sauce, and continue until all duck and sauce are used. Cover with lid or foil and let stand unrefrigerated for 30–60 minutes. Place covered casserole in 325° oven for 1 hour.

Increase sauce by half if ducks are large mallards.

Southern Accent
THE JUNIOR LEAGUE OF PINE BLUFF, ARKANSAS

. . . .

Doves

Salt and pepper to taste
Flour
14–16 doves
½ cup salad oil
½ cup chopped green onions with tops
1½ cups water
1 cup sherry
¼ cup chopped parsley

Salt, pepper, and flour doves. Brown in oil in roasting pan in 400° oven. After browned, add chopped onions and water. Cover. Reduce heat to 350°. Cook until tender, about 1½ hours, basting during cooking.

Add sherry and cook 30 minutes longer, basting several times. Add parsley to gravy before serving over rice.

YIELD: 2–3 DOVES PER SERVING

The Blue Denim Gourmet
THE JUNIOR LEAGUE OF ODESSA, TEXAS

. . . .

Dove à la Como

12 doves, ready to cook
Salt
Flour
1 cup butter
2 10½-ounce cans condensed consommé
½ can water
1 tablespoon cracked black pepper
Salt to taste
Buttered whole wheat toast
4 cups crumbled crisp-fried bacon
½ cup sherry

Rinse doves. Lightly salt. Roll in flour. Brown in butter.

Add consommé, water, pepper, and salt to taste. Cover and simmer, breast down, for 1½ hours.

When done, serve on buttered toast. Completely cover dove with bacon and serve with gravy, to which you have added the sherry. The bacon is the secret!

YIELD: 4 SERVINGS

Little Rock Cooks
THE JUNIOR LEAGUE OF LITTLE ROCK, ARKANSAS

.   .   .   .

Doves London Style

4–6 doves
Salt and pepper
Paprika
Flour
¾ cup butter
1 cup water plus 1 beef bouillon cube or 1 cup canned condensed bouillon
½ pound sliced sautéed mushrooms

Recipe continues . . .

Dress doves, wash carefully, and pat dry. Shake salt, pepper, and paprika liberally over entire surface. Coat with flour.

Melt butter in heavy iron skillet and brown birds. Add water with bouillon cube or consommé. Add sautéed mushrooms. Cover pan and simmer slowly 3 hours.

YIELD: 2 SERVINGS

That Something Special
THE JUNIOR LEAGUE OF DURHAM, NORTH CAROLINA

. . . .

Dove au Vin

12 doves, ready to cook
Salt and pepper to taste
Flour
¾ stick butter
1 cup chopped celery
1 cup chopped onion
1 small green pepper, chopped
1 10½-ounce can condensed consommé
½ cup red wine

Season doves with salt and pepper and roll in flour. In a skillet, brown doves slowly in butter until brown on both sides. Transfer to a casserole and add celery, onion, pepper, and consommé. Put top on casserole and bake at 350° for 2 hours. Add wine last 30 minutes of cooking time.

YIELD: 4–6 SERVINGS

Party Potpourri
THE JUNIOR LEAGUE OF MEMPHIS, TENNESSEE

. . . .

Doves and Grapes

Salt and pepper to taste
8 doves, cleaned and dressed
Sifted flour
1 stick butter
1 cup water
1 cup seedless white grapes
Juice of 1 lemon
½ cup slivered blanched almonds
Decrusted toast squares

Salt and pepper doves inside and out and sprinkle liberally with flour, inside and out.

Melt butter in skillet and brown doves on all sides. Add 1 cup water. Cover and cook very slowly until tender. Do not let water evaporate; add more if fire is too high.

Add white grapes and cook about 20 minutes longer.

Remove birds and keep warm. Add lemon juice and almonds to skillet, simmer a few minutes, and pour over doves.

Serve doves on toast with sauce spooned over.

YIELD: 2–3 SERVINGS

Recipe Jubilee
THE JUNIOR LEAGUE OF MOBILE, ALABAMA

. . . .

Doves à la Bailey

Salt and pepper
Flour
Doves, ready to cook
Butter or bacon drippings
1 onion, finely chopped
Celery
Water

Recipe continues . . .

Salt, pepper, and very lightly flour doves with sifter. Brown in butter or bacon drippings in large, heavy frying pan. Pour off excess fat. Add onion and an equal amount of chopped celery. Add water so that doves are about half covered. Cover pan and simmer for at least 2 hours or until tender, adding water if needed.

To make gravy, remove doves from pan, add 1 heaping teaspoon flour, and brown on high heat. Add water, stirring constantly.

This recipe is excellent for all small game birds. Wild ducks should be quartered or halved and cooked slightly longer.

YIELD: 3 DOVES PER SERVING

300 Years of Carolina Cooking
THE JUNIOR LEAGUE OF GREENVILLE, SOUTH CAROLINA

. . . .

Roast Quail with White Grapes

4 quail
6 tablespoons butter
Salt
Freshly ground black pepper
About 30 Thompson seedless grapes, peeled
(if not available, use Belgian White Muscat or California
Emperor grapes, peeled, halved, and seeded)
2–3 tablespoons cognac
¼ cup dry sherry, white wine, or vermouth
1 cup chicken stock
1½ teaspoons arrowroot
1 teaspoon grated lemon rind
1–2 teaspoons lemon juice

Rub quail generously with butter, salt, and pepper. Put a lump of butter, salt, pepper, and 3–4 grapes in the cavity. Sprinkle with cognac. Place in a roasting pan and roast 12–15 minutes at 450°, basting thoroughly two or three times.

While the quail are roasting, gently heat the remaining grapes in sherry and chicken stock in a small saucepan. Remove grapes with a slotted spoon, add to quail, and roast 5 more minutes. Remove quail to heated serving platter. Mix arrowroot into sherry and chicken stock and add to pan juices with grated lemon rind and lemon juice. Stir well, scraping up brown bits on bottom, and simmer until slightly thickened. Check seasoning. Pour sauce over quail and serve immediately.

YIELD: 2 SERVINGS

The Dallas Jr. League Cookbook
THE JUNIOR LEAGUE OF DALLAS, TEXAS

· · · · · · · · · · · · · · · · · · ·

Fried Quail

Salt and pepper
12 quail
Flour
Fat for frying

Salt, pepper, and roll quail in flour. Fry in deep fat until brown (save drippings for cream gravy). Wrap quail tightly in foil and cook in oven for 2 hours at 250°.

Serve with hot biscuits, gravy, and rice.

YIELD: 4–6 SERVINGS

The Blue Denim Gourmet
THE JUNIOR LEAGUE OF ODESSA, TEXAS

· · · · · · · · · · · · · · · · · ·

Quail in Wine

¼ pound margarine or butter
Quail or doves
Flour
Salt and pepper
2 cups water
½ cup sherry

Melt margarine or butter in bottom of Dutch oven or in heavy frying pan with close-fitting top.

Roll cleaned and picked quail in flour; salt and pepper well; brown in butter on each side. Add water and ¼ cup sherry. Cover closely and bake at 425° for 1 hour. Fifteen minutes before quail are done, pour over them another ¼ cup sherry and bake uncovered for the remaining 15 minutes.

(Dove may be cooked by same method, but should bake at least 2½ hours at 400° and should be watched so that more water may be added occasionally as birds become dry.)

Serve with wild rice or whole hominy.

YIELD: 2 BIRDS PER SERVING

The Cotton Blossom Cookbook
THE JUNIOR LEAGUE OF ATLANTA, GEORGIA

· · · · · · · · · · · · · · · · · · · ·

Quail or Dove Suprême

Salt
12 quail or dove breasts
⅓ cup cooking oil
1 carrot, finely chopped
1 medium onion, minced
1 tablespoon minced green pepper
2 heaping tablespoons flour
2 10½-ounce cans condensed beef consommé, heated
1 cup canned sliced mushrooms
⅓ cup white wine

Salt birds lightly and brown in oil. Remove to oblong casserole. Brown carrot, onion, and pepper in same oil; blend in flour; gradually add heated consommé. Salt to taste. Add mushrooms and wine. Pour sauce over birds.

Cover with foil and bake at 350° for 45 minutes.

YIELD: 4–6 SERVINGS

Of Pots and Pipkins
THE JUNIOR LEAGUE OF ROANOKE VALLEY, VIRGINIA

Roasted Quail with Mushrooms

4 quail
4 slices thin bacon
1 tablespoon butter
¼ cup lemon juice
½ cup hot water
½ cup mushrooms, sautéed in butter (if large, cut into pieces)
Brown rice

Prepare quail. Wrap in bacon and fasten with picks.

Place in shallow, buttered pan and cover. Bake at 350° for 45–60 minutes, basting often with lemon juice and hot water mixture. When tender, remove from oven, add mushrooms, and serve over brown rice.

YIELD: 2 SERVINGS

300 Years of Carolina Cooking
THE JUNIOR LEAGUE OF GREENVILLE, SOUTH CAROLINA

Smothered Quail

6 quail
6 tablespoons butter
3 tablespoons flour
2 cups chicken broth
½ cup sherry
Salt and pepper
Rice

Clean quail. Brown in butter in heavy skillet or Dutch oven. Remove to baking dish. Add flour to butter in skillet and stir well. Slowly add chicken broth, sherry, salt, and pepper. Blend well and pour over quail.

Cover baking dish and bake at 350° for 1 hour.

Serve with rice.

YIELD: 3 SERVINGS

Little Rock Cooks
THE JUNIOR LEAGUE OF LITTLE ROCK, ARKANSAS

Wild Turkey Steaks

This is a 60-year-old recipe taken from a rare book about wild turkey hunting. The book says, "Having eaten turkey this way, you would not care for baked or roast turkey again."

Take a sharp knife, run the blade down alongside the keel bone, removing the flesh from one end to the other. By this process, each half breast can be taken off whole.

Lay the slab of white meat skin side down and cut off ½-inch-thick steaks until all the meat is gone. Sprinkle with salt and pepper and pile the steaks up together—thus the salt will quickly penetrate. *Do not salt steaks more than you want for one meal.* As soon as salt dissolves and juices begin to flow, spread out steaks, and sprinkle dry flour lightly on both sides. Take care to do this right or you will get the flour too thick. The flour mixes with the juices, forming a crust around the steak, like batter.

Have the frying pan on the stove with plenty of sizzling hot fat so that the steak will fry the moment it touches the fat. Brown on both sides.

By this method you retain all the juice from the meat and the flour prevents any fat from penetrating the meat. Will melt in mouth.

For a rich, brown gravy, add ½ pint cold water to pan drippings and about ½ teaspoon of the leftover fat in hot frying pan. Let boil about 5 minutes and season.

Little Rock Cooks
THE JUNIOR LEAGUE OF LITTLE ROCK, ARKANSAS

Stuffings and Condiments

Mama's Corn Bread Dressing

2 quarts cold, crumbled corn bread (packaged mix can be used)
3 slices loaf bread or cold biscuits
2 cups chopped celery
1 cup chopped onion
2 teaspoons poultry seasoning
1 tablespoon sugar (if packaged mix is not used for corn bread)
2 cups stock from turkey
1 10¾-ounce can chicken broth
4 eggs, well beaten

Mix all ingredients well. Spoon into a greased pan and bake at 350° for 20–25 minutes or just until set. Do not overcook.

YIELD: ABOUT 3 QUARTS

Gator Country Cooks
THE JUNIOR LEAGUE OF GAINESVILLE, FLORIDA

· · · · · · · · · · · · · · · ·

Peanut Dressing

1 cup shelled, parched peanuts (or peanut butter)
2 cups corn bread crumbs
2 tablespoons melted butter
1 egg yolk
Broth from turkey
Salt and pepper

Grind peanuts; add crumbs, melted butter, and egg yolk. Moisten with a little broth made by cooking the giblets and neck. Season with salt and pepper.

YIELD: ENOUGH FOR NECK END OF A TURKEY

VARIATION:

Use 1 pound ground salted peanuts, without other ingredients.

Charleston Receipts
THE JUNIOR LEAGUE OF CHARLESTON, SOUTH CAROLINA

· · · · · · · · · · · · · · · ·

Hot Mustard

1 cup dry mustard
1 cup vinegar
½ cup sugar
2 eggs, well beaten

Soak mustard and vinegar together overnight. Add sugar. Stir well and add eggs. Cook in double boiler until thickened. Stir often.

YIELD: 2 CUPS

Home Cookin'
THE JUNIOR LEAGUE OF WICHITA FALLS, TEXAS

· · · · · · · · · · · · · · · ·

Horseradish Jelly

3¼ cups sugar
½ cup prepared horseradish
½ cup cider vinegar
½ cup liquid pectin

In large pan, heat and stir sugar, horseradish, and vinegar until sugar dissolves. Bring to boil, then stir in pectin all at once. Bring to full rolling boil while stirring.

Recipe continues . . .

Take off heat and skim foam off top. Pour at once into hot sterilized jelly jars. Seal with paraffin.

Excellent with roast beef or chicken.

YIELD: 3 HALF PINTS

Southern Sideboards
THE JUNIOR LEAGUE OF JACKSON, MISSISSIPPI

· · · · · · · · · · · · · · ·

Currant Jelly Sauce

1 part currant jelly
1 part catsup
1 part sherry

Heat jelly and catsup. Add sherry when ready to serve. This is good with duck or lamb.

300 Years of Carolina Cooking
THE JUNIOR LEAGUE OF GREENVILLE, SOUTH CAROLINA

· · · · · · · · · · · · · · ·

Pepper Jelly

¾ cup chopped hot green pepper
¾ cup chopped sweet green pepper
¼ cup cider vinegar
6 cups sugar
1 cup cider vinegar
8 ounces liquid pectin
Red or green food coloring

Put peppers in blender jar. Add ¼ cup vinegar and blend until thin and soupy. Pour into pot and add sugar and 1 cup vinegar. Bring all to a boil and then remove from heat and skim.

Add pectin and food coloring. Reheat and boil hard for 1 minute.

Remove from heat and fill jars to ½ inch from top and seal with paraffin.

Serve with pork, ham, or turkey. Also good on crackers with cream cheese.

NOTE: Be sure to wear rubber gloves when making this recipe.

YIELD: 4 PINTS

Gator Country Cooks
THE JUNIOR LEAGUE OF GAINESVILLE, FLORIDA

· · · · · · · · · · · · · ·

Brandied Cranberries

1 pound fresh cranberries
2 cups sugar
4 tablespoons brandy
¼ cup sugar

Place berries in a shallow pan. Sprinkle with 2 cups sugar. Bake covered at 350° for 1 hour.

Remove from oven and sprinkle with brandy and remaining sugar. Refrigerate.

YIELD: ABOUT 3 CUPS

Southern Accent
THE JUNIOR LEAGUE OF PINE BLUFF, ARKANSAS

· · · · · · · · · · ·

Peeled Fig Preserves

6 cups sugar
4 pounds peeled figs
1 lemon, sliced

Layer sugar, figs, and lemon slices in large pot and cook covered on very low heat until sugar dissolves (about 1 hour).

Uncover and cook about 45 minutes longer, until figs are transparent.

Lift out figs with a slotted spoon and cook the syrup about 15 minutes longer, until thicker. Put figs back into pot and let sit overnight.

The following morning, heat figs to a boil and seal in jars.

YIELD: 7 HALF PINTS

Southern Sideboards
THE JUNIOR LEAGUE OF JACKSON, MISSISSIPPI

Curried Fruit

1 16-ounce can apricot halves
1 16-ounce can peach halves
1 16-ounce can pear halves
1 15-ounce can pineapple chunks
1 cup golden raisins
¾ cup brown sugar
½ cup melted butter
3 teaspoons curry powder
3 tablespoons lemon juice

Mix drained fruit and raisins and place in 2-quart ovenproof casserole. Mix last four ingredients and pour over fruit. Bake 1 hour at 325°. Cover and chill. Reheat following day.

Especially good with salty meats.

YIELD: 10–12 SERVINGS

Mountain Measures
THE JUNIOR LEAGUE OF CHARLESTON, WEST VIRGINIA

Brandied Peaches

4 pounds sugar
4 pounds peaches
1 pint brandy

Put sugar in pot with enough water to dissolve and let come to a boil. Add fruit and cook 5 minutes.

Remove fruit, boil syrup 15 minutes, and add brandy.

Remove from fire at once, and pour over fruit which has been packed in glass jars, and seal.

YIELD: ABOUT 6 PINTS

Spartanburg Secrets II
THE JUNIOR LEAGUE OF SPARTANBURG, SOUTH CAROLINA

. . . .

Peach Chutney

4 quarts chopped peaches
1 cup chopped onion
1 clove garlic, chopped
1 pod hot pepper
1 cup raisins
1 quart vinegar
2 tablespoons ground ginger
¼ cup mustard seeds
3 cups brown sugar
2 teaspoons salt

Mix all ingredients. Cook until thick, stirring frequently. Pour into hot sterilized jars. Seal immediately.

YIELD: 4 PINTS

That Something Special
THE JUNIOR LEAGUE OF DURHAM, NORTH CAROLINA

. . . .

Strawberry Preserves

4 cups sugar
1 cup water
4 cups whole strawberries

Boil together 2 cups sugar and 1 cup water until syrup spins a thread. Add 2 cups whole strawberries. Boil 10 minutes. Add 2 more cups strawberries and 2 more cups sugar. Boil 10 more minutes. Skim and set aside until following day.

Stir well and seal cold in sterile jars.

YIELD: ABOUT 4 HALF PINTS

A Cook's Tour of Shreveport
THE JUNIOR LEAGUE OF SHREVEPORT, LOUISIANA

Chili Salsa

½ onion, finely chopped
1 clove garlic, minced
Olive oil
2 jalapeño peppers, chopped
8–10 long green chilies, chopped
3 small tomatoes, peeled and chopped
Salt

Sauté onion and garlic over very low heat in oil. Add jalapeño peppers and chilies and simmer for about 5 minutes. Add tomatoes and salt. Cook 10 more minutes.

Cool and serve as a garnish.

YIELD: 2 CUPS

Seasoned with Sun: Recipes from the Southwest
THE JUNIOR LEAGUE OF EL PASO, TEXAS

Old Timey Chowchow

2 gallons chopped tomatoes
1 gallon chopped cabbage
12 sweet peppers (red or green)
12 hot peppers
12 large onions
¾ cup salt
6 cups sugar
½ gallon vinegar
2 tablespoons ground ginger
2 tablespoons dry mustard
2 tablespoons turmeric
2 tablespoons cinnamon

Hand chop vegetables uniformly. Add salt. Drain in colander for 2 hours. Place in large granite or stainless steel pan. Add remaining ingredients. Bring to hard boil for 2 full minutes. Place in jars and seal.

YIELD: 8 QUARTS

The Blue Denim Gourmet
THE JUNIOR LEAGUE OF ODESSA, TEXAS

· · · · · · · · · · · · · · · ·

Grandmother's Tomato Relish

30 large tomatoes
10 large onions
5 large green peppers
1 teaspoon cinnamon
1 teaspoon allspice
1 teaspoon cloves
3 tablespoons salt
1½ cups sugar
2 cups cider vinegar

Recipe continues . . .

Peel tomatoes. Chop tomatoes, onions, and peppers. Combine with rest of ingredients and cook on medium to low heat for several hours until relish turns a deep red color and is very thick.

Put in sterile jars and seal.

This is excellent on hamburger patties, leftover roast, and black-eyed peas. It can be made with canned tomatoes (about 7 large cans of a good brand) and frozen chopped onions and green peppers.

YIELD: 6–8 HALF PINTS

Southern Sideboards
THE JUNIOR LEAGUE OF JACKSON, MISSISSIPPI

·   ·   ·   ·   ·   ·   ·   ·   ·   ·   ·   ·   ·   ·   ·   ·

Green Tomato Pickle

1 peck green tomatoes
2 quarts onions
Salt
2 quarts vinegar
2 pounds brown sugar
½ pound white mustard seed
½ ounce ground mace
1 tablespoon celery seed
1 tablespoon ground cloves
½ tablespoon cayenne
1 tablespoon dry mustard
1 teaspoon turmeric
½ cup olive oil

Slice tomatoes and onions very thin. Place on large platters and sprinkle with salt. Let stand overnight. Drain through colander.

Add 1 quart vinegar to vegetables and boil slowly until tender and clear. Drain.

Mix sugar, mustard seed, mace, celery seed, and cloves with remaining vinegar and boil 5 minutes. Mix drained vegetables with cayenne, mustard, and turmeric and add to vinegar mixture. Mix well, add olive oil, and seal in jars.

YIELD: 8 QUARTS

Charleston Receipts
THE JUNIOR LEAGUE OF CHARLESTON, SOUTH CAROLINA

Quick Corn Relish

¼ cup sugar
½ teaspoon salt
½ teaspoon celery seed
¼ teaspoon mustard seed
½ cup vinegar
¼ teaspoon Tabasco
1 12-ounce can whole kernel corn
2 tablespoons chopped green pepper
1 tablespoon chopped pimento
1 tablespoon instant minced onion

In small pan, heat sugar, salt, seeds, vinegar, and Tabasco to boiling. Boil 2 minutes.

Remove from heat, and stir in remaining ingredients. Cool and refrigerate. For better flavor, let stand several days.

YIELD: ABOUT 1 CUP

The Blue Denim Gourmet
THE JUNIOR LEAGUE OF ODESSA, TEXAS

Jerusalem Artichoke Relish

3 quarts (4 pounds) Jerusalem artichokes
1 quart (2 pounds) ground onions
6 green peppers, ground
2 heads cauliflower, broken into small flowerets
1 gallon water
1 pint salt
½ cup flour
2 cups sugar
2 tablespoons dry mustard
1 tablespoon turmeric
2½ quarts white vinegar
2 4-ounce jars pimentos, chopped
1 tablespoon mustard seed
2 teaspoons celery seed

Scrub and chop artichokes. Add ground onions, peppers, and cauliflower. Soak overnight in water with salt. Drain well in colander and rinse with clear water.

Mix flour, sugar, mustard, and turmeric and add enough vinegar to make a paste. Heat remaining vinegar in large roaster or preserving kettle and add paste mixture. Cook about 5 minutes to blend. Add vegetables, pimento, mustard seed, and celery seed and bring to a boil.

Seal in pint jars.

YIELD: 8–10 PINTS

Home Cookin'
THE JUNIOR LEAGUE OF WICHITA FALLS, TEXAS

Jane's Cucumber Pickle

4 quarts sliced cucumbers
1½ cups sliced white onion
2 large cloves garlic
½ cup salt
4 cups sugar
1½ teaspoons turmeric
1½ teaspoons mustard seed
3 cups white vinegar

Wash, drain, and slice cucumbers. Add onion, garlic, and salt. Mix thoroughly. Cover with ice and allow to stand 3 hours in a crock.

Remove garlic. Combine remaining ingredients and heat to boiling; add cucumbers and onion to this mixture. Return to boil, lower heat, and heat 5 minutes. Fill sterilized jars ½ inch from top. Process 5 minutes in boiling water.

YIELD: 5–6 PINTS

Mountain Measures
THE JUNIOR LEAGUE OF CHARLESTON, WEST VIRGINIA

· · · · · · · · · · · · · · ·

Buffet Pickles

1 large onion
6 small cucumbers
2 tablespoons sugar
1 teaspoon dill seed
¼ cup cold water
1 tablespoon salt
½ cup white vinegar

Slice onion and cucumbers thin. Pack in quart jar. Combine remaining ingredients and pour over cucumbers and onion.

Recipe continues . . .

Cover and refrigerate for several days.
As pickles are used, add more cucumbers to liquid.

YIELD: 1 QUART

Fun Foods
THE JUNIOR LEAGUE OF GREATER LAKELAND, FLORIDA

.   .   .   .

Bread and Butter Pickles

These are called bread and butter pickles because they are delicious when
served with just bread and butter!

6 quarts cucumbers
1 quart sliced onions (optional)
4 sweet green peppers
9 cups water
1 cup salt
3 pints vinegar
3 pounds white sugar
1 tablespoon turmeric
1 teaspoon white mustard seed
1 teaspoon celery seed

Wash and slice cucumbers without peeling. Combine with onions and
peppers. Cover vegetables with water mixed with salt. Let stand 3 hours.
Drain.

Combine remaining ingredients and heat to boiling.

Add vegetables. Bring to boiling point again but do not boil. Seal in
sterilized jars.

Chill before serving.

YIELD: APPROXIMATELY 12 QUARTS

The Cotton Blossom Cookbook
THE JUNIOR LEAGUE OF ATLANTA, GEORGIA

.   .   .   .

Centennial Pickled Peaches

5–10 whole cloves
6–12 sticks cinnamon
2 tablespoons whole allspice
1 quart water
1 pint vinegar
2 quarts sugar
Peaches

Put spices in cloth bag and boil in the water mixed with vinegar and sugar. Peel peaches and add to liquid. Cook until tender.

Put in hot sterilized jars and pour hot syrup over and seal.

YIELD: 12 PINTS

Home Cookin'
THE JUNIOR LEAGUE OF WICHITA FALLS, TEXAS

Pickled Squash

2 pounds yellow or summer squash
3 medium onions
¼ cup salt
2 cups white vinegar
2 cups sugar
1 teaspoon celery seed
1 teaspoon turmeric
2 teaspoons mustard seed

Wash squash and slice thin. Peel onions and slice thin. Cover both with water and add salt. Let stand 1–2 hours. Drain.

Bring vinegar, sugar, and seasonings to boil and pour over vegetables. Let stand 3–4 minutes. Bring to boil, stirring, and boil 4 minutes.

Pour into hot sterilized jars and seal.

YIELD: ABOUT 4 PINTS

Southern Accent
THE JUNIOR LEAGUE OF PINE BLUFF, ARKANSAS

Pickled Okra

3¼ pounds okra
1 quart white vinegar
2 tablespoons salt
2 tablespoons pepper
1 tablespoon dry parsley flakes
1 tablespoon dill weed
1 clove garlic, crushed
1 tablespoon Worcestershire sauce
1 teaspoon Tabasco
3 cloves
1 medium onion, chopped

Wash okra; soak in cold water 1 hour. Place in hot sterilized jars. Put other ingredients in pan; bring to boil. Pour over okra in hot jars. Seal.

Okra is better if refrigerated a day before using, to insure crispness.

YIELD: 4 PINTS

Huntsville Heritage Cookbook
THE JUNIOR LEAGUE OF HUNTSVILLE, ALABAMA

Watermelon Pickle

3½ pounds watermelon rind (about ½ watermelon)
2 teaspoons alum
3½ pounds sugar
½ cup water
1½ cups cider vinegar
¼ teaspoon oil of cloves
¼ teaspoon oil of cinnamon
Cinnamon sticks
Whole cloves

Trim off dark green part of rind and most of the pink pulp. Cut rind into strips 1 inch by ½ inch wide. Parboil rind until tender (about 1 hour) but not soft or mushy. Drain well in colander. Place in crock, glass, or enamel bowl and cover with enough ice cubes so that when ice melts it will provide ice water to cover rind. When ice has melted, sprinkle alum over rind. Leave in ice water 4 hours.

Combine sugar, water, vinegar, oil of cloves, and oil of cinnamon in saucepan and bring to a boil.

Pour ice water from rind in colander. Drain well. Return rind to bowl and pour heated mixture over rind. Cover with lid, plate, or heavy towel and allow to stand at room temperature for 4 nights.

During the 4-day standing period, drain off syrup mixture and heat to boiling point each morning; pour syrup back over rind and cover. On the fourth day place rind in clean jars with tight-fitting lids; add the heated syrup and one cinnamon stick and several whole cloves per jar. Seal with wax paper and lids and refrigerate.

Pickles should be allowed to mellow several weeks before use.

Serve with beef, pork, or fowl.

YIELD: 4 PINTS

Mountain Measures
THE JUNIOR LEAGUE OF CHARLESTON, WEST VIRGINIA

. . . .

Savory Sauces

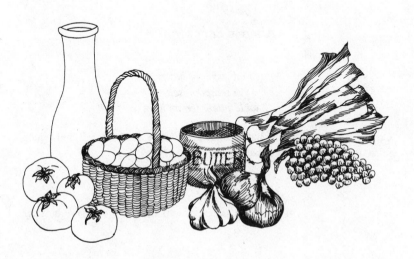

Parsley and Garlic Butter Sauce for Fish

2 tablespoons chopped parsley
2 cloves garlic, crushed
½ cup melted butter

Add parsley and garlic to melted butter and use to baste any bland fish or pour over cooked fish. May also be used for dipping fish.

YIELD: ½ CUP

Seafood Sorcery
THE JUNIOR LEAGUE OF WILMINGTON, NORTH CAROLINA

. . . .

Almond Sauce for Fish

½ cup almonds, slivered
3 tablespoons butter
½ teaspoon salt
2 tablespoons lemon juice

Cook the almonds in the butter until golden tan. Add the salt and lemon juice. Pour over broiled or baked fish.

YIELD: ¾ CUP

Seafood Sorcery
THE JUNIOR LEAGUE OF WILMINGTON, NORTH CAROLINA

. . . .

Grape Sauce for Fish

¼ cup butter
½ cup white wine
1 cup white seedless grapes

Simmer all ingredients gently for 8 minutes. Serve on broiled fish.

YIELD: 1¾ CUPS

Seafood Sorcery
THE JUNIOR LEAGUE OF WILMINGTON, NORTH CAROLINA

· · · · · · · · · · · · · · · · · · · ·

Tennessee Blender Hollandaise Sauce

3 egg yolks
2 tablespoons lemon juice
½ teaspoon salt
⅛ teaspoon pepper
½ cup soft butter
½ cup boiling water

Put all ingredients except water in blender container. Blend until smooth. Add boiling water slowly as you continue blending.

Pour in top of double boiler and stir often over boiling water until sauce thickens. Remove from heat immediately.

Can be kept indefinitely in refrigerator and may be reheated.

YIELD: ABOUT 1½ CUPS

Nashville Seasons Encore
THE JUNIOR LEAGUE OF NASHVILLE, TENNESSEE

· · · · · · · · · · · · · · · · · · ·

Carolina Blender Hollandaise Sauce

This is the only "can't fail" that really can't fail.

½ pound butter or margarine
4 egg yolks
2 tablespoons lemon juice
¼ teaspoon salt
Pinch cayenne

Heat butter or margarine just to bubbling. Put egg yolks, lemon juice, salt, and cayenne into blender jar. Cover; turn blender on high speed. Immediately remove cover and add hot butter in steady stream.

To keep, store in refrigerator.

YIELD: 1¼ CUPS

Spartanburg Secrets II
THE JUNIOR LEAGUE OF SPARTANBURG, SOUTH CAROLINA

· · · · · · · · · · · · · · · · · ·

Pit Barbecue Sauce

½ pound butter
1 pint catsup
1 pint vinegar
1 tablespoon Tabasco
½ cup Worcestershire sauce
1 tablespoon brown sugar
1 tablespoon onion juice
1½ cloves garlic, chopped fine
Dash red pepper
Dash black pepper
1–3 tablespoons salt

Bring all ingredients to a boil. Add more salt if desired.
Save leftover sauce. Refrigeration is not necessary.

YIELD: SLIGHTLY LESS THAN 2 QUARTS

The Memphis Cook Book
THE JUNIOR LEAGUE OF MEMPHIS, TENNESSEE

. . . .

Georgia Barbecue Sauce

1 9-ounce jar prepared mustard
⅔ cup sugar
1 14-ounce bottle catsup
⅛–¼ teaspoon cayenne
1–2 cups distilled vinegar (depending on thickness desired)

Mix mustard and sugar well in large pan on top of stove. Mix in catsup
and cayenne; then add vinegar. Simmer about 15 minutes. Excellent with
pork or chicken.

YIELD: 1 QUART

Winston-Salem's Heritage of Hospitality
THE JUNIOR LEAGUE OF WINSTON-SALEM, NORTH CAROLINA

. . . .

George Major's Barbecue Sauce for Chicken

2 sticks butter
Juice and rind of 2 lemons
2 onions
1 10-ounce bottle Worcestershire sauce
2 6-ounce bottles steak sauce

Recipe continues . . .

Melt butter in saucepan. Squeeze lemon juice into melted butter. Cut onions into six slices and add with lemon rinds to butter mixture. Simmer 20 minutes. Add Worcestershire and steak sauces, simmering an additional 5 minutes.

Use generously on chicken roasted on a barbecue pit.

YIELD: ABOUT 3 CUPS

Recipe Jubilee
THE JUNIOR LEAGUE OF MOBILE, ALABAMA

Huntsville Barbecue Sauce

¼ cup olive or salad oil
¾ cup chopped onion
1 clove garlic, chopped
1 cup honey
1 cup catsup
1 cup wine vinegar
½ cup Worcestershire sauce
1 tablespoon dry mustard
1½ teaspoons salt
1 teaspoon oregano
1 teaspoon black pepper
½ teaspoon thyme

Put oil in large pot and sauté onions and garlic. Add remaining ingredients and simmer 20 minutes, stirring frequently.

Especially good for basting chicken or pork chops. Can be stored in refrigerator.

YIELD: ABOUT 1 QUART

Huntsville Heritage Cookbook
THE JUNIOR LEAGUE OF HUNTSVILLE, ALABAMA

Barbecue Sauce for Pork (Backbone or Spareribs)

1 cup butter
½ cup lemon juice
4 tablespoons horseradish
4 tablespoons vinegar
4 tablespoons catsup
4 teaspoons salt
3 teaspoons Worcestershire sauce
1½ teaspoons Tabasco
Garlic to taste

Combine all ingredients.

Cook ribs until almost done in foil in oven if desired, then put on grill and baste frequently with sauce. Or cook very slowly on grill, basting often.

YIELD: ABOUT 2 CUPS

Furniture City Feasts
THE JUNIOR LEAGUE OF HIGH POINT, NORTH CAROLINA

Tartar Sauce for Fish

1 cup mayonnaise
1 teaspoon finely minced onion
1 tablespoon capers
1 teaspoon finely minced pickle
1 tablespoon tarragon vinegar

Mix and chill. May substitute pickle relish for pickle.

YIELD: 1¼ CUPS

Seafood Sorcery
THE JUNIOR LEAGUE OF WILMINGTON, NORTH CAROLINA

Cocktail Sauce

2 tablespoons lemon juice
1 cup catsup
1 tablespoon finely chopped celery
1 tablespoon horseradish
1 tablespoon finely chopped onion
1 teaspoon Worcestershire sauce
½ teaspoon salt
3 drops Tabasco

Combine all ingredients, mix thoroughly, and chill.

YIELD: 1¼ CUPS

Seafood Sorcery
THE JUNIOR LEAGUE OF WILMINGTON, NORTH CAROLINA

. . . .

Cocktail Sauce for Shrimp, Crab, or Raw Vegetables

1 cup mayonnaise
1 teaspoon lemon juice
1 teaspoon curry powder
½ teaspoon finely minced onion
½ teaspoon Worcestershire sauce
½ teaspoon Tabasco
¼ cup chili sauce
Salt and pepper to taste

Mix all ingredients well and keep in refrigerator until ready to serve.

YIELD: ABOUT 1¼ CUPS

Charleston Receipts
THE JUNIOR LEAGUE OF CHARLESTON, SOUTH CAROLINA

. . . .

Blender Béarnaise Sauce for Fish or Beef

2 teaspoons dried tarragon
2 tablespoons white vinegar
¼ teaspoon dry mustard
3 green onions, chopped fine
2 large eggs
3 tablespoons white vinegar
1 teaspoon salt
Dash Tabasco
½ teaspoon Worcestershire sauce
1 pint salad oil

Soak the tarragon in 2 tablespoons vinegar for 5 minutes. Add the mustard and the green onions. Set aside.

Blend the eggs, 3 tablespoons white vinegar, salt, Tabasco, and Worcestershire sauce together on slow speed for 15 seconds. Turn speed control to high and slowly add the salad oil until the sauce is thick. Turn off blender and add the tarragon mixture. Blend well for 15 seconds.

For fillet of flounder (or other fish): Bake fillets and just as they begin to flake, coat generously with Béarnaise Sauce and return to cook until done. The broiler may be turned on at this point, but watch carefully, and remove when the fillets are just slightly brown.

For fillet of beef: Chop a dill pickle fine. Place in clean dish towel and squeeze juice from pickle. Add to the Béarnaise Sauce. Serve this sauce on the side of cooked fillet.

YIELD: ABOUT 2½ CUPS

Gator Country Cooks
THE JUNIOR LEAGUE OF GAINESVILLE, FLORIDA

Curry Sauce for Chicken or Lamb

½ cup chopped celery
½ cup chopped onion
1 cup butter
2 tablespoons ground cumin
2 tablespoons turmeric
2 tablespoons ground coriander
½ teaspoon cayenne
1 teaspoon salt
¾ cup flour
3 cups chicken broth
2 cups milk
1 cup heavy cream
1 tablespoon lemon juice

Sauté celery and onion in butter until onions are yellow. Add spices and salt and cook, stirring over low heat for 4 minutes. Add flour and stir over low heat for 5 minutes. Add chicken broth and bring to a boil, stirring with a wire whisk. Boil, stirring, for 2 minutes. Turn off heat and add milk. Simmer for 10 minutes stirring occasionally. Add cream and lemon juice and cook 2 minutes more.

Add 6 cups of chicken or lamb and simmer about 15 minutes and serve.

The sauce may be made the day before. It will thicken when refrigerated and thin out when heated.

YIELD: 12 SERVINGS

The Dallas Jr. League Cookbook
THE JUNIOR LEAGUE OF DALLAS, TEXAS

Tomato Sauce

½ cup olive oil
1 green pepper, finely chopped
2 medium onions, finely chopped
2 stalks celery, finely chopped
1 clove garlic, finely chopped
3 sprigs parsley, finely chopped
2 pounds coarsely ground lean beef
½ teaspoon sugar
1 teaspoon salt
¼ teaspoon freshly ground pepper
½ teaspoon oregano
½ teaspoon bitters
1 teaspoon Worcestershire sauce
2 bay leaves
1 teaspoon monosodium glutamate
3 6-ounce cans tomato paste
1 1-gallon can tomato purée (Italian-style tomatoes are best)
2 cups very dry red wine
1 8-ounce can whole mushrooms (optional)

Heat olive oil in large skillet; add and cook until lightly browned all the chopped vegetables. Add beef, and stir until brown. Add remaining ingredients (except mushrooms), and simmer very slowly for 2 hours. If sauce is too thick, thin with tomato juice.

Remove bay leaves; add mushrooms.

A delicious sauce for spaghetti, lasagna, manicotti, pizza, or omelets, or as a base for chili. The sauce will freeze well.

YIELD: 6 QUARTS

The Gasparilla Cookbook
THE JUNIOR LEAGUE OF TAMPA, FLORIDA

Louisiana Marchand de Vin Sauce

2 tablespoons fat
2 tablespoons flour
1 small onion, finely chopped
2 cups chicken or beef broth
3 tablespoons tomato sauce
Salt and pepper
4 shallots, chopped fine
4 tablespoons butter
½ cup red wine
1 tablespoon butter
Dash lemon juice

Make a roux with fat and flour. Add onion and cook until wilted. Add broth and tomato sauce and cook until thickened. Simmer down to 1 cup and season to taste with salt and pepper.

Sauté shallots in 4 tablespoons butter. Add the red wine and reduce liquid by half. Add to tomato sauce mixture and simmer a few minutes. Add remaining butter and lemon juice. Serve over steak.

YIELD: ABOUT 1½ CUPS

Talk About Good!
THE JUNIOR LEAGUE OF LAFAYETTE, LOUISIANA

Alabama Marchand de Vin Sauce

½ stick butter
2 cloves garlic, chopped fine
3 green onions, chopped
¼ teaspoon freshly ground black pepper
Pinch marjoram
½ cup red wine
1 tablespoon flour
3 cups beef stock
½ pound mushrooms, sautéed in butter
2 tablespoons sherry
2 tablespoons brandy
Salt

Braise in butter: garlic, green onions, pepper, and marjoram. Add red wine. Cook to a paste. Add flour and beef stock. Simmer until reduced by half. Add sautéed mushrooms, sherry, and brandy. Season to taste with salt.

YIELD: ABOUT 2 CUPS

Recipe Jubilee
THE JUNIOR LEAGUE OF MOBILE, ALABAMA

· · · · · · · · · · · · · · · ·

Sour Cream Sauce for Roast Beef or Steak

1 teaspoon sugar
1 teaspoon vinegar
1½ tablespoons moist horseradish
Several drops Worcestershire sauce
1 cup sour cream
Paprika

Mix ingredients well and add paprika for color. Refrigerate until used.

YIELD: ABOUT 1 CUP

That Something Special
THE JUNIOR LEAGUE OF DURHAM, NORTH CAROLINA

Eggs, Cheese, and Pasta

Fried Cheese Patties

1 pound creamed cottage cheese
2 eggs
1 cup flour
1 teaspoon salt
2 tablespoons sugar
¼ cup butter
1 cup sour cream

In large bowl mix cheese, eggs, flour, salt, and sugar. (Mixture will be thick.)

Melt butter in 12-inch skillet over medium heat. Drop five ½-cup mounds of cheese mixture in hot butter. Using a pancake turner, shape each mound into a 3-inch round patty. Fry 8–10 minutes until lightly browned, turning once. Remove patties to a warm platter and keep warm.

Repeat with remaining mixture to make 10 patties.

To serve, dot with sour cream and sprinkle with sugar.

YIELD: 10 PATTIES

Southern Accent
THE JUNIOR LEAGUE OF PINE BLUFF, ARKANSAS

· · · · · · · · · · · · · · ·

Snappy Cheese Bake

2 4-ounce cans green chilies
1 pound cheddar cheese, shredded
6 eggs
1½ cups biscuit mix
1 quart milk

Butter a 12 × 7-inch shallow baking dish. Split and seed chilies; spread flat on bottom of dish and cover with cheese.

Beat eggs, biscuit mix, and milk, and pour over cheese. Bake at 350° for 1 hour.

A nice change from potatoes or rice, or may be used as a base for meat sauce, creamed dishes, etc.

YIELD: 8 SERVINGS

Home Cookin'
THE JUNIOR LEAGUE OF WICHITA FALLS, TEXAS

.   .   .   .

Sausage Strata

6 slices bread
1½ pounds pork sausage
1 teaspoon prepared mustard
1 cup (¼ pound) shredded Swiss cheese
4 eggs, slightly beaten
1½ cups milk
¾ cup light cream
½ teaspoon salt
Dash pepper
Dash nutmeg
1 teaspoon Worcestershire sauce

Trim crust from bread and fit bread into bottom of greased 10 × 16 × 1½-inch casserole. Brown sausage. Drain off all excess fat. Stir in mustard. Spoon sausage evenly over bread and sprinkle with cheese. Combine remaining ingredients and pour over cheese and sausage. Bake at 350° for 25–30 minutes.

This can be made early in the afternoon and put in refrigerator until time to bake.

YIELD: 6 SERVINGS

Furniture City Feasts
THE JUNIOR LEAGUE OF HIGH POINT, NORTH CAROLINA

.   .   .   .

Hot Crab Sandwich

16 slices bread
8 slices Old English cheddar cheese
2 6½-ounce cans crabmeat
5 eggs
3⅓ cups milk
1 teaspoon Worcestershire sauce
Dash cayenne
1½ teaspoons salt
1½ cups cornflakes
1 stick butter, melted

Remove bread crusts. Arrange 8 bread slices in buttered 9¾ × 15-inch baking dish. Top each slice with cheese slice; sprinkle with crabmeat. Top with remaining bread slices.

Beat eggs, milk, and seasonings; pour over sandwiches. Cover dish with plastic wrap; refrigerate overnight.

One hour before serving, sprinkle with cornflakes and drizzle with melted butter. Bake 1 hour at 350°.

Delicious with citrus fruit salad.

YIELD: 8 SERVINGS

Huntsville Heritage Cookbook
THE JUNIOR LEAGUE OF HUNTSVILLE, ALABAMA

Cheese Strata

6 slices bread, buttered
½ pound sliced American cheese
3 eggs, beaten
2 cups half and half
Pinch salt

Remove bread crusts. In small buttered casserole, layer 3 bread slices, then half of cheese. Repeat. Mix eggs, milk, and salt; pour into casserole. Refrigerate several hours or overnight. Set in pan of hot water; bake 40–60 minutes at 325° or until knife stuck in center comes out clean.

YIELD: 4 SERVINGS

Huntsville Heritage Cookbook
THE JUNIOR LEAGUE OF HUNTSVILLE, ALABAMA

· · · · · · · · · · · · ·

Mac's Brunch Egg Casserole

¼ cup butter
¼ cup flour
1 cup milk
1 cup light cream
¼ teaspoon thyme
¼ teaspoon marjoram
¼ teaspoon basil
¾ pound sharp cheddar cheese, shredded
1½ dozen hard-boiled eggs, sliced thin
1 pound bacon, sautéed, drained, crumbled
¼ cup finely chopped parsley
Buttered bread crumbs

Melt butter in saucepan. Stir in flour. Gradually stir in milk and cream and cook, stirring, until cream sauce is smooth and thickened.

Add thyme, marjoram, basil, and cheese, and cook, stirring, until cheese is melted.

Place layer of sliced eggs in casserole; sprinkle bacon over eggs; sprinkle parsley over bacon. Add layer of cheese sauce. Repeat two more

Recipe continues . . .

layers. Sprinkle top with buttered bread crumbs. Bake uncovered at 350° for 30 minutes. Can be made a day ahead.

YIELD: 10 SERVINGS

That Something Special
THE JUNIOR LEAGUE OF DURHAM, NORTH CAROLINA

. . . .

Quiche Lorraine

PASTRY:
1 cup flour
½ teaspoon salt
½ cup butter or margarine
3–4 tablespoons cold water

Sift flour and salt together; cut in butter or margarine. Add water and work into dough. Roll out on lightly floured board. Place in oblong ovenproof dish or pie pan.

QUICHE FILLING:
½ pound bacon, fried until crisp
1 pound Swiss or American cheese, shredded
3 whole eggs, slightly beaten
2 cups milk or light cream
1 teaspoon salt
Red and black pepper to taste
Dash Worcestershire sauce
Dash Tabasco
1 medium onion, minced
1 4-ounce can mushrooms (optional)
2 tablespoons butter
Paprika

Crumble bacon into pie shell; cover with cheese. Mix eggs, milk or cream, salt, peppers, Worcestershire sauce, and Tabasco. Set aside.

Sauté minced onion and mushrooms in butter until onion is transparent. Add them to egg mixture. Pour over cheese and bacon layers. Garnish with paprika.

Bake at 400° for 35–45 minutes.

Allow to cool for about 5 minutes before serving.

This makes a wonderful Sunday night supper, served with a fruit bowl.

NOTE: See other quiche recipes in Index.

YIELD: 4 SERVINGS

A Cook's Tour of Shreveport
THE JUNIOR LEAGUE OF SHREVEPORT, LOUISIANA

· · · · · · · · · · · · · · · ·

French Egg Casserole

¼ cup butter
¼ cup flour
1 cup nondairy creamer
2 cups boiling water
¾ teaspoon salt
Pinch cayenne
⅛ teaspoon white pepper
½ pound Gruyère cheese, shredded
1 tablespoon prepared mustard
2 egg yolks, beaten with 2 tablespoons water
½ cup butter
4 large onions, sliced thin
¼ pound fresh mushrooms, sliced thin
12 hard-boiled eggs
Paprika

In heavy saucepan, melt ¼ cup butter over low heat until frothy. Blend in flour with wire whisk and cook, stirring, for 1 minute. (Do not allow to

Recipe continues . . .

brown.) Add the creamer, then boiling water all at once, beating with wire whisk to blend. Increase heat to moderately high. Cook until sauce comes to a boil and thickens, stirring constantly. Fold in seasonings, cheese, and mustard. Continue stirring and cook *only* until cheese melts.

Remove from fire; add egg yolks which have been beaten with 2 table-spoons water. Return to fire and heat until *just* heated through. Do not boil!

Melt ½ cup butter in a skillet. Sauté onions until tender. Remove onions, add mushrooms to skillet, and sauté until tender. Mix onions and mushrooms and place in a shallow 2-quart casserole. Blend in 1 cup of sauce. Cut each egg into 4 slices and layer over vegetables. Top with re-maining sauce and sprinkle with paprika.

Bake at 350° for 15 minutes, then brown *briefly* under broiler.

YIELD: 8 SERVINGS

Southern Accent
THE JUNIOR LEAGUE OF PINE BLUFF, ARKANSAS

. . . .

Deviled Eggs and Asparagus

2 10-ounce packages frozen asparagus
10 hard-boiled eggs
1 6-ounce can deviled ham
1 teaspoon grated onion
½ teaspoon Worcestershire sauce
¾ teaspoon dry mustard
1 teaspoon heavy cream
6 tablespoons butter
6 tablespoons flour
3 cups milk
2 cups shredded cheddar cheese
¼ teaspoon dry mustard
1 teaspoon salt
Dash pepper
2 cups crushed cornflakes
2 tablespoons melted butter

Cook asparagus according to directions on package; drain and cut up. Place on the bottom of a buttered casserole.

Slice eggs in half. Mix yolks with ham, onion, Worcestershire, ¾ teaspoon dry mustard, and cream. Stuff egg whites and place on top of asparagus.

Make a cheese sauce by melting butter in a saucepan and adding flour. Gradually add milk; stir until thick. Add cheese, ¼ teaspoon dry mustard, 1 teaspoon salt, and dash pepper and pour over casserole. Top with crushed cornflakes mixed with melted butter.

Bake at 350° for 20 minutes.

YIELD: 8–10 SERVINGS

Little Rock Cooks

THE JUNIOR LEAGUE OF LITTLE ROCK, ARKANSAS

·   ·   ·   ·   ·   ·   ·   ·   ·   ·   ·   ·   ·

Cheese Soufflé

Guaranteed not to fall!

¾ cup milk
¼ cup butter
¼ cup flour
½ pound sharp cheddar cheese, shredded
½ teaspoon salt
6 eggs, separated
1½ tablespoons cold water

For this dish, upstate New York hoop cheese with a good snappy taste is preferred. Never use soft processed cheese.

First make cream sauce as follows: Scald but do not boil milk. Melt butter in flat-bottomed saucepan, blend in flour, add milk, and beat with wire whisk until smooth. Cook over low heat, stirring constantly until thick. Add shredded cheese and cook till smooth. Cool; stir in salt and beaten egg yolks.

Recipe continues ...

Using an electric or rotary beater, whip the whites with the cold water until stiff and dry. Fold the cheese mixture *into* the egg whites; keep turning the bowl and folding until it is blended.

Pour into a *hot* buttered 2-quart casserole and place in pan of hot water.

Bake 10 minutes at 400°. Reduce heat to 325° and bake 20 minutes longer. *Do not peep* for at least 20 minutes!

The secret of this soufflé is in the beating of the whites. A good rule is to beat them until you fall down, get up and beat again!

YIELD: 4–6 SERVINGS

> *Spartanburg Secrets II*
> THE JUNIOR LEAGUE OF SPARTANBURG, SOUTH CAROLINA

· · · · · · · · · · · · · · · ·

Peña Blanca Eggs

Olive oil
6 cloves garlic
Oregano
Salt
Parsley
6 eggs

Pour into large muffin tins enough olive oil to cover bottoms. To each tin add 1 clove garlic, dash of oregano, salt, and parsley. Put in preheated 400° oven.

When the container is spitting oil, remove from oven and remove garlic. Drop an egg into each container. The eggs cook without returning to the oven. Cover with Chili Sauce to serve.

YIELD: 6 SERVINGS

CHILI SAUCE:
1 tomato, chopped
1 jalapeño pepper, chopped and seeded
1 small onion, chopped
Salt and pepper
Chopped fresh cilantro (or 1 teaspoon ground coriander)

Mix all ingredients together. Cover eggs with sauce to serve. Sauce may be kept covered in refrigerator.

> *Seasoned with Sun: Recipes from the Southwest*
> THE JUNIOR LEAGUE OF EL PASO, TEXAS

·   ·   ·   ·   ·   ·   ·   ·   ·   ·   ·   ·   ·   ·   ·   ·   ·

Creole Eggs

3 onions, chopped
3 green peppers, chopped
2 cloves garlic
1 stick butter
2 1-pound cans tomatoes
½ cup flour
1 pint milk
Salt and pepper
10 hard-boiled eggs, sliced
Cracker crumbs

Brown onions, peppers, and garlic in 2 tablespoons butter. Add tomatoes; simmer.

Make thick white sauce of remaining butter, flour, milk, and seasonings. Blend with tomato mixture.

In greased casserole, alternate layers of eggs, tomato sauce, and crumbs. Bake at 350° for a half hour.

YIELD: 6 SERVINGS

> *Huntsville Heritage Cookbook*
> THE JUNIOR LEAGUE OF HUNTSVILLE, ALABAMA

·   ·   ·   ·   ·   ·   ·   ·   ·   ·   ·   ·   ·   ·   ·   ·   ·

Capered Eggs

1 dozen hard-boiled eggs, halved
1 minced jalapeño pepper with juice
2 cups mayonnaise
1 cup sour cream
1 2¼-ounce bottle capers, undrained
Dash red pepper
¼ cup fresh or frozen chives
2 teaspoons dill weed
2 teaspoons chopped parsley, fresh or dry
½ medium onion, minced
Seasoned salt
Pepper

Arrange egg halves in 9 × 13-inch ovenproof glass baking dish and top each with jalapeño pepper and a little juice.

Mix all other ingredients and pour over eggs.

Bake at 200° for 30 minutes.

YIELD: 12 SERVINGS

Home Cookin'
THE JUNIOR LEAGUE OF WICHITA FALLS, TEXAS

·   ·   ·   ·   ·   ·   ·   ·   ·   ·   ·   ·   ·   ·   ·

Eggs Hussarde

Canadian bacon
English muffins, split
Butter
Marchand de Vin Sauce
Tomato slices
Poached eggs
Hollandaise Sauce (see Index)
Paprika

Lay slices of grilled Canadian bacon cut ¼ inch thick on buttered, toasted halves of English muffins. Cover with Marchand de Vin Sauce. Top with uncooked or grilled tomato slices, then soft-poached eggs. Ladle Hollandaise Sauce over all and garnish with paprika.

Two servings each will satisfy even the hungriest of men.

NOTE: You can poach a number of eggs at a time by placing eggs in well-greased muffin tins. Place muffin tins over large pan of boiling water and seal tightly with an aluminum foil tent. Watch closely or eggs will cook hard. Or break eggs into greased ramekins, place ramekins in utensil containing 1 inch of boiling water, and cover.

MARCHAND DE VIN SAUCE:
½ cup butter (no substitutes)
⅓ cup finely chopped mushrooms
½ cup minced ham
⅓ cup shallots, finely chopped, or green onions
½ cup finely chopped onion
2 or 3 cloves garlic, minced
2 tablespoons flour
⅛ teaspoon pepper
Dash cayenne
¾ cup beef stock
½ cup claret

In a skillet, melt butter and lightly sauté the mushrooms, ham, shallots, onion, and garlic. When the onion is tender, add the flour, pepper, and cayenne. Brown about 7–10 minutes, stirring constantly. Blend in the stock and wine. Cover and simmer over low heat about 30 minutes, stirring now and then.

The sauce can be made ahead and reheated very slowly. Eggs Hussarde can be cooked and assembled in about 30 minutes if the Marchand de Vin Sauce is made ahead.

YIELD: 1½ CUPS

Party Potpourri
THE JUNIOR LEAGUE OF MEMPHIS, TENNESSEE

Oeufs à la Procter

6 medium, firm tomatoes
1 pound chicken livers, preferably fresh
½ stick butter
¼ cup finely chopped onion
Salt
Black pepper
1 4-ounce can sliced or button mushrooms, drained
Fresh bread crumbs
4 sprigs parsley, chopped
2 tablespoons chopped green onion
6 eggs
Butter
White pepper
6 slices crisp buttered toast

Scoop out tomatoes. Cut chicken livers into two or three pieces each and sauté in iron skillet with ½ stick butter and chopped onion. Season lightly with salt and black pepper and add mushrooms. Simmer until tender.

Add 4 tablespoons of pulp scooped from center of tomatoes and cook with rest of sauce until slightly thickened. If too thin, add a little fresh bread crumbs until right consistency. Add parsley and green onion.

Pour ingredients into tomatoes and top each with a raw egg and dab of butter. Sprinkle egg lightly with salt and white pepper. Place tomatoes on cookie sheet and bake at 350° until egg is poached.

Serve on hot crisp buttered toast. Delicious for brunch.

YIELD: 6 SERVINGS

Talk About Good!
THE JUNIOR LEAGUE OF LAFAYETTE, LOUISIANA

Chiliquillas

A Mexican brunch dish.

10 or 11 tortillas, cut into bite-size pieces
Cooking oil
Salt
1 large tomato, peeled and chopped
½ onion, chopped
1 or ½ fresh jalapeño pepper, minced
4 eggs
Sour cream
Mozzarella cheese, finely shredded

Fry the tortillas until crisp in hot oil. Pour off most of the grease, leaving enough to cook the eggs in. Salt the pan of tortillas well.

Mix together the tomato, onion, jalapeño, and eggs. Add to the skillet of crisp tortillas and scramble together until the eggs are done.

Put the sour cream and shredded cheese over each serving.

Excellent with a fresh fruit salad and hot coffee or Mexican hot chocolate.

YIELD: 3–4 SERVINGS

The Dallas Jr. League Cookbook
THE JUNIOR LEAGUE OF DALLAS, TEXAS

. . . .

Party Eggs

3 dozen eggs
1⅓ cups light cream
3 teaspoons salt
Pepper to taste
¼ cup butter
2 cups medium cream sauce (see page 355)
Chopped parsley

Recipe continues . . .

Beat eggs with cream, salt, and pepper.

Melt butter in large frying pan. Pour in egg mixture, stirring occasionally until almost set. Fold in hot white sauce while eggs are still creamy. Keep hot in a very slow oven (140°–200°) or place over hot water on top of range. Sprinkle with parsley.

These eggs are great for late-night breakfast. They stay very moist in a chafing dish. They can also be served over hot toast with deviled ham.

YIELD: 18 SERVINGS

Little Rock Cooks

THE JUNIOR LEAGUE OF LITTLE ROCK, ARKANSAS

Meat Balls and Spaghetti

1½ pounds ground chuck
1 cup grated Parmesan cheese
8 small crackers, soaked in water and squeezed
3 large eggs
2 teaspoons salt
1 teaspoon pepper
2 dashes Tabasco
1 large bunch green onions, chopped
½ cup olive oil
2 8-ounce cans tomato purée
2 pints water
2 large cloves garlic, minced
1 cup finely chopped parsley
1 teaspoon salt
½ teaspoon red pepper
1 teaspoon oregano
Additional grated Parmesan cheese

Combine first seven ingredients. Make into small meat balls about 1½ inches in diameter. Brown meat balls and green onions in olive oil.

Remove meat; add tomato purée and water. Add garlic, parsley, and seasonings to taste. Cook one hour or until reduced to about one-half.

Add meat balls. Simmer 1 hour.

Serve over buttered spaghetti. Pass additional cheese.

YIELD: 4–6 SERVINGS

A Cook's Tour of Shreveport
THE JUNIOR LEAGUE OF SHREVEPORT, LOUISIANA

. . . .

Vermicelli with Clam Sauce

3 cloves garlic, cut in half
⅔ cup olive oil
1 cup bottled clam juice
¼ teaspoon salt
Pepper to taste
½ teaspoon oregano
3 7½-ounce cans minced clams
½ cup chopped fresh parsley
½ cup chopped green onions and tops
1 pound vermicelli, cooked
Freshly grated Parmesan cheese
Fresh clams, if available

Sauté garlic in the oil, mashing it as it cooks. Add clam juice, salt, pepper, and oregano and simmer for 5 minutes. Add canned clams with their juice and cook uncovered so liquid will reduce. Add parsley and onions and cook 10 minutes longer.

Toss half the sauce with hot vermicelli and some Parmesan cheese. Pour remaining sauce on top, and arrange freshly steamed clams around sides of dish. Serve with additional grated Parmesan.

YIELD: 4–6 SERVINGS

Winston-Salem's Heritage of Hospitality
THE JUNIOR LEAGUE OF WINSTON-SALEM, NORTH CAROLINA

. . . .

Chicken Tetrazzini

1 3½-pound stewing chicken
2 teaspoons salt
⅛ teaspoon pepper
½ pound fine noodles
7 tablespoons butter
½ pound sliced mushrooms
¼ cup flour
½ teaspoon salt
1 cup light cream
¼ cup sherry or cooking sherry
1½ cups shredded natural cheddar cheese or
⅓ cup grated Parmesan cheese
Paprika

Simmer chicken with 2 quarts water, 2 teaspoons salt, and pepper, covered, for 3–4 hours. Remove chicken from broth; refrigerate separately.

One hour before serving, bring broth to boil, add noodles, and cook 8 minutes. Drain, reserving broth; boil down to 2 cups; strain.

Cut meat into pieces.

In 3 tablespoons hot butter sauté mushrooms. Set aside. Melt 4 tablespoons butter and stir in flour, ½ teaspoon salt, broth, and cream. Cook until thickened. Add chicken, mushrooms, and sherry; heat.

Place noodles in greased casserole and pour sauce over them. Top with cheese and paprika.

Bake 10 minutes at 450°.

YIELD: 8 SERVINGS

The Gasparilla Cookbook
THE JUNIOR LEAGUE OF TAMPA, FLORIDA

Chicken Maison Theodore

1 hen
¼ pound butter
2 shallots or onions, finely chopped
1 tablespoon flour
1 wineglass good dry sherry
1 pint milk
A few fresh mushrooms (optional)
2 bay leaves
1 pound noodles
1 teaspoon butter
6 tablespoons whipped cream
3 beaten egg yolks
3 tablespoons grated Parmesan cheese

Boil hen until very tender. Cool. Cut into bite-size pieces.

Put water on for noodles.

Put ¼ pound butter in frying pan and brown shallots or onions. Add flour and blend well. Add chicken, then sherry and milk. Add mushrooms, if desired, and bay leaves. Simmer this mixture gently for 10 minutes while noodles are cooked and drained.

Swirl noodles into casserole with 1 teaspoon butter. Pour over chicken mixture. Top casserole with whipped cream blended with egg yolks and grated Parmesan cheese.

Bake at 325°–350° until golden brown.

Can freeze all but whipped cream topping.

YIELD: 6–8 SERVINGS

That Something Special
THE JUNIOR LEAGUE OF DURHAM, NORTH CAROLINA

Breast of Chicken Tropicale

2 chicken breasts, halved
Salt and pepper
¼ cup butter
8 ounces noodles
Salt, pepper, and butter
1 pound mushrooms, chopped
2 tablespoons minced onion
5–6 sprigs parsley
½ cup fine, dry bread crumbs
1 8-ounce can sliced pineapple
¼ cup grated Parmesan cheese

Season breasts with salt and pepper; sauté in butter until slightly brown. Cover and cook until done, turning occasionally.

Cook noodles and drain well. Then season with salt, pepper, and butter and put in flat baking dish. Top noodles with chicken and keep warm.

Cook mushrooms and onion in butter remaining in skillet. Add parsley and bread crumbs; mix well and season. Place a pineapple slice on each breast and top with a mound of mushroom mixture. Pour Pineapple Cream Sauce over and sprinkle with grated cheese. Brown under broiler.

YIELD: 4 SERVINGS

PINEAPPLE CREAM SAUCE:
3 tablespoons butter
3 tablespoons flour
2½ cups milk
½ cup pineapple juice
2 egg yolks, well beaten
½ cup heavy cream, whipped

Melt butter and blend in flour. Add milk and juice; cook until thickened. Add a little of mixture to egg yolks; return to saucepan. Cook, then fold in cream and season to taste.

Huntsville Heritage Cookbook
THE JUNIOR LEAGUE OF HUNTSVILLE, ALABAMA

Easy Chicken Tetrazzini

1 8-ounce can mushrooms (reserve liquid)
2 tablespoons butter
1 teaspoon salt
½ teaspoon pepper
2 cups diced, cooked chicken (or more)
Chicken broth (optional)
2 10¾-ounce cans condensed cream of celery soup
1 cup sour cream
5½ ounces noodles, cooked
Grated Parmesan cheese

Sauté mushrooms in butter. Add salt, pepper, chicken, undiluted soup, and sour cream. Mix well. Drain noodles and arrange in layers with chicken mixture in baking dish. Sprinkle liberally with Parmesan cheese. Bake at 350° for 25 minutes.

Add some mushroom juice and chicken broth if the mixture is too thick.

YIELD: 6–8 SERVINGS

Furniture City Feasts
THE JUNIOR LEAGUE OF HIGH POINT, NORTH CAROLINA

. . . .

Saxapahash

1 pound ground beef
1 teaspoon salt
1 teaspoon sugar
Garlic salt
1 16-ounce can tomato sauce
6 green onions
1 cup sour cream at room temperature
1 3-ounce package cream cheese, softened
8 ounces small noodles
Shredded cheddar cheese

Recipe continues . . .

Brown beef. Add salt, sugar, garlic salt, and tomato sauce. Simmer 20 minutes.

Chop onions and mix with sour cream and cream cheese.

Cook noodles as directed.

In buttered casserole, place a layer of noodles, a layer of cream cheese mixture, and a layer of meat mixture. Repeat. Top with cheddar cheese. Bake at 350° for 20–25 minutes.

YIELD: 6 SERVINGS

300 Years of Carolina Cooking
THE JUNIOR LEAGUE OF GREENVILLE, SOUTH CAROLINA

• • • • • • • • • • • • • •

Divine Casserole

1 pound small egg noodles
2 pounds ground beef
2 6-ounce cans tomato sauce
1 tablespoon Worcestershire sauce
Salt to taste
8 ounces cream-style cottage cheese
1 8-ounce package cream cheese
1 cup sour cream
3 or 4 green onions, chopped
1 stick butter or margarine

Boil, drain, and rinse noodles under hot water. Brown meat well; add tomato sauce, Worcestershire, and salt.

Mix cottage cheese, cream cheese, sour cream, and onions. Melt butter or margarine.

Grease two 2-quart casseroles. Place one-fourth of noodles in each casserole, pour a little melted butter over noodles, and add half of cheese mixture to each casserole. Add remaining noodles, more butter, and top with meat mixture.

Bake at 350° for 30–45 minutes. Freezes well.

YIELD: 8–10 SERVINGS

Recipe Jubilee
THE JUNIOR LEAGUE OF MOBILE, ALABAMA

·　·　·　·　·　·　·　·　·　·　·　·　·　·

Macaroni and Cauliflower au Gratin

4 ounces elbow macaroni
3 tablespoons butter
3 tablespoons flour
1½ teaspoons salt
½ teaspoon paprika
1½ cups milk
1 cup shredded American cheese
1½ cups coarsely chopped steamed cauliflower
¼ cup buttered bread crumbs

Cook macaroni in boiling salted water for 10 minutes. Drain and rinse.

Melt butter and stir in flour, salt, and paprika. Gradually add milk, stirring until thickened. Add cheese and steamed cauliflower. Fold in macaroni.

Pour into greased casserole and sprinkle with bread crumbs. Bake 15 minutes at 350°.

YIELD: 4 SERVINGS

Recipe Jubilee
THE JUNIOR LEAGUE OF MOBILE, ALABAMA

·　·　·　·　·　·　·　·　·　·　·　·　·　·

Cymbaline

3 tablespoons butter
4 tablespoons flour
2 cups milk
1 cup shredded sharp cheddar cheese
1½ teaspoons salt
1 teaspoon pepper
¼ cup chopped green pepper
¼ cup chopped pimento
3 hard-boiled eggs, sliced
1 cup shell macaroni, cooked

Melt butter in saucepan. Stir in flour. Gradually stir in milk and cook, stirring, until sauce is smooth and thickened. Add half the cheese and cook, stirring until cheese is melted.

Mix sauce with remaining ingredients except reserved cheese. Empty into 6-cup casserole, sprinkle with reserved cheese, and bake at 325° for 35 minutes.

YIELD: 6–7 SERVINGS

The Cotton Blossom Cookbook
THE JUNIOR LEAGUE OF ATLANTA, GEORGIA

Pastitsio

2 pounds ground chuck (include a little ground beef fat)
2 medium onions, chopped
2 tablespoons chopped parsley
½ teaspoon cinnamon
Salt and pepper to taste
1 1-pound can tomato purée
1 pound elbow macaroni
⅓ cup grated Parmesan or Romano cheese
¼ teaspoon nutmeg

Sauté meat in heavy skillet. Add onions, parsley, cinnamon, salt, and pepper and sauté lightly. Add tomato purée and simmer for 1 hour. Meanwhile cook macaroni according to package directions and drain.

Toss macaroni and meat mixture together and place in an 11 × 16-inch baking tray. Sprinkle with grated cheese and add Egg Sauce. Sprinkle with a little nutmeg. Bake at 325° for 45 minutes or until topping is a golden even brown.

If you prefer Pastitsio in layers, then start by placing macaroni in tray first; then add layer of meat sauce. Repeat this until macaroni and sauce are used, ending with macaroni. Pour Egg Sauce over this, sprinkle with cheese and nutmeg, and bake. When cool, cut in squares.

Pastitsio is served in Greece as a first course. It makes a good main dish or it may be served for a buffet.

YIELD: 20 SERVINGS

EGG SAUCE:
¼ pound butter
1¼ cups flour
1¼ quarts milk
6 egg yolks, slightly beaten
Salt and pepper to taste

Recipe continues . . .

Melt butter in a heavy saucepan; stir in the flour until thoroughly blended and smooth. Add the milk gradually, while stirring, and cook until smooth and thickened. Now add egg yolks, salt, and pepper.

The Gasparilla Cookbook
THE JUNIOR LEAGUE OF TAMPA, FLORIDA

. . . .

Chicken Lasagne

8 ounces (12 strips) wide lasagne noodles
2 quarts salted water
1 10¾-ounce can condensed cream of mushroom soup
⅔ cup milk
½ teaspoon poultry seasoning
1 teaspoon salt
1 8-ounce package cream cheese, softened
1 8-ounce container cottage cheese
⅓ cup minced onions
⅓ cup chopped green pepper
⅓ cup chopped stuffed olives
1 teaspoon chopped parsley
2 2-pound chickens, cooked, boned, and diced
1 cup buttered bread crumbs

Boil noodles in salted water until tender, about 30 minutes. Rinse in cold water and drain. Heat soup, milk, poultry seasoning, and salt. Add cheeses while still warm.

Combine onions, green pepper, olives, and parsley.

In lasagne dish, arrange 1 layer noodles, 1 layer cheese mixture, 1 layer onion mixture, and 1 layer diced chicken. Repeat until dish is full. Cover with bread crumbs.

Bake at 325° for 30 minutes. Let stand for 5 minutes.

YIELD: 12 SERVINGS

Furniture City Feasts
THE JUNIOR LEAGUE OF HIGH POINT, NORTH CAROLINA

. . . .

Green Chili Lasagne

1 16-ounce package medium noodles
1 teaspoon margarine
3 pounds lean ground beef
5 8-ounce cans tomato sauce
1 tablespoon sugar
2 teaspoons salt
1 teaspoon garlic salt
½ teaspoon pepper
2 cups large-curd cottage cheese
1 8-ounce package cream cheese, softened
1 cup sour cream
1 cup thinly sliced green onions and tops
2 4-ounce cans green chilies, chopped
½ cup grated Parmesan cheese

Grease two 9 × 13-inch baking dishes. Cook noodles according to directions. Drain and add margarine.

Brown beef in small amount of fat.

In a large saucepan, combine tomato sauce, sugar, salts, and pepper. Add browned meat and simmer until meat is tender, about 30 minutes. Skim off fat.

In a separate bowl, combine cottage cheese, cream cheese, sour cream, onions, and green chilies. Mix until smooth and creamy.

Recipe continues ...

Fill baking dishes in this order: Put ¼ cooked noodles in the bottom of each of the pans. Cover with ¼ meat sauce in each pan. Next, divide the cheese mixture between both pans—use all of it for one thick layer. Spread remaining noodles evenly over cheese. Use remaining meat sauce over noodles and finish with heavy coating of Parmesan cheese. Cover with foil and refrigerate.

Before serving, heat in 350° oven for 45 minutes. Better if made the day before.

YIELD: 24 SERVINGS

Fiesta: Favorite Recipes of South Texas
THE JUNIOR LEAGUE OF CORPUS CHRISTI, TEXAS

· · · · · · · · · · · · · · · · · ·

Cannelloni

MEAT FILLING:
4 cloves garlic
1 medium onion
2 tablespoons butter
2 tablespoons olive oil
½ pound ground chuck
½ pound Italian sausage
1 10-ounce package frozen chopped spinach, thawed and drained
5 tablespoons grated Parmesan cheese
½ teaspoon oregano
Salt and pepper to taste
2 eggs, beaten
2 tablespoons heavy cream
1 package manicotti noodles, cooked and drained

CREAM SAUCE:
4 tablespoons butter
4 tablespoons flour
1 cup milk
1 cup heavy cream
1 teaspoon salt
White pepper to taste

TOMATO SAUCE:
1 small onion
2 tablespoons olive oil
2 1-pound cans Italian-style tomatoes
3 tablespoons tomato paste
1 teaspoon basil
½ teaspoon salt
1 teaspoon sugar
Black pepper to taste

TOPPING:
3 tablespoons grated Parmesan cheese
Butter

Meat Filling: Blend garlic and onion to a paste in blender. Heat butter and olive oil and cook onion/garlic paste for 5 minutes. Add ground beef and sausage and brown. Add spinach and cook until moisture is nearly gone. Add cheese and seasonings. Cool and add eggs which have been beaten with cream.

Stuff cooked noodles with mixture.

Cream Sauce: Melt butter and stir in flour. Cook 2 minutes, stirring. Add milk and cream and stir until thick. Add seasonings.

Tomato Sauce: Blend onion to a paste in a blender. Heat olive oil and sauté onion paste briefly. Blend the tomatoes and juice in blender and add to onion mixture. Add tomato paste and seasonings. Simmer for 30–40 minutes.

Recipe continues ...

To assemble: Pour small amount of tomato sauce in a large rectangular casserole and spread it over the bottom of dish. Put in one layer only of stuffed manicotti. Cover with cream sauce and then tomato sauce. Sprinkle Parmesan cheese on top and dot with butter.

Bake at 350° for 20–30 minutes or until hot and bubbly.

YIELD: 8 SERVINGS

Winston-Salem's Heritage of Hospitality
THE JUNIOR LEAGUE OF WINSTON-SALEM, NORTH CAROLINA

Grains, Beans, and Peas

Couch-Couch Acadian Style

2 cups corn meal
1½ teaspoons salt
1 teaspoon baking powder
1½ cups milk or water
½ cup oil

Mix thoroughly corn meal, salt, baking powder, and milk or water and add to hot oil in skillet over high heat. Let a crust form.

Give a good stir and reduce flame to low. Cover and cook about 15 minutes; stir often. Serve with milk and sugar or with cane syrup and crisp bacon for breakfast or brunch.

YIELD: 6 SERVINGS

Talk About Good!
THE JUNIOR LEAGUE OF LAFAYETTE, LOUISIANA

. . . .

Old Fashioned Grits and Cheese Soufflé

1 cup grits
1 cup shredded New York State sharp cheddar cheese
¼ cup milk
4 eggs, well beaten
½ teaspoon baking powder

Cook grits according to package directions.

Thoroughly mix with remaining ingredients and pour into greased 1½-quart casserole.

Bake at 400° for about 30 minutes.

YIELD: 4—6 SERVINGS

Huntsville Heritage Cookbook
THE JUNIOR LEAGUE OF HUNTSVILLE, ALABAMA

. . . .

Louisiana Garlic-Cheese Grits Casserole

1 cup grits
4 cups water
1 teaspoon salt
1 roll garlic cheese
1 stick butter
2 eggs, well beaten
Salt and pepper to taste
¼ cup milk

Cook grits in water with salt added. After grits are cooked, add garlic cheese and butter. Stir in well-beaten eggs, salt and pepper to taste, and milk. Put in a 1½ -quart casserole and bake 40 minutes to 1 hour at 300°– 350°.

YIELD: 8 SERVINGS

VARIATION:

Separate the eggs and fold in the beaten egg whites before putting in casserole to bake.

Talk About Good!
THE JUNIOR LEAGUE OF LAFAYETTE, LOUISIANA

. . . .

Carolina Garlic-Cheese Grits Casserole

1 cup grits
1 stick butter
1½ tablespoons Worcestershire sauce
¾ pound or more shredded American cheese
1 clove garlic, grated
Dash Tabasco
2 egg whites

Recipe continues . . .

Cook grits according to package directions, to a thick but not stiff consistency. When still hot, add butter, Worcestershire, cheese, garlic, and Tabasco. Let cool. Beat egg whites until stiff. Fold into grits. Pour into 2-quart casserole.

Just before serving, bake at 400° for 20 minutes or until slightly brown on top.

This can be put in refrigerator in the morning and baked at night.

YIELD: 12 SERVINGS

300 Years of Carolina Cooking
THE JUNIOR LEAGUE OF GREENVILLE, SOUTH CAROLINA

. . . .

Chili-Cheese Grits

1½ cups grits
6 cups water
2 teaspoons salt
3 eggs, beaten
1 pound longhorn cheese, shredded
3 teaspoons seasoned salt
Dash Tabasco
Dash paprika
½ cup butter
Dash Worcestershire sauce
1 4-ounce can chopped green chilies

Bring water to a boil. Cook grits in water according to package instructions. Add remaining ingredients. Mix well.

Bake in oblong dish at 250° for 1½–2 hours.

This may be prepared ahead and refrigerated. Good with barbecued beef or chicken.

YIELD: 10–12 SERVINGS

Seasoned with Sun: Recipes from the Southwest
THE JUNIOR LEAGUE OF EL PASO, TEXAS

. . . .

Wine Rice

1 cup raw rice
1 cup chopped fresh tomatoes
½ cup chopped onion
1 pound fresh mushrooms, sliced
Chicken broth
½ cup red wine
2 teaspoons salt
¼ teaspoon pepper
1 cup canned tiny green peas, heated and drained
½ cup butter
¼ –½ cup grated Parmesan cheese

Place rice, tomatoes, onion, and mushrooms in large skillet. Add amount of chicken broth equal to amount of liquid called for on rice package, less ½ cup. Add wine, salt, and pepper; mix well.

Cover and simmer for 30–40 minutes, or until liquid is absorbed and rice is tender.

Stir in peas and butter; sprinkle with cheese and serve immediately.

YIELD: 8 SERVINGS

Little Rock Cooks
THE JUNIOR LEAGUE OF LITTLE ROCK, ARKANSAS

· · · · · · · · · · · · · · · · · ·

Picnic Pride Rice

1½ cups raw rice
3 cups water
2 bouillon cubes
2 tablespoons bacon drippings
Salt and pepper to taste
½ cup chopped peanuts
½ cup chopped raisins
½ cup cut-up celery
1 teaspoon concentrated beef extract

Recipe continues . . .

Wash rice. Cook in steamer with 1 cup water in which bouillon cubes have been dissolved and bacon drippings, salt, and pepper added. When half cooked, or when rice has soaked up all the water, add peanuts (which have been mashed with a rolling pin), raisins, celery, beef extract, and remaining 2 cups water. A ham skin may be cooked with the rice, if desired. Cover tightly and cook about 1½ hours or until done.

Fine for picnics with cold meat or hash.

YIELD: 6 SERVINGS

Charleston Receipts

THE JUNIOR LEAGUE OF CHARLESTON, SOUTH CAROLINA

. . . .

Chicken Jambalaya

1 cup chopped onions
1 cup chopped green pepper
2 cloves garlic, minced
2 tablespoons salad oil
1 cup cooked, diced ham
12 small pork sausage links, cut into rounds
1 cup cooked, diced chicken
2 16-ounce cans tomatoes
1 cup uncooked rice
1½ cups chicken broth
½ teaspoon thyme
1 teaspoon salt
1 tablespoon chopped parsley

Sauté onions, green pepper, and garlic in hot salad oil in a skillet, stirring frequently until tender. Stir in meats and cook for 5 minutes.

Add all remaining ingredients and place in greased casserole dish. Cover dish and bake at 350° for 1 hour.

YIELD: 8 SERVINGS

Southern Sideboards

THE JUNIOR LEAGUE OF JACKSON, MISSISSIPPI

. . . .

James Island Shrimp "Pie"

This recipe dates back to about 1860.

1 cup raw rice
1 teaspoon salt
2 cups water
¼ cup butter
2 eggs
Pinch mace
5 tablespoons catsup
2½ tablespoons Worcestershire sauce
Salt and pepper to taste
2 pounds shrimp, cooked and cleaned
About 1 cup milk

Cook rice in salted water until very soft and stir butter into it. Combine all ingredients with cooked shrimp, adding enough milk to make mixture the consistency of thick custard.

Put in buttered casserole and bake at 350° until brown on top, about 30 minutes.

YIELD: 8 SERVINGS

Charleston Receipts
THE JUNIOR LEAGUE OF CHARLESTON, SOUTH CAROLINA

Paella Valenciana

This takes time to prepare but it is not at all hard and is well worth the trouble!

¼ cup oil
2 9-inch pepperonis, sliced thick
8 boned chicken breasts, halved
1 large onion, chopped
1 clove garlic, minced
2 7-ounce cans minced clams, drained (reserve juice)
1½ pounds shelled and deveined shrimp (fresh or frozen)
2 cups raw converted rice
1 teaspoon freshly ground black pepper
2 teaspoons salt
10–15 pieces of saffron (or about ¼ teaspoon powdered saffron)
4 cups liquid (including the reserved clam broth)
2 teaspoons instant chicken bouillon granules
½ teaspoon monosodium glutamate
Garnish of clam shells, pimento, black olives, asparagus, peas, etc.

In a large skillet or paella pan, heat oil until smoky hot and brown the pepperoni slices. Remove pepperoni with slotted spoon, drain, and reserve. Add the chicken breasts and brown in the same oil; then set aside. Add the chopped onion and garlic and sauté until translucent; then remove. Stir in the drained, minced clams and shrimp and cook until shrimp are almost done. Set aside.

In remaining oil (adding a tiny bit more if necessary), add the rice, black pepper, salt, and saffron, and brown slightly; then stir in onion mixture, 4 cups liquid, chicken bouillon granules, and monosodium glutamate. Cover pan tightly and cook about 10 minutes; then uncover and add the reserved pepperoni, chicken breasts, and seafood.

It can be prepared ahead to this point; you may have to add a little more liquid. Before serving, bake uncovered at 400° another 20–30 minutes, or until rice is done.

The more traditional way, if you have a paella pan, is to cook uncovered in the oven the whole cooking time. Serve at once after garnishing attractively with whatever garnishes you have chosen, but especially with shells if possible. If you can obtain the brand of canned clams with clams in the shells, arrange them around the top of the paella pan before the last baking time.

Wonderful preceded by gazpacho, and served with hard, crusty bread and butter, and lots of sangría!

YIELD: 8 SERVINGS

Southern Accent
THE JUNIOR LEAGUE OF PINE BLUFF, ARKANSAS

. . . .

Hampton Plantation Shrimp Pilau

4 slices bacon
2 cups water
1 cup raw rice
3 tablespoons butter
½ cup finely chopped celery
2 tablespoons chopped green pepper
2 cups cleaned shrimp
1 teaspoon Worcestershire sauce
1 tablespoon flour
Salt and pepper to taste

Fry bacon until crisp. Save to use later. Add bacon drippings to'the water and cook rice.

In another pot, melt butter and add celery and green pepper. Cook a few minutes; add shrimp which have been sprinkled with Worcestershire sauce and dredged with flour. Stir and simmer until flour is cooked. Season with salt and pepper.

Recipe continues . . .

Now add cooked rice and mix until rice is "all buttery" and "shrimpy." You may want to add more butter. Into this stir the crisp bacon, crumbled. Serve hot.

YIELD: 6 SERVINGS

Charleston Receipts
THE JUNIOR LEAGUE OF CHARLESTON, SOUTH CAROLINA

. . . .

Baked Herb Rice

2 cups raw rice
⅔ stick butter
4 cups undiluted canned consommé
¼ teaspoon oregano
¼ teaspoon thyme
Salt and pepper to taste
¾ cup chopped fresh parsley (or 1 tablespoon dry flakes)
¾ cup finely chopped celery
½ cup finely chopped onion
1 cup slivered almonds or pecans

Brown raw rice in butter for 5 minutes; keep stirring. Heat 3¼ cups consommé. Put the browned rice, heated consommé, and herbs in warmed 2-quart casserole. Cover and bake 1 hour at 350°, stirring several times during baking.

Heat remaining ¾ cup consommé and add to casserole along with chopped vegetables and nuts. Stir well. Return casserole to oven, cover, and bake ¾ hour longer.

YIELD: 8–10 SERVINGS

That Something Special
THE JUNIOR LEAGUE OF DURHAM, NORTH CAROLINA

. . . .

Greenville Green Rice

2 cups raw rice
1½ cups milk
½ cup salad oil
1 cup chopped parsley
1 cup chopped green pepper
2 cloves garlic, chopped
1 pound shredded New York State sharp cheddar cheese
1 cup chopped green onions with tops
Salt and pepper to taste

Cook rice as usual. When done, add milk and other ingredients. Mix well. Pour into greased casserole and bake covered at 350° for 1 hour.

Good with chicken.

YIELD: 10–12 SERVINGS

> *300 Years of Carolina Cooking*
> THE JUNIOR LEAGUE OF GREENVILLE, SOUTH CAROLINA

· · · · · · · · · · · · · · · ·

Tampa Green Rice

1 cup raw rice
2 teaspoons salt
2½ cups boiling water
4 eggs, separated
1 green pepper, finely chopped
1 small onion, finely chopped
½ cup minced parsley
5 tablespoons grated Parmesan cheese
1 teaspoon paprika
1 cup heavy cream, whipped

Recipe continues . . .

Add rice and 1 teaspoon salt to boiling water (½ teaspoon garlic salt and ½ teaspoon salt may be used). Cover and cook over low heat until rice is tender and water is absorbed (20–25 minutes). Beat egg yolks and combine with green pepper, onion, parsley, cheese, paprika, and the remaining 1 teaspoon salt. Blend mixture with the cooked rice. Fold in whipped cream. Beat egg whites until foamy and fold into the mixture. Turn into greased 2-quart casserole or ring mold. Place in pan of hot water and bake at 350° until set (50–60 minutes).

YIELD: 6–8 SERVINGS

The Gasparilla Cookbook
THE JUNIOR LEAGUE OF TAMPA, FLORIDA

· · · · · · · · · · · · · · · ·

Chili Cheese Rice

¾ cup raw rice
2 cups sour cream
Salt to taste
½ pound Monterey Jack cheese, cut into 1¼-inch cubes
4 4-ounce cans chopped green chilies
½ cup shredded Monterey Jack cheese
Butter

Cook rice. Combine with sour cream and season with salt.

Arrange half the mixture in buttered ovenproof casserole. Cover with a layer of cheese cubes and chopped chilies. Top with the remaining rice mixture. Sprinkle the shredded cheese over top. Dot with butter. Bake at 350° for 30 minutes.

This recipe can be prepared ahead and refrigerated, or frozen, then thawed for 1 hour and baked.

YIELD: 10 SERVINGS

Seasoned with Sun: Recipes from the Southwest
THE JUNIOR LEAGUE OF EL PASO, TEXAS

· · · · · · · · · · · · · · · ·

"Dirty" Rice

1 12-ounce package brown rice
2 onions
2 green peppers
4 stalks celery with tops
1 clove garlic
2 tablespoons bacon drippings
½ pound chicken livers, chopped
⅛ pound ground beef or pork
(optional, but good when cooked in large quantities)
4 tablespoons pecans or walnuts (optional)
Tabasco
Worcestershire sauce
Salt
Cayenne
Black pepper

Boil rice according to directions on package. Drain. Brown rice has a slightly coarser grain than white.

Chop onions, peppers, celery, and garlic fine (use blender).

In bacon drippings, sauté chopped vegetables until the mixture cooks down, about 30 minutes. Add chicken livers and ground meat and cook until done, then mash. The mixture looks "dirty" and soupy. Add nuts and seasonings to taste, and mix with rice.

May be prepared in morning and reheated. Additional water may be needed.

YIELD: 8 LARGE SERVINGS

A Cook's Tour of Shreveport
THE JUNIOR LEAGUE OF SHREVEPORT, LOUISIANA

Red Rice

4 strips bacon, cubed
2 onions, chopped fine
1 6-ounce can tomato paste
1½–2 cans water
3 teaspoons salt
2–3 teaspoons sugar
Good dash pepper
2 cups raw rice
8 tablespoons bacon drippings

Fry bacon, remove from pan; sauté onions in drippings remaining in pan. Add tomato paste, water, salt, sugar, and pepper. Cook uncovered slowly, about 10 minutes, then add to rice in top section of steamer. Add the 8 tablespoons additional bacon drippings, steam for ½ hour, then add bacon, crumbled, and stir with a fork. Cook 30–45 minutes longer.

YIELD: 6–8 SERVINGS

Charleston Receipts
THE JUNIOR LEAGUE OF CHARLESTON, SOUTH CAROLINA

· · · · · · · · · · · · · ·

Oyster and Wild Rice Casserole

2 cups raw wild rice
¼ pound butter
2 pints small oysters
Salt and pepper to taste
1 10¾-ounce can condensed cream of celery soup
1 cup light cream
1½ tablespoons chopped onion
¾ teaspoon thyme
Parsley

Cook rice until open and soft; drain well. Slice butter and mix with wild rice until melted.

Butter large shallow baking dish and spread rice evenly over dish. Cover with well-drained oysters and sprinkle with salt and pepper. Heat soup, diluted with cream. Add onion and thyme. Pour over rice as evenly as possible.

Bake at 300° for 45 minutes. Garnish with parsley.

This can be done the day ahead, saving out liquid to add just before putting it in the oven. Long-grain and wild rice mixture may be used also.

YIELD: 10–12 SERVINGS

Of Pots and Pipkins
THE JUNIOR LEAGUE OF ROANOKE VALLEY, VIRGINIA

Charlotte Wild Rice Casserole

1 cup raw wild rice or long-grain and wild rice mix
3 cups boiling water
1 teaspoon salt
2 tablespoons butter
4 tablespoons minced onion
2 tablespoons chopped green pepper
1 4-ounce can sliced mushrooms, drained
1 10¾-ounce can cream of mushroom soup, undiluted
¾ cup half and half
¼ teaspoon dried marjoram
⅛ teaspoon dried basil
⅛ teaspoon dried tarragon
½ teaspoon curry powder
½ teaspoon salt
¼ teaspoon pepper
8 whole mushrooms, buttered, for garnish

Wash the rice in three or four changes of cold water. Then, to the boiling water in a saucepan, add 1 teaspoon salt and stir in rice. Simmer covered about 30 minutes, or until all water is absorbed.

While rice is cooking, prepare the following: In another saucepan melt 2 tablespoons butter and sauté the onion, green pepper, and drained canned mushrooms for about 5 minutes. Then stir in soup, half and half, marjoram, basil, tarragon, curry powder, salt, and pepper. Heat the combined mixture *slowly* for about 10 minutes.

When wild rice is ready, rinse it in a colander and then add the rice to the cream sauce mixture. Pour into a greased 2-quart casserole, add the fresh buttered mushrooms for garnish, and heat 8–10 minutes in preheated 350° oven.

Better made the day before so herbs can blend better.

YIELD: 8 SERVINGS

The Charlotte Cookbook
THE JUNIOR LEAGUE OF CHARLOTTE, NORTH CAROLINA

Mobile Wild Rice Casserole

1 pound sausage
1 8-ounce can sliced mushrooms (or 1 pound fresh)
1 cup sliced onions
2 cups raw wild rice
¼ cup flour
½ cup heavy cream
2½ cups condensed chicken broth
1 teaspoon monosodium glutamate
Pinch each of oregano, thyme, and marjoram
Salt and pepper to taste
½ cup toasted almonds or pine nuts

Sauté sausage, drain, and break into small pieces. Sauté mushrooms and onions in sausage fat (or butter). Add sausage.

Cook rice in boiling, salted water 20–30 minutes. Drain.

Mix flour with cream until smooth. Add chicken broth and cook until thickened. Add seasonings.

Combine rice with sausage mixture. Pour into casserole and bake 25–30 minutes in 350° oven. Sprinkle nuts around sides of casserole before serving.

If prepared in advance, rice will absorb liquid, so add a little more chicken broth before baking.

YIELD: 18 SERVINGS

Recipe Jubilee
THE JUNIOR LEAGUE OF MOBILE, ALABAMA

Margaret Walsh's Hopping John

Hopping John, made of cow peas and rice, is eaten in the stateliest of houses and in the humblest cabins and always on New Year's Day. "Hoppin' John eaten then will bring good luck" is an old tradition. (*Charleston Receipts*, THE JUNIOR LEAGUE OF CHARLESTON, SOUTH CAROLINA)

1 cup dried black-eyed peas
2 cups boiling water
⅓ pound salt pork or fat bacon
1 large onion, sliced
1 sprig celery leaves
1 small bay leaf
2½ teaspoons salt
⅛ teaspoon pepper
2 cups boiling water
½ cup raw rice
2 tablespoons minced parsley

Place peas and 2 cups boiling water in saucepan. Cover and let stand 2 hours. Do not drain.

Cut salt pork or bacon into squares and brown in hot skillet. Sauté onion and celery leaves in this and add to soaked peas, along with bay leaf, salt, and pepper. Add 2 more cups boiling water. Simmer in covered saucepan until peas are nearly tender. Discard bay leaf. Add rice and simmer covered until rice is done. More water may be added if necessary.

Top with chopped parsley to serve.

YIELD: 6 SERVINGS

Fiesta: Favorite Recipes of South Texas
THE JUNIOR LEAGUE OF CORPUS CHRISTI, TEXAS

Cassoulet

2 quarts water
1 pound dried white Great Northern beans
4 garlic cloves
4 cups sliced onion
4 sprigs parsley
2 tablespoons salt
4 whole cloves
½ pound sliced bacon, cut into 1-inch pieces
2 pounds lean pork, cut into 1-inch pieces or 2 pounds boned
chicken cut into large chunks
2 10½-ounce cans condensed beef broth, undiluted
1½ cups tomato purée
1 teaspoon thyme
3 bay leaves
1 pound Polish sausage
½ cup dry white wine

Bring water to boiling in a 4-quart kettle and add beans. Return to boiling point and boil for 2 minutes. Remove from heat; let stand 1 hour.

Crush 2 of the garlic cloves and add to the beans along with 2 cups of the onion, parsley sprigs, 1 tablespoon of the salt, and cloves. Bring to a boil; reduce heat and simmer covered for 1½ hours. Drain. Remove cloves and discard.

Recipe continues . . .

While beans are cooking, sauté bacon in a large skillet until crisp. Remove bacon and set aside; pour off drippings. Return 2 tablespoons drippings to skillet and brown pork or chicken on all sides. Remove and set aside.

Crush remaining 2 garlic cloves; add them with remaining 2 cups of onion to skillet and sauté until golden, about 5 minutes. Return bacon and pork to skillet. (If using chicken, do not add until the final baking step because it will cook to shreds.) Add 1 tablespoon salt, beef broth, tomato purée, thyme, and bay leaves to meat mixture and bring to a boil. Reduce heat. Simmer covered for 1½ hours. Remove bay leaves and discard.

While the pork is cooking, make cuts in sausage in several places to prevent curling or cut sausage into 2-inch lengths. Cook in boiling water for 30 minutes.

Add drained beans and the wine to meat mixture. Turn into a 3-quart casserole and top with sausage. Bake uncovered at 350° for 1 hour. Stir beans before serving.

If prepared ahead, refrigerate and heat, covered, at 350° until hot and bubbly, about 1½ hours.

YIELD: 8–10 SERVINGS

Mountain Measures
THE JUNIOR LEAGUE OF CHARLESTON, WEST VIRGINIA

Louisiana Red Beans with Rice

1 pound red beans
8 ounces ham hock
2 quarts water
1 tablespoon salt
3 cups chopped onion
1 bunch green onions, chopped
2 cloves garlic, minced
1 cup chopped green pepper
1 cup minced parsley
1 teaspoon cayenne
1 teaspoon black pepper
⅛ teaspoon Tabasco
1 tablespoon Worcestershire sauce
1 8-ounce can tomato sauce
¼ teaspoon oregano
¼ teaspoon thyme

Soak red beans overnight. (These are not red kidney beans but a smaller, distinctive bean.)

Put drained beans and ham hock in large soup kettle, add water and salt, bring to boil, and cook slowly for 45 minutes.

Add all other ingredients and cook slowly for 2 hours or until beans are tender and liquid thick. Serve over steamed rice. Beans (but not rice) can be frozen.

YIELD: 12 SERVINGS

Fiesta: Favorite Recipes of South Texas
THE JUNIOR LEAGUE OF CORPUS CHRISTI, TEXAS

Patio Beans

4 slices bacon
1 medium onion, chopped
1 1-pound can baked beans in tomato sauce
1 1-pound can kidney beans, drained
1 1-pound can lima beans, drained
¼ pound sharp cheddar cheese, cubed
½ cup brown sugar
⅓ cup catsup
2 teaspoons Worcestershire sauce
Grated Parmesan cheese

Fry bacon until crisp. Sauté onion in bacon drippings. Combine in large casserole the beans, cubed cheese, brown sugar, and seasonings. Stir in the onion and bacon, which has been crumbled. Sprinkle with grated Parmesan cheese.

Bake at 350° until heated thoroughly and bubbly.

YIELD: 6 SERVINGS

> *The Charlotte Cookbook*
> THE JUNIOR LEAGUE OF CHARLOTTE, NORTH CAROLINA

Vegetables

Artichoke Hearts with Roquefort Dressing

¼ pound butter
1 wedge Roquefort cheese, crumbled
Lemon juice to taste
1 1-pound can artichoke hearts

Melt butter in double boiler; add Roquefort and lemon juice. Drain hearts, add to butter sauce, and serve hot.

Good served with steak.

YIELD: 2–4 SERVINGS

The Memphis Cook Book
THE JUNIOR LEAGUE OF MEMPHIS, TENNESSEE

· · · · · · · · · · · ·

Stuffed Artichokes

6–8 artichokes
1 can Italian-style seasoned bread crumbs
1 cup freshly grated Romano cheese
3 cloves garlic, crushed
2 cups finely chopped parsley
1½ teaspoons salt
1 teaspoon black pepper
¼ pound butter
1 lemon, thinly sliced
1 cup cooking oil

Remove stems of artichokes and trim the tips of leaves. Pound each artichoke on a board until the leaves open and discard choke.

Combine bread crumbs, cheese, garlic, parsley, salt, and pepper. Stuff each leaf and the center of the artichoke. Top each artichoke with a large pat of butter and a thin slice of lemon. Pour over all the artichokes the cooking oil, then place them in a large pot and add lightly salted water that reaches about ½ inch high on the artichokes, or use a steamer. Cover and cook over medium heat, being sure that the water stays at the same level by adding additional hot water as necessary.

Artichokes should cook in about 1 hour, but the best test is to pull a large bottom leaf; when it pulls easily, the artichokes are done.

May be served cold, but best hot.

YIELD: 6–8 SERVINGS

A Cook's Tour of Shreveport
THE JUNIOR LEAGUE OF SHREVEPORT, LOUISIANA

Artichokes and Mushrooms

3 14-ounce cans artichoke hearts
1½ pounds mushrooms, sliced
½ stick butter
2 tablespoons olive oil
2 tablespoons wine vinegar
½ clove garlic, crushed
1 teaspoon celery seed
½ teaspoon paprika
¼ teaspoon seasoned salt
⅛ teaspoon cayenne
Patty shells or buttered bread crumbs

Rinse, drain, and slice artichokes. Sauté mushrooms in butter. Combine oil, vinegar, garlic, celery seed, paprika, seasoned salt, and cayenne, and toss the vegetables in them. Stir this mixture into the Cheese Cream Sauce.

Serve either in patty shells, or as a casserole. If used as a casserole, cover thickly with buttered bread crumbs and bake at 350° for 30 minutes.

YIELD: 8 SERVINGS

Recipe continues . . .

CHEESE CREAM SAUCE:
½ stick butter
¼ cup flour
1½ cups hot rich chicken stock
½ cup heavy cream
1 teaspoon lemon juice
Salt and pepper to taste
1½ cups shredded cheddar cheese

Melt butter and blend in flour. Add hot chicken stock and stir until thickened. Add cream and lemon juice gradually. Add salt, pepper, and cheese, stirring until combined and smooth. Combine sauce with artichoke mixture and keep warm, or reheat over hot water.

Winston-Salem's Heritage of Hospitality
THE JUNIOR LEAGUE OF WINSTON-SALEM, NORTH CAROLINA

. . . .

Natural Asparagus

1–1½ pounds fresh asparagus
Salt and pepper to taste
3 tablespoons butter

Rinse and trim asparagus. Do not peel unless very tough. Place asparagus in one or two layers in a flat dish, just large enough to hold them. Sprinkle with salt and pepper and dot with butter.

Cover tightly and bake at 300° for 30 minutes. Asparagus will be crunchy and will not lose its color.

YIELD: 4 SERVINGS

Winston-Salem's Heritage of Hospitality
THE JUNIOR LEAGUE OF WINSTON-SALEM, NORTH CAROLINA

. . . .

Brussels Sprouts in Celery Sauce

1 quart Brussels sprouts
1½ cups chopped celery
3 tablespoons butter
3 tablespoons flour
½ cup water that celery cooked in
1 cup milk
Celery salt, pepper, and nutmeg to taste

Cook Brussels sprouts in boiling salted water until tender. Drain. Cook celery in 1 cup boiling salted water until tender. Save water from celery.

In top of double boiler, let butter melt. Add flour and gradually stir in ½ cup celery water and milk. Cook until thick. Season with celery salt, pepper, and a pinch of grated nutmeg. Add celery. Pour over hot Brussels sprouts.

YIELD: 6 SERVINGS

The Cotton Blossom Cookbook
THE JUNIOR LEAGUE OF ATLANTA, GEORGIA

Tangy Green Beans

2 cans whole string beans
Bacon strips, cut in half

VINAIGRETTE SAUCE:
3 tablespoons butter
2 tablespoons vinegar
1 tablespoon tarragon vinegar
1 teaspoon salt
1 teaspoon paprika
1 tablespoon chopped parsley
1 teaspoon grated onion

Recipe continues . . .

Wrap 6 or 7 string beans in half piece of bacon. Secure with pick. Repeat with remaining string beans. Broil until bacon is done.

Combine all sauce ingredients and bring to a boil. Pour hot sauce over beans and serve.

YIELD: 8 SERVINGS

Southern Sideboards
THE JUNIOR LEAGUE OF JACKSON, MISSISSIPPI

· · · · · · · · · · · · · · · ·

Sweet and Sour Broccoli

3 slices bacon
1 10-ounce package frozen chopped broccoli
½ teaspoon salt
⅛ teaspoon pepper
¼ cup water
¼ cup sweet pickle relish
1 hard-boiled egg

In large skillet, fry bacon until crisp; remove bacon, drain on absorbent paper, and crumble. Add frozen broccoli, salt, pepper, and water to bacon drippings in skillet. Cover and cook over low heat, stirring occasionally, until broccoli pieces are separated. Add relish and cook until broccoli is tender-crisp, about 5 minutes. Place in serving bowl. Slice egg; place on top of broccoli and sprinkle with crumbled bacon.

YIELD: 2 SERVINGS

Furniture City Feasts
THE JUNIOR LEAGUE OF HIGH POINT, NORTH CAROLINA

· · · · · · · · · · · · · · · ·

Sesame Broccoli

1 pound fresh broccoli
1 tablespoon salad oil
1 tablespoon vinegar
1 tablespoon soy sauce
4 teaspoons sugar
1 tablespoon toasted sesame seeds

Cook broccoli in small amount of boiling salted water about 15 minutes, or just until tender. Drain.

In a small saucepan, combine oil, vinegar, soy sauce, sugar, and sesame seeds. Heat to boiling. Pour sauce over hot broccoli, turning to coat. Serve hot.

YIELD: 4–5 SERVINGS

That Something Special
THE JUNIOR LEAGUE OF DURHAM, NORTH CAROLINA

·   ·   ·   ·   ·   ·   ·   ·   ·   ·   ·   ·   ·   ·   ·

Baked Stuffed Carrots

4 large carrots
1 medium onion (or ½ large onion)
½ green or red sweet pepper
Salt and pepper to taste
3 tablespoons butter or margarine

Boil carrots whole for 30 minutes or until mildly cooked. Cut in halves. Scoop out centers and mash.

Chop onion and green or red pepper and add salt, pepper, and 2 table-

Recipe continues . . .

spoons butter. Add to mashed carrot centers and stuff the eight carrot shells.

Bake in a dish greased with 1 tablespoon butter for about 30 minutes at 350°.

YIELD: 8 SERVINGS

Mountain Measures
THE JUNIOR LEAGUE OF CHARLESTON, WEST VIRGINIA

· · · · · · · · · · · · · ·

Carrot Casserole

12 carrots, peeled and sliced
1 small onion, sliced
¼ cup flour
¼ cup margarine
1 teaspoon salt
¼ teaspoon celery salt
¼ teaspoon dry mustard
¼ teaspoon pepper
2 cups milk
1 cup shredded sharp cheddar cheese
2 cups fresh buttered bread crumbs

Cook the carrots until tender. Add the onion and cook for 2 or 3 more minutes. Set aside.

Make a cream sauce of the flour, margarine, salt, celery salt, mustard, pepper, and milk. Heat until thick, then stir in cheese and stir until melted.

Pour over carrots which you have placed in a casserole. Top with buttered bread crumbs. Bake at 350° for 25–30 minutes.

YIELD: 5–6 SERVINGS

Furniture City Feasts
THE JUNIOR LEAGUE OF HIGH POINT, NORTH CAROLINA

· · · · · · · · · · · · · ·

Creole Cauliflower au Gratin

4 tablespoons butter
1 onion, chopped
½ green pepper, chopped
2 tablespoons flour
2 cups mashed cooked tomatoes
Salt and pepper to taste
3 cups cooked chopped cauliflower
½ cup shredded cheese

Melt butter in a saucepan, add onion and green pepper, and brown lightly. Blend in flour and add tomatoes and salt and pepper.

Heat to boiling point and cook 3 minutes, stirring constantly. Add cauliflower and heat thoroughly.

Place mixture in a casserole and cover with shredded cheese. Bake at 350° until cheese has melted and mixture is hot and bubbly.

YIELD: 6 SERVINGS

Talk About Good!
THE JUNIOR LEAGUE OF LAFAYETTE, LOUISIANA

. . . .

Celery and Pecan Casserole

3 cups diced celery
1 tablespoon sugar
1 cup pecan halves
½ stick butter
3 tablespoons flour
½ pint light cream
1 teaspoon salt
½ teaspoon red pepper
1 egg, well beaten
Cracker crumbs

Recipe continues . . .

Place celery and sugar in water to cover. Cook until tender. Drain and mix with pecans.

Make cream sauce by melting butter and adding flour. Cook, stirring, for 2 minutes, then gradually add milk, stirring until thick. Add salt, red pepper, and beaten egg. Mix with celery and nuts.

Pour into buttered 1½-quart casserole; top with cracker crumbs. Bake ½ hour at 325°.

YIELD: 4 SERVINGS

Huntsville Heritage Cookbook
THE JUNIOR LEAGUE OF HUNTSVILLE, ALABAMA

. . . .

Corn and Sour Cream

2 tablespoons chopped onion
2 tablespoons butter
2 tablespoons flour
1 teaspoon salt
½ pound bacon
1 cup sour cream
2 12-ounce cans whole kernel corn
1 tablespoon chopped parsley

Cook onion in butter until soft; blend in flour and salt. Cook bacon and drain. Add sour cream to first mixture gradually, stirring constantly. Heat to boiling. Add corn, return to boil, and fold in ½ cup crumbled bacon.

Turn into serving dish and garnish with remaining bacon and parsley.

YIELD: 4 SERVINGS

Recipe Jubilee
THE JUNIOR LEAGUE OF MOBILE, ALABAMA

. . . .

Middleburg Plantation Corn Pudding

1 pint fresh corn cut from cob
4 eggs, well beaten
2 cups light cream
1 tablespoon butter
Pepper and salt to taste

Combine all ingredients.
Bake in buttered dish in pan of hot water for 30–40 minutes at 350°.

YIELD: 6 SERVINGS

Charleston Receipts
THE JUNIOR LEAGUE OF CHARLESTON, SOUTH CAROLINA

· · · · · · · · · · · · · · · ·

Fried Corn à la Limestone County

12 ears corn
6 tablespoons bacon drippings or butter
1 cup water
1 cup milk or cream
Salt and pepper to taste

Make a slit down each row of corn kernels with a sharp knife, then scrape the ears. (Use deep container when cutting corn to lessen spatter.)

Heat drippings or butter in heavy saucepan or iron skillet. Add corn and water and bring to boil, stirring constantly. Lower heat, cover, and cook slowly for a half hour. Stir occasionally and add more water to prevent burning.

Just before serving, remove from stove and add milk or cream, salt, and pepper. Return to stove at higher setting, bring to boil, and serve.

YIELD: 6 LARGE SERVINGS

Huntsville Heritage Cookbook
THE JUNIOR LEAGUE OF HUNTSVILLE, ALABAMA

· · · · · · · · · · · · · · · ·

"Maque Choux" (Stewed Corn and Tomatoes)

8 ears corn
1 onion, chopped
¼ green pepper, chopped
½ cup peeled and chopped tomato
1 teaspoon sugar
Salt and pepper to taste
½ cup bacon drippings or shortening

Clean corn thoroughly and cut lengthwise ¼ inch from top and scrape corn with side of blade of knife to get juice.

Mix all ingredients except drippings. In skillet, heat drippings to very hot. Add corn mixture and reduce fire to low. Cook ¾ hour, covered. Stir occasionally.

YIELD: 4–6 SERVINGS

Talk About Good!
THE JUNIOR LEAGUE OF LAFAYETTE, LOUISIANA

· · · · · · · · · · · · · · ·

Corn with Tamales

1 onion, chopped
½ green pepper, diced
1 4-ounce jar pimentos
1 15-ounce can hot tamales
2 1-pound cans creamed corn
Salt and pepper to taste
1 cup shredded sharp cheddar cheese

Stew onion, pepper, and pimentos in juice from tamales. Cut tamales into bite-size pieces. Add corn, tamales, salt, and pepper to sauce mixture.

Bake in 1½-quart casserole at 350° for 1 hour or until mixture thickens. Top with grated cheese just before serving and return to oven until cheese melts.

YIELD: 6–8 SERVINGS

Cooking Through Rose Colored Glasses
THE JUNIOR LEAGUE OF TYLER, TEXAS

. . . .

Ned's Eggplant Sticks

3 medium eggplants
1 cup seasoned bread crumbs
1 teaspoon salt
1 teaspoon pepper
¼ cup milk
3 eggs
Shortening for frying

Peel eggplant and cut into finger-size slices, ½ × 3 inches. Soak in ice water for 30 minutes. Drain well.

Mix bread crumbs, salt, and pepper. Beat together milk and eggs. Dip eggplant in milk and eggs, then in bread crumbs. Place in refrigerator for half hour to allow coating to set.

Deep fry in fat until golden brown. Drain on absorbent paper. Serve as a vegetable as is or as an hors d'oeuvre with a chili sauce dip.

YIELD: 8 SERVINGS

Party Potpourri
THE JUNIOR LEAGUE OF MEMPHIS, TENNESSEE

. . . .

Ruby's Eggplant Casserole

1 medium eggplant
½ stick butter
3 tablespoons flour
¾ cup milk
2 eggs
1 tablespoon grated onion
Dash Worcestershire sauce
Dash Tabasco
Salt and pepper to taste
Shredded sharp cheddar cheese

Peel eggplant and cut into 1-inch-square pieces. Soak in salt water about 1 hour, rinse, and drain. Boil in plain water until tender. Drain.

Make thick cream sauce of butter, flour, and milk. Beat in eggs when sauce is cool. Mix with eggplant. Add onion and seasonings.

Put in casserole dish, cover with shredded sharp cheese, and bake for 30 minutes at 350°.

YIELD: 4 SERVINGS

Spartanburg Secrets II
THE JUNIOR LEAGUE OF SPARTANBURG, SOUTH CAROLINA

·   ·   ·   ·   ·   ·   ·   ·   ·   ·   ·   ·   ·   ·   ·   ·   ·   ·

Long Pond Eggplant

1 large eggplant
4 tablespoons butter or ¼ cup olive oil
6 slices bacon, cut in half
6 ½-inch-thick slices tomato
Monosodium glutamate
Salt and pepper
Grated Parmesan cheese
6 slices Swiss, American, or mozzarella cheese

Peel and cut eggplant into ¾-inch slices. Soak eggplant slices 3–4 hours in salty water, then drain and place on paper towels.

Sauté eggplant in butter or olive oil until slightly brown but not completely done. Place on cookie sheet.

Fry bacon slightly and drain. On each slice of eggplant place 1 slice of tomato and sprinkle each with monosodium glutamate, salt, pepper, and Parmesan. Then place 1 slice bacon and 1 slice Swiss, American, or mozzarella cheese on top of tomato slices.

Place cookie sheet on bottom rack in oven. Broil until cheese is melted and bacon is cooked.

YIELD: 6 SERVINGS

Gator Country Cooks
THE JUNIOR LEAGUE OF GAINESVILLE, FLORIDA

Creole Eggplant

1 medium eggplant
5 tablespoons butter
3 tablespoons flour
2 cups chopped canned tomatoes
1 small green pepper, chopped
1 small onion, chopped
Salt and pepper to taste
1 tablespoon brown sugar
Bread crumbs
Butter
Grated cheese, preferably Parmesan

Peel eggplant, cut up, and boil in salted water about 10 minutes. Drain and place in buttered baking dish.

Melt 3 tablespoons butter and stir thoroughly into eggplant; sift flour

Recipe continues . . .

over it and mix. Mix tomatoes, green pepper, onion, salt, pepper, and sugar and cook for 5 minutes; add to eggplant mixture. Mix well. Top casserole with bread crumbs and dot with remaining butter and cheese.

Bake at 350° for 40 minutes.

YIELD: 6 SERVINGS

Mountain Measures
THE JUNIOR LEAGUE OF CHARLESTON, WEST VIRGINIA

· · · · · · · · · · · · · · · · · ·

Baked Eggplant

1 medium eggplant
2 strips bacon, minced
¼ cup minced onion
¼ cup minced green pepper
1 16-ounce can Italian-style tomatoes
¼ cup diced celery
1 4-ounce can chopped mushrooms
Salt and pepper
Dry bread crumbs
Grated cheese

Cut eggplant in half lengthwise. Scoop out and chop the meat, reserving the shells. Heat bacon in 12-inch skillet and add onion and green pepper. Cook until bacon is done. Add eggplant, tomatoes, and celery. Simmer 30 minutes. Beat with fork until well blended. Add mushrooms, salt, and pepper.

Place in eggplant shells. Cover with bread crumbs and grated cheese. Bake in 350° oven for 20 minutes or until very hot.

YIELD: 4 SERVINGS

That Something Special
THE JUNIOR LEAGUE OF DURHAM, NORTH CAROLINA

· · · · · · · · · · · · · · · · · ·

Mushrooms in Cream

20–24 large mushrooms
½ cup butter, softened
2 tablespoons chopped fresh parsley
1½ teaspoons chopped chives
1½ shallots, minced
Salt to taste
¼–½ teaspoon lemon juice
1 cup heavy cream

Remove stems from mushrooms and stuff caps with a mixture of the butter, parsley, chives, shallots, salt, and lemon juice. Put in a shallow baking dish and pour the cream over all. Bake at 450° for 10 minutes.

YIELD: 8 SERVINGS

The Dallas Jr. League Cookbook
THE JUNIOR LEAGUE OF DALLAS, TEXAS

· · · · · · · · · · · · · ·

Russian Mushrooms

1 pound mushrooms
Salt
Flour
½ cup butter
Sour cream
Grated Parmesan cheese

Wash and peel mushrooms, leaving stems attached. Dry and cut each into four or five parts. Sprinkle with salt. Sift flour over dried pieces until well covered (or shake in bag).

Recipe continues . . .

Heat butter in frying pan and brown mushrooms. Place in baking dish, cover with sour cream, and sprinkle with cheese.

Bake at 350° until brown. Serve hot in same dish with meat. steak, roast, etc.

YIELD: 4 SERVINGS

That Something Special
THE JUNIOR LEAGUE OF DURHAM, NORTH CAROLINA

· · · · · · · · · · · · · ·

Mushrooms Divine

2 pounds fresh mushrooms
3 medium onions, chopped
1 stick butter
1½ teaspoons salt
1½ teaspoons ground black pepper
Juice of 1½ lemons
Freshly ground nutmeg

Wash mushrooms thoroughly (do not soak). Remove stems.

Over low heat, very gently sauté onions in ½ stick butter.

Place mushrooms cap side down on top of onions in large skillet. Fill each cavity with pat of butter. Sprinkle with remaining ingredients. Cover and cook on medium heat about 12–15 minutes. Set aside 5 minutes.

Serve in chafing dish as hors d'oeuvre or as vegetable with steak or chicken.

YIELD: 6–8 SERVINGS AS DINNER VEGETABLE

Huntsville Heritage Cookbook
THE JUNIOR LEAGUE OF HUNTSVILLE, ALABAMA

· · · · · · · · · · · · ·

Mushroom Pie

2 pounds fresh mushrooms
6 tablespoons butter
Salt and pepper
Lemon juice
Dash soy sauce
3 tablespoons flour
1½ cups chicken stock
½ cup Madeira wine
½ cup heavy cream, heated
1 stick pie crust mix
1 egg, beaten

Wash, dry, and remove stems from mushrooms.

Heat 4 tablespoons butter, add mushrooms, and sprinkle with salt, pepper, lemon juice, and soy sauce. Cover and cook 10 minutes, stirring occasionally.

Arrange mushrooms in buttered 1-quart casserole, piling them high in the center.

To the juice in the pan, add remaining butter. Stir in flour and stock. Cook, stirring constantly, until thick. Add wine, cream, and salt and pepper to taste. Pour sauce over mushrooms.

Roll out pie crust and cover mushrooms. Brush crust with beaten egg and make a few slits in the top. Bake for 15 minutes at 450°, then 15 minutes at 300°.

YIELD: 8 SERVINGS

Party Potpourri
THE JUNIOR LEAGUE OF MEMPHIS, TENNESSEE

Creamed Mushrooms

2 pounds fresh mushrooms
4 tablespoons butter
4 tablespoons dry sherry
2 cups sour cream
1 cup (½ pound) grated Parmesan cheese
1 teaspoon salt
½ teaspoon freshly ground pepper
1 teaspoon monosodium glutamate

Leave mushroom caps whole but chop the stems; sauté in butter for 2 minutes. Add sherry and cook 1 minute. Blend in sour cream, cheese, salt, pepper, and monosodium glutamate. Cook over low heat until thickened. Serve on buttered toast.

This can also be served from a chafing dish as an appetizer after thickening slightly with flour. A wonderful accompaniment for rare roast beef.

YIELD: 8 SERVINGS

Party Potpourri
THE JUNIOR LEAGUE OF MEMPHIS, TENNESSEE

· · · · · · · · · · · · · · · · · ·

Onion Tart

1¼ cups cracker crumbs
10 tablespoons butter, softened
4 cups thinly sliced onions
4 tablespoons flour
1 cup hot milk
½ cup hot chicken stock
½ cup sour cream
1 egg yolk, beaten
Salt and pepper
1–1½ cups shredded longhorn cheese

With fingers, mix cracker crumbs with 4 tablespoons softened butter. Press into bottom and sides of a 9-inch pie plate.

Sauté onions in 2 tablespoons butter in a heavy-bottomed pan until tender. Melt 4 tablespoons butter, stir in flour, and cook 1 minute. Take off heat and stir in hot milk and chicken stock. Return to heat and stir until thickened. Add sour cream mixed with egg yolk. Season to taste with salt and pepper. Mix sauce with onions and pour into crust.

Spread cheese over top and bake at 350° about 25–30 minutes.

Good with roast beef, pork tenderloin, and leg of lamb. Can be prepared in advance and baked when ready to serve. Can also be frozen.

YIELD: 8 SERVINGS

The Dallas Jr. League Cookbook
THE JUNIOR LEAGUE OF DALLAS, TEXAS

. . . .

Stuffed Baked Onions

Peel 6 large onions and parboil in salted water 10 minutes or until almost tender. Drain and reserve liquid. Remove and save centers of onions, leaving enough exterior to make shells. Fill with desired stuffing and place in shallow baking dish. Pour 1 cup reserved liquid around onions. Bake 30 minutes at 375°.

YIELD: 6 SERVINGS

HAM STUFFING:
2 tablespoons butter
1 cup soft bread crumbs
Dash pepper
2 teaspoons minced parsley
4 tablespoons (1 small can) deviled ham
6 tablespoons chili sauce
Buttered crumbs

Recipe continues . . .

Chop reserved onion centers and sauté in butter. Add bread crumbs, pepper, parsley, and deviled ham. Mix well with fork. Top each onion with a tablespoon of chili sauce and sprinkle with buttered crumbs.

BEEF STUFFING:
½ pound ground beef
1 package stuffing mix (or bread crumbs)
Salt and pepper to taste
Buttered crumbs
Shredded sharp cheddar cheese

Chop reserved onion centers. Combine with ground beef and stuffing mix. Salt and pepper to taste. Top onions with crumbs or cheese or both.

Huntsville Heritage Cookbook
THE JUNIOR LEAGUE OF HUNTSVILLE, ALABAMA

· · · · · · · · · · · · · · · · · · ·

French Onion Casserole

4 medium onions, sliced
3 tablespoons butter
2 tablespoons flour
Salt to taste
Dash pepper
¾ cup beef bouillon
¼ cup sherry (optional)
1½ cups plain croutons
2 tablespoons melted butter
½ cup shredded Swiss cheese
3 tablespoons grated Parmesan cheese (optional)

Cook onions in 3 tablespoons butter, just until tender. Blend in flour, salt, and pepper. Add bouillon and sherry. (If sherry is omitted, use 1 cup beef bouillon instead of ¾ cup.) Cook and stir until thickened and bubbly.

Turn into 1-quart casserole. Toss croutons with 2 tablespoons melted butter and spoon on the onion mixture. Sprinkle with Swiss cheese (and Parmesan if desired).

Broil until cheese melts, about 1 minute. Serve immediately.

YIELD: 4–5 SERVINGS

Winston-Salem's Heritage of Hospitality
THE JUNIOR LEAGUE OF WINSTON-SALEM, NORTH CAROLINA

Peas Orientale

2 10¾-ounce cans condensed cream of mushroom soup
3 10-ounce packages frozen peas, cooked
2 4-ounce cans water chestnuts, drained and sliced thin
2 16-ounce cans bean sprouts, drained
1 pound button mushrooms, sautéed in butter
2 3½-ounce cans French fried onion rings

Beat soup with fork. Mix vegetables with soup and place in large buttered casserole. Bake at 350° approximately 30 minutes. Top with French fried onions and continue baking another 15–20 minutes. This is a wonderful vegetable casserole for buffet dinners, and goes well with almost any meat or poultry dish. It is easy to prepare in advance, and has an unusual and distinctive flavor.

YIELD: 12 SERVINGS

Nashville Seasons
THE JUNIOR LEAGUE OF NASHVILLE, TENNESSEE

Sweet Potato Surprise

1 1-pound can sweet potatoes, cut lengthwise
1¼ cups brown sugar
1½ tablespoons cornstarch
¼ teaspoon salt
⅛ teaspoon cinnamon
1 teaspoon shredded orange peel
1 1-pound can apricot halves
2 tablespoons butter
½ cup pecan halves

Place sweet potatoes in greased 10 × 6 × 1½-inch baking dish. Combine sugar, cornstarch, salt, cinnamon, and orange peel in saucepan.

Drain apricots, reserving syrup. Stir 1 cup syrup into cornstarch mixture. Cook and stir over medium heat until boiling. Boil 2 minutes, then add apricots, butter, and pecans. Pour over sweet potatoes. Bake uncovered at 375° for 25 minutes.

YIELD: 6 SERVINGS

Huntsville Heritage Cookbook
THE JUNIOR LEAGUE OF HUNTSVILLE, ALABAMA

.   .   .   .

Brandied Sweet Potatoes

6 large yams
2 teaspoons cornstarch
½ teaspoon nutmeg or cinnamon
2 teaspoons salt
½ cup sugar
1 cup water
1 tablespoon lemon juice
⅓ cup brandy
Miniature marshmallows (optional)

One and a quarter hours before serving: Cook the unpared yams in boiling salted water for 25 minutes or until tender. Drain and cool. In a 1-quart saucepan, mix the cornstarch, nutmeg or cinnamon, salt, and sugar. Stir in water. Cook over low heat until sauce is clear. Stir in lemon juice and brandy.

Heat oven to 375°. Peel potatoes and slice crosswise, ¼- to ½-inch thick. Put into buttered shallow baking dish. Pour on sauce, then bake 30 minutes or until glazed; basting occasionally.

When glazed, sprinkle with miniature marshmallows and broil until golden, if desired.

YIELD: 6–8 SERVINGS

Talk About Good!

THE JUNIOR LEAGUE OF LAFAYETTE, LOUISIANA

·   ·   ·   ·   ·   ·   ·   ·   ·   ·   ·   ·   ·   ·   ·   ·   ·

"*Likker*" *Pudding*

2½ cups milk
3 medium yams
3 eggs
2 cups sugar
2 teaspoons cinnamon
½ cup blanched, slivered almonds
¼ stick butter
½ cup whiskey or rum

Put milk into 2-quart casserole. Grate yams, adding to milk as you grate to prevent potatoes from turning dark. Beat eggs well and add sugar gradually. Add cinnamon and almonds and mix well with potatoes. Dot generously with butter and bake at 300° for 2 hours.

Just before serving, pour the whiskey or rum over the pudding.

Delicious with turkey. May be used without "likker."

YIELD: 6 SERVINGS

Charleston Receipts

THE JUNIOR LEAGUE OF CHARLESTON, SOUTH CAROLINA

·   ·   ·   ·   ·   ·   ·   ·   ·   ·   ·   ·   ·   ·   ·   ·

Mozzarella and Potato Pie

2 pounds potatoes, peeled
¼ cup butter, softened
Salt and pepper to taste
Butter
Flour
½ pound mozzarella cheese
3 tomatoes, peeled
1 teaspoon oregano
1 teaspoon basil
½ cup freshly grated Parmesan cheese
¼ cup butter, melted

Boil peeled potatoes in salted water to cover until they are tender. Drain and mash them. Stir in softened butter and season with salt and pepper.

Butter and lightly flour a deep 9½-inch pie plate. Spread in the mashed potatoes. Cut the mozzarella cheese into ¼-inch-thick slices. Arrange half of the cheese on the potatoes and top it with the peeled tomatoes cut into ½-inch-thick slices. Sprinkle with oregano, basil, salt, and pepper. Top the tomatoes with remaining mozzarella, Parmesan, and melted butter.

Bake the pie at 425° for 20–25 minutes or until cheese is melted and lightly browned. Can be made ahead and refrigerated until baking time.

YIELD: **4–6** SERVINGS

The Dallas Jr. League Cookbook
THE JUNIOR LEAGUE OF DALLAS, TEXAS

. . . .

Scalloped Potatoes

5 cups diced cooked potatoes
2 cups creamy cottage cheese
¼ cup minced green onion
2 teaspoons salt
1 cup sour cream
1 clove garlic, minced (optional)
½ cup shredded American cheese

Boil potatoes in jackets. Peel and dice.

Combine cottage cheese, onion, salt, sour cream, and garlic. Fold in potatoes.

Place in 1½-quart baking dish. Top with American cheese and bake at 350° for 40–45 minutes.

YIELD: 6–8 SERVINGS

Home Cookin'
THE JUNIOR LEAGUE OF WICHITA FALLS, TEXAS

. . . .

Party Potatoes

8–10 medium-size potatoes
1 cup sour cream
1 8-ounce package cream cheese, softened
4 tablespoons butter
⅓ cup chopped chives
Salt and pepper to taste
Additional butter
Paprika

Boil peeled potatoes until tender. Beat sour cream and cheese together, add hot potatoes, and beat until smooth. Add butter, chives, and salt and pepper to taste.

Recipe continues ...

Pour into a well-greased 2-quart casserole, dot with butter, and sprinkle paprika on top. Bake at 350° for 25 minutes. Wonderful do-ahead dish for company.

YIELD: 8–10 SERVINGS

The Charlotte Cookbook
THE JUNIOR LEAGUE OF CHARLOTTE, NORTH CAROLINA

. . . .

Baker's Potatoes

2 pounds potatoes
1 medium-size onion
2 tablespoons chopped parsley
Salt and pepper to taste
½ cup margarine
1 10½-ounce can consommé, undiluted

Slice potatoes and onion thin and arrange in shallow glass baking dish. Sprinkle with parsley and salt and pepper to taste. Dot with margarine. Spoon consommé on top, almost covering the potatoes entirely. Bake at 350° for 1 hour.

YIELD: 6–8 SERVINGS

Furniture City Feasts
THE JUNIOR LEAGUE OF HIGH POINT, NORTH CAROLINA

. . . .

Spinach Rouen

4 pounds spinach
⅓ pound butter, melted
1 cup heavy cream
Salt and pepper

Cook spinach till tender. Chop up very fine or put through a grinder. Drain all juice from spinach. Replace juice with melted butter.

Bake in a glass dish in oven for 20 minutes at 400° or until quite dry. Add cream, a little salt, and a dash of pepper, and replace in oven till hot.

YIELD: 6 SERVINGS

The Cotton Blossom Cookbook
THE JUNIOR LEAGUE OF ATLANTA, GEORGIA

. . . .

Spinach Casserole

1 10-ounce package frozen chopped spinach
1 teaspoon sugar
1 10¾-ounce can condensed cream of chicken soup
1 egg, beaten
1 cup shredded sharp cheddar cheese
2 slices bread, cubed
3 tablespoons melted butter
Dash garlic salt
Dash red pepper

Cook spinach, using ½ cup water and 1 teaspoon sugar. Drain thoroughly, mashing out *all* liquid.

Combine spinach, soup, egg, and cheese.

Pour into greased 1½-quart casserole. Toss the bread cubes in the melted butter, to which the garlic salt and red pepper have been added. Place on top of the spinach and bake 1 hour at 350°.

YIELD: 4 SERVINGS

The Charlotte Cookbook
THE JUNIOR LEAGUE OF CHARLOTTE, NORTH CAROLINA

. . . .

Spinach-Artichoke Casserole

2 10-ounce packages frozen chopped spinach
½ cup finely chopped onion
1 stick butter
1 1-pound can artichokes
1 pint sour cream
½ cup grated Parmesan cheese
Salt and pepper

Cook spinach as directed on box. Drain. Sauté onion in butter. Mix all ingredients together and place in casserole. Stir Parmesan cheese into casserole and also sprinkle some on top. Bake at 350° for 20 or 30 minutes.

YIELD: 6 SERVINGS

Talk About Good!
THE JUNIOR LEAGUE OF LAFAYETTE, LOUISIANA

.   .   .   .

Baked Squash

6 yellow squash
6 tablespoons grated Parmesan cheese
6 tablespoons butter
Salt and pepper to taste
1 cup milk

Slice squash in half lengthwise. Place in 9 × 9-inch baking pan, cut side up. Sprinkle on enough Parmesan cheese to cover each squash half. Dot with butter, salt, and pepper. Carefully pour milk into pan to approximately ½-inch depth. Avoid letting milk wash cheese off the squash.

Bake at 350° for 45 minutes, until tops of squash are golden brown.

YIELD: 4–6 SERVINGS

A Taste of Tampa
THE JUNIOR LEAGUE OF TAMPA, FLORIDA

.   .   .   .

Summer Squash Casserole

3 cups cubed summer squash
¼ cup sour cream
1 tablespoon melted butter
1 tablespoon shredded cheese
½ teaspoon salt
⅛ teaspoon paprika
1 egg yolk, beaten
1 tablespoon chopped chives
2 tablespoons softened butter
½ cup grated Parmesan cheese
½ cup dry bread crumbs

Simmer squash until tender and drain.

Combine sour cream, melted butter, cheese, salt, and paprika. Stir mixture over low heat until cheese is melted.

Stir in egg yolk and chopped chives. Mix squash into mixture. Place mixture in buttered baking dish. Dot with butter, grated cheese, and bread crumbs.

Bake at 350° until bubbly and brown, approximately 25–30 minutes.

YIELD: 4 SERVINGS

Furniture City Feasts
THE JUNIOR LEAGUE OF HIGH POINT, NORTH CAROLINA

.   .   .   .

Winter Squash Casserole

A substitute for sweet potatoes at your holiday dinner table.

2 large acorn or butternut squash (or 1 hubbard)
¼ pound butter
2 eggs, whipped
2 teaspoons pumpkin pie seasoning

Recipe continues . . .

TOPPING:
¼ cup half and half
1 cup brown sugar
¾ cup pecans or Brazil nuts, chopped

Bake squash whole at 350° for 1 or 2 hours or until a fork penetrates easily. Cut and remove seeds and skin. With an electric mixer, mash the squash and beat in remaining ingredients. Put in casserole and either bake or freeze.

To serve, combine the topping ingredients, cover the squash with the mixture, and bake at 375° for 45 minutes.

YIELD: 6–8 SERVINGS

Nashville Seasons Encore
THE JUNIOR LEAGUE OF NASHVILLE, TENNESSEE

. . . .

Grilled Tomatoes

6 large tomatoes (not too ripe)
1 stick butter
2 tablespoons dry onion flakes
1 or 2 sprigs fresh parsley, chopped
2–3 tablespoons brown sugar
Salt, basil, and thyme to taste
2 cups fine, dry bread crumbs

Cut tomatoes in half, squeeze out seeds and juice, salt well, and turn upside down on cake rack to drain while preparing stuffing.

Melt butter; add onion, parsley, sugar, and seasonings. Add enough of the 2 cups crumbs to make stuffing the right consistency. Press stuffing into each tomato half and place in compartments of a muffin tin. (Muffin tin helps them keep their shape.)

Bake at 350° just long enough to heat through (usually 5 to 10 minutes). Gently remove from tin with spoons and place on heated platter.

YIELD: 12 TOMATO HALVES

That Something Special
THE JUNIOR LEAGUE OF DURHAM, NORTH CAROLINA

· · · · · · · · · · · · · · · ·

Caramelized Tomatoes

2 stalks celery, chopped
⅓ green pepper, chopped
1 small onion, chopped
1 cup brown sugar
2 teaspoons flour
1 teaspoon salt
2 tablespoons lemon juice
1 teaspoon oregano
4 tomatoes, peeled and cored
Salt and pepper to taste
Margarine

In saucepan, combine first four ingredients. Cook over low heat about 15 minutes.

Make paste of flour, salt, lemon juice, oregano, and a little water. Stir into vegetable mixture and cook until thick and smooth.

Fill tomatoes with mixture. Salt, pepper, and dot with margarine before baking for 20 minutes at 375°.

YIELD: 4 SERVINGS

Huntsville Heritage Cookbook
THE JUNIOR LEAGUE OF HUNTSVILLE, ALABAMA

· · · · · · · · · · · · · · ·

Cherry Tomatoes in Cream

3 tablespoons butter
3 tablespoons brown sugar
½ teaspoon salt
1 box cherry tomatoes
1 pint heavy cream

Melt butter, sugar, and salt in heavy skillet. Add washed tomatoes. Stir with wooden spoon. When tomatoes begin to split open, add cream.

Serve in individual bowls.

YIELD: 4 SERVINGS

Southern Sideboards
THE JUNIOR LEAGUE OF JACKSON, MISSISSIPPI

. . . .

Turnips and Peas à la Crème

7–8 white turnips, peeled and sliced very thin
2 tablespoons minced onion
3 tablespoons butter
½ cup sugar
½ cup heavy cream
1 cup cooked green peas
Salt and pepper
Chopped parsley

Cook turnips until tender. Drain well.

Sauté onion with butter and sugar for approximately 1 minute. Add turnips and cook until hot.

Add cream and peas and simmer until cream is reduced. Add seasonings and sprinkle with chopped parsley.

YIELD: 4 SERVINGS

Home Cookin'
THE JUNIOR LEAGUE OF WICHITA FALLS, TEXAS

. . . .

Scalloped Tomatoes

2 cups thinly sliced onion
4 tablespoons margarine
1½ cups dry bread crumbs
2 teaspoons salt
¼ teaspoon pepper
½ teaspoon celery salt
2 tablespoons brown sugar
2 cups canned tomatoes

Sauté onions until transparent in 2 tablespoons of the margarine. Remove from pan and drain. Do not brown.

Sauté bread crumbs in the remaining 2 tablespoons margarine until browned. Set aside. Add seasonings and sugar to onions. Mix with tomatoes which have been well drained. Pour into greased casserole. Top with bread crumbs. Bake uncovered for 1 hour at 350°.

YIELD: 6 SERVINGS

Furniture City Feasts
THE JUNIOR LEAGUE OF HIGH POINT, NORTH CAROLINA

· · · · · · · · · · · · · · · · · ·

White Turnip Casserole

3 pounds fresh white turnip roots
Bacon drippings (optional)
¼ cup butter
1½ teaspoons sugar
1½ teaspoons salt
Dash pepper
3 eggs
1 cup fresh bread crumbs
1½ teaspoons lemon juice
Paprika

Recipe continues . . .

Peel and dice turnips. Cook in boiling salted water to which a little bacon drippings may be added. Boil for about 25 minutes. Drain and put in electric mixer. Add butter, sugar, salt, and pepper. Beat until smooth.

Add eggs, one at a time. Turn off mixer. Stir in crumbs and lemon juice.

Pour into greased oblong casserole and sprinkle with paprika.

Bake uncovered at 375° for 50 minutes.

YIELD: 8 SERVINGS

Gator Country Cooks
THE JUNIOR LEAGUE OF GAINESVILLE, FLORIDA

. . . .

Zucchini Flan

3 tablespoons chopped onion
2 tablespoons butter
6 firm and unblemished zucchini, sliced thin
1 cup heavy cream (or evaporated milk)
2 eggs, slightly beaten
¼ teaspoon nutmeg
Salt and pepper to taste
½ cup shredded Swiss or Gruyère cheese

Cook onion in butter until transparent. Add sliced zucchini and cook until tender.

In buttered casserole, blend cream, eggs, nutmeg, salt, and pepper. Add zucchini to cream mixture and sprinkle top with cheese.

Bake at 350° until custard is lightly set, about 30 minutes.

YIELD: 6 SERVINGS

Mountain Measures
THE JUNIOR LEAGUE OF CHARLESTON, WEST VIRGINIA

. . . .

Ratatouille

⅓ cup olive oil
1 medium onion, chopped very fine
1 clove garlic, chopped very fine
1½ pounds eggplant, peeled and cubed
3 small zucchini, unpeeled and sliced
1 green pepper, cut into strips
Salt and pepper
Pinch basil
6 small tomatoes (or 3 medium), peeled and seeded, or
1 1-pound 4-ounce can solid-pack tomatoes
Additional oil (optional)
Lemon juice (optional)

Heat olive oil in large pot. Sauté onion and garlic until soft. Add eggplant and zucchini and toss well. Add pepper strips, salt and pepper to taste, and basil. Simmer covered until vegetables are soft.

Add tomatoes and let them cook down with the vegetables until mixture is thick and well blended.

Serve hot or chilled, with additional oil and lemon juice if desired.

YIELD: 6 SERVINGS

Spartanburg Secrets II
THE JUNIOR LEAGUE OF SPARTANBURG, SOUTH CAROLINA

. . . .

Green Vegetables with Egg Sauce

1 10-ounce package frozen baby lima beans
1 10-ounce package frozen small peas
1 16-ounce can whole green beans

Cook vegetables separately, according to package directions. Mix together and heat. Drain and serve with Egg Sauce.

Recipe continues . . .

EGG SAUCE:
2 hard-boiled eggs
¼ teaspoon dry mustard
1 cup mayonnaise
2½ teaspoons Worcestershire sauce
½ teaspoon chopped onion
2 tablespoons olive oil

Grate eggs finely and mix together with remaining ingredients. Serve at room temperature over the hot vegetables.

YIELD: 8 SERVINGS

Party Potpourri
THE JUNIOR LEAGUE OF MEMPHIS, TENNESSEE

. . . .

Okra, Corn, and Tomato Mélange

4 strips bacon
4 tablespoons bacon drippings
1 onion, chopped fine
1 pint okra, cut into ¼-inch rings
4 ears corn, scraped
3 large tomatoes, peeled and diced
1 small green pepper, chopped
1 teaspoon sugar
Salt and pepper to taste
Dash Tabasco

Fry bacon until crisp, drain, and reserve 4 tablespoons drippings. Stir onion and okra into drippings, add corn kernels, and cook for 10 minutes, stirring constantly. Add tomatoes, green pepper, and seasonings. Cover and simmer until done (about 25 minutes), stirring occasionally.

Correct seasoning, pour into serving dish, and sprinkle with crumbled bacon.

YIELD: 6 SERVINGS

Southern Accent
THE JUNIOR LEAGUE OF PINE BLUFF, ARKANSAS

. . . .

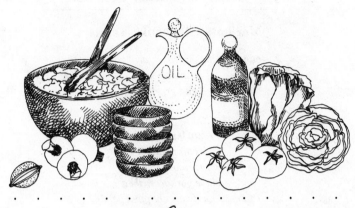

Salads and Salad Dressings

Marinated Artichoke Hearts

2 9-ounce packages frozen artichoke hearts
1 teaspoon salt
Salad greens

VEGETABLE MARINADE:
¼ cup lemon juice
¼ cup salad oil
¼ cup red wine vinegar
1 clove garlic, crushed
1 tablespoon finely chopped parsley
1 tablespoon finely chopped onion
½ teaspoon oregano
½ teaspoon salt
¼ teaspoon pepper

Cook artichoke hearts according to directions on package, using 1 teaspoon salt in water. Drain and cool slightly.

Combine marinade ingredients in pint jar and shake vigorously, or blend in blender. Pour marinade over artichokes. Toss to coat well, cover, and refrigerate several hours (or overnight), stirring occasionally.

Add to a tossed green salad, or serve on lettuce leaves.

YIELD: 6 SERVINGS

A Cook's Tour of Shreveport
THE JUNIOR LEAGUE OF SHREVEPORT, LOUISIANA

. . . .

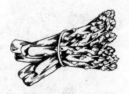

Asparagus Vinaigrette

2 14½-ounce cans green asparagus
2 hard-boiled eggs

Drain asparagus. Arrange in serving dish and marinate in the dressing a few hours in refrigerator.

Grate eggs on top just before serving.

YIELD: 6–8 SERVINGS

VINAIGRETTE DRESSING:
½ teaspoon prepared mustard
2 tablespoons vinegar
6 tablespoons salad oil
½ teaspoon salt
Dash pepper
1 teaspoon finely grated onion

Combine all ingredients and blend thoroughly.

Winston-Salem's Heritage of Hospitality
THE JUNIOR LEAGUE OF WINSTON-SALEM, NORTH CAROLINA

. . . .

Bermuda Salad Bowl

1 small head cauliflower
½ large Bermuda onion
½ cup sliced stuffed olives (preferably large ones)
⅔ cup French dressing
½ cup crumbled Roquefort cheese
1 head lettuce

Separate cauliflower into flowerets; slice thin crosswise. Slice onion in rings. Marinate cauliflower, onion, and olives in French dressing 30 minutes before serving.

Recipe continues . . .

Just before serving, add cheese and lettuce torn into bite-size pieces. Toss lightly and serve.

YIELD: 6 SERVINGS

The Cotton Blossom Cookbook
THE JUNIOR LEAGUE OF ATLANTA, GEORGIA

Gilded Green Beans

6 tablespoons vinegar
¾ cup salad or olive oil
2 medium onions, minced
Salt and pepper
2 pounds whole green beans, cooked
8 slices crisp bacon, crumbled

Prepare marinade by combining vinegar, oil, onions, salt, and pepper. Chill beans in marinade several hours. Remove beans from marinade and add crumbled bacon to them. Heap in salad bowl. Top with Egg Dressing.

YIELD: 8 SERVINGS

EGG DRESSING:
8 hard-boiled eggs, chopped
6 tablespoons mayonnaise
4 teaspoons vinegar
2 teaspoons prepared mustard
Salt

Combine all ingredients and blend thoroughly.

Home Cookin'
THE JUNIOR LEAGUE OF WICHITA FALLS, TEXAS

Broccoli Vinaigrette

2 pounds fresh or frozen broccoli
2 cups oil and vinegar dressing
½ cup chopped dill pickle relish
½ cup minced green pepper
¼ cup snipped parsley
¼ cup capers
Pimento (optional)

Cook broccoli until barely tender; drain. Put remaining ingredients in jar; shake until well mixed. Pour over broccoli in flat dish. Chill a few hours or overnight. Garnish with strips of pimento.

YIELD: 8 SERVINGS

Little Rock Cooks
THE JUNIOR LEAGUE OF LITTLE ROCK, ARKANSAS

. . . .

Slaw

1 medium cabbage, shredded fine
1 onion, shredded
1 cup sugar
1 cup vinegar
¾ cup oil
1 teaspoon dry mustard
1 teaspoon celery seed
1 tablespoon salt

Put cabbage and onion in bean pot; top with sugar.

Combine vinegar, oil, mustard, celery seed, and salt. Bring to boil. Pour hot mixture over cabbage and cool. Cover and refrigerate for at least 2 days.

YIELD: 6–8 SERVINGS

300 Years of Carolina Cooking
THE JUNIOR LEAGUE OF GREENVILLE, SOUTH CAROLINA

. . . .

Swedish Cucumbers

½ teaspoon salt
½ teaspoon sugar
1 pound cucumbers, peeled and sliced thin

WHITE SALAD DRESSING:
2 tablespoons minced parsley
1 tablespoon salt
1 tablespoon sugar
2 tablespoons white vinegar
1 tablespoon water
½ teaspoon black pepper

Salt and sugar the cucumbers. Squeeze out after 15 minutes to drain thoroughly.

Combine dressing ingredients and add to cucumbers at least 1 hour before serving.

YIELD: 6 SERVINGS

Winston-Salem's Heritage of Hospitality
THE JUNIOR LEAGUE OF WINSTON-SALEM, NORTH CAROLINA

· · · · · · · · · · · · · ·

Mushroom Salad

1 pound fresh mushrooms
1 cup chopped celery (inner stalks and tiny leaves)
2 pimentos, cut into strips
1 hard-boiled egg, sliced
2 tablespoons minced chives or green onions
Oil and vinegar dressing
Salt and pepper

Rinse mushrooms lightly and dry well. Cut caps and stems into bite-size pieces. Mix all ingredients in bowl and toss with dressing. Marinating salad in refrigerator 30 minutes adds to flavor.

Sprinkle lightly with salt and freshly ground black pepper. Remove salad from dressing and arrange with lettuce or romaine leaves on salad plates.

May also be tossed with a variety of greens and artichoke hearts. Bottled Italian dressing can be used. The marinated ingredients could be done an hour or so ahead, but greens should be tossed at the last minute.

YIELD: 4–6 SERVINGS

Seasoned with Sun: Recipes from the Southwest
THE JUNIOR LEAGUE OF EL PASO, TEXAS

. . . .

Marinated Artichokes and Mushrooms

2 pounds fresh mushrooms
2 7-ounce cans artichokes, drained
1 cup vinegar
½ cup oil
1 clove garlic
1½ tablespoons salt
½ tablespoon freshly ground pepper
½ teaspoon thyme
½ teaspoon oregano
1 tablespoon dry parsley flakes
1 onion, sliced in rings

Wash and drain mushrooms. Drain artichokes. Combine all other ingredients in bowl. Mix well; add artichokes and mushrooms. Marinate overnight in refrigerator.

Serve on platter covered with fresh spinach leaves.

YIELD: 6–8 SERVINGS

Of Pots and Pipkins
THE JUNIOR LEAGUE OF ROANOKE VALLEY, VIRGINIA

. . . .

Pineapple Cheese Salad

1 cup crushed pineapple
¾ cup sugar
Juice of one lemon
1 envelope unflavored gelatin
½ cup cold water
1 cup boiling water
1 cup heavy cream, whipped
1 cup shredded cheddar cheese

Boil together for 5 minutes the pineapple, sugar, and lemon juice. Add the unflavored gelatin to cold water in order to soften, then add the boiling water and combine with pineapple mixture. Put in refrigerator until partially set. Remove from refrigerator and stir in whipped cream and cheese.

YIELD: 8 SERVINGS

Furniture City Feasts
THE JUNIOR LEAGUE OF HIGH POINT, NORTH CAROLINA

Irma Price's Neighbor Tater Stuff

8 medium potatoes
1½ cups mayonnaise
1 cup sour cream
1½ teaspoons horseradish
1 teaspoon celery seed
½ teaspoon salt
1 cup chopped parsley
2 medium onions, finely chopped, or ½ cup chives, chopped

Boil potatoes in jackets until done; peel and cut into ⅛-inch slices. Combine mayonnaise, sour cream, horseradish, celery seed, and salt. Set aside.

In another bowl, mix parsley (do not omit or decrease) and onions or chives.

In large serving bowl arrange layer of potatoes; salt lightly, cover with layer of mayonnaise mixture, then layer of parsley-onion mixture. Continue layering, ending with parsley-onion mix. *Do not stir.* Cover and store in refrigerator at least 8 hours before serving.

Better made the day before.

YIELD: 8–10 SERVINGS

Furniture City Feasts
THE JUNIOR LEAGUE OF HIGH POINT, NORTH CAROLINA

. . . .

Hot Potato Salad

6 potatoes
1 small onion, chopped
6 slices bacon
Mayonnaise or salad dressing
1 tablespoon Worcestershire sauce
1 tablespoon celery seed
1 3-ounce jar Spanish olives, sliced
½ pound mild cheese, cubed
Dash each of sugar, salt, and pepper

Boil potatoes until done. Cook onion and bacon together. Add this and drippings to cooked, diced potatoes. Add enough mayonnaise or salad dressing to moisten, then Worcestershire sauce and celery seed.

Add olives, cheese, and dashes of sugar, salt, and pepper.

Place in oblong baking dish and heat in 350° oven until cheese melts (about 30–40 minutes).

This may be prepared a day ahead or even prepared and frozen.

YIELD: 6–8 SERVINGS

Little Rock Cooks
THE JUNIOR LEAGUE OF LITTLE ROCK, ARKANSAS

. . . .

Sara Thompson's Rice Salad

1 tablespoon vinegar
2 tablespoons corn oil
¾ cup mayonnaise
1 teaspoon salt
½ teaspoon curry powder
1⅓ cups hot cooked rice
2 tablespoons chopped onion
1 cup chopped celery
1 10-ounce package frozen small peas (undercooked)

Mix vinegar, oil, mayonnaise, salt, and curry powder. Cook rice until just done. Add rice to mixture, then add chopped onion while rice is hot. When cooled, add celery and peas.

This is better the second day.

YIELD: 6–8 SERVINGS

Cooking Through Rose Colored Glasses
THE JUNIOR LEAGUE OF TYLER, TEXAS

· · · · · · · · · · · · · · · · · ·

German Potato Salad

8–10 medium-size new potatoes
Pinch salt
¼ onion, chopped very fine
1 tablespoon bacon drippings
1 tablespoon flour
1 cup vinegar
½ cup water
¾ cup sugar
8 pieces bacon
Chopped parsley (optional)

Boil unpeeled potatoes in enough water to cover them. Add pinch salt to the water. Cook the potatoes until almost done; then cool and cut into thin slices. Mix the potatoes and onion. Make a sauce of bacon drippings, flour, vinegar, water, and sugar as follows: Warm the drippings and add the flour, stirring constantly. Mix well the vinegar, water, and sugar. Add to the drippings and flour and stir until the mixture begins to thicken. Pour this over the potatoes and onions and refrigerate for at least 12 hours.

Warm *slightly* before serving, add crumbled pieces of fried bacon, and mix well.

This potato salad should be served only slightly above room temperature. If desired, chopped parsley may be added.

YIELD: 6–8 SERVINGS

Nashville Seasons
THE JUNIOR LEAGUE OF NASHVILLE, TENNESSEE

Golden Rice Salad

¼ cup salad oil
2 tablespoons vinegar
1½ teaspoons salt
⅛ teaspoon black pepper
⅛ teaspoon red pepper
4½ cups hot cooked rice (1½ cups raw rice) cooked in
3 cups chicken broth
1 cup ripe olives, cut into large pieces
2 hard-boiled eggs, diced
1½ cups sliced celery
¼ cup chopped dill pickle
1 small onion, minced
½ cup mayonnaise
2 tablespoons prepared mustard
Parsley and green onion tops (optional)

Recipe continues ...

Blend together salad oil, vinegar, salt, and peppers; pour over hot cooked rice. Toss and set aside to cool.

Add remaining ingredients; toss. Chill thoroughly. Parsley and green onion tops may be added.

YIELD: 6 SERVINGS

Talk About Good!
THE JUNIOR LEAGUE OF LAFAYETTE, LOUISIANA

. . . .

Spinach Salad

1 bunch fresh spinach, cleaned, dried, and torn into bite-size pieces
2 hard-boiled eggs
6 slices crisp, cooked bacon

DRESSING:
⅔ cup salad oil
¼ cup wine vinegar with garlic
2 tablespoons white wine
2 teaspoons soy sauce
1 teaspoon sugar
1 teaspoon dry mustard
½ teaspoon curry powder
1½ teaspoons salt
Freshly ground pepper

Combine dressing ingredients in a jar and set aside until ready to use.

Arrange spinach in individual salad dishes or bowls or in a large glass bowl. Pour dressing over spinach and mix. Top with crisp crumbled bacon and chopped eggs.

YIELD: 4–6 SERVINGS

Furniture City Feasts
THE JUNIOR LEAGUE OF HIGH POINT, NORTH CAROLINA

. . . .

Watercress à la Dennis

Bacon
Green onions
Watercress

For each portion of salad chop 1 slice of crisp cooled bacon and 1 chopped green onion. Toss with watercress; add dressing. Toss again.

DRESSING:
1 cup olive oil
⅓ cup cider vinegar
½ teaspoon white pepper
½ teaspoon horseradish
1 teaspoon paprika
¼ teaspoon dry mustard
1 teaspoon salt
1 teaspoon Worcestershire sauce
1 tablespoon sugar

Put all ingredients in bowl with piece of ice about size of an egg. Whip until completely mixed.

YIELD: 4–5 SERVINGS

Huntsville Heritage Cookbook
THE JUNIOR LEAGUE OF HUNTSVILLE, ALABAMA

· · · · · · · · · · · · · · ·

Tossed Salad with Greek Cheese

*Mixed salad greens (Boston, Bibb, iceberg, few spinach
leaves for color)*
Onions, sliced thin and soaked in ice water until translucent
Feta cheese, broken in pieces (about 1 tablespoon per person)
Olive oil
Lemon juice
Salt
Freshly ground black pepper

Toss all ingredients lightly in a large salad bowl. For variety, smoked
oysters, avocado, ripe olives, artichoke hearts, or tomatoes may be added,
singly or in various combinations to suit your taste.

The Gasparilla Cookbook
THE JUNIOR LEAGUE OF TAMPA, FLORIDA

. . . .

Marinated Vegetable Salad

1 16-ounce can tiny green peas
1 12-ounce can tiny white shoe peg corn (small-kernel white corn)
1 16-ounce can French-style green beans
1 medium-size onion, chopped
¾ cup finely chopped celery
Chopped pimento to taste

Drain canned vegetables and combine with onion, celery, and pimento.
Pour dressing over all, tossing well.

SWEET AND SOUR DRESSING:
½ cup salad oil
½ cup wine vinegar
¾ cup sugar
1 teaspoon salt
½ teaspoon pepper

Combine all ingredients thoroughly and heat to boiling.

The salad should be prepared a day ahead. It will keep in the refrigerator several weeks.

YIELD: 8–10 SERVINGS

Of Pots and Pipkins
THE JUNIOR LEAGUE OF ROANOKE VALLEY, VIRGINIA

· · · · · · · · · · · · · · · · · ·

Cooked Green Vegetable Salad

1 10-ounce package frozen cut broccoli
1 10-ounce package frozen French-style green beans
1 10-ounce package frozen cut asparagus
1 green pepper, chopped
1 cucumber, diced
1 6-ounce can marinated artichoke hearts, sliced
Romaine lettuce

DRESSING:
½ cup half and half
2 tablespoons lemon juice
2 tablespoons garlic vinegar
1 cup mayonnaise
¾ cup chopped parsley
¼ cup chopped onions
2 tablespoons anchovy paste (optional)
Salt to taste

Recipe continues . . .

Cook broccoli, green beans, and asparagus together about 5 minutes. Drain and cool. Break into bite-size pieces.

Add pepper, chopped cucumber, artichoke hearts. Chill.

Combine all dressing ingredients. Add dressing before serving. Serve in bowl lined with romaine.

YIELD: 8–10 SERVINGS

The Blue Denim Gourmet
THE JUNIOR LEAGUE OF ODESSA, TEXAS

· · · · · · · · · · · · · · · · ·

Gourmet Delight

1 pound celery hearts, chopped
2 6-ounce cans pitted black olives, drained and sliced
2 5-ounce jars stuffed green olives, drained and sliced
1 head cauliflower, broken into flowerets
1 pint cherry tomatoes, cut in half
2 8½-ounce cans artichoke hearts, sliced
1 pound carrots, chopped

Mix above ingredients in large salad bowl. Pour over dressing. Chill. *Marinate for 24 hours.*

YIELD: 18–20 SERVINGS

FRENCH DRESSING:
1½ cups salad oil
⅔ cup white vinegar
2½ teaspoons salt
1 teaspoon pepper
2 cloves garlic, crushed
1½ teaspoons sugar

Combine ingredients and mix well.

Home Cookin'
THE JUNIOR LEAGUE OF WICHITA FALLS, TEXAS

· · · · · · · · · · · · · · · · ·

Taco Salad

1½ pounds ground beef
1½ cups chopped onion
1 cup chopped celery
1 cup chopped green pepper
3 cloves garlic, minced
1 teaspoon salt
1 teaspoon chili powder
½ teaspoon ground cumin
1 large head lettuce
2 large fresh tomatoes
⅓ 11-ounce package corn chips
1 10-ounce can tomatoes and green chilies
1 pound soft processed cheese, cubed

Brown ground beef and set aside.

Sauté chopped onion, celery, and pepper with minced garlic in remaining juices. Combine meat with mixture and spices; simmer for 20 minutes.

Cut lettuce coarsely and dice tomatoes; toss together in a large bowl and add slightly crushed corn chips.

In top of double boiler, put canned tomatoes and chilies with cubed cheese. Stir frequently until melted.

When ready to serve, add hot meat to lettuce and toss to mix. Pour cheese sauce in bowl to use as dressing for salad.

YIELD: 10 SERVINGS

Seasoned with Sun: Recipes from the Southwest
THE JUNIOR LEAGUE OF EL PASO, TEXAS

· · · · · · · · · · · · · · ·

Chicken and Avocado Salad

2½ cups diced, cooked chicken
¾ cup diced celery
¾ cup small raw cauliflower flowerets
⅓ cup French dressing
½ cup sour cream
¼ cup mayonnaise
⅓ cup chopped toasted almonds
Salt and pepper to taste
3 avocados, chilled
1 head lettuce

Mix chicken and vegetables. Marinate with French dressing; let stand in refrigerator several hours.

Shortly before serving, add sour cream, mayonnaise, almonds, salt, and pepper.

Peel and halve avocados; arrange halves in lettuce cups and fill with chicken salad.

YIELD: 6 SERVINGS

300 Years of Carolina Cooking
THE JUNIOR LEAGUE OF GREENVILLE, SOUTH CAROLINA

· · · · · · · · · · · · · · · · · · · ·

Cold Beef Salad

SALAD:
2 cups beef, cooked rare, chilled, and slivered
½ cup sliced celery
⅓ cup chopped sour pickle
¼ cup chopped green onions
¼ cup drained capers

DIJON DRESSING:
½ cup salad oil
3 tablespoons vinegar
1 tablespoon Dijon mustard
½ clove garlic
Dash hot pepper sauce
Salt and pepper to taste

Combine salad ingredients and toss.

Combine dressing ingredients. Let stand at room temperature. When ready to serve, remove garlic clove from dressing. Add dressing to salad and serve at room temperature.

YIELD: 4 SERVINGS

Winston-Salem's Heritage of Hospitality
THE JUNIOR LEAGUE OF WINSTON-SALEM, NORTH CAROLINA

·   ·   ·   ·   ·   ·   ·   ·   ·   ·   ·   ·   ·   ·   ·   ·

Salpicon (Mexican Shredded Beef)

8 pounds top sirloin or eye of round
2 cloves garlic
1 bay leaf
1 12-ounce can tomatoes
¼ cup chopped fresh cilantro (coriander leaves)
Salt and pepper to taste
1 8-ounce bottle Italian-style salad dressing
1 cup cooked garbanzo beans
½ pound Monterey Jack cheese, cut into ½-inch squares
1 cup chopped green chilies (fresh or canned)
2 avocados, cut into strips
1 bunch parsley

Place beef in heavy pot; cover with water and add garlic, bay leaf, tomatoes, cilantro, salt, and pepper. Cook over medium heat about 5 hours.

Recipe continues . . .

Remove meat from broth, cool meat, and cut into 2-inch squares. Shred and arrange in a 9 × 11-inch glass dish.

Cover beef with salad dressing and allow to marinate overnight in refrigerator.

Before serving, arrange the following in layers over beef: beans, cheese, chilies, and avocados. Decorate with parsley. This is a perfect dish for a buffet table.

YIELD: 16–20 SERVINGS

Seasoned with Sun: Recipes from the Southwest
THE JUNIOR LEAGUE OF EL PASO, TEXAS

. . . .

Exotic Chicken Salad

4½–5 pounds chicken breasts, split
Melted butter
Salt and pepper
3 3¼-ounce packages slivered almonds
2 cups mayonnaise, preferably homemade
1 tablespoon curry powder
2 tablespoons soy sauce
2 cups sliced celery
3 6-ounce cans water chestnuts, sliced
2 pounds seedless grapes
Boston or Bibb lettuce

Brush chicken breasts with melted butter and sprinkle with salt and pepper. Wrap in heavy-duty aluminum foil and seal edges tightly. Place in shallow pan and bake in 350° oven for 1 hour. Cool, bone, and cut into bite-size pieces; there should be 2 quarts.

Coat almond slivers with melted butter and spread on cookie sheet. Roast in 350° oven about 30 minutes or until they are a mellow brown.

Spread on paper towels, sprinkle with salt, and set aside until just before serving. All this can be done the day before.

A few hours before serving, mix mayonnaise with curry powder and soy sauce. If mayonnaise is not homemade with lemon juice, add 2 tablespoons lemon juice. Combine with chicken, celery, water chestnuts, and grapes. Chill until time to serve.

Arrange lettuce leaves around edge of large porcelain or silver platter. Mound chicken salad in center. Also interesting served in a dark wooden salad bowl. Sprinkle almonds over all.

YIELD: 12 SERVINGS

VARIATION:

One large can pineapple chunks, drained, may be added to this, along with additional mayonnaise. Place individual servings in half a hollowed pineapple (cut pineapple lengthwise, leaving crown on).

Party Potpourri
THE JUNIOR LEAGUE OF MEMPHIS, TENNESSEE

. . . .

Curried Chicken Salad

4 cups cooked chicken, cubed
1 1-pound 4-ounce can water chestnuts, drained and sliced
1 pound seedless white grapes, halved
1 cup sliced celery
¼ cup sliced and toasted almonds
1 cup mayonnaise
1 or 2 tablespoons curry powder, to taste
1 tablespoon soy sauce
Juice of 1 lemon

Recipe continues . . .

Combine chicken, water chestnuts, grapes, celery, and almonds. Mix all remaining ingredients and add to chicken. Toss well. Chill several hours. Serve on lettuce.

YIELD: 12 SERVINGS

Furniture City Feasts
THE JUNIOR LEAGUE OF HIGH POINT, NORTH CAROLINA

· · · · · · · · · · · · · · ·

Chicken Enchiladas

1 3-pound chicken
1 cup sour cream
Jalapeño juice
Salt
Sugar
Tortillas
Oil
1 head lettuce
2 tomatoes
½ cup chopped onion

Boil and bone chicken.

Dilute sour cream with some juice from a can of jalapeño peppers. (Dilute to the consistency of salad dressing and to the degree of hotness desired.) Add a dash of salt and sugar. Mix well.

Dip tortillas in hot oil for a few seconds to tenderize tortillas. Place about ¼ cup chicken in each tortilla and add a spoonful of sauce. Chop lettuce, 2 tomatoes, and onion and add enough of your sauce to coat the salad. Toss and place on top of the tortillas and roll up like a cigar.

YIELD: 4 SERVINGS

The Blue Denim Gourmet
THE JUNIOR LEAGUE OF ODESSA, TEXAS

· · · · · · · · · · · · · ·

Curried Chicken and Rice Salad

2 cups cooked chicken, cut into bite-size pieces
1½ cups chopped celery
1½ cups cold cooked rice
½ cup toasted almonds
¼ cup capers

SOUR CREAM DRESSING:
½ cup sour cream
½ cup Italian-style salad dressing
1 teaspoon salt
1 teaspoon curry powder

Combine chicken, celery, rice, almonds, and capers. Mix dressing ingredients and pour over chicken mixture. Toss thoroughly.

This salad is best prepared several hours before serving.

Good served on sliced pineapple with toasted coconut curls sprinkled on top.

YIELD: 6–8 SERVINGS

A Cook's Tour of Shreveport
THE JUNIOR LEAGUE OF SHREVEPORT, LOUISIANA

. . . .

Chicken Salad

1 5- or 6-pound hen
1 carrot, cut into 3 sections
1 stalk celery, cut into 3 sections
1 medium onion, quartered
1½–2 cups finely chopped celery
1½–2 cups finely chopped blanched almonds
Mayonnaise
Salt

Recipe continues . . .

Simmer hen with carrot, celery, and onion until meat falls from bone. Cut meat with scissors into small pieces.

Combine the cooked dressing and the chicken the night before or several hours before serving. Add the celery and almonds last. Add extra mayonnaise and salt to taste.

Serve on lettuce leaves or use for stuffing tomatoes.

YIELD: 12–14 SERVINGS

COOKED DRESSING:
3 tablespoons sugar
1 teaspoon salt
1 teaspoon prepared mustard
1½ tablespoons flour
1 egg, beaten
¾ cup milk
4 tablespoons vinegar
1 tablespoon butter

Blend the first seven ingredients in the order given and cook over hot water in a double boiler, stirring constantly, until thick. Add the butter and blend thoroughly. Cool before using.

Southern Sideboards
THE JUNIOR LEAGUE OF JACKSON, MISSISSIPPI

. . . .

Turkey Salad Deluxe

10 cups chopped celery
20 cups chopped cooked turkey breast
2 pounds fried bacon, crumbled
5 8-ounce cans whole mushrooms
5 8-ounce containers sour cream
1 quart plus ½ pint mayonnaise
Salt, pepper, and onion salt to taste

Combine all ingredients, seasoning *well* with salt, pepper, and lots of onion salt. Chill. Serve on lettuce leaves.

YIELD: 50 SERVINGS

The Blue Denim Gourmet
THE JUNIOR LEAGUE OF ODESSA, TEXAS

· · · · · · · · · · · · · · · ·

Avocado Stuffed with Crabmeat

6 avocados
Lemon juice
1 pound crabmeat
About 2 tablespoons mayonnaise
About 2 tablespoons sour cream
1 teaspoon Worcestershire sauce
1 tablespoon capers
Dash red pepper
Dash grated onion

Slice each avocado in half, peel, remove seed, and roll in lemon juice. Mix crabmeat and remaining ingredients. Stuff avocados and refrigerate until ready to serve on lettuce.

YIELD: 12 SERVINGS

Seafood Sorcery
THE JUNIOR LEAGUE OF WILMINGTON, NORTH CAROLINA

· · · · · · · · · · · · · · · ·

Crabmeat Salad

1 pound crabmeat
1 cup diced celery
⅛ teaspoon pepper
1 green pepper, chopped
2 hard-boiled eggs, diced
½ cup mayonnaise or salad dressing
½ teaspoon salt

Remove any shell from the crabmeat. Combine all the ingredients and serve on lettuce.

Shrimp may be used instead of crabmeat.

YIELD: 6 SERVINGS

Charleston Receipts
THE JUNIOR LEAGUE OF CHARLESTON, SOUTH CAROLINA

. . . .

Lobster Chunks with Green Goddess Dressing

GREEN GODDESS DRESSING:
1 clove garlic, minced
½ teaspoon salt
½ teaspoon dry mustard
1 teaspoon Worcestershire sauce
3 tablespoons tarragon wine vinegar

2 tablespoons anchovy paste
3 tablespoons grated onion
⅓ cup chopped parsley
1 cup mayonnaise
½ cup sour cream
⅛ teaspoon pepper

Combine all ingredients the day before serving. Allow to season, covered, in refrigerator until serving time.

Serve over lobster in lettuce cups or over mixed greens topped with croutons. Dressing may also be used as a dip.

LOBSTER:
4 1-pound frozen lobster tails

Cook lobster the day it is to be used. Drop tails in boiling salted water and cook 3 minutes per pound, based on weight of largest tail. Cool and cut into bite-size chunks.

YIELD: ABOUT 20 SERVINGS

The Charlotte Cookbook
THE JUNIOR LEAGUE OF CHARLOTTE, NORTH CAROLINA

.   .   .   .

Florida Shrimp Remoulade

3 pounds shrimp
4 tablespoons vinegar
4 tablespoons lemon juice
2 teaspoons salt
1 teaspoon pepper
2 tablespoons catsup
4 tablespoons prepared mustard
4 tablespoons horseradish
1 cup salad oil
½ cup finely chopped celery
½ cup sliced onion
Lettuce

Clean and boil shrimp. Mix in large bowl: vinegar, lemon juice, salt, pepper, catsup, mustard, and horseradish. Slowly add 1 cup oil beating with rotary beater. Then add celery and onion. Pour over the boiled shrimp.

Recipe continues ...

Marinate in refrigerator at least 2 hours.

To serve, shred lettuce on a large platter, spread shrimp, and pour dressing on top.

YIELD: 8 SERVINGS

That Something Special
THE JUNIOR LEAGUE OF DURHAM, NORTH CAROLINA

Shrimp Arnaud

1½ pounds cleaned, uncooked shrimp
1 large slice lemon
½ green pepper
½ onion
Cayenne
Salt

DRESSING:
2 tablespoons vinegar
4 tablespoons oil (preferably olive oil)
2 green onions with tops, minced
1 tablespoon Creole (hot) mustard
¼ stalk celery, minced
Salt and pepper to taste

Remove shells and black vein from shrimp. Wash and put in pot of cold water. Add lemon, green pepper, onion, lots of cayenne, and salt. Boil 30 minutes. Remove, let cool in same water, then drain and place on ice.

Combine all dressing ingredients. Mix with chilled shrimp and let set about 2 hours.

YIELD: 4–6 SERVINGS

The Cotton Blossom Cookbook
THE JUNIOR LEAGUE OF ATLANTA, GEORGIA

Shrimp Remoulade

Lettuce
1 pound cooked shrimp
½ pound cooked king crab legs, removed from shells and cut into chunks
Hard-boiled eggs
Cucumber
Tomatoes
Ripe olives
Radishes
Green pepper, sliced

SAUCE:
2 cups mayonnaise
2 tablespoons finely chopped cucumber pickle or relish
2 tablespoons drained capers, chopped
2 tablespoons prepared mustard
2 tablespoons finely chopped parsley
¼ cup crushed tarragon
½ teaspoon crushed chervil
1½ teaspoons anchovy paste
Dash Tabasco
2 tablespoons fresh lemon juice

Mix all of the sauce ingredients together. To serve, line center of individual plates with lettuce leaves. Place some shredded lettuce in the center of each plate. Mound shrimp and crab on lettuce.

On the rim of plate put a quartered egg, quartered cucumber, quartered tomato, ripe olive, radishes, and slices of green pepper. Spoon sauce generously over the shrimp and crab. Pass additional sauce.

YIELD: 4–6 SERVINGS

The Dallas Jr. League Cookbook
THE JUNIOR LEAGUE OF DALLAS, TEXAS

Melon Ball and Shrimp Salad

2 pounds cooked shrimp
2 tablespoons lemon juice
2 teaspoons grated onion
1½ cups chopped celery
1½ teaspoons salt
1 cup mayonnaise
1½ tablespoons curry powder
6 tablespoons sour cream
1 large honeydew melon, cut into balls
1 large cantaloupe, cut into balls
Bibb lettuce
Shredded coconut (optional)

Combine shrimp, lemon juice, onion, celery, salt, and mayonnaise.

Blend curry powder into sour cream. Combine the two mixtures. Mix well. Chill several hours.

Add melon balls before serving.

Serve on a bed of Bibb lettuce and top with coconut if desired.

This recipe is perfect for lunch or as a first course for a seated dinner.

YIELD: **6–8** SERVINGS

Nashville Seasons Encore
THE JUNIOR LEAGUE OF NASHVILLE, TENNESSEE

· · · · · · · · · · · · · · · · · · ·

Cedar Key Island Hotel Tropical Salad

4 cups sliced palm hearts
1 cup cubed pineapple
¼ cup chopped dates
½ cup chopped candied or preserved ginger

DRESSING:
2 tablespoons vanilla ice cream
2 tablespoons mayonnaise
2 tablespoons crunchy peanut butter
Pineapple juice or preserved ginger juice
A few drops green food coloring (optional)

Toss salad ingredients and chill. Mix ice cream, mayonnaise, and peanut butter thoroughly.

Thin with pineapple juice or ginger juice. Add a few drops green food coloring if desired. Pour over salad and serve.

YIELD: 6 SERVINGS

Gator Country Cooks
THE JUNIOR LEAGUE OF GAINESVILLE, FLORIDA

. . . .

Midsummer Salad

½ watermelon
1 large cantaloupe
1 large honeydew melon
1 cup canned pineapple chunks
1 cup seedless green grapes (cut into halves if they are large)
1 cup strawberries, cut into halves or large pieces
¾ cup sugar
½ cup water
1 tablespoon grated lemon rind
1 tablespoon grated orange rind
¼ cup lemon juice
3 tablespoons lime juice

Cut melons into balls with melon baller. Mix all fruit and put in glass bowl.

Recipe continues . . .

Mix together remaining ingredients; stir until sugar is dissolved. Boil 5 minutes. Cool; pour over mixed fruit. Chill for a few hours or overnight.

YIELD: 10–15 SERVINGS

Fiesta: Favorite Recipes of South Texas
THE JUNIOR LEAGUE OF CORPUS CHRISTI, TEXAS

Frozen Tomato Salad

2 1-pound cans tomatoes, well drained
1⅓ cups mayonnaise
Juice of 1 lemon
3 teaspoons green onion, finely chopped
1 teaspoon Worcestershire sauce
2 drops Tabasco
1 teaspoon salt
A shake of cracked pepper to taste
1 envelope gelatin dissolved in ⅓ cup water

Combine all ingredients in blender and whip on high until well blended.

Place liquid in container in freezer and beat a couple of times as it freezes. When frozen, scoop out with ice cream scoop, refreeze individual servings. (This is highly seasoned, so homemade mayonnaise is sufficient for topping. If you really like it rich, a sliced hard-boiled egg and horse-radish dressing is a grand topping.)

YIELD: 6–8 SERVINGS

Horseradish Dressing

1 cup mayonnaise
½ cup sour cream
¼ teaspoon dry mustard
4 teaspoons undrained horseradish
2 cloves garlic, pressed
2 teaspoons chives

Put all ingredients except chives in blender and blend until smooth. Stir in the chives and refrigerate.

Serve on Frozen Tomato Salad or fried shrimp.

YIELD: 1½ CUPS

Recipe Jubilee
THE JUNIOR LEAGUE OF MOBILE, ALABAMA

.   .   .   .

Avocado Salad

2 packages lime gelatin
2 cups boiling water
½ cup salad dressing
1 cup chopped celery
1 small onion, grated
1 green pepper, minced
4 3-ounce packages cream cheese, softened
2 or more ripe avocados, mashed
Salt, lemon juice, and Tabasco to taste

Dissolve lime gelatin in water and cool. Combine all other ingredients and add to lime gelatin. Pour into molds and chill.

YIELD: 16 SERVINGS

A Cook's Tour of Shreveport
THE JUNIOR LEAGUE OF SHREVEPORT, LOUISIANA

.   .   .   .

Cranberry Salad

1 1-pound can whole cranberry sauce
1 cup boiling water
1 package cherry-flavored gelatin
Dash salt
½ cup mayonnaise
1 apple, diced
¼ cup nuts

Heat cranberry sauce. Drain and pour hot juice and boiling water over cherry-flavored gelatin, with salt. Chill in refrigerator until grainy.

Whip mayonnaise into gelatin and add cranberries, apple, and nuts. Pour into a 1-quart mold or 6 individual molds. Chill in refrigerator until firm.

YIELD: 6 SERVINGS

300 Years of Carolina Cooking
THE JUNIOR LEAGUE OF GREENVILLE, SOUTH CAROLINA

Grapefruit Salad

3 grapefruits
4 cups fruit juice
1 envelope unflavored gelatin
½ cup cold water
2 packages lemon gelatin
1 4-ounce can crushed pineapple
1 4-ounce jar maraschino cherries, sliced

Cut grapefruits in half and scrape out sections with knife or spoon; reserve shells. Drain juice from fruits and add enough other fruit juice to make 4 cups.

Soak plain gelatin in water. Divide fruit juices into 3 parts. Boil 1 part and in it dissolve lemon gelatin and soaked plain gelatin. Freeze 1 part and chill 1 part. Add chilled juice to dissolved gelatins, then add frozen juice. Stir until mixture begins to thicken, then add fruit.

Put into grapefruit shells and refrigerate several hours.

When ready to serve, cut grapefruit halves and put ¼ grapefruit on lettuce. Top with Fruit Salad Dressing.

YIELD: 12 SERVINGS

FRUIT SALAD DRESSING:

3 tablespoons sugar
1 tablespoon flour
⅓ cup pineapple juice
1 egg yolk, beaten
4 marshmallows
⅓ pint heavy cream, whipped with 1 tablespoon sugar
½ cup chopped nuts

Mix sugar and flour. Boil pineapple juice and pour over sugar and flour; then pour over egg yolk. Cook in double boiler, stirring until thick. Add marshmallows and stir until dissolved. Cool and stir in sweetened cream and nuts. Keep refrigerated.

Huntsville Heritage Cookbook
THE JUNIOR LEAGUE OF HUNTSVILLE, ALABAMA

·   ·   ·   ·   ·   ·   ·   ·   ·   ·   ·   ·   ·   ·

Pear-Pecan Salad

1 1-pound 4-ounce can pears
1 3-ounce package lemon gelatin
1 8-ounce package cream cheese
1 cup chopped pecans
1 cup heavy cream

Recipe continues . . .

Drain pears reserving 1 cup of juice. Bring juice to boil and remove; add gelatin and chill until partially set.

Blend pears and cheese in blender until creamy. Stir in gelatin mixture and pecans.

Whip cream and fold in with other ingredients.

Pour into large mold or 16 individual molds.

YIELD: 16 SERVINGS

Home Cookin'
THE JUNIOR LEAGUE OF WICHITA FALLS, TEXAS

· · · · · · · · · · · · · · · · · ·

Fresh Fruit Salad

2 cups boiling water
2 3-ounce packages apple gelatin
1 envelope unflavored gelatin
¼ cup water
¾ cup sugar
5 or 6 peaches, sliced and sweetened
1½ cups sliced green grapes, seeded and sweetened
4 oranges, sectioned
3 pears, diced
3 bananas, diced
1 cantaloupe, cut into balls
1 basket blueberries
Juice from fresh fruits
½ pint sweetened whipped cream
Mayonnaise to taste

Pour boiling water over packages of apple gelatin. Add unflavored gelatin which has been softened in ¼ cup water. Stir until dissolved. Add sugar and fruit to gelatin. Add enough water to juice to make 2 cups. Add to gelatin and fruit. Pour into molds and congeal.

Combine whipped cream and mayonnaise for dressing. When ready to serve, unmold salad and top with dressing.

YIELD: 30 SERVINGS

Winston-Salem's Heritage of Hospitality
THE JUNIOR LEAGUE OF WINSTON-SALEM, NORTH CAROLINA

Paper-Cup Frozen Salad

2 cups sour cream
2 tablespoons lemon juice
½ cup sugar
⅛ teaspoon salt
1 8-ounce can crushed pineapple, well drained
1 banana, diced
¼ cup chopped pecans
4 drops red food coloring (optional)
1 1-pound can pitted bing cherries, drained

Combine sour cream, lemon juice, sugar, salt, pineapple, banana, pecans, coloring (if used), and cherries. Spoon into large, fluted paper muffin cups which have been placed in 3-inch muffin pans. Cover with plastic wrap and freeze.

Remove from freezer about 15 minutes before serving. Peel off paper cup and place salad on greens.

YIELD: 12 LARGE SERVINGS

The Blue Denim Gourmet
THE JUNIOR LEAGUE OF ODESSA, TEXAS

Strawberry Salad

2 3-ounce packages strawberry gelatin
1½ cups boiling water
2 10-ounce packages frozen strawberries, unthawed
2–3 bananas, mashed
1 20-ounce can crushed pineapple, drained
1 cup chopped nuts
1 cup sour cream or heavy cream, whipped

Mix gelatin and boiling water until the gelatin is dissolved. Add the frozen strawberries and stir until thick. Add the bananas, pineapple, and nuts.

Pour half of the mixture in a 13 × 9 × 2-inch pan; refrigerate until set. Spread with sour cream or whipped cream; then cover with the remaining gelatin mixture. Refrigerate.

This salad is good also as a dessert.

YIELD: 10–12 SERVINGS

Mountain Measures
THE JUNIOR LEAGUE OF CHARLESTON, WEST VIRGINIA

· · · · · · · · · · · · ·

Molded Crab

2 tablespoons unflavored gelatin
¼ cup vinegar
3 tablespoons lemon juice
½ teaspoon salt
2 cups flaked crabmeat
¾ cup chopped celery
2 tablespoons minced onion (juice included)
½ cup mayonnaise

Soak gelatin in 4 tablespoons cold water. Then dissolve in ¼ cup boiling water. Add remaining ingredients and pour into a mold which has been rinsed in cold water.

If you have a fish mold, use a sliced stuffed olive for the eye and line the fish mold with red pimentos.

Serve on lettuce and garnish tray with radishes and tomatoes. Serve with crackers.

YIELD: A 1-QUART MOLD

Seafood Sorcery
THE JUNIOR LEAGUE OF WILMINGTON, NORTH CAROLINA

· · · · · · · · · · · · · · · · ·

Salmon Mousse

2 envelopes unflavored gelatin
½ cup cold water
1 cup boiling water
1 tablespoon vinegar
3 tablespoons lemon juice
1 1-pound can salmon
1 cup mayonnaise
1 cup heavy cream, firmly whipped
½ teaspoon salt
1 tablespoon Worcestershire sauce
2 cups finely chopped cucumber or celery
1 medium-size onion, grated

Soak gelatin in cold water and dissolve in boiling water. Add vinegar and lemon juice and place in refrigerator to thicken.

Flake salmon, combine with mayonnaise and with whipped cream, and add to all other ingredients.

Recipe continues . . .

Pour into oiled 6-cup mold and chill until firm, preferably overnight. Serve on chilled platter.

YIELD: 6 CUPS

That Something Special
THE JUNIOR LEAGUE OF DURHAM, NORTH CAROLINA

Tomato Aspic

3 cups tomato-vegetable juice
1 stalk celery
1 onion, sliced
1 bay leaf
1 teaspoon salt
1 or 2 lemons, sliced thin
⅛ teaspoon pepper
2 envelopes unflavored gelatin
⅔ cup tomato-vegetable juice
¼ cup vinegar

Combine first seven ingredients and bring to a boil. Lower heat and simmer for 10–15 minutes.

Sprinkle gelatin over ⅔ cup juice and vinegar in order to soften the gelatin.

Drain hot mixture, pressing well to extract all juices. Pour hot mixture over cold gelatin. Mix and stir until gelatin is thoroughly dissolved. Pour into mold and refrigerate until set.

YIELD: 8–10 SERVINGS

Furniture City Feasts
THE JUNIOR LEAGUE OF HIGH POINT, NORTH CAROLINA

Tomato Aspic and Cream Cheese Salad

CHEESE LAYER:
6 ounces cream cheese, softened
½ cup mayonnaise
½ teaspoon salt
1 teaspoon unflavored gelatin
4 teaspoons lemon juice
4 tablespoons boiling water
½ cup finely chopped celery
2 tablespoons chopped chives or onion

Blend softened cream cheese with mayonnaise and salt.

Soften the gelatin in lemon juice and dissolve in boiling water.

Combine with remaining ingredients and put in bottom of oiled individual molds or one large mold. Chill until firm before adding aspic layer.

ASPIC:
2 envelopes unflavored gelatin (from which the above 1
teaspoon gelatin has already been used)
¼ cup cold water
1 cup boiling water
1 15-ounce can seasoned tomato sauce
2 tablespoons lemon juice
1 teaspoon salt

Soften gelatin in cold water; dissolve in boiling water. Add remaining ingredients and pour over cream cheese layer. Chill until firm.

Depending on the size of the mold used, there may be some of the tomato sauce mixture left over, which can be used molded alone.

YIELD: ABOUT 6 CUPS

Mountain Measures
THE JUNIOR LEAGUE OF CHARLESTON, WEST VIRGINIA

· · · · · · · · · · · · ·

Aunt Alice's Grapefruit and Avocado Salad Dressing

1 teaspoon dry mustard
1 teaspoon salt
¼ cup sugar
2 teaspoons grated onion
1 cup cold salad oil
2 tablespoons red wine vinegar
½–1 teaspoon celery seed
Paprika

Mix mustard, salt, and sugar in small, deep bowl. Then add onion to make smooth paste. Add salad oil, dripping in a little at a time and beating constantly with an electric beater. The dressing should be very thick. When it gets too thick, thin it down by beating in a little of the wine vinegar. Repeat until all the oil and all the vinegar have been used. Then stir in celery seed to taste and enough paprika to give the dressing an attractive rosy color. (Be sure the oil is very cold, and that you never let it "puddle" while mixing. Also, store the dressing in the bowl in which it was made. Often it will separate if it is transferred to another container.)

Use on an avocado and grapefruit salad. This is also good on a fruit salad made of grapefruit sections, orange sections, pineapple chunks, white grapes, and mandarin orange slices.

YIELD: 2 CUPS

Gator Country Cooks
THE JUNIOR LEAGUE OF GAINESVILLE, FLORIDA

Dore's French Dressing

6 ounces vegetable or salad oil
2 ounces cider vinegar
Juice of 1 lemon
1 clove garlic
½ teaspoon salt
¼ teaspoon black pepper
½ teaspoon seasoned salt

Mix all ingredients together well. The dressing may be served on any tossed green salad but is a "must" for spinach salad.

YIELD: 1 CUP

The Memphis Cook Book
THE JUNIOR LEAGUE OF MEMPHIS, TENNESSEE

Koiner's Dressing

1¼ cups salad oil
6 tablespoons vinegar
2 teaspoons salt
⅛ teaspoon red pepper
1 tablespoon celery salt
1 tablespoon chili sauce
1 tablespoon lemon juice
1 whole clove garlic

Mix oil and vinegar and add remaining ingredients. Shake vigorously to blend well.

YIELD: 2 CUPS

Of Pots and Pipkins
THE JUNIOR LEAGUE OF ROANOKE VALLEY, VIRGINIA

Green Salad Dressing

1 teaspoon salt
1 egg
1 teaspoon sugar
Dash Tabasco
3 tablespoons vinegar
1 clove garlic
1 cup chives (or green onion tops)
1 cup parsley
¾ cup salad oil

Put all ingredients except salad oil into blender and blend a few seconds. Add salad oil and blend until dressing is smooth. Serve on green salads.

YIELD: 1 PINT

Fiesta: Favorite Recipes of South Texas
THE JUNIOR LEAGUE OF CORPUS CHRISTI, TEXAS

. . . .

Lime Honey Dressing

2–3 tablespoons lime juice
½ cup honey
2 eggs, well beaten
½ pint heavy cream, whipped stiff

Add lime juice to honey. Stir in well-beaten eggs, mixing thoroughly. Cook over simmering hot water until thickened, stirring constantly.
   Cool. Fold in whipped cream.

YIELD: ABOUT 1½ CUPS

Cooking Through Rose Colored Glasses
THE JUNIOR LEAGUE OF TYLER, TEXAS

. . . .

Mayonnaise

2 whole eggs
2 teaspoons sugar
2 teaspoons salt
2 teaspoons dry mustard
1 teaspoon paprika
Dash pepper
1 quart salad oil
Juice of 2 lemons (or more to taste)
2 tablespoons boiling water

Beat eggs in mixer. Add all dry ingredients. Beat in oil, a little at a time, making certain it is well mixed before adding more. As mixture thickens, turn mixer speed up. When ½ of oil has been added, pour in lemon juice. Beat in remaining oil, then boiling water.

This recipe halves nicely.

YIELD: 1 QUART

Nashville Seasons Encore
THE JUNIOR LEAGUE OF NASHVILLE, TENNESSEE

. . . .

Onion Salad Dressing

Onions
2 teaspoons salt
2 teaspoons black pepper
2 teaspoons dry mustard
2 teaspoons paprika
½ cup sugar
¾ cup vinegar
Salad oil

Fill a quart jar half full of finely chopped onions. Add salt, black pepper,

Recipe continues . . .

dry mustard, and paprika. Stir well. Let stand about 10 minutes, shaking or stirring a few times. Add sugar and vinegar. Finish filling jar with salad oil. Mix thoroughly.

Keep refrigerated. Keeps long and well. Better after at least a few days.

YIELD: 1 QUART

Spartanburg Secrets II
THE JUNIOR LEAGUE OF SPARTANBURG, SOUTH CAROLINA

· · · · · · · · · · · · · · · · · · ·

Piquant Dressing

½ cup vinegar
2 teaspoons salt
1 teaspoon sugar
½ teaspoon pepper
1 teaspoon paprika
1 teaspoon dry mustard
1½ cups salad oil
2 teaspoons prepared mustard
1 teaspoon Worcestershire sauce
8 drops Tabasco
¼ onion

Combine first six ingredients. Shake well, then add next four. Shake again. Put ¼ of a cut onion in jar with dressing to season. Do not pour onion out on salad.

This is *particularly* good on all salad greens.

YIELD: ABOUT 2 CUPS

The Charlotte Cookbook
THE JUNIOR LEAGUE OF CHARLOTTE, NORTH CAROLINA

· · · · · · · · · · · · · · · · · · ·

Poppy Seed Dressing

¾ cup sugar
1 teaspoon dry mustard
¼ teaspoon salt
½ cup vinegar
1½ tablespoons grated onion
1 cup salad oil
1½ tablespoons poppy seed

Mix first four ingredients. Gradually add onion and oil, and then poppy seed. Refrigerate.

Serve over fruit salad. This keeps well in refrigerator.

YIELD: ABOUT 2 CUPS

300 Years of Carolina Cooking
THE JUNIOR LEAGUE OF GREENVILLE, SOUTH CAROLINA

.   .   .   .

Shrimp Remoulade

1½ cups mayonnaise
¼ cup brown mustard
1 teaspoon seasoned pepper
2 teaspoons seasoned salt
1 small onion, chopped
¼ cup lime juice
1 teaspoon Tabasco
Dash cayenne
Dash garlic salt
Chilled boiled shrimp
Hard-boiled eggs

Blend all ingredients thoroughly and refrigerate for at least 12 hours. Serve over chilled boiled shrimp or hard-boiled eggs.

YIELD: 4–6 SERVINGS

Fun Foods
THE JUNIOR LEAGUE OF GREATER LAKELAND, FLORIDA

.   .   .   .

Roquefort Dressing

1 cup sour cream
1 cup mayonnaise
2 ounces Roquefort or blue cheese
Juice of ½ lemon
1 clove garlic, minced, or ¼ teaspoon garlic powder (not garlic salt)

Mix all ingredients until smooth in a blender or electric mixer. Let the dressing ripen in the refrigerator for several hours before using it.

This is also a good dip for raw vegetables.

YIELD: 2½ CUPS

300 Years of Carolina Cooking
THE JUNIOR LEAGUE OF GREENVILLE, SOUTH CAROLINA

.   .   .   .

White Dressing

3 eggs
1 large or 2 small cloves garlic
¼ medium onion
1 teaspoon dry mustard
1 teaspoon salt
Dash Tabasco
1 teaspoon white pepper
2 ounces white vinegar
2 tablespoons lemon juice
2 cups salad oil

Mix in blender as follows: Beat whole eggs well, add garlic, onion, mustard, salt, Tabasco, and white pepper. Blend. Add vinegar and lemon juice. Pour salad oil in slowly as it is blending. Good on fish or vegetable salads or tossed with salad greens.

YIELD: ABOUT 2 CUPS

300 Years of Carolina Cooking
THE JUNIOR LEAGUE OF GREENVILLE, SOUTH CAROLINA

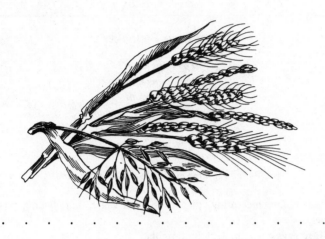

Breads

Best Ever Pancakes

1¾ cups flour
2 teaspoons sugar
1 teaspoon salt
1½ teaspoons baking powder
1 teaspoon baking soda
2 eggs, well beaten
2 cups buttermilk
2–4 tablespoons melted butter or margarine

Sift flour before measuring, then resift with sugar, salt, baking powder, and soda.

Beat eggs, then mix with buttermilk.

Combine the dry and liquid ingredients with a few quick strokes, then add melted butter or margarine. Mix ingredients well but with as few strokes as possible. Batter will be lumpy.

Bake on hot griddle until browned on both sides.

YIELD: ABOUT 20 4-INCH CAKES

Southern Sideboards
THE JUNIOR LEAGUE OF JACKSON, MISSISSIPPI

· · · · · · · · · · · · · · · ·

Breakfast Crêpes and Apples

¾ cup flour
1 teaspoon baking powder
2 tablespoons confectioners' sugar
½ teaspoon salt
2 eggs, beaten
⅔ cup milk
⅓ cup water
¾ teaspoon vanilla or grated lemon rind
Sausages
Butter

Sift together the flour, baking powder, sugar, and salt. Beat together the eggs, milk, water, and vanilla or lemon rind. Pour the liquid into the dry ingredients and combine with a few stirs. Do not try to get rid of lumps as they will take care of themselves as the crepes cook.

Grease a small skillet and heat till drops of water dance on it. Add a small quantity of batter and tip the skillet to coat. When one side is brown, turn the crepe and brown the other side. Stack the crepes between layers of waxed paper. They may be refrigerated overnight or frozen until needed. Reheat on cookie sheet in 250° oven.

Fill each crepe with a spoonful of the hot apple filling and roll up. Place two on each breakfast plate with fried sausage and top each crepe with a dab of butter.

YIELD: ABOUT 14 5-INCH CAKES

APPLE FILLING:
12 cooking apples
4 tablespoons butter
1 cup sugar

In a skillet, cook about a dozen peeled, cored, and thinly sliced cooking apples in butter. After about 5 minutes, add sugar and cook the apples, covered, stirring often until they are soft.

Mountain Measures
THE JUNIOR LEAGUE OF CHARLESTON, WEST VIRGINIA

. . . .

Kitty's Biscuits

2 cups sifted self-rising flour
1 teaspoon sugar
½ cup plus 1 rounded tablespoon shortening
¾ cup very cold milk

Sift flour and sugar into bowl and work shortening into flour with fingers.

Recipe continues . . .

Pour milk into mixture, enough to make a soft dough. Handle lightly, using upward motions instead of pressing down. Toss onto floured board and lightly roll out with floured rolling pin to about ½-inch thickness for fluffy biscuits, ¼-inch for crusty biscuits. Cut out with a small biscuit cutter. Dip cutter in flour often for easy cutting.

Place on greased cookie sheet and bake on top rack in preheated 450° oven for 5–7 minutes until golden brown.

To freeze, place pan of unbaked biscuits in freezer until firm, then package in plastic bags. They will keep as long as two weeks. Take out as many as needed and place on greased pan and thaw. Follow same baking instructions.

YIELD: ABOUT 2½ DOZEN BISCUITS

Gator Country Cooks
THE JUNIOR LEAGUE OF GAINESVILLE, FLORIDA

· · · · · · · · · · · · · · · ·

Sopaipilla Dulce (Mexican Fried Cookie)

4 cups flour
1 teaspoon salt
2 teaspoons baking powder
4 tablespoons lard
4 eggs
1 cup sugar
Water or milk
2 teaspoons cinnamon

Sift flour with salt and baking powder; cut in lard. Beat eggs and add ½ cup sugar to flour mixture. Add enough milk or water to make a medium dough, neither stiff nor soft. Let dough stand for 30 minutes.

Roll out ¼ inch thick; cut into 1½-inch squares and fry in deep fat until brown. Drain.

To remaining ½ cup sugar, add cinnamon and mix well. While the sopaipillas are still hot, roll in sugar and cinnamon mixture.

YIELD: 2 DOZEN

Seasoned with Sun: Recipes from the Southwest
THE JUNIOR LEAGUE OF EL PASO, TEXAS

· ·

Hush Puppies

1½ cups corn meal
½ cup flour
⅛ teaspoon salt
2 tablespoons baking powder
½ teaspoon baking soda
1 egg, beaten
1 cup buttermilk
4 tablespoons bacon drippings, melted
1 onion, chopped

Mix all ingredients and drop by teaspoonfuls into hot fat and brown. Serve with fried fish.

YIELD: 1 DOZEN

Talk About Good!
THE JUNIOR LEAGUE OF LAFAYETTE, LOUISIANA

· ·

Cream Cheese Biscuits

1 3-ounce package cream cheese
1 stick margarine
1 cup flour

Recipe continues . . .

Soften cream cheese and margarine at room temperature and cream together. Blend in flour and shape into rolls in waxed paper.

Chill several hours or overnight in refrigerator. Slice and bake for about 10 minutes (until brown) at 400° on ungreased cookie sheet.

These are good for a buffet since they don't need to be buttered.

YIELD: ABOUT 3 DOZEN BISCUITS

300 Years of Carolina Cooking
THE JUNIOR LEAGUE OF GREENVILLE, SOUTH CAROLINA

· · · · · · · · · · · · · · · ·

Middleton Gardens's Sesame Seed Biscuits

2 cups flour
1 teaspoon baking powder
½ teaspoon salt
½ cup shortening
½ cup cold milk
½ cup roasted sesame seeds

Combine flour, baking powder, and salt, and cream with shortening. Add milk. Mix in sesame seeds. Roll out on floured bread board very thin. Cut out with small biscuit cutter.

Bake at 350° 7–9 minutes. Sprinkle with salt while hot.

YIELD: ABOUT 5 DOZEN BISCUITS

Charleston Receipts
THE JUNIOR LEAGUE OF CHARLESTON, SOUTH CAROLINA

· · · · · · · · · · · · · · · ·

Biscuits Supreme

2 cups sifted flour
4 teaspoons baking powder
½ teaspoon salt
½ teaspoon cream of tartar
2 teaspoons sugar
½ cup shortening
⅔ cup milk

Sift dry ingredients together and cut in shortening. Add milk and mix well. Knead gently ½ minute. Pat and roll ½ inch thick. Bake on ungreased cookie sheet for 10–12 minutes in 450° oven.

YIELD: 16 MEDIUM BISCUITS

Recipe Jubilee
THE JUNIOR LEAGUE OF MOBILE, ALABAMA

. . . .

Pecan Muffins

1 cup sugar
2 cups flour
¼ teaspoon salt
2 teaspoons baking powder
4 teaspoons cinnamon
1 cup chopped pecans
1 cup milk
½ cup shortening (butter and lard mixed), melted
2 eggs, beaten

Sift dry ingredients together. Add nuts. Mix together milk, melted shorten-

Recipe continues . . .

ing, and eggs. Combine dry and liquid ingredients quickly with little stirring. Bake in muffin tins in hot oven (425°) about 15 minutes.

YIELD: 1 DOZEN MUFFINS

The Cotton Blossom Cookbook
THE JUNIOR LEAGUE OF ATLANTA, GEORGIA

. . . .

French Breakfast Puffs

⅓ cup shortening
½ cup sugar
1 egg
1½ cups sifted flour
1½ teaspoons baking powder
½ teaspoon salt
¼ teaspoon nutmeg
½ cup milk
⅓ cup butter, melted
½ cup sugar
1 teaspoon cinnamon

Blend the shortening and ½ cup sugar thoroughly. Add egg, mixing well.

Sift together the flour, baking powder, salt, and nutmeg and add to shortening mixture alternately with milk.

Fill greased muffin cups ⅔ full. Bake at 350° for 20–25 minutes until golden brown. Immediately roll in melted butter, then in mixture of ½ sugar and cinnamon.

Serve hot.

YIELD: 12–16 MUFFINS

Gator Country Cooks
THE JUNIOR LEAGUE OF GAINESVILLE, FLORIDA

. . . .

Date Muffins

1 cup flour
1 cup wheat germ
⅔ cup sugar
3 teaspoons baking powder
½ cup margarine, softened
1 cup milk
2 eggs, beaten
½ cup dates, cut up

Grease muffin tins very well or use paper cupcake liners, as dates tend to stick.

Combine dry ingredients; add margarine, milk, and eggs; stir, but do not beat. Fold in dates.

Pour into muffin tins; bake at 425° for 20 minutes.

YIELD: 12 MUFFINS

Little Rock Cooks
THE JUNIOR LEAGUE OF LITTLE ROCK, ARKANSAS

. . . .

Orange Muffins

1 cup sugar
½ cup margarine
2 eggs
2 cups flour
1 teaspoon baking soda
½ teaspoon salt
1 cup buttermilk
Rind and juice of 1 orange
1 cup raisins
½ cup chopped pecans
⅓ cup sugar

Recipe continues . . .

Make a batter out of the first seven ingredients in the order they are listed. Grate orange rind. Add rind, raisins, and pecans to batter. Pour in greased muffin tins. Bake at 350° for 25–30 minutes.

Combine juice of orange and ⅓ cup sugar. Bring to boil. Glaze muffins.

YIELD: 1 DOZEN

A Cook's Tour of Shreveport
THE JUNIOR LEAGUE OF SHREVEPORT, LOUISIANA

· · · · · · · · · · · · · · · ·

Hattie's Refrigerator Gingerbread Muffins

1 cup sugar
1 cup shortening
1 cup dark molasses
4 eggs, beaten
3½ cups flour
1 teaspoon cinnamon
1 teaspoon ginger
1 teaspoon nutmeg
½ teaspoon salt
1 cup buttermilk
1 teaspoon baking soda
1 teaspoon hot water
1 teaspoon vanilla
1 cup raisins
1 cup pecans

Cream sugar and shortening. Add molasses and stir. Add beaten eggs.

Sift flour with cinnamon, ginger, nutmeg, and salt. Add dry ingredients and buttermilk alternately to the molasses and sugar mixture. Add baking soda that has been dissolved in 1 teaspoon hot water and beat. Add vanilla. Stir in raisins and pecans.

Put gingerbread batter in greased muffin tins. Bake in preheated 375° oven for about 30 minutes. Batter can be kept in refrigerator for several days before baking.

YIELD: 2 DOZEN MUFFINS

Fiesta: Favorite Recipes of South Texas
THE JUNIOR LEAGUE OF CORPUS CHRISTI, TEXAS

Spoon Bread

1 cup corn meal
½ teaspoon salt
1½ cups boiling water
2 eggs, separated
1 tablespoon melted butter
1 cup buttermilk
½ teaspoon baking soda

Mix corn meal and salt. Add water and egg yolks, then add butter and buttermilk.

Beat egg whites, add soda, and fold into batter. Put in greased 2-quart baking dish. Bake 45 minutes at 325° and serve immediately.

YIELD: 6–8 SERVINGS

Huntsville Heritage Cookbook
THE JUNIOR LEAGUE OF HUNTSVILLE, ALABAMA

Cheese Spoon Bread

2 cups milk
1 cup corn meal
1 teaspoon salt
4 tablespoons butter
4 eggs, separated
½ cup shredded mild cheddar cheese

Heat milk in double boiler. When hot, add corn meal. Stir until thick. Add salt, butter, egg yolks, and cheese.

Beat egg whites and fold into corn meal mixture. Bake in 2-quart casserole at 350° for 35 minutes.

YIELD: 8 SERVINGS

Mountain Measures
THE JUNIOR LEAGUE OF CHARLESTON, WEST VIRGINIA

. . . .

West Texas Corn Bread

2 eggs
½ cup salad oil
1 cup sour cream
1 cup yellow corn meal
1 cup cream-style corn
3 teaspoons baking powder
1 cup shredded cheddar cheese
1 4-ounce can chopped green chilies or chopped hot
jalapeño peppers

Mix all ingredients. Bake at 400° in a well-greased bundt cake pan for 35–40 minutes or in a large, well-greased iron skillet for 30–40 minutes.

YIELD: 12 SERVINGS

Seasoned with Sun: Recipes from the Southwest
THE JUNIOR LEAGUE OF EL PASO, TEXAS

. . . .

Banana Bread

2 cups sifted flour
1 teaspoon salt
½ teaspoon baking soda
½ cup shortening or 1 stick margarine
1 cup sugar
2 eggs
1½ cups mashed bananas (3–5 bananas)
1 teaspoon vanilla
⅔ cup chopped nuts

Sift together flour, salt, and soda. Cream shortening; add sugar slowly; cream well. Add eggs and beat. Add bananas, then dry ingredients. Add vanilla and nuts.

Bake for approximately 1 hour and 15 minutes at 325° in a greased 2-quart loaf pan. Test center for doneness.

Cool thoroughly, wrap in foil, and keep in refrigerator. Best for slicing after at least one day.

YIELD: 1 LOAF

The Gasparilla Cookbook
THE JUNIOR LEAGUE OF TAMPA, FLORIDA

Lemon Cream Loaf

2½ cups flour
1 tablespoon baking powder
1 teaspoon salt
1⅔ cups sugar
½ cup shortening
2 eggs
1 8-ounce package cream cheese, cut into ¼-inch cubes
1 cup milk
½ cup nuts
2 tablespoons grated lemon peel
¼ cup lemon juice

Sift flour with baking powder and salt. Add 1⅓ cups sugar to shortening. Cream with electric mixer at high speed. Blend in eggs. Add dry ingredients. Fold in cream cheese, milk, nuts, and lemon peel.

Pour into 5 × 9-inch loaf pan lined with wax paper. Bake at 375° for 50 minutes. Combine remaining sugar and lemon juice. Brush over hot loaf. Cool 30 minutes.

YIELD: 1 LARGE LOAF

The Blue Denim Gourmet
THE JUNIOR LEAGUE OF ODESSA, TEXAS

· · · · · · · · · · · · · · · · ·

Potato Ice Box Rolls

1 cake compressed yeast
¾ cup warm water
1 cup hot mashed potatoes
1 cup shortening
1 cup sugar
1 teaspoon salt
1½ cups milk
6–7 cups flour

Dissolve yeast cake in water.

In large bowl, mix potatoes, shortening, sugar, and salt. Mix yeast with potato mixture. Add alternately milk and flour. Cover dough with cloth and refrigerate until double in size.

If using immediately, form into desired shapes and allow to rise until double in size—about 3 hours. Bake at 350° for about 15 minutes or until brown.

Will keep in refrigerator about 2 weeks.

YIELD: 3–4 DOZEN

Recipe Jubilee
THE JUNIOR LEAGUE OF MOBILE, ALABAMA

· · · · · · · · · · · · · · · · ·

Orange Nut Bread

Juice and rind of 1 medium orange
1 cup raisins or dates
2 tablespoons melted shortening
1 teaspoon vanilla
1 egg, beaten
2 cups flour
¼ teaspoon salt
1 teaspoon baking powder
½ teaspoon baking soda
1 cup sugar
½ cup chopped nuts

Pour juice from orange into 8-ounce measuring cup; add boiling water to fill cup.

Remove most of white membrane from orange rind; force rind through food chopper with raisins or dates, using coarse blade. Add diluted orange juice. Stir in shortening, vanilla, and egg.

Add flour sifted with salt, baking powder, soda, and sugar. Beat well. Stir in nut meats.

Recipe continues . . .

Bake in wax paper-lined 5 × 9-inch loaf pan in moderate oven (350°) about 1 hour.

For a lighter bread, leave out the raisins or dates.

YIELD: 1 LOAF

Spartanburg Secrets II
THE JUNIOR LEAGUE OF SPARTANBURG, SOUTH CAROLINA

· · · · · · · · · · · · · · · · · · ·

Strawberry Nut Bread

1 cup butter
1½ cups sugar
1 teaspoon vanilla
¼ teaspoon lemon extract
4 eggs
3 cups sifted flour
1 teaspoon salt
1 teaspoon cream of tartar
½ teaspoon baking soda
1 cup strawberry jam or preserves
½ cup sour cream
1 cup broken walnuts

Cream butter, sugar, vanilla, and lemon extract until fluffy. Add eggs, one at a time, beating well after each addition. Sift together flour, salt, cream of tartar, and soda. Combine jam and sour cream. Add jam mixture alternately with dry ingredients to creamed mixture, beating until well combined. Stir in nuts.

Divide among five greased and floured 4½ × 2¾ × 2½-inch loaf pans. Bake 50 minutes (or until done) at 350°. Cool 10 minutes in pans. Remove from pans and cool completely on wire rack.

Serve with whipped cream cheese flavored with strawberry jam.

YIELD: 5 SMALL LOAVES

Cooking Through Rose Colored Glasses
THE JUNIOR LEAGUE OF TYLER, TEXAS

.   .   .   .

Pumpkin Bread

2⅔ *cups sugar*
⅔ *cup butter*
2 *cups mashed cooked pumpkin (fresh if possible)*
4 *eggs, beaten*
3⅓ *cups flour*
2 *teaspoons baking soda*
½ *teaspoon baking powder*
1½ *teaspoons salt*
1 *teaspoon cloves*
2 *teaspoons cinnamon*
1 *teaspoon pumpkin pie spice*
1 *teaspoon nutmeg*
⅔ *cup water*
1½ *teaspoons vanilla*
1 *cup nuts*
1 *cup white raisins*

Cream sugar and butter. Add pumpkin and eggs. Combine all dry ingredients and add along with water and vanilla. Mix well. Add nuts and raisins. Put into 4 small oiled loaf pans. Bake at 350° for 45–55 minutes. Freezes well. Warm and slice to serve. Spread with cream cheese.

YIELD: 4 SMALL LOAVES

Winston-Salem's Heritage of Hospitality
THE JUNIOR LEAGUE OF WINSTON-SALEM, NORTH CAROLINA

.   .   .   .

Angel Biscuits

2 cups buttermilk
1 cup vegetable shortening
1 package dry yeast
¼ cup warm water
4 tablespoons sugar
5 cups flour
1 teaspoon salt
1 tablespoon baking powder
Melted butter

Warm buttermilk and add shortening, stirring to melt. Cool. Add the yeast which has been softened in ¼ cup warm water. Add sugar.

Sift together flour, salt, and baking powder. Add to buttermilk mixture. Stir to mix and cover with a damp cloth and an inverted plate. Chill overnight.

At this point, the dough will keep about five days to be used as needed. The sixth or seventh day, use the dough as cobbler topping or for fried pies.

When ready to use dough, roll out ¼ inch thick, cut into 1½-inch rounds, brush each round with melted butter, and stack two together. Place in greased pan, almost touching. Let rise 1 hour, then bake at 400° for 10 minutes or until done.

YIELD: 5 DOZEN

Mountain Measures
THE JUNIOR LEAGUE OF CHARLESTON, WEST VIRGINIA

· · · · · · · · · · · · · · · · ·

Refrigerator Rolls

2 packages dry yeast
1 cup warm water
1 cup shortening
1 cup sugar
1 cup boiling water
2 eggs
6 cups unsifted flour
1 tablespoon salt
Melted butter or margarine

Sprinkle yeast on top of warm water in small bowl and set aside.

Cream shortening and sugar in large bowl. Add boiling water. Beat the eggs until thick and add to shortening and sugar mixture. When luke-warm, stir in yeast mixture. Sift in flour and salt and mix well.

Tightly cover bowl and set in refrigerator overnight or until ready to use. It will keep for a week.

Two and a half to three hours before ready to use, roll out the dough to ½-inch thickness and cut into rounds with a biscuit cutter. Place small bits of butter on the round, fold over, and pinch together the edges. Place on lightly greased pans and brush with melted butter or margarine.

Let rise 2–3 hours, then bake in hot oven (400°) about 5 minutes or until lightly browned on top.

YIELD: 3–4 DOZEN

Furniture City Feasts
THE JUNIOR LEAGUE OF HIGH POINT, NORTH CAROLINA

. . . .

Crescent Rolls

¾ cup milk
½ cup melted butter
½ cup melted shortening
4 cups unsifted bread flour
Large pinch salt
½ cup sugar
3 eggs, beaten
1 package dry yeast
¼ cup warm water
Additional melted butter

Combine milk with melted butter and shortening. Combine flour, salt, and sugar. Stir in milk mixture and beaten eggs.

Soften yeast in the warm water and stir into flour mixture. Beat thoroughly. Then, with hands, slap dough hard against pastry board or table top until it becomes a greasy ball. Cover and leave in refrigerator overnight. Will keep about four days.

When ready to bake, divide dough into 4 equal parts. Roll each part out separately on floured board into a large round. Brush with melted butter and cut into 12 pie-shaped wedges. Start rolling with wide edge into crescents.

Arrange crescents on greased cookie sheet and brush with melted butter. Let rise for 1–1½ hours.

Bake at 450° for 12 minutes.

YIELD: 4 DOZEN CRESCENTS

Spartanburg Secrets II
THE JUNIOR LEAGUE OF SPARTANBURG, SOUTH CAROLINA

Hot Corn Meal Rolls

⅓ cup corn meal
½ cup sugar
1 teaspoon salt
½ cup melted shortening
2 cups milk
1 cake or package dry, active yeast
¼ cup warm water
2 eggs, beaten
4 cups flour
Melted butter

Cook corn meal, sugar, salt, shortening, and milk over medium heat until thick. Cool to lukewarm.

Dissolve yeast in warm water. Add to mixture with two beaten eggs. Let mixture rise for 2 hours, covered, in a warm place. Then add flour to form soft dough. Knead well and let rise 1 hour, or until doubled.

Knead again and roll out about ½ inch thick. Cut with biscuit cutter, brush with melted butter, crease, and fold over like Parker House rolls.

Let rise 1 hour. Bake at 375° for 15 minutes on greased cookie sheet.

YIELD: 4 DOZEN

Mountain Measures
THE JUNIOR LEAGUE OF CHARLESTON, WEST VIRGINIA

Cinnamon Sticky Buns

1 package dry yeast
¼ cup warm water
1 cup milk, scalded
4 tablespoons shortening
4 tablespoons sugar
1 teaspoon salt
1 egg, beaten well
3½–4 cups sifted flour
6 tablespoons melted butter
1 cup light corn syrup
1½ pounds light brown sugar
Additional melted butter
2 teaspoons cinnamon
½–1 cup chopped nuts

Soften yeast in warm water. Pour scalded milk over shortening, sugar, and salt in large bowl. Cool to lukewarm. Add softened yeast and beaten egg. Gradually stir in flour to form a soft dough. Beat vigorously, cover, and let rise until double (about 2 hours).

Prepare three flat, round 8-inch pans. In each put 2 tablespoons melted butter, ⅓ cup corn syrup, and ⅓ box brown sugar. Mix and melt over low heat.

Turn out risen dough onto lightly floured board and divide dough in half. Roll half into an oblong about ¼-inch thick. Brush with melted butter and sprinkle with ¼ cup brown sugar, 1 teaspoon cinnamon, and ¼–½ cup chopped nuts. Roll up like jelly roll, seal edges, and cut into slices about ¾-inch thick. Repeat on second half of dough. You should have about 18 rolls from each half.

Place rolls over mixture in pans. Cover and let rise until double (about 1½ hours). Bake at 375° for 25–30 minutes or until done.

Remove immediately from pan by inverting onto aluminum foil or serving plate. Let pan remain over rolls for a few minutes so all of syrup will run down onto rolls. Freezes well.

YIELD: 3 DOZEN BUNS

Nashville Seasons Encore
THE JUNIOR LEAGUE OF NASHVILLE, TENNESSEE

· · · · · · · · · · · · · ·

Ethel Field's Hot Rolls

This recipe makes the easiest and most irresistibly light rolls imaginable.

1 cup milk
½ cup butter
½ cup sugar
2 teaspoons salt
1 cake or package dry, active yeast
¼ cup warm water
3 eggs
5 cups flour
Melted butter

Scald milk; add butter, sugar, and salt. Let cool.

Dissolve yeast in the warm water. Add eggs to milk mixture, then add yeast-water mixture. Add flour, mixing gradually as you add. Allow dough to rise in warm place.

After approximately 2 hours, punch down and shape. Pinch off small quantity, roll on floured surface, and cut with biscuit cutter. Score in center, dip half of roll in melted butter, and fold over as for Parker House rolls. Let rolls rise 1 hour.

Bake at 400° for 8 minutes.

YIELD: 6 DOZEN

Of Pots and Pipkins
THE JUNIOR LEAGUE OF ROANOKE VALLEY, VIRGINIA

· · · · · · · · · · · · · ·

Yeast Bread

1 cup shortening
1 cup sugar
1¼ cups hot milk
8 cups flour
2 teaspoons salt
1 package plus 1 teaspoon dry yeast
1 teaspoon sugar
1 cup warm water
2 eggs, beaten

In large bowl, mix together shortening, sugar, and hot milk. Let cool to lukewarm.

Stir in 4 cups flour and salt.

Soften yeast with the 1 teaspoon sugar in warm water. Beat into flour mixture.

Add beaten eggs to mixture.

Let dough rise in a warm place until double in bulk. Punch down and work in about 4 more cups flour. Turn out on board or table top and knead long and hard. Let rise again until double in bulk.

Shape dough into 3 loaves, place in greased pans, and let rise until double in bulk.

Bake at 325° for 1 hour.

YIELD: 3 LOAVES

Spartanburg Secrets II
THE JUNIOR LEAGUE OF SPARTANBURG, SOUTH CAROLINA

Elizabeth Young's Homemade Bread

2 tablespoons sugar
1 package dry yeast (2 may be used on a cold day)
2½ cups lukewarm water
½ cup sugar
1½ teaspoons salt
2½ tablespoons melted bacon fat (or any other drippings)
6 cups unsifted flour
Butter or margarine

Stir 2 tablespoons sugar and yeast into water. Let mixture sit 5–15 minutes. Add ½ cup sugar, salt, and drippings. Stir in flour, cup by cup, until too thick to stir, then work in by hand. Turn onto floured board; add more flour if necessary and knead at least 10 minutes. Place in large greased bowl and brush top with melted butter or margarine. Cover and let rise in warm place (76°–85°) until doubled (about 1½ hours).

Gently divide into two equal portions. *Do not knead.* Mold into 2 loaves. Place into greased 9¼ × 5¼ × 2¾-inch loaf pans. Brush entire top surface of loaves with melted margarine. Cover pans with light cloth and let rise about 1½ hours.

Bake at 375° for 15 minutes, lower temperature to 275°, and bake 15–20 minutes. Test loaf for doneness by trying to slip it out of pan. If it doesn't come out easily, return to oven for 5–10 minutes.

Remove from oven. Brush margarine on tops of loaves while still in pan. Lift loaves gently out of pan. Let cool on wire rack. For softer crust, brush sides of loaves with butter while hot. Leave loaves uncovered while cooling.

YIELD: **2 LOAVES**

Southern Accent
THE JUNIOR LEAGUE OF PINE BLUFF, ARKANSAS

Grandma's Oatmeal Bread

2 packages dry yeast
½ cup warm water
1¼ cups boiling water
1 cup quick-cooking rolled oats
½ cup dark molasses
⅓ cup shortening
1 tablespoon salt
6–6¼ cups flour
2 eggs, beaten
4 tablespoons rolled oats
1 egg white
1 tablespoon water

Soften yeast in ½ cup warm water. Combine 1¼ cups boiling water, quick-cooking rolled oats, molasses, shortening, and salt; cool to luke-warm.

Sift flour. Stir in 2 cups sifted flour; beat well. Add beaten eggs and the yeast; beat well. Add enough remaining flour to make a soft dough. Turn out onto lightly floured surface; cover and let rest 10 minutes. Knead until smooth. Place in a lightly greased bowl, turning dough once. Cover and let rise until double (about 1½ hours).

Punch down. Coat two well-greased 8½ × 4½ × 2½-inch loaf pans with 2 tablespoons rolled oats each. Divide dough in half. Shape in loaves and place in pans. Cover and let double (45–60 minutes). Brush with mixture of 1 egg white and 1 tablespoon water; sprinkle lightly with rolled oats. Bake at 375° for 40 minutes. Cover with foil after baking 15 minutes if tops are getting too brown.

YIELD: 2 LOAVES

Mountain Measures
THE JUNIOR LEAGUE OF CHARLESTON, WEST VIRGINIA

Whole Wheat Bread

1 package dry yeast
2 cups warm water
½ teaspoon sugar
3 cups whole wheat flour
3 cups white flour
½ cup sugar
½ cup wheat germ
1½ tablespoons salt
1–1⅓ cups dry milk (amount to make 1 quart liquid;
look on the box. It varies with the brand of dry milk used,
but use it dry)
2 beaten eggs
½ cup salad oil
Margarine

Dissolve yeast in warm water with the ½ teaspoon sugar. Mix all dry ingredients. Beat the eggs into the yeast mixture. Alternately mix salad oil and yeast-egg mixture into the dry ingredients. Knead on floured board. You will need to use ½–¾ cup more white flour to work the dough until it is not gummy.

Let rise to double (3 hours or more, depending on heat in room). Punch down and let rise again (will take shorter time). Knead and form into loaves.

Put into greased loaf pan. Let rise.

Bake at 325° for 35–45 minutes, until golden brown. Last 5 minutes of baking, rub margarine over top.

YIELD: 2 LARGE OR 4 SMALL LOAVES

A Cook's Tour of Shreveport
THE JUNIOR LEAGUE OF SHREVEPORT, LOUISIANA

Sally Lunn

1 stick butter
1 cup milk, scalded
2 eggs, well beaten
2 teaspoons salt
3 tablespoons sugar
1 package yeast dissolved in ½ cup warm water
4 cups sifted flour
A little additional melted butter

Add butter to scalded milk, allowing it to melt. Beat eggs in large bowl and add milk and butter, salt, and sugar.

When cooled to lukewarm, add dissolved yeast. Beat in flour with mixer until smooth. Cover and let rise in warm place until doubled.

Punch down and put in greased bundt pan. Let rise to top of pan. Pour a little melted butter on top. Bake at 350° for 45 minutes to 1 hour.

Very pretty bread for a buffet.

YIELD: 10–12 SERVINGS

Nashville Seasons Encore
THE JUNIOR LEAGUE OF NASHVILLE, TENNESSEE

Monkey Bread

⅔ cup sugar
1 teaspoon salt
1 cup mashed potatoes
1 package dry yeast
½ cup lukewarm water
⅔ cup butter
⅔ cup margarine
1 cup milk
6 cups sifted flour
2 eggs
Additional butter

Mix sugar, salt, and potatoes in bowl. Dissolve yeast in water. Melt butter and margarine in milk over low heat and add to potato mixture. Cool to lukewarm. Add yeast and half of flour. Beat eggs; add to remaining flour. Combine the two mixtures and mix well. Let rise about 1 hour. Stir down and place in refrigerator.

When ready to bake, melt more butter and dip small elongated rolls of dough in it. Place rolls of dough in well-buttered ring mold, making only two layers. Bake at 350° for 30–40 minutes.

When serving, tear bread off with fingers instead of cutting with a knife.

YIELD: 8–10 SERVINGS

Party Potpourri
THE JUNIOR LEAGUE OF MEMPHIS, TENNESSEE

. . . .

Dilly Bread

1 package dry yeast
¼ cup warm water
1 cup cottage cheese
2 tablespoons sugar
1 tablespoon dry onion soup mix
1 tablespoon butter or margarine
2 teaspoons dill seed
1 teaspoon salt
¼ teaspoon baking soda
1 egg
2¼ – 2½ cups flour

Dissolve yeast in water. Heat cottage cheese to lukewarm. Combine sugar, onion soup, butter or margarine, dill seed, salt, soda, and egg in a bowl with cheese and yeast mixture. Add flour to form stiff dough. Cover and let rise until double in bulk. Stir dough down. Turn into well-greased 1½-quart casserole or two small loaf pans. Let rise 30–40 minutes or until double. Bake at 350° for 40–45 minutes. Baking time may be reduced if the two small pans are used. Brush with butter and sprinkle with salt. Delicious sliced and toasted and spread with butter.

YIELD: 2 SMALL LOAVES OR 1 LARGE LOAF

Cooking Through Rose Colored Glasses
THE JUNIOR LEAGUE OF TYLER, TEXAS

. . . .

Batter Bread

¼ cup sugar
1½ cups warm water
1 package dry yeast
3 eggs, beaten
3½ cups flour
1 cup rolled wheat or oats
1½ teaspoons salt
½ cup dry milk
½ cup melted butter
Additional oats and soft butter

Dissolve sugar in water; add yeast.

Combine beaten eggs with yeast mixture and then slowly stir in dry ingredients. Mix in melted butter last.

Spread in lightly greased 9 × 13-inch pan. Brush with butter and sprinkle with more oats.

Let rise 1 hour or until double. Bake at 375° for 30 minutes or until done. Cut into squares and serve hot with butter.

YIELD: 12 SERVINGS

Home Cookin'
THE JUNIOR LEAGUE OF WICHITA FALLS, TEXAS

. . . .

Desserts and Candy

Apple Dumplings with Different Pastry

PASTRY:
⅔ cup shortening
2 cups flour
1 teaspoon salt
3 tablespoons confectioners' sugar
4 tablespoons ice water

Mix half of the shortening with dry ingredients. Then mix in other half and add ice water. Blend with fork until dough can be pressed together. Divide into six equal portions and roll out each separately. Each one should be about a 7-inch square in order to encase the apple.

APPLES AND FILLING:
6 apples, peeled and cored
Sugar
Butter
¾ teaspoon cinnamon
Nutmeg

Place an apple on each pastry square. Fill cavities with sugar, butter, ⅛ teaspoon cinnamon, and a sprinkling of nutmeg. Add more butter and sugar at top. Moisten points of pastry and bring opposite corners up over apple, sealing well. Place about 2 inches apart in a buttered oblong casserole.

SYRUP:
1 cup sugar
2 cups water
3 tablespoons butter
¼ teaspoon cinnamon
1 teaspoon vanilla

Boil all ingredients together for 3 minutes. Pour around but not over dumplings. Bake at 425° for 40–45 minutes. If they seem to be browning too much, turn oven to 375° for the last 15 or 20 minutes.

YIELD: 6 SERVINGS

Home Cookin'
THE JUNIOR LEAGUE OF WICHITA FALLS, TEXAS

· · · · · · · · · · · · · · ·

Fried Apple Rings

8 medium apples
⅓ cup butter
Sugar
Cinnamon

Core apples and slice crosswise. Melt butter in large skillet. Place apples in and sprinkle with sugar and cinnamon. Cover and cook slowly for ½ hour. Baste but do not turn the apples.

YIELD: 8 SERVINGS

The Cotton Blossom Cookbook
THE JUNIOR LEAGUE OF ATLANTA, GEORGIA

· · · · · · · · · · · · · · ·

Bananas Caramel

1⅓ cups brown sugar, firmly packed
¼ cup half and half
¼ cup butter or margarine
1½ teaspoons vanilla
6 bananas, sliced
1 cup sour cream
¼ cup confectioners' sugar

Recipe continues . . .

Mix brown sugar, half and half, and butter or margarine. Cook over low heat, stirring constantly until the consistency of mayonnaise. Remove from heat and add vanilla.

Arrange sliced bananas in serving dish. Pour sauce over bananas and cool.

Mix sour cream and confectioners' sugar well. Spoon over banana mixture and chill before serving.

This should be served the same day it is prepared. It is especially attractive served in parfait glasses.

YIELD: 8–10 SERVINGS

Home Cookin'
THE JUNIOR LEAGUE OF WICHITA FALLS, TEXAS

· · · · · · · · · · · · · · · · · · ·

Banana Pancakes

This recipe came from a native cook at Round Hill, Montego Bay, Jamaica.

1 egg
1 tablespoon sugar
3 tablespoons flour
½ teaspoon baking powder
3 ripe bananas, peeled and mashed
Butter
Sugar

Beat egg with sugar. Add flour, baking powder, and bananas. Mix together with a fork.

Drop a tablespoonful at a time into a hot buttered frying pan. Turn when bubbles appear. These cook quickly. Be careful not to burn the butter. Add more butter to frying pan as needed. Remove to platter and sprinkle with granulated sugar. These are so delicious that no syrup is needed.

It is better to make two batches of pancake batter than to double the recipe. Recipe can be doubled if blender is used.

YIELD: 14–16 SMALL PANCAKES

The Gasparilla Cookbook
THE JUNIOR LEAGUE OF TAMPA, FLORIDA

Prize Peach Cobbler

¾ cup flour
Less than ⅛ teaspoon salt
2 teaspoons baking powder
1 cup sugar
¾ cup milk
½ cup butter or margarine
2 cups fresh sliced peaches
1 cup sugar

Sift flour, salt, and baking powder. Mix with 1 cup sugar; slowly stir in milk to make batter.

Melt butter in 8 × 8 × 2-inch baking pan. Pour batter over melted butter. Do not stir. Mix the peaches and 1 cup sugar thoroughly and carefully spoon them over the batter.

Bake 1 hour at 350°. Serve hot or cold, with cream if desired.

YIELD: 6 SERVINGS

The Gasparilla Cookbook
THE JUNIOR LEAGUE OF TAMPA, FLORIDA

Orange-Poached Pears

24 medium-size Bosc pears
Juice of 2 lemons
3 cups water
1½ cups sugar
2 cups white wine
1 cup orange-flavored liqueur
10 cloves
3 wide strips orange peel
½ cup brandy

Carefully peel pears, leaving the stems intact. Drop the pears as they are peeled into a bowl of cold water, acidulated with juice of 2 lemons.

In a saucepan, bring 3 cups water and sugar to a boil over moderate heat and simmer the syrup for 5 minutes. Arrange the pears on their sides in one layer in a 14 × 10-inch baking dish and pour over them mixture of white wine, liqueur, the syrup, and cloves. Add orange peel and bring to a simmer on top of the stove. Cover with aluminum foil and bake pears in a 375° oven for 30 minutes.

Remove foil and turn pears onto other sides, lifting them carefully by the stems. Replace the foil and bake the pears 20–30 minutes more or until tender. Carefully transfer the pears by the stems to a deep dish, add brandy to juices, and ladle the juices over the pears. Let pears cool and chill overnight.

Serve with the juices and pass a bowl of slightly sweetened whipped cream flavored with orange liqueur, or serve with chocolate sauce.

YIELD: 8 SERVINGS

The Dallas Jr. League Cookbook
THE JUNIOR LEAGUE OF DALLAS, TEXAS

Strawberry Pizza

1 cup flour
¼ cup confectioners' sugar
1 stick margarine
8 ounces cream cheese
½ cup sugar
3 10-ounce boxes frozen strawberries
4 tablespoons sugar
4 teaspoons cornstarch

Cut together first three ingredients as for pie crust. Sprinkle evenly over 12 or 13-inch pizza pan. Press firmly and bake at 325° for 15–20 minutes, until light brown. Cool.

Combine cream cheese and ½ cup sugar and spread over cooled crust. Chill.

Thaw and drain berries; combine 1 cup berry juice, sugar, and cornstarch; cook until thick. Add berries. Chill. Spread over cheese filling. This is a real waist-stretcher!

YIELD: 12 SERVINGS

The Blue Denim Gourmet
THE JUNIOR LEAGUE OF ODESSA, TEXAS

. . . .

Crème Brûlée with Pêches Flambées

An elegant-looking dessert but very simple to make and always a hit!

1 large can peaches (or equivalent in fresh fruit)
Maple syrup
2 wineglasses brandy

Place drained canned or fresh peeled fruit (peaches preferably) in shallow baking dish, adding maple syrup to almost cover fruit, and heat thoroughly

Recipe continues . . .

in oven. Brown under broiler for 1 minute. Pour brandy over top, light, and bring to table flaming. Pass separately the ice cold Crème Brûlée.

YIELD: 6 SERVINGS

COLD CRÈME BRÛLÉE:
4 eggs
1½ pints heavy cream
Pinch salt
Brown sugar

Beat eggs together with cream and salt. Cook over hot water, stirring constantly until smooth and thick.

When cool, pour into lightly buttered shallow casserole. Chill thoroughly. Sprinkle top completely with layer of sifted brown sugar. Run under broiler until sugar melts and forms a crust.

Chill in refrigerator several hours before serving.

Spartanburg Secrets II
THE JUNIOR LEAGUE OF SPARTANBURG, SOUTH CAROLINA

Bread Pudding with Whiskey Sauce

3–4 slices bread
3½ cups milk
4 tablespoons sugar
4 eggs, separated
1 tablespoon vanilla
Pinch salt
Raisins (optional)
½ stick butter
8 level tablespoons sugar

Break bread into ovenproof dish of at least 1½-quart capacity. Soften bread with small amount of milk. Beat 4 tablespoons sugar and egg yolks.

Add remaining milk and stir well. Add vanilla and salt. Pour milk mixture over bread. Fold in raisins if desired. Dot with butter.

Place dish in pan of water and bake at 300° for 40–50 minutes or until silver knife inserted comes out clean. Remove from oven and raise temperature to 350°.

Make meringue using 2 level tablespoons sugar to each egg white. Spread over pudding and return to 350° oven until brown.

WHISKEY SAUCE:
½ cup sugar
¼ cup water
¼ stick butter
Whiskey to taste

Cook first three ingredients until butter is melted and sugar dissolved. Remove from heat and add whiskey to taste. Serve with Bread Pudding.

YIELD: 8 SERVINGS

Talk About Good!
THE JUNIOR LEAGUE OF LAFAYETTE, LOUISIANA

· · · · · · · · · · · · · ·

Steamed Cranberry Pudding

2 cups raw cranberries, halved
¼ cup white corn syrup
¼ cup black strap molasses
⅓ cup hot water
2 teaspoons baking soda
1½ cups flour
1 egg, beaten

Mix ingredients in order. Place in greased mold with tight cover or in greased loaf pan, covering with foil and holding foil in place with rubber band. Steam for 1½–2 hours. May use a trivet in a Dutch oven and

Recipe continues . . .

partially cover. Place hot water in Dutch oven so that the level is about halfway up the loaf pan while bubbling gently.

SAUCE:

1 cup sugar
½ cup butter
½ cup heavy cream

Mix sauce ingredients and simmer until well blended. Serve pudding warm with hot sauce.

May be prepared several days in advance and frozen. To freeze, turn out of pan and wrap in foil. Reheat before serving by resteaming, or dampen and heat in top of double boiler.

YIELD: 12 SERVINGS

Cooking Through Rose Colored Glasses
THE JUNIOR LEAGUE OF TYLER, TEXAS

.   .   .   .

Rice Impératrice Pudding

This recipe comes from the famous Greenbriar Hotel, nestled in the Appalachian Mountains at White Sulphur Springs, West Virginia.

½ 3-ounce package red gelatin
1 cup boiling water
¾ cup rice
2 cups water
4 cups milk
⅞ cup sugar
4 envelopes unflavored gelatin
¾ cup cold water
2 cups heavy cream
¾–1 teaspoon lemon extract or grated lemon rind
1 teaspoon vanilla

Dissolve red gelatin in boiling water. Pour into custard cups or shallow 3-quart dish. Let set partially. Cook rice in water until dry. Add milk to rice and cook until thick, about 1 hour. Stir sugar into rice.

Soften unflavored gelatin in cold water; stir into rice. Let rice cool.

Whip cream and fold whipped cream and flavorings into rice. Carefully spoon onto partially set red gelatin. Refrigerate until set, about 3 hours.

Traditionally served with Melba Sauce, but may also be served with brandied fruit, Rumtopf, or any other fruit sauce.

YIELD: 12–15 SERVINGS

MELBA SAUCE:
3 cups raspberries, strained to remove seeds
¾ cup sugar
1 tablespoon cornstarch (optional)
¼ cup water (optional)

Combine berries and sugar; cook for 10 minutes over low heat. For a slightly thicker sauce, soften cornstarch in water and add to sugar-berry mixture, cooking until sauce is thickened and clear.

Mountain Measures
THE JUNIOR LEAGUE OF CHARLESTON, WEST VIRGINIA

. . . .

Grand Marnier Soufflé

3 tablespoons butter
2 tablespoons flour
1 cup heavy cream
6 tablespoons sugar
5 egg yolks
5 tablespoons Grand Marnier
½ teaspoon cream of tartar
6 egg whites

Recipe continues . . .

Melt butter in top of double boiler and add flour. Mix well and cook for a moment. Pour in cream, stirring constantly until mixture thickens, then add sugar. When sugar is dissolved, remove from heat and allow to cool. When cool, beat yolks and stir in along with Grand Marnier. Sprinkle cream of tartar over the egg whites while beating them into stiff, moist peaks.

Take one-third of the beaten whites and mix vigorously into the Grand Marnier custard. Dribble custard over the remaining egg whites and fold thoroughly and carefully.

Butter sides and bottom of a 2-quart soufflé dish, then sprinkle thoroughly with sugar. Pour mixture into prepared dish and place in a pre-heated 350° oven for about 25–30 minutes. Test to be sure soufflé is done before removing from oven by shaking to see if firm. Serve immediately, passing sauce to spoon over individual servings.

YIELD: 6 SERVINGS

GRAND MARNIER SAUCE:
½ cup sugar
3 tablespoons strong black coffee
3 tablespoons Grand Marnier

In a small, heavy iron skillet, melt the sugar and stir until a rich brown (be very careful not to burn). Remove from heat and stir in coffee and Grand Marnier. Return to heat for a moment and stir until blended. If caramelized sugar does not dissolve after a few minutes, add 1–2 tablespoons water and stir over heat until it does dissolve. This sauce can be used hot, cold, or lukewarm.

Southern Sideboards
THE JUNIOR LEAGUE OF JACKSON, MISSISSIPPI

Soufflé au Rhum

4 egg yolks
1 teaspoon salt
½ cup confectioners' sugar
6 tablespoons rum
8 egg whites
Guava jelly
Powdered or superfine sugar

Beat the egg yolks, salt, confectioners' sugar, and 2 tablespoons of rum until light; fold in the beaten egg whites.

Cook slowly in hot buttered omelet pan until puffed and faintly browned on under side. Place on center rack in oven to finish cooking the top. Spread with jelly. Fold one half over the other. Turn onto platter and sprinkle with powdered or superfine sugar. Pour the rest of the rum around it and bring to the table lighted.

YIELD: 2 SERVINGS

The Cotton Blossom Cookbook
THE JUNIOR LEAGUE OF ATLANTA, GEORGIA

· · · · · · · · · · · · · · · · · · ·

Chocolate Soufflé

2 envelopes unflavored gelatin
½ cup water
⅔ cup crème de cacao
1¼ cups brown sugar
1 12-ounce package semisweet chocolate morsels
8 eggs, separated
½ teaspoon salt
2 cups heavy cream, whipped
½ cup chopped pistachio nuts or ground almonds

Recipe continues . . .

Sprinkle gelatin over water and crème de cacao in a saucepan. Add ½ cup of the sugar and place over low heat. Stir constantly until gelatin and sugar are dissolved. Add chocolate and stir until melted. Remove from heat. Beat in egg yolks, one at a time. Cool.

Beat egg whites and salt until stiff but not dry. Gradually beat in remaining sugar and continue beating until very stiff. Fold egg whites into the gelatin mixture. Fold in whipped cream.

Turn into a 2-quart soufflé dish with a 2-inch collar, or into a 3-quart serving bowl. Chill several hours or overnight.

Sprinkle with pistachio nuts or ground almonds.

YIELD: 12–14 SERVINGS

Furniture City Feasts
THE JUNIOR LEAGUE OF HIGH POINT, NORTH CAROLINA

· ·

Cold Lemon Soufflé with Wine Sauce

1 envelope unflavored gelatin
¼ cup cold water
5 eggs, separated
¾ cup fresh lemon juice
2 teaspoons grated lemon rind
1½ cups sugar
1 cup heavy cream

Sprinkle gelatin over cold water to soften. Mix egg yolks with lemon juice, rind, and ¾ cup of the sugar. Place in double boiler over boiling water and cook, stirring constantly, until lemon mixture is slightly thickened (about 8 minutes). Remove from heat and stir in gelatin until dissolved. Chill 30–40 minutes or until mixture mounds slightly when dropped from spoon.

Beat egg whites until they begin to hold their shape; then gradually add ¾ cup sugar until all has been added and whites are stiff. Beat cream until stiff. Fold whites and cream into yolk mixture until no white streaks remain. Pour into a 2-quart soufflé dish and chill 4 hours or more. Serve with Wine Sauce.

YIELD: 8 SERVINGS

WINE SAUCE:
½ cup sugar
1 tablespoon cornstarch
½ cup water
3 tablespoons fresh lemon juice
1 teaspoon grated lemon rind
2 tablespoons butter
½ cup dry white wine

In a small saucepan, mix together sugar and cornstarch. Stir in water, lemon juice, and rind until smooth. Add butter. Bring to a boil, lower heat, and cook until thickened (about 3 minutes). Remove from heat and stir in wine. Chill, stirring occasionally.

Party Potpourri
THE JUNIOR LEAGUE OF MEMPHIS, TENNESSEE

.   .   .   .

Flan with Caramel Topping

2½ cups sugar
1 tablespoon water
8 eggs
1 teaspoon vanilla
½ teaspoon salt
1 quart milk, scalded

Caramelize 1 cup sugar over low heat. Add water and cook 1 minute, stirring constantly. Pour caramel into 12 custard cups, one at a time, tilting each cup to coat the sides.

Recipe continues ...

Lightly beat eggs. Add remaining sugar, vanilla, and salt. Stir in milk. Pour into custard cups. Set cups in a pan with 1 inch hot water. Bake in a preheated 350° oven for 30 minutes or until a silver knife near the edge comes out clean. Unmold before serving.

YIELD: 12 SERVINGS

Fiesta: Favorite Recipes of South Texas
THE JUNIOR LEAGUE OF CORPUS CHRISTI, TEXAS

. . . .

Czarina Cream

1 pint heavy cream
½ cup sugar
1 envelope unflavored gelatin
¼ cup cold water
1 teaspoon vanilla
¼ cup sherry
¼ cup blanched, slivered almonds
Frozen raspberries

Whip cream, slowly adding sugar. Soak gelatin in cold water and dissolve over hot water. Let cool and add to whipped cream. Add vanilla, sherry, and slivered almonds.

Put in a 1½-quart ring mold and refrigerate until set.

Unmold on serving plate. In the center, place a glass or silver sauce dish of thawed frozen raspberries to spoon over the slices of Czarina Cream.

YIELD: 4 SERVINGS

300 Years of Carolina Cooking
THE JUNIOR LEAGUE OF GREENVILLE, SOUTH CAROLINA

. . . .

Chocolate Yummy-Rummy

½ cup strong coffee
1 12-ounce package semisweet chocolate morsels
6 eggs, separated
3–4 tablespoons rum

Heat coffee to boiling and add nuggets. When completely melted, remove from fire and gradually stir in 6 well-beaten egg yolks. Add rum. Fold in the stiffly beaten egg whites. Pour into individual dessert cups and refrigerate for at least 12 hours before serving.

You may "gild the lily" if you desire by topping with whipped cream and/or chopped nuts . . . but it doesn't need a thing.

YIELD: 8–10 SERVINGS

Nashville Seasons
THE JUNIOR LEAGUE OF NASHVILLE, TENNESSEE

. . . .

Grandmother Allen's Charlotte Russe

1½ dozen lady fingers
2 envelopes unflavored gelatin
½ cup cold water
2 cups milk
6 egg yolks
1 cup sugar
Vanilla to taste
2 cups heavy cream, whipped

Line angel cake pan or mold with lady fingers. Soften gelatin in cold water. Scald milk, beat yolks and sugar well, then stir into milk. Cook until mixture begins to thicken. Just before removing from fire, add gelatin and stir until well dissolved. Add vanilla and set aside.

Recipe continues . . .

When thoroughly cool, fold in whipped cream and place in mold lined with lady fingers. Chill. To serve, unmold on cake plate and slice like cake.

YIELD: 8 SERVINGS

VARIATION:

2 squares melted bitter chocolate may be added to hot custard.

The Memphis Cook Book
THE JUNIOR LEAGUE OF MEMPHIS, TENNESSEE

·   ·   ·   ·   ·   ·   ·   ·   ·   ·   ·   ·   ·   ·   ·   ·   ·

Sherry Bavarian Cream

1 envelope unflavored gelatin
2 tablespoons cold water
½ cup sugar
¾ cup boiling water
1 tablespoon lemon juice
Pinch salt
½ cup good sherry
1 cup heavy cream, whipped

Soften gelatin in cold water for 10 minutes, then dissolve with sugar in boiling water. Add lemon juice. Cool slightly; add salt and sherry. When almost at the setting point, fold in whipped cream.

Turn into large mold or several individual molds, previously moistened with cold water. Chill thoroughly. Unmold for serving and garnish with slices of any desired fruit.

YIELD: 4–6 SERVINGS

Spartanburg Secrets II
THE JUNIOR LEAGUE OF SPARTANBURG, SOUTH CAROLINA

·   ·   ·   ·   ·   ·   ·   ·   ·   ·   ·   ·   ·   ·   ·   ·   ·

Old-Time Homemade Ice Cream

5 eggs
2½ cups sugar
½ gallon milk
2 13-ounce cans evaporated milk
2 13-ounce cans condensed milk
At least 4 tablespoons vanilla (or more to taste)

Make custard of eggs, sugar, and milk. Heat very slowly until mixture coats a spoon. Remove and cool thoroughly.

Add evaporated milk, condensed milk, and vanilla.

Freeze in electric freezer. Recipe can be halved to make two refrigerator ice trays full.

YIELD: 1 GALLON

Recipe Jubilee
THE JUNIOR LEAGUE OF MOBILE, ALABAMA

.   .   .   .

Fresh Peach Custard Mousse

1 envelope unflavored gelatin
½ cup orange juice
¼ cup lemon juice
1 cup sugar
¼ cup flour
¼ teaspoon salt
1 cup milk
3 egg yolks, slightly beaten
1 tablespoon grated lemon rind
5 or 6 medium fresh peaches, crushed
3 egg whites
3 tablespoons sugar
18 lady fingers, split in half
1 cup heavy cream

Recipe continues . . .

Soften gelatin in orange and lemon juice.

Mix sugar, flour, and salt in pan. Gradually add milk. Cook over medium heat, stirring constantly, until thickened. Cook 2 more minutes.

Blend small amount of hot mixture into egg yolks; return all to pan and cook 1 minute. (Do not boil.) Stir in softened gelatin until dissolved. Add lemon rind. Cool.

Crush peaches and add custard. Beat egg whites until frothy; beat in sugar 1 tablespoon at a time; beat until mixture forms stiff peaks. Fold into cooled custard.

Line bottom and sides of 7 × 11-inch pan with lady fingers. Pour in peach mixture. Cover and refrigerate for 2–3 hours. Spread with whipped cream just before serving.

YIELD: 6 SERVINGS

The Charlotte Cookbook
THE JUNIOR LEAGUE OF CHARLOTTE, NORTH CAROLINA

• • • • • • • • • • • • • • •

Caramel Ice Cream

3 egg yolks
½ cup sugar
1 scant cup sugar
1 pint milk
1 tablespoon unflavored gelatin
1 pint heavy cream

Cream egg yolks with ½ cup sugar. Place in a frying pan 1 scant cup sugar and stir over the fire until it becomes a deep golden brown—not too dark or the caramel flavor will be lost, or too light as it will be tasteless.

Pour this hot caramel slowly into the pint of milk heated in a double boiler with the gelatin, and stir until dissolved. Remove mixture from stove and pour it slowly into the creamed yolks and sugar. Stir well. Return this mixture to the double boiler and stir constantly until it thickens or the custard coats the spoon. Remove instantly when it reaches this point. Strain mixture and let cool.

Just before freezing, add a pint of cream which has been whipped fairly stiff. Freeze in a regular ice cream freezer.

YIELD: 6 SERVINGS

The Cotton Blossom Cookbook
THE JUNIOR LEAGUE OF ATLANTA, GEORGIA

· · · · · · · · · · · · · · · · · ·

Coffee Tortoni

A farmhouse of the Civil War era is the setting for Country Road Inn, located at Zela, near Summersville, West Virginia. The inn serves mostly Italian cuisine and delights guests with homemade specialties such as this.

2 tablespoons grated coconut
2 tablespoons chopped almonds
1 egg white
1 heaping teaspoon instant coffee
½ cup plus 2 teaspoons sugar
1 cup heavy cream
1 teaspoon vanilla
⅛ teaspoon almond extract

Toast coconut and chopped almonds. Whip egg white with coffee; gradually add 2 teaspoons sugar. Whip cream; add remaining ½ cup sugar, vanilla, and almond extract. Fold cream into egg mixture; add coconut and almonds.

Pour into fluted paper baking cups. Sprinkle with additional coconut if desired. Freeze 2 hours or more.

YIELD: 6 SERVINGS

Mountain Measures
THE JUNIOR LEAGUE OF CHARLESTON, WEST VIRGINIA

· · · · · · · · · · · · · · · · · ·

Chocolate Ice Cream

Idiot's ice cream—it's so easy to make!

⅓ cup slivered blanched almonds
⅔ cup chocolate syrup
⅔ cup sweetened condensed milk
2 cups heavy cream
½ teaspoon vanilla

Toast almonds. Allow to cool. Combine remaining ingredients and chill. Whip until fluffy. Fold in almonds, reserving a few for topping. Pour into containers and freeze.

May also be put into individual parfait glasses and frozen. When served, top with a few almonds. Very rich.

YIELD: 8 SERVINGS

Furniture City Feasts
THE JUNIOR LEAGUE OF HIGH POINT, NORTH CAROLINA

. . . .

Regal Chocolate Sauce

½ cup light corn syrup
1 cup sugar
1 cup water
3 1-ounce squares unsweetened chocolate
1 teaspoon vanilla
1 cup evaporated milk

Combine syrup, sugar, and water. Cook to soft ball stage (235° on candy thermometer).

Remove from heat; add chocolate and stir until melted. Add vanilla and *slowly* add evaporated milk, mixing thoroughly. Store in refrigerator.

YIELD: 2 CUPS

The Gasparilla Cookbook
THE JUNIOR LEAGUE OF TAMPA, FLORIDA

. . . .

Hot Fudge Sauce

2 squares unsweetened chocolate
4 tablespoons butter
¾ cup sugar
½ cup evaporated milk

Melt chocolate and butter and add sugar. Stir in evaporated milk.

YIELD: 1½ CUPS

Furniture City Feasts
THE JUNIOR LEAGUE OF HIGH POINT, NORTH CAROLINA

. . . .

Chocolate Crème de Menthe Sauce

2 squares unsweetened chocolate
4 tablespoons water
½ cup sugar
Dash salt
3 tablespoons butter
1 miniature bottle crème de menthe

Melt chocolate squares in water over low heat, stirring until mixture is smooth.

Recipe continues . . .

Add sugar and dash of salt. Cook and stir until smooth and slightly thickened. Stir in butter and crème de menthe.

Serve over vanilla ice cream.

YIELD: ABOUT 1 CUP

A Taste of Tampa
THE JUNIOR LEAGUE OF TAMPA, FLORIDA

Raspberry Sauce

1 16-ounce package frozen red raspberries
1 teaspoon cornstarch
1 tablespoon water
¼ cup sugar
½ cup red currant jelly
4 tablespoons Cointreau

Thaw berries, heat, and strain through sieve.

Mix cornstarch with water. Add to strained berries and simmer 5 minutes. Add sugar and red currant jelly. Dissolve thoroughly and add Cointreau.

Serve over fresh sliced peaches, cantaloupe, or ice cream. Keeps well in refrigerator.

YIELD: 6 SERVINGS

Of Pots and Pipkins
THE JUNIOR LEAGUE OF ROANOKE VALLEY, VIRGINIA

Sherry Sauce

This sauce is so easily and quickly made and makes something really special of vanilla ice cream.

½ cup milk
1 cup sugar
4 tablespoons butter
2 tablespoons sherry

Boil milk, sugar, and butter together for 5 minutes. Add sherry.

YIELD: 1 CUP

Charleston Receipts

THE JUNIOR LEAGUE OF CHARLESTON, SOUTH CAROLINA

. . . .

Fresh Coconut Cake

3 cups cake flour, sifted
2 teaspoons baking powder
Pinch salt if shortening is used
1 cup butter or shortening
2 cups sugar
1 cup milk
1 teaspoon vanilla
6 egg whites, beaten stiff
Coconut milk plus enough water to equal 1 cup
⅔ cup sugar
Grated fresh coconut

Sift together flour and baking powder. Add pinch salt if shortening is to be used. If cake flour is not available, ⅞ cup all-purpose flour may be substituted for each cup cake flour.

Cream butter or shortening and sugar. Add milk and vanilla alternately with flour mixture. Fold in egg whites. Bake in 2 greased 9-inch round pans lined with wax paper.

Bake at 350° until cakes begin to pull from side of pans or until a toothpick inserted comes out clean. While cakes are baking, put coconut

Recipe continues ...

milk, water, and sugar into saucepan and boil vigorously for 5 minutes. Set aside to cool. When cakes are done, pour syrup over them immediately.

When cakes are cool, remove from pan and frost top and sides with Seven-Minute Frosting. Sprinkle generously with grated coconut.

YIELD: 12 SERVINGS

SEVEN-MINUTE FROSTING:
1½ cups sugar
2 tablespoons white corn syrup
½ teaspoon cream of tartar
2 egg whites
⅓ cup water
½ teaspoon vanilla

Place all ingredients except vanilla in top of double boiler and cook over boiling water, beating constantly with rotary or electric mixer, for 7 minutes or until icing stands in peaks. Remove from heat; beat in vanilla.

Home Cookin'
THE JUNIOR LEAGUE OF WICHITA FALLS, TEXAS

· · · · · · · · · · · · · · · · · · ·

1, 2, 3, 4 Cake

3 cups sifted cake flour
1 tablespoon baking powder
½ teaspoon salt
1 cup butter
2 cups sugar
4 eggs, separated
1 cup milk
1 teaspoon vanilla

Grease and flour three 9-inch round pans, or line bottoms of greased pans with greased brown paper. Sift together the flour, baking powder, and salt.

(If cake flour is not available, use ⅞ cup all-purpose flour for each cup cake flour.)

Cream butter and sugar well. Add egg yolks; beat. Add flour alternately with milk, beginning and ending with flour. Fold in stiffly beaten egg whites and vanilla. Bake at 350° for 25–30 minutes. Use Pineapple Filling between layers and frost with Boiled White Icing.

YIELD: A 9-INCH 3-LAYER CAKE

PINEAPPLE FILLING:
1 cup sugar
1 heaping tablespoon flour
1 8¼ -ounce can crushed pineapple
3 egg yolks, beaten
1½ tablespoons lemon juice
1 tablespoon butter

Blend sugar and flour; combine with pineapple. Add egg yolks, lemon juice, and butter. Cook over low heat, stirring constantly, until thick and smooth, about 20 minutes. Cool and spread between layers of cake.

BOILED WHITE ICING:
2 cups sugar
1 cup water
2 tablespoons light corn syrup
2 egg whites
⅛ teaspoon salt
⅛ teaspoon cream of tartar
1 teaspoon vanilla

Mix sugar, water, and syrup and cook, stirring often, until sugar is dissolved. Boil until syrup reaches soft ball stage (234° on a candy thermometer).

Beat egg whites with salt until frothy. Add one-third of boiling syrup to the egg whites in a thin stream, beating constantly. Then return syrup to heat and cook a little more. Add second third of boiling syrup in the same manner. Place remainder of syrup on heat to reach crack stage (about 290°); add to egg whites. Add cream of tartar and vanilla. Whip until

Recipe continues . . .

creamy. If icing gets too hard and stiff, add a few drops of water at a time until it is right consistency for smooth spreading. Ice top and sides of cake.

Fiesta: Favorite Recipes of South Texas
THE JUNIOR LEAGUE OF CORPUS CHRISTI, TEXAS

. . . .

Lady Baltimore Cake

Owen Wister immortalized Charleston's Lady Baltimore Tea Room and its glamorous cake in his book *Lady Baltimore*.

1 cup butter
2 cups sugar
4 eggs
4 teaspoons baking powder
3½ cups cake flour
1 cup milk
1 cup sugar
½ cup water
2 teaspoons almond extract
2 teaspoons vanilla

Use electric mixer, if possible; cream butter, add 2 cups sugar gradually, and beat until the consistency of whipped cream. Add eggs, one at a time, and beat thoroughly. Sift baking powder and flour three times and add alternately with milk, using a wooden spoon for blending. Bake in two 11-inch greased cake pans at 350° for 30 minutes.

Make a thick syrup of 1 cup sugar and ½ cup water. Flavor with almond extract and vanilla. Spread this over layers as soon as you remove them from the pans.

When cool, spread frosting between layers and on top and sides of cake.

YIELD: ONE LARGE 2-LAYER CAKE

LADY BALTIMORE FROSTING:
2 cups sugar
⅔ cup water
2 teaspoons corn syrup
2 egg whites, beaten stiff
2 cups seeded raisins
2 cups pecans or walnuts
12 figs
Sherry or brandy (optional)
Vanilla and almond extract

Mix sugar, water, and corn syrup. Cook until mixture forms a firm ball in cold water. Pour gradually into the stiff egg whites, beating constantly.

Add raisins, nuts, and figs, all cut fine. Raisins and figs may be soaked overnight in small amount of sherry or brandy, if desired. Add vanilla and almond extract to taste.

Charleston Receipts
THE JUNIOR LEAGUE OF CHARLESTON, SOUTH CAROLINA

· · · · · · · · · · · · · · · · ·

Sour Cream Pound Cake

1 cup butter
3 cups sugar
6 eggs, separated
¼ teaspoon baking soda
3 cups sifted flour
1 cup sour cream

Cream butter and sugar thoroughly. Stir in egg yolks one at a time. Add soda to flour. Add flour and sour cream alternately to creamed mixture. Beat egg whites stiff and fold in.

Recipe continues . . .

Bake in large tube pan, greased and floured, at 300° for 1½–2 hours, or until a toothpick inserted in center of cake comes out clean. Should have nice brown crust on top. Let stand 15 minutes before taking out of pan.

No flavoring needed. The longer you keep this cake the more moist it gets!

YIELD: 12 SERVINGS

The Gasparilla Cookbook
THE JUNIOR LEAGUE OF TAMPA, FLORIDA

· · · · · · · · · · · · · · · ·

Rum Cake de Maison

This cake should be baked, filled, and frosted 24 hours before serving.

2 cups sifted cake flour
2 teaspoons baking powder
¼ teaspoon baking soda
¼ teaspoon salt
½ cup butter
¾ cup sugar
2 egg yolks, unbeaten
1 teaspoon grated orange rind
½ cup orange juice
2 tablespoons white rum
¼ teaspoon vanilla
¼ teaspoon almond extract
2 egg whites
¼ cup sugar
8 tablespoons white rum
1½ cups walnuts

Sift first four ingredients and set aside. (If cake flour is not available, substitute ⅞ cup all-purpose flour for each cup cake flour.)

In large bowl, cream butter, add ¾ cup sugar, and mix until light and fluffy. Beat in egg yolks one at a time. Add orange rind. Add flour alternately with orange juice combined with 2 tablespoons rum. Add vanilla and almond extract.

In medium bowl, beat egg whites, gradually adding ¼ cup sugar. Beat until stiff peaks form. Gently fold batter into egg whites, pour into two greased 9-inch cake pans, and bake 25 minutes at 350°.

Cool cakes and split into four layers. Sprinkle each layer with 2 tablespoons rum. Put three layers together with Whipped-Cream Filling. Top fourth layer with Chocolate Frosting.

YIELD: A 9-INCH 4-LAYER CAKE

WHIPPED-CREAM FILLING:
2 teaspoons unflavored gelatin
2 tablespoons hot water
2 cups heavy cream
½ cup confectioners' sugar
⅓ cup white rum

Dissolve gelatin in water. Cool slightly.

Beat cream with sugar until stiff. Gradually beat in rum. Add gelatin slowly, beating until stiff.

CHOCOLATE FROSTING:
4 squares unsweetened chocolate
1 cup sugar
2 tablespoons hot water
2 eggs
6 tablespoons soft butter

In double boiler over hot water, melt chocolate. Remove from heat.

Recipe continues . . .

Beat in sugar and hot water. Beat in eggs, one at a time, beating very well. Beat in butter, 2 tablespoons at a time, until smooth.

That Something Special
THE JUNIOR LEAGUE OF DURHAM, NORTH CAROLINA

. . . .

Spicy Carrot Cake

2 cups sugar
2 cups flour
2 teaspoons baking soda
2 teaspoons cinnamon
1 teaspoon salt
4 eggs
1½ cups oil
3 cups grated carrots

Combine dry ingredients and mix well. Add eggs and oil and mix well. Now add carrots and beat on medium speed with electric mixer about 2 minutes.

Grease and flour three 9-inch cake pans. Preheat oven for 10 minutes at 350°. Pour batter into the three cake pans and bake 25–30 minutes.

Cool for 10 minutes. Then turn out onto cake racks. When cool, put layers together and frost top with filling.

YIELD: A 3-LAYER CAKE

CREAM CHEESE FILLING:
1 stick butter
1 8-ounce package cream cheese
1 box confectioners' sugar
1 teaspoon vanilla
1 cup chopped pecans (optional)

Cream butter and cheese until light and fluffy. Beat in sugar gradually. Add vanilla and pecans.

Talk About Good!
THE JUNIOR LEAGUE OF LAFAYETTE, LOUISIANA

. . . .

Old-Fashioned Pound Cake

2 sticks butter
2 cups sugar
5 eggs
2 cups sifted cake flour
2 teaspoons vanilla
1 tablespoon lemon juice
¼ teaspoon salt

Cream butter and sugar until light and fluffy. Beat in whole eggs, one at a time. Sift flour before measuring 2 cups. (If necessary, ⅞ cup all-purpose flour may be substituted for each cup cake flour.) Sift again and add to mixture. Add vanilla, lemon juice, and salt. Pour into greased and floured bundt or tube pan. Bake at 325° for 1 hour.

This cake can be frozen.

YIELD: 12–15 SERVINGS

Cooking Through Rose Colored Glasses
THE JUNIOR LEAGUE OF TYLER, TEXAS

· · · · · · · · · · · · · · · · · ·

Carrot Cake

2 cups sugar
1½ cups oil
4 eggs, beaten
2 cups flour
1 teaspoon salt
2 teaspoons baking soda
2 teaspoons cinnamon
½ cup chopped nuts (optional)
3 cups grated carrots

Mix sugar, oil, and beaten eggs together. Sift flour, salt, soda, and

Recipe continues ...

cinnamon together. Add flour mixture to egg mixture in four parts, then fold in nuts and carrots.

Bake in slightly oiled tube pan at 350° for 55–60 minutes or in 13 × 9 × 2-inch pan at 300° for 60–70 minutes. Cool and ice. Keep in refrigerator. Freezes well.

YIELD: ABOUT 12 SERVINGS

CREAM CHEESE ICING:
1 stick butter
1 8-ounce package cream cheese
1 box confectioners' sugar
2 teaspoons vanilla
½ cup chopped nuts

Have butter and cream cheese at room temperature. Cream together well. Add sugar and vanilla and beat well. Stir in nuts. Spread on Carrot Cake.

The Charlotte Cookbook
THE JUNIOR LEAGUE OF CHARLOTTE, NORTH CAROLINA

· · · · · · · · · · · · · · · · · ·

White Chocolate Cake

½ pound white chocolate
1 cup butter
2 cups sugar
4 eggs, separated
2½ cups flour
1 teaspoon baking powder
½ teaspoon salt
1 cup buttermilk
1 cup chopped pecans
1 cup flaked coconut
1 teaspoon vanilla

Melt chocolate over hot water.

Cream butter and sugar. Add egg yolks; beat. Add chocolate to creamed mixture.

Sift flour, baking powder, and salt together. Add alternately with buttermilk to chocolate mixture. Add pecans, coconut, and vanilla.

Beat egg whites until stiff and fold into batter. Pour into ungreased tube pan. Bake at 325° for 1 hour and 10 minutes. Cool for a few minutes, then turn out onto cake rack to cool.

YIELD: 8–10 SERVINGS

Mountain Measures
THE JUNIOR LEAGUE OF CHARLESTON, WEST VIRGINIA

. . . .

Butter Crumb Cake

¼ cup butter
½ cup flour
½ cup brown sugar
2 cups sifted flour
2 teaspoons baking powder
½ teaspoon baking soda
½ teaspoon salt
½ cup butter
1 8-ounce package cream cheese
1¼ cups sugar
2 eggs, unbeaten
1 teaspoon vanilla
½ cup milk
½ cup broken nuts

Make crumbs by cutting ¼ cup butter into ½ cup flour and the brown sugar.

Sift together 2 cups flour, baking powder, soda, and salt.

Recipe continues . . .

Cream ½ cup butter with cream cheese. Gradually add 1¼ cups sugar. Cream well. Blend in unbeaten eggs and vanilla. Beat well. Add milk alternately with dry ingredients, beginning and ending with dry ingredients.

Pour into 9 × 13-inch greased pan; sprinkle with crumb mixture and ½ cup broken nuts. Bake at 350° for 35–45 minutes.

YIELD: ABOUT 12 SERVINGS

That Something Special
THE JUNIOR LEAGUE OF DURHAM, NORTH CAROLINA

· · · · · · · · · · · · · ·

Chocolate Cake Deluxe

1 cup butter
2 cups sugar
2 eggs
2 squares unsweetened chocolate
2 teaspoons vanilla
1 cup sour cream
2 teaspoons baking soda
2½ cups flour
¼ teaspoon salt
1 cup boiling water

Cream butter and sugar. Mix in eggs. Melt chocolate and add vanilla to it. Blend into butter mixture. In separate bowl, mix sour cream and soda. Sift flour and salt together. Add sour cream mixture and flour mixture alternately to chocolate mixture. Add 1 cup boiling water last.

Grease and flour round tube pan. Bake at 325° for 1–1¼ hours. Frost when cool.

YIELD: ONE TUBE CAKE

ICING DELUXE:
1 6-ounce package chocolate morsels
⅓ cup evaporated milk
2 cups confectioners' sugar

Melt chocolate; add milk, then sugar. Add more milk if icing is too thick.

The Charlotte Cookbook
THE JUNIOR LEAGUE OF CHARLOTTE, NORTH CAROLINA

. . . .

Mama B's Chocolate Cake

2 sticks butter or 1 cup shortening
2 cups sugar
2 eggs, beaten
3½ cups flour
1½ teaspoons baking soda
3 tablespoons plus 1 teaspoon cocoa
2 cups buttermilk
2 teaspoons vanilla

Cream butter or shortening with sugar. Add beaten eggs. Sift flour with soda and cocoa. Add to creamed mixture alternately with buttermilk, beginning and ending with flour mixture. Add vanilla.

Pour batter into four greased and floured 8-inch cake pans. Bake at 350° for 20–30 minutes. Spread filling between cooled layers and frost with Mama B's Chocolate Icing.

YIELD: AN 8-INCH 4-LAYER CAKE

FILLING:
1 stick butter
1 cup pecans, toasted slowly until brown
⅓ cup milk
2 cups confectioners' sugar

Melt butter; add toasted pecans and milk. Sift sugar into mixture and mix well.

Recipe continues . . .

MAMA B'S CHOCOLATE ICING:
1 stick butter
2 cups confectioners' sugar
3 tablespoons cocoa
Milk

Melt butter and sift in sugar. Add cocoa and small amount of milk, if needed, to make mixture of spreading consistency.

Cooking Through Rose Colored Glasses
THE JUNIOR LEAGUE OF TYLER, TEXAS

. . . .

Siren's Chocolate Cake

Strong men melt, weak men feel like Atlas when confronted with this cake!

4 1-ounce squares bitter chocolate
1 stick butter
2 eggs
2 cups buttermilk
2 teaspoons vanilla
2½ cups flour
½ teaspoon salt
2 cups sugar
2 teaspoons baking soda

Melt chocolate and butter together in double boiler. Cool.

Beat eggs with buttermilk and add vanilla. Sift dry ingredients and add to egg mixture, then add butter and chocolate. Beat thoroughly. Pour into two greased 8-inch cake pans and bake about 30 minutes at 350°. Put layers together and frost with Siren's Chocolate Icing.

YIELD: AN 8-INCH 2-LAYER CAKE

SIREN'S CHOCOLATE ICING:
1 scant cup evaporated milk
2 teaspoons vanilla
1 pound confectioners' sugar, sifted
4 squares bitter chocolate
1 stick butter

Add milk and vanilla to sifted sugar.

Melt chocolate and butter together and add to first mixture. If icing is not thick enough to spread nicely, add more sifted sugar.

The Memphis Cook Book
THE JUNIOR LEAGUE OF MEMPHIS, TENNESSEE

.   .   .   .

Chocolate Pound Cake

½ pound butter
½ cup shortening
3 cups sugar
5 eggs
3 cups flour
½ teaspoon baking powder
½ teaspoon salt
4 heaping teaspoons cocoa
1 cup milk
1 tablespoon vanilla

Cream butter, shortening, and sugar together thoroughly. Add eggs. Add sifted dry ingredients alternately with milk. Add vanilla.

Bake in well-greased and floured tube cake pan at 325° for 1 hour and 20 minutes.

Ice cake while hot.

Recipe continues . . .

YIELD: ONE TUBE CAKE

ICING:
⅔ stick butter
⅔ box sifted confectioners' sugar
1 heaping tablespoon cocoa
1 teaspoon vanilla
3 tablespoons hot coffee

Cream butter and add sifted sugar gradually. Add remaining ingredients and mix well.

Recipe Jubilee
THE JUNIOR LEAGUE OF MOBILE, ALABAMA

· · · · · · · · · · · · ·

French Chocolate Torte

5½ ounces semisweet chocolate
1½ cups pecans, pulverized
2 tablespoons flour
1½ sticks butter, softened
¾ cup sugar
6 eggs, separated

Melt chocolate in top of double boiler set over hot water. Let chocolate cool to room temperature.

Stir together pulverized pecans and flour. With electric mixer, cream together butter and sugar until mixture is light and fluffy. Add 6 egg yolks, one at a time, beating well after each addition. Stir in the melted chocolate and the pecan mixture.

Beat egg whites until they hold stiff peaks and fold them gently but thoroughly into egg yolk mixture. Pour batter into a 10-inch round cake pan which is 2 inches deep. To remove cake easily, cover bottom of pan with foil, then grease and flour.

Bake in a preheated oven at 350° for 30 minutes, or until cake tests done. Let cake cool. Turn cake out of pan and frost it thickly.

Chill the cake for at least 2 hours before serving.

YIELD: 12 SERVINGS

FROSTING:
¼ cup hot water
1 tablespoon instant espresso coffee
¼ cup sugar
3½ ounces semisweet chocolate, grated
2 egg yolks
1 cup heavy cream

In a saucepan, combine water and coffee. Add sugar and chocolate, and cook mixture over moderate heat, stirring, until chocolate is melted and sugar is dissolved. Let mixture cool, stirring occasionally, for 5 minutes.

Add egg yolks, one at a time, beating well after each addition. Let mixture cool to room temperature.

Whip cream until stiff and fold into chocolate mixture. Chill frosting for 20 minutes or until it is of spreading consistency.

Southern Sideboards
THE JUNIOR LEAGUE OF JACKSON, MISSISSIPPI

· · · · · · · · · · · · · · · · ·

Plantation Pecan Torte

2 tablespoons cake flour
2 teaspoons baking powder
¼ teaspoon salt
3 cups finely chopped pecans
6 eggs, separated
1½ cups sugar
1 pint heavy cream
¼ cup confectioners' sugar
1 teaspoon vanilla

Recipe continues . . .

Combine flour, baking powder, and salt with pecans chopped to resemble fine corn meal. Beat egg yolks with 1½ cups sugar until thick and lemon-colored. Fold beaten egg whites into nut mixture. Fold egg white–nut mixture into yolk-sugar mixture.

Pour into two greased paper-lined 8-inch round cake pans. Use either wax paper or brown paper. Bake at 350° for 20–25 minutes. Cool.

Whip cream with confectioners' sugar and vanilla. Spread between cooled layers and over top of cake.

YIELD: AN 8-INCH 2-LAYER CAKE

A Cook's Tour of Shreveport
THE JUNIOR LEAGUE OF SHREVEPORT, LOUISIANA

· · · · · · · · · · · ·

Viennese Torte

This rich dessert takes all morning because you have to wait until each step cools. However, the recipe is not difficult. It is better not to make it a day ahead!

6 eggs, separated
½ teaspoon salt
1 teaspoon vanilla
¾ cup sugar
1 cup flour, sifted
1½ cup pecans, finely chopped

Combine egg yolks, salt, and vanilla; beat until *very* light and lemon-colored.

Beat in ½ cup sugar gradually; continue beating until very light and fluffy (about 5 minutes at medium speed). Stir in flour and 1 cup pecans. Make sure they are combined well.

Beat egg whites until they form soft peaks; beat in remaining ¼ cup sugar gradually and continue beating until glossy. Fold into egg yolk mixture.

Divide batter equally into three 8-inch layer pans and spread *just enough* to level. Bake 20–25 minutes at 300°. Cool in pans for 10 minutes; remove from pans and cool *thoroughly* on rack before filling.

Put layers together with Cream Filling, using one-third of filling on each layer. Sprinkle top with ½ cup chopped pecans. Chill in refrigerator until filling is firm before frosting sides.

YIELD: 12–16 SERVINGS

CREAM FILLING:
1 6-ounce package semisweet chocolate morsels
¾ cup cold butter
1¼ cup confectioners' sugar, sifted
⅛ teaspoon salt
1 egg
3 tablespoons rum or 2 teaspoons vanilla

Melt chocolate and cool, stirring often during cooling. (Chocolate must be cold, but not chilled.) Whip butter until fluffy. Mix in sugar and salt and beat at medium-high speed until very light and fluffy (about 6 minutes). Add egg and continue beating until mixture is smooth (about 2 minutes). Fold in flavoring and chocolate quickly but carefully. Cool in refrigerator to stiffen slightly before spreading on torte layers.

FROSTING:
1 cup sugar
¼ cup cornstarch
¼ teaspoon salt
1 cup boiling water
2 ounces unsweetened chocolate, melted
3 tablespoons butter

Combine sugar, cornstarch, and salt in saucepan; mix well. Add water gradually, stirring constantly during addition. Place over low heat and cook until smooth and thickened, stirring constantly. Add melted chocolate

Recipe continues . . .

and butter. Continue cooking until smooth and thick. Chill over ice water until proper consistency for spreading, stirring frequently. Scrape any excess filling off sides of torte and cover sides with frosting. Chill and serve.

Of Pots and Pipkins
THE JUNIOR LEAGUE OF ROANOKE VALLEY, VIRGINIA

. . . .

Pumpkin Pie

This is so outstanding even non-pumpkin eaters love it. It takes time from start to finish, but is worth every minute!

¾ cup milk
2 cups canned pumpkin
1½ cups brown sugar
⅛ teaspoon salt
¾ teaspoon ginger
¾ teaspoon cinnamon
⅓ teaspoon nutmeg
5 egg yolks
2 envelopes unflavored gelatin
⅓ cup cold water
5 egg whites
1½ cups heavy cream
⅓ cup sugar
1 10-inch baked pie shell
Caramelized Almonds (see page 539)
Butterscotch sauce
Whipped cream

Heat milk with pumpkin, brown sugar, salt, and spices. Beat egg yolks slightly and add hot mixture gradually to yolks. Mix well and cook in double boiler until thick, stirring constantly.

Soften gelatin in cold water and add to hot custard. Stir until dissolved. Cool until it begins to thicken.

Beat egg whites until stiff but not dry. Fold in custard. Cool a little while, but not until set. Whip cream. Fold the ⅓ cup sugar into whipped cream, then fold cream into pumpkin mixture. Chill until very thick and pour into baked pie shell. (If making your own pie shell, add toasted sesame seeds to dough before baking.) Chill until set.

Before serving, sprinkle each piece with caramelized almonds, dribble with butterscotch sauce, and top with whipped cream. This pie is not complete without the almonds, sauce, and whipped cream.

YIELD: 8 SERVINGS

CARAMELIZED ALMONDS:
½ cup sugar
1 cup slivered blanched almonds

Stir sugar and almonds constantly in heavy skillet until light caramel color. Spread on greased cookie sheet. Break apart when crisp. These will keep indefinitely in an airtight container. (They are also delicious on coffee ice cream.)

Cooking Through Rose Colored Glasses
THE JUNIOR LEAGUE OF TYLER, TEXAS

. . . .

Huguenot Torte

4 eggs
3 cups sugar
½ cup flour
5 teaspoons baking powder
½ teaspoon salt
2 cups chopped tart cooking apples
2 cups chopped pecans or walnuts
2 teaspoons vanilla
Whipped cream
Additional chopped nuts

Recipe continues . . .

Beat whole eggs in electric mixer or with rotary beater until very frothy and lemon-colored. Add sugar. Add flour gradually, and then add other ingredients in order listed, except for the whipped cream and additional chopped nuts. Mix well and pour into two *well-buttered* baking pans about 8 × 12 inches. Bake at 325° for about 45 minutes or until crusty and brown.

To serve, scoop up with pancake turner (keeping crusty part on top), pile on large plate, and cover with whipped cream and a sprinkling of the chopped nuts.

YIELD: 16 SERVINGS

Charleston Receipts
THE JUNIOR LEAGUE OF CHARLESTON, SOUTH CAROLINA

· · · · · · · · · · · · · ·

Prune Cake with Buttermilk Glaze

2 cups flour
1 teaspoon baking soda
1 teaspoon allspice
1 teaspoon nutmeg
½ teaspoon salt
1 cup vegetable oil
1½ cups sugar
3 eggs, beaten
1 cup buttermilk
1 teaspoon vanilla
1 cup cooked prunes, drained and chopped

Sift first five ingredients together. Gradually mix in oil, sugar, and beaten eggs. Then add buttermilk, vanilla, and prunes. Beat at medium speed until well blended.

Pour into greased and floured 9 × 14-inch baking pan. Bake at 350° approximately 40 minutes. Remove from oven, cool, and top with Buttermilk Glaze.

BUTTERMILK GLAZE:
1 cup sugar
½ cup buttermilk
½ stick butter
1 teaspoon vanilla

Combine ingredients and boil 3 minutes. Let cool, then beat a few minutes with mixer until thickened. Pour over cooled cake.

Cooking Through Rose Colored Glasses
THE JUNIOR LEAGUE OF TYLER, TEXAS

. . . .

Prune Cake

1½ cups sugar
1 cup oil
3 eggs, beaten
2 cups flour
1 teaspoon baking soda
1 teaspoon cinnamon
1 teaspoon nutmeg
1 teaspoon allspice
½ teaspoon salt
1 cup sour milk or buttermilk
1 cup chopped nuts
1 cup cooked prunes, pitted
1 teaspoon vanilla

Blend sugar and oil. Add beaten eggs and beat well. Sift dry ingredients together three times and add alternately with sour milk or buttermilk, beating well after each addition. Add nuts, chopped prunes, and vanilla; stir to distribute evenly through batter. Pour batter into buttered 9 × 13 × 2-inch

Recipe continues . . .

pan and bake at 300° for 1 hour. While cake is baking, prepare Buttermilk Sauce. Pour it over cake while it is still hot. Leave cake in pan.

YIELD: 10–12 SERVINGS

BUTTERMILK SAUCE:
1 cup sugar
½ cup buttermilk
½ teaspoon baking soda
2 teaspoons vanilla
¼–½ cup butter

Combine all ingredients in saucepan. Boil for 1 minute without beating.

Mountain Measures
THE JUNIOR LEAGUE OF CHARLESTON, WEST VIRGINIA

·   ·   ·   ·   ·   ·   ·   ·   ·   ·   ·   ·   ·   ·   ·   ·   ·

Special Cheese Cake

CRUST:
14 zwieback crackers, crumbled
½ cup butter, melted
½ cup sugar

Mix all ingredients together. Press into bottom of a 9½ × 3-inch cheese cake pan.

FILLING:
3 pounds cream cheese, softened
6 eggs
½ cup plus 2 tablespoons flour
2½ cups sugar
1½ cups heavy cream
1 teaspoon vanilla
Juice of 1 lemon

Mix all ingredients well and pour into crust-lined cake pan. Place a pan with an inch of water in it under cake while baking. Bake at 350° for 1 hour or until cake begins to brown on top. Then turn off oven and let cake remain in oven for 30 minutes with oven door closed.

Chill before unmolding.

Freezes beautifully.

YIELD: ABOUT 20 SERVINGS

Little Rock Cooks
THE JUNIOR LEAGUE OF LITTLE ROCK, ARKANSAS

· · · · · · · · · · · · · · ·

Christmas Cake

¾ cup raisins
3 ounces chopped, candied citron
3 ounces candied orange peel
1½ ounces candied lemon peel
1 cup flour
¼ teaspoon baking soda
1 teaspoon each salt, nutmeg, cloves, and cinnamon
¼ cup butter
¼ cup brown sugar
¼ cup molasses
2 eggs

Mix fruit together with flour, soda, spices, and salt.

Cream butter; add sugar, molasses, and beaten eggs. Stir in fruit mixture.

Turn into loaf pan and bake at 275–300° for 2½ hours.

YIELD: 1 LOAF

The Cotton Blossom Cookbook
THE JUNIOR LEAGUE OF ATLANTA, GEORGIA

· · · · · · · · · · · · · · ·

Big Mamma's Fruit Cake

1 cup butter
2 cups sugar
6 eggs, separated
4 cups flour (save 1 cup for flouring fruit)
2 teaspoons baking powder
Pinch salt
1 cup good bourbon
2 teaspoons freshly grated nutmeg
2 teaspoons vanilla
1 pound candied cherries
1 pound pitted dates
1 pound raisins
1 pound pecans
½ pound English walnuts
1 pound candied pineapple

Cream butter thoroughly, then add sugar gradually. Beat until light and fluffy. Beat in egg yolks one at a time. Sift and measure 3 cups flour; resift three times with the baking powder and salt. Add alternately (flour first and last) with the whiskey. Add nutmeg and vanilla.

Flour fruit with the remaining cup of flour (sifted) and fold into the batter. As this needs a very large container, you can use a roasting pan, and use your hands to mix fruit into batter thoroughly. Finally, fold in egg whites, which have been beaten stiff but not dry.

Put batter into tube, loaf, and other deep pans, greased and lined with wax paper. Bake at 275° for 2 or more hours. Test with a toothpick for doneness of batter; you do not want cake to be too dry.

Makes wonderful Christmas presents.

YIELD: 1 LARGE AND 2 SMALL CAKES

A Cook's Tour of Shreveport
THE JUNIOR LEAGUE OF SHREVEPORT, LOUISIANA

· · · · · · · · · · · · · · ·

Blueberry Torte

16 double graham crackers, rolled into crumbs
2 cups sugar
½ cup butter
2 eggs
1 8-ounce package cream cheese
5 tablespoons cornstarch
2 tablespoons lemon juice
1 can blueberries
½ pint heavy cream, whipped

Combine crumbs, ½ cup sugar, and butter. Mix and line a 10-inch square pan. Beat eggs, ½ cup sugar, and cream cheese until smooth. Pour over crumb mixture and bake for 20 minutes at 350°.

While this bakes, make topping. Blend cornstarch, 1 cup sugar, lemon juice, and juice of blueberries. Cook until thick. Cool and add blueberries. Pour over baked mixture.

When ready to serve, spread with whipped cream. Can be made a day ahead.

YIELD: 10–12 SERVINGS

The Charlotte Cookbook
THE JUNIOR LEAGUE OF CHARLOTTE, NORTH CAROLINA

Cheese Cake

1½ cups graham cracker crumbs
1½ cups sugar
1 teaspoon cinnamon
⅓ cup butter, melted
4 eggs
2 pounds cream cheese
1 tablespoon lemon juice
Dash salt
⅛ teaspoon vanilla
2 cups sour cream

Mix with the crumbs ¼ cup of the sugar, cinnamon, and butter; press into bottom of 10-inch spring-form pan, reserving ½ cup for topping.

Beat eggs and 1 cup of the sugar until thick and lemon-colored. Without washing beaters, beat cheese until fluffy and smooth. Add beaten eggs to cheese with lemon juice and dash salt. Beat well. Pour in crumb-lined pan and bake at 375° for 30 minutes.

Remove from oven. Fold remaining ¼ cup sugar and vanilla into sour cream and spread over cake. Sprinkle with remaining crumbs. Bake at 475° for 10 minutes.

Cool and refrigerate 2–3 hours. Let stand at room temperature 1 hour before serving.

YIELD: ONE 10-INCH CAKE

Furniture City Feasts
THE JUNIOR LEAGUE OF HIGH POINT, NORTH CAROLINA

Lady Finger Torte

4 packages lady fingers
Milk
1–3 tablespoons rum
½ pound butter
2 cups confectioners' sugar
2 eggs
8 ounces semisweet chocolate morsels, melted
1 tablespoon instant coffee
⅔ cup toasted almonds
½ pint heavy cream
4 tablespoons confectioners' sugar
1 tablespoon rum

Dip split lady fingers in milk flavored with rum. Line bottom and sides of 9-inch spring-form cake pan with lady fingers.

Cream butter and sugar; add eggs; melted chocolate, coffee, and almonds.

Fill pan with alternate layers of chocolate mixture and lady fingers. Chill for at least 4 hours.

Whip cream and stir in 4 tablespoons confectioners' sugar and 1 tablespoon rum.

Unmold and spread cream on top. Decorate with chocolate chips.

YIELD: 6 SERVINGS

Recipe Jubilee
THE JUNIOR LEAGUE OF MOBILE, ALABAMA

· · · · · · · · · · · · · · ·

Ruth's Chocolate Refrigerator Cake

This is very rich. It may be used as a birthday cake for a special party.

Recipe continues . . .

2 4-ounce bars German chocolate
1 tablespoon water
4 eggs, separated
1 tablespoon sugar
1½ cups heavy cream
1 teaspoon vanilla
2 dozen lady fingers
Additional whipped cream
Toasted slivered almonds

Melt the chocolate with water in double boiler. Beat egg yolks in large bowl with sugar. Mix chocolate with yolks.

Beat whites stiff. Whip cream and add vanilla. Fold egg whites and cream into chocolate mixture.

Line greased spring-form pan with split lady fingers and pour in half of chocolate mixture. Cover with another layer of lady fingers and pour in rest of mixture. Let stand in refrigerator 24 hours.

Serve with additional whipped cream on top and toasted slivered almonds.

YIELD: 6–8 SERVINGS

300 Years of Carolina Cooking
THE JUNIOR LEAGUE OF GREENVILLE, SOUTH CAROLINA

. . . .

Garden of Eden Apple Pie

CHEESE PASTRY:
½ cup shortening
2 cups flour
¾ teaspoon salt
1 cup shredded New York State cheddar cheese (or ½ cup
American and ½ cup cheddar cheese)
6–8 tablespoons cold water
Melted fat

Cut shortening into sifted flour and salt until mixture resembles peas in size. Mix in cheese lightly with fork. Add enough water to hold together. Roll lightly and put into 9-inch pie pan. Brush bottom crust with melted fat to prevent soaking.

APPLE FILLING:
5 or 6 large tart apples
¾ cup sugar
2 teaspoons flour
⅛ teaspoon salt
1 teaspoon cinnamon
1 teaspoon nutmeg (optional)
2 tablespoons butter (or more)

Pare, core, and slice apples. Lay slices in pie plate lined with cheese pastry. Mix sugar, flour, salt, cinnamon, and nutmeg. Sprinkle over each layer of apples, dot with butter, and cover with crust. Press edges together and slash top. Bake at 450° for 10 minutes or until edges are brown. Reduce oven to 350° and bake about 30 minutes longer.

YIELD: 6–8 SERVINGS

The Memphis Cook Book
THE JUNIOR LEAGUE OF MEMPHIS, TENNESSEE

·   ·   ·   ·   ·   ·   ·   ·   ·   ·   ·   ·

Key Lime Pie

1 13-ounce can condensed milk
4 eggs, separated
½ cup lime juice
1 9-inch frozen pie shell
6 tablespoons sugar
½ teaspoon cream of tartar

Combine condensed milk, egg yolks, and lime juice in mixing bowl. Beat 1 egg white stiff. Fold into mixture and turn into pie shell.

Recipe continues . . .

Beat 3 egg whites and gradually add sugar and cream of tartar. Spread meringue over filling and bake at 350° for about 20 minutes or until egg whites are golden brown.

YIELD: 6 SERVINGS

A Taste of Tampa
THE JUNIOR LEAGUE OF TAMPA, FLORIDA

· · · · · · · · · · · · · · · · · · · ·

Sherry Pie

PASTRY:
1 cup sifted flour
½ teaspoon salt
1 tablespoon confectioners' sugar
⅓ cup shortening
3 tablespoons heavy cream

Sift flour, salt, and sugar together in a bowl. Work in shortening with a pastry blender or two knives until mixture looks like fine bread crumbs. Sprinkle in cream gradually, mixing with fork until pastry holds together. Roll on lightly floured board and line 9-inch pie pan. Prick sides and bottom with fork. Bake at 450° for 7–8 minutes or until golden brown. Cool.

FILLING:
1 envelope unflavored gelatin
1¼ cups cold milk
3 eggs, separated
½ cup sugar
Dash salt
¼ teaspoon nutmeg
½ cup sherry
1 cup heavy cream

Sprinkle gelatin over ¼ cup cold milk to soften. Combine egg yolks, sugar, and 1 cup milk in top of double boiler. Cook over bubbling water, stirring constantly, until slightly thick. Remove from heat; stir in gelatin, salt, and nutmeg. Slowly stir in sherry. Chill until thick as raw egg whites.

Beat egg whites until they hold a shape. Beat cream until stiff. Combine gelatin mixture, egg whites, and cream and pour into cool pastry shell. Chill until firm. Garnish with shaved chocolate if desired.

YIELD: 6–8 SERVINGS

Spartanburg Secrets II
THE JUNIOR LEAGUE OF SPARTANBURG, SOUTH CAROLINA

· · · · · · · · · · · · · · · · ·

Greta's Coconut Pie

1 tablespoon gelatin
¼ cup cold water
3 eggs, separated
½ cup sugar
½ teaspoon salt
1 cup evaporated milk, scalded
1 teaspoon vanilla
⅛ teaspoon cream of tartar
¼ cup sugar
1 10-inch or 2 8-inch baked pie shells
Whipped cream, sweetened to taste
Toasted coconut

Soften gelatin in cold water. Beat egg yolks with ½ cup sugar and salt; add to scalded milk. Cook until slightly thickened (do not overcook); add softened gelatin and vanilla. Blend. Cool until the consistency of unbeaten egg whites.

Beat egg whites until frothy; add cream of tartar and beat to soft peaks, gradually adding ¼ cup sugar. Fold meringue into cooled custard mixture. Pour into baked shell; chill until set. Top with a layer of sweetened whipped cream and sprinkle with toasted coconut.

YIELD: 8–10 SERVINGS

Recipe continues . . .

VARIATIONS:

Substitute fresh strawberries, slivered semisweet chocolate, or freshly grated nutmeg for coconut.

Southern Accent
THE JUNIOR LEAGUE OF PINE BLUFF, ARKANSAS

Chocolate Chiffon Pie

1 envelope unflavored gelatin
¼ cup cold water
6 tablespoons cocoa or 2 squares chocolate
½ cup boiling water
4 eggs, separated
1 cup sugar
½ teaspoon salt
1 teaspoon vanilla
1 9-inch baked pie shell
Whipped cream

Soften gelatin in cold water. Mix cocoa or chocolate and boiling water until smooth. Add gelatin to hot chocolate mixture, stirring thoroughly. Add egg yolks, slightly beaten, ½ cup sugar, salt, and vanilla. Cool, and when mixture begins to thicken, fold in stiffly beaten egg whites to which the other ½ cup sugar has been added.

Fill baked pie shell and chill. Just before serving, spread over pie a thin layer of whipped cream.

YIELD: 8 SERVINGS

The Cotton Blossom Cookbook
THE JUNIOR LEAGUE OF ATLANTA, GEORGIA

Pecan Cream Pie

1 cup sugar
1 cup heavy cream
4 egg yolks
1 cup toasted pecans (coarsely chopped, if desired)
1 baked pie shell
4 egg whites
¾ cup sugar

Cook 1 cup sugar and cream in a heavy saucepan for 12 minutes, stirring occasionally. Beat egg yolks. Stir a little of the hot mixture into yolks, then return yolks to pan and continue cooking and stirring another 2 minutes. Remove from heat. Add pecans and pour into pie shell. Make meringue by beating egg whites until stiff. Add ¾ cup sugar gradually, beating until glossy. Cover pie with meringue and bake at 325° for about 20 minutes.

Cool before slicing. This pie is best made and eaten the same day.

YIELD: 8 SERVINGS

Southern Sideboards
THE JUNIOR LEAGUE OF JACKSON, MISSISSIPPI

. . . .

Buttermilk Pecan Pie

This was a family recipe often prepared by a career U.S. Navy chef for such dignitaries as the late President Harry S Truman. Through the years of his military career, the chef refused to share his recipe. Finally, when he retired, he allowed it to be published in a Navy newspaper.

Recipe continues . . .

½ cup butter
2 cups sugar
2 teaspoons vanilla
3 eggs
3 tablespoons flour
¼ teaspoon salt
1 cup buttermilk
½ cup chopped pecans
1 9-inch unbaked pie shell

Preheat oven to 300°. Cream butter and sugar, adding ½ cup sugar at a time. Blend in vanilla. Stir in eggs, one at a time. Combine flour and salt; add small amount at a time. Stir in buttermilk. Sprinkle pecans in bottom of pie crust, pour custard mix over the pecans, and bake 1 hour and 30 minutes.

Best served at room temperature.

YIELD: 6–8 SERVINGS

Fiesta: Favorite Recipes of South Texas
THE JUNIOR LEAGUE OF CORPUS CHRISTI, TEXAS

· · · · · · · · · · · · · · · · ·

Blueberry Pecan Pie

1 13-ounce can condensed milk
Juice of 2 lemons
1 cup heavy cream
1 cup pecan halves
1 16-ounce can blueberries, drained
1 9-inch baked pie shell

Mix condensed milk with lemon juice and ½ cup of whipping cream (not whipped). Stir in pecan halves and drained blueberries. Pour into baked pie shell.

Top with remainder of cream, whipped. Store in refrigerator until served. This may be made the day before or several hours before serving.

YIELD: 8 SERVINGS

Cooking Through Rose Colored Glasses
THE JUNIOR LEAGUE OF TYLER, TEXAS

. . . .

Pecan Pie

3 eggs
1 cup sugar
3 tablespoons flour
1 cup white corn syrup
1 cup shelled pecans
3 tablespoons melted butter or soft margarine
1 tablespoon vanilla
1 9-inch unbaked pastry shell

Beat eggs thoroughly. Add sugar, flour, and syrup gradually. Add pecans and butter or margarine, then vanilla. Pour into unbaked pastry shell. Bake at 350° for approximately 45 minutes.

A Cook's Tour of Shreveport
THE JUNIOR LEAGUE OF SHREVEPORT, LOUISIANA

. . . .

Fudge Pie

1 stick butter
2 squares unsweetened chocolate
¼ cup flour, sifted
Dash salt
1 cup sugar
2 eggs, beaten
1 teaspoon vanilla
Whipped cream or ice cream

Recipe continues . . .

Melt butter with chocolate. Stir in flour and dash salt. Add sugar. Beat eggs and add to the above ingredients. Add vanilla. Pour into greased pan and bake for 30 minutes at 350°. Serve with whipped cream or ice cream.

YIELD: 6–8 SERVINGS

That Something Special
THE JUNIOR LEAGUE OF DURHAM, NORTH CAROLINA

Osgood Pie

1 stick margarine
1 cup sugar
2 eggs, separated
½ cup chopped pecans
½ cup raisins
½ teaspoon allspice
½ teaspoon cinnamon
2 teaspoons cocoa
1 teaspoon vinegar
1 9-inch unbaked pie shell

Cream margarine, sugar, and beaten egg yolks. Add pecans, raisins, spices, cocoa, and vinegar. Mix well, then stir in stiffly beaten egg whites. Pour into unbaked pie shell. Bake at 375° for 10 minutes; reduce heat to 325° and bake for 30 minutes. Freezes well.

YIELD: 6–8 SERVINGS

Cooking Through Rose Colored Glasses
THE JUNIOR LEAGUE OF TYLER, TEXAS

Ice Cream Pie with Chocolate Sauce

3 egg whites
1 teaspoon baking powder
¼ teaspoon salt
1 cup sugar
1 cup graham cracker crumbs
½ cup pecans, chopped
1 quart coffee ice cream

Beat egg whites stiff. Add baking powder and salt. Slowly add sugar, beating constantly. Fold in graham cracker crumbs and pecans. Pour into well-greased and floured 10-inch pie pan. Bake for 30 minutes at 350°. Cool and fill with 1 quart of coffee ice cream. Serve with Chocolate Sauce.

YIELD: 8 SERVINGS

CHOCOLATE SAUCE:
4 squares unsweetened chocolate
2 cups sugar
1 13-ounce can condensed milk
1 tablespoon butter
Pinch salt
2 teaspoons vanilla

Put all ingredients in a saucepan and cook over low heat. Stir occasionally and cook until thick. Do not boil. This makes more sauce than is needed. Save leftover sauce for future ice cream snacks.

The Charlotte Cookbook
THE JUNIOR LEAGUE OF CHARLOTTE, NORTH CAROLINA

Chocolate Ice Box Pie

2 cups crushed vanilla wafers
⅓ cup soft butter
1 12-ounce package semisweet chocolate morsels
1 whole egg
2 eggs, separated
1 teaspoon rum
1 pint heavy cream
Grated chocolate

Combine wafer crumbs and butter and press into a spring-form pan or deep pie pan.

Melt chocolate over simmering water in double boiler. Beat 1 whole egg and 2 egg yolks well and add to melted chocolate, then add rum. Whip ½ pint cream and beat egg whites stiff. Fold both into chocolate mixture. Pour into crust and freeze for several hours.

Top with other ½ pint cream, whipped, before serving. To decorate for company, put cream through a pastry tube and top with grated chocolate. The pie can be returned to freezer. The cream will freeze and keep.

YIELD: 6–8 SERVINGS

300 Years of Carolina Cooking
THE JUNIOR LEAGUE OF GREENVILLE, SOUTH CAROLINA

·　·　·　·　·　·　·　·　·　·　·　·　·　·

1850 Blackberry Pie

1 unbaked 10-inch pie shell
1 quart blackberries
1 cup flour
2 cups sugar
1 cup milk

Fill shell with berries. Mix flour, sugar, and milk. Pour mixture over berries. Bake at 350° for 45–50 minutes, until center is set. If desired, brown under broiler.

YIELD: 8 SERVINGS

Mountain Measures
THE JUNIOR LEAGUE OF CHARLESTON, WEST VIRGINIA

· · · · · · · · · · · · · · · · ·

Angel Berry Pie

MERINGUE CRUST:
3 egg whites
1 cup sugar
2 teaspoons white vinegar

Beat egg whites until stiff, add sugar gradually, then vinegar. Bake in greased 9-inch ovenproof pie dish for 1½ hours at 300° on second rack of oven. Cool.

CUSTARD FILLING:
3 egg yolks, beaten
½ cup sifted sugar
1 heaping tablespoon sifted flour
1 cup milk
1 teaspoon vanilla
Pinch salt
Strawberries
½ pint heavy cream, whipped

Cook all ingredients except strawberries and cream in top of double boiler, stirring constantly, until thick.

Pour Custard Filling into meringue crust. Let set for a while, then

Recipe continues . . .

cover filling with cut-up strawberries. Cover strawberries with whipped cream and garnish with whole strawberries.

YIELD: 8 SERVINGS

A Cook's Tour of Shreveport
THE JUNIOR LEAGUE OF SHREVEPORT, LOUISIANA

· · · · · · · · · · · · · · ·

Lemon Luscious Pie

1 cup sugar
3 tablespoons cornstarch
¼ cup butter
1 tablespoon grated lemon rind
¼ cup lemon juice
3 unbeaten egg yolks
1 cup milk
1 cup sour cream
1 9-inch baked pie shell
Whipped cream
Chopped walnuts

Combine sugar and cornstarch in saucepan. Add butter, lemon rind, lemon juice, and egg yolks. Stir in milk. Cook over medium heat, stirring constantly until thick. Cool. Fold in sour cream.

Spoon into baked pie shell. Chill at least 2 hours. Serve with whipped cream and chopped walnuts sprinkled over the top, or top with meringue.

YIELD: 6–8 SERVINGS

The Charlotte Cookbook
THE JUNIOR LEAGUE OF CHARLOTTE, NORTH CAROLINA

· · · · · · · · · · · · · · ·

Banana-Caramel Pie

10 candy caramels
2 cups milk
⅓ cup flour
⅓ cup sugar
¼ teaspoon salt
3 egg yolks, slightly beaten
1 teaspoon vanilla
2 bananas
1 9-inch baked pie shell
1 cup heavy cream, whipped

Melt caramels in milk over low heat. Combine flour, sugar, and salt in double boiler. Add caramel-milk mixture and cook over hot water until thick, stirring constantly. Add beaten egg yolks to which a little hot mixture has been added. Cook 5 minutes longer, stirring. Remove from heat. Add vanilla, cover, and chill.

Arrange 2 sliced bananas in baked pie shell. Cover with filling. Top with whipped cream.

YIELD: 6–8 SERVINGS

Cooking Through Rose Colored Glasses
THE JUNIOR LEAGUE OF TYLER, TEXAS

. . . .

Brown Sugar Pie

1 cup brown sugar, firmly packed
1 egg, slightly beaten
2 tablespoons flour
3 tablespoons milk
¼ teaspoon salt
1 teaspoon vanilla
2 tablespoons melted butter
1 9-inch unbaked pie shell

Recipe continues . . .

Combine ingredients in order given. Pour into an unbaked pie shell. Bake at 325°–350° for approximately 15 minutes.

YIELD: 6–8 SERVINGS

That Something Special
THE JUNIOR LEAGUE OF DURHAM, NORTH CAROLINA

· · · · · · · · · · · · · · · · · · · ·

Grasshopper Pie

1½ cups finely crushed chocolate wafers
¼ cup butter, melted
¼ cup sugar
1½ teaspoons unflavored gelatin
⅓ cup heavy cream
4 egg yolks
¼ cup sugar
¼ cup white crème de cacao
¼ cup green crème de menthe
1 cup heavy cream, whipped
Mint-flavored chocolate or additional whipped cream and crème de menthe

Crush wafers with a rolling pin and force through sieve to make fine crumbs. Mix with melted butter and ¼ cup sugar. Butter a pie plate generously and pat crumbs thickly over bottom and sides. Bake in a very hot oven (450°) for 5 minutes. Cool.

Soften gelatin in ⅓ cup cream and dissolve over hot water. In another bowl, beat egg yolks until thick. Add ¼ cup sugar. Stir in crème de cacao, crème de menthe, and gelatin mixture. Chill until slightly thickened. Fold in whipped cream.

Pour filling into crust and chill until firm. Sprinkle with crushed mint-flavored chocolate or cover top of pie with whipped cream swirled with crème de menthe.

YIELD: 6 SERVINGS

A Cook's Tour of Shreveport
THE JUNIOR LEAGUE OF SHREVEPORT, LOUISIANA

· · · · · · · · · · · · · · · · · · · ·

Chess Pie

1½ cups sugar
½ cup water
1½ tablespoons corn meal
1½ tablespoons flour
½ cup melted butter
6 egg yolks
1 teaspoon vanilla
1 9-inch unbaked pie shell

Combine ingredients and pour into unbaked pie shell. Bake at 250° for about 1 hour or until firm in the middle.

YIELD: 6–8 SERVINGS

Recipe Jubilee
THE JUNIOR LEAGUE OF MOBILE, ALABAMA

·　·　·　·　·　·　·　·　·　·　·　·　·　·　·

Lemon Cheese Tarts

PASTRY:
1 cup shortening
4 cups flour
Pinch salt
2 eggs beaten with 1 or 2 tablespoons ice water

Cut shortening into flour mixed with salt. Add eggs beaten with water. Store in refrigerator at least 24 hours before making tart shells. Fill shells with Lemon Cheese Filling. Bake at 400° for about 7–8 minutes. Do not brown.

YIELD: 5–6 DOZEN

Recipe continues . . .

LEMON CHEESE FILLING:
½ stick butter
1 cup sugar
Juice and rind of 2 large lemons
2 eggs, beaten

Melt butter and sugar in top of double boiler. Add finely grated rind and juice of lemons. Heat slowly until sugar is dissolved. Add beaten eggs and stir constantly until thick. Cool before filling shells.

Filling will keep for about 2 weeks in a covered jar in refrigerator.

Gator Country Cooks
THE JUNIOR LEAGUE OF GAINESVILLE, FLORIDA

. . . .

Pecan Tassies

CREAM CHEESE PASTRY:
1 3-ounce package cream cheese
½ cup butter
1 cup sifted flour

FILLING:
1 egg
¾ cup brown sugar
1 tablespoon soft butter or margarine
1 teaspoon vanilla, or 1 teaspoon grated orange rind plus
½ teaspoon orange extract
Dash salt
⅔ cup coarsely broken pecans

Allow cream cheese and butter to soften at room temperature; blend together. Stir in flour. Chill slightly for 1 hour. Shape into 2 dozen 1-inch balls. Place in tiny ungreased 1¾-inch muffin cups. Press dough against bottom and sides of cups.

Beat together egg, sugar, butter or margarine, flavoring, and salt, until just smooth.

Divide half of pecans among pastry-lined cups; add egg mixture and top with remaining pecans. Bake at 325° for 25 minutes or until filling is set. Cool and remove from pans.

These tiny pecan pies are wonderful for an open house or reception and make a nice twosome served with little cream puffs filled with chicken salad. They may be frozen, or made several days ahead.

YIELD: 24 PASTRIES

A Cook's Tour of Shreveport
THE JUNIOR LEAGUE OF SHREVEPORT, LOUISIANA

· · · · · · · · · · · · · · · · · · ·

Baklava

5 cups sugar
5 cups water
1 tablespoon honey
Juice of 1 lemon
1 pound blanched almonds, chopped fine
½ teaspoon grated nutmeg
1 pound pastry sheets (phyllo)
½ pound butter, melted

Combine sugar, water, and honey and boil about 20 minutes. Add lemon juice and boil another minute. While syrup is being made, start putting Baklava together.

Combine chopped almonds with nutmeg and mix well.

Line a buttered 9 × 14-inch baking pan with 1 sheet of phyllo (these may be bought from Greek bakery or delicatessen). Brush with melted butter and add 1 more sheet of pastry. Repeat this one more time. Now add 3–4 tablespoons chopped almonds (enough to form thin layer). Place 1 sheet on top of this layer, brush with butter, and add another layer of

Recipe continues ...

almonds. Repeat until all ingredients are used, ending with 2 or 3 whole pastry sheets brushed with butter.

When top sheet is brushed with butter, take a sharp knife and score the top sheets in diamond shapes. Bake at 300° for 1 hour or until golden brown. Remove from oven and pour hot syrup gradually over Baklava. If syrup is not absorbed, do not add more until it is. All the syrup doesn't have to be used. Cool. Cut the pieces through and allow time for them to absorb the syrup before serving.

This very sweet Greek dessert is good cut into bite-size pieces and served with coffee.

YIELD: 24–30 SERVINGS

The Gasparilla Cookbook
THE JUNIOR LEAGUE OF TAMPA, FLORIDA

· · · · · · · · · · · · · · · · ·

Pecan Tarts

1 3-ounce package cream cheese
½ cup butter
1 cup sifted flour
1 egg
¾ cup brown sugar
1 tablespoon soft butter
1 teaspoon vanilla
Dash salt
⅔ cup chopped pecans
24 half pecans

Let cheese and ½ cup butter soften at room temperature. Blend them together and stir in flour. Chill for 1 hour. Shape dough into 2 dozen 1-inch balls. Press balls into bottom and sides of small muffin tins.

Beat egg, sugar, 1 tablespoon butter, vanilla, and salt until smooth.

Add chopped nuts. Fill cups. Place a half pecan on top of each. Bake for 25 minutes at 325°.

YIELD: 24 TARTS

Recipe Jubilee
THE JUNIOR LEAGUE OF MOBILE, ALABAMA

· · · · · · · · · · · · · · ·

English Toffee Squares

1 cup vanilla wafer crumbs (about 18 wafers, rolled)
1 cup chopped pecans
¼ pound butter
1 cup confectioners' sugar
3 egg yolks, beaten
1½ ounces bitter chocolate, melted
½ teaspoon vanilla
3 egg whites, at room temperature
Whipped cream for topping

Mix together crumbs and chopped nuts. Spread half of wafer mixture evenly over the bottom of a buttered 9 × 9-inch pan.

With a hand or electric mixer, cream the butter and sugar well. Add the beaten egg yolks, melted chocolate, and vanilla. Carefully fold in stiffly beaten egg whites. Spread evenly over the wafer mixture. Sprinkle remaining wafer mixture over the top. Cover tightly with plastic wrap and refrigerate overnight.

Cut into squares and serve with lightly sweetened whipped cream.

YIELD: 6 SERVINGS

Gator Country Cooks
THE JUNIOR LEAGUE OF GAINESVILLE, FLORIDA

· · · · · · · · · · · · · · ·

Chocolate Mint Sticks

2 1-ounce squares unsweetened chocolate
½ cup butter
2 eggs
1 cup sugar
1 teaspoon vanilla
½ cup flour
¼ teaspoon baking powder
¼ teaspoon salt
½ cup chopped nuts

Melt chocolate and butter together. Cool. Add eggs, sugar, vanilla, flour, baking powder, and salt. Mix well. Add nuts.

Pour into greased 9 × 13-inch pan and bake at 350° for 15 minutes. Cool and frost with Chocolate Mint Icing. Cut into 1 × 3-inch sticks.

YIELD: 36 STICKS

CHOCOLATE MINT ICING:
3 tablespoons butter
1 tablespoon heavy cream
1 cup confectioners' sugar
¾ teaspoon peppermint extract
1 1-ounce square unsweetened chocolate

Combine 2 tablespoons of the butter, cream, sugar, and peppermint extract and frost cake. Chill until firm.

Then melt chocolate with 1 tablespoon butter and drizzle over white frosting.

Mountain Measures
THE JUNIOR LEAGUE OF CHARLESTON, WEST VIRGINIA

Texas Brownies

Double this recipe—the first pan will go too fast!

1 cup butter
2 squares unsweetened chocolate
4 eggs
2 cups sugar
Pinch salt
2 tablespoons vanilla
1 cup flour, sifted
1 cup chopped nuts

Melt butter and chocolate over hot water in double boiler and set aside to cool. Beat eggs and add sugar, salt, and vanilla. Add cooled chocolate mixture. Fold in flour and chopped nuts.

Pour into greased and floured 9 × 13-inch pan. Bake at 350° for 45 minutes over pan of hot water.

Pour icing over brownies, cool, and cut into squares.

YIELD: 24 BROWNIES

ICING:
¼ cup cocoa
¼ cup butter
¼ cup milk
1 cup sugar
1 teaspoon vanilla

Combine all ingredients except vanilla and boil 1 minute. Add vanilla and beat a few minutes. Pour over brownies.

Cooking Through Rose Colored Glasses
THE JUNIOR LEAGUE OF TYLER, TEXAS

Summit Lemon Squares

2 sticks butter, softened
2 cups flour
½ cup confectioners' sugar
4 eggs
2 cups sugar
6 tablespoons lemon juice
1 tablespoon flour
½ teaspoon baking powder
1 cup pecans (optional)
Additional confectioners' sugar

Mix butter, flour, and confectioners' sugar and press into 10 × 14-inch pan. Bake at 325° for 15 minutes.

Beat eggs slightly. Add sugar, lemon juice, flour, baking powder, and pecans. Mix and pour on top of pastry. Bake at 325° for 40–50 minutes. Sprinkle with additional confectioners' sugar.

Cool and cut into squares.

YIELD: 2–3 DOZEN

Winston-Salem's Heritage of Hospitality
THE JUNIOR LEAGUE OF WINSTON-SALEM, NORTH CAROLINA

· · · · · · · · · · · · · · · ·

Meltaways

¼ pound butter
1 ounce unsweetened chocolate
¼ cup sugar
1 teaspoon vanilla
1 egg, beaten
2 cups graham cracker crumbs
1 cup grated coconut
½ cup chopped nuts
4 ounces unsweetened chocolate, melted

Melt butter and 1 ounce chocolate. Blend sugar, vanilla, egg, graham cracker crumbs, coconut, and nuts into chocolate-butter mixture. Press into 9 × 13-inch pan. Refrigerate while making filling.

Spread filling over crumb mixture. Chill.

Pour melted unsweetened chocolate over top. Refrigerate. Cut into squares before topping gets too hard.

YIELD: 2–3 DOZEN

FILLING:
4 tablespoons butter
2 cups confectioners' sugar
1 tablespoon milk
1 teaspoon vanilla

Cream butter. Slowly add sugar, milk, and vanilla.

Of Pots and Pipkins
THE JUNIOR LEAGUE OF ROANOKE VALLEY, VIRGINIA

· · · · · · · · · · · · · · · · · ·

Charleston Devils

1 cup milk
4 squares chocolate
½ stick butter
1 cup sugar
1 egg
2 cups flour
1 teaspoon baking soda
Pinch salt
¾ cup buttermilk
1 teaspoon vanilla

Recipe continues . . .

Cook milk, chocolate, and butter in top of double boiler, stirring until thick. Set aside to cool. Cream sugar and egg together; add to cooled chocolate mixture.

Sift flour, soda, and salt three times; add to mixture alternately with buttermilk. Add vanilla. Pour into 9 × 13-inch pan lined with wax paper and bake 25 minutes in a slow oven (325°). Cut into squares. Cool and ice.

YIELD: 3 DOZEN CAKES

ICING:
1 box confectioners' sugar
4 heaping tablespoons cocoa
½ stick butter or margarine, melted
1 teaspoon vanilla

Combine first three ingredients. Add enough boiling water to mix. Stir until smooth and add vanilla. If icing is runny, add more sugar.

Charleston Receipts
THE JUNIOR LEAGUE OF CHARLESTON, SOUTH CAROLINA

· ·

Les Oreilles de Cochon ("Pig Ears")

2 cups flour
½ teaspoon baking powder
½ teaspoon salt
½ stick butter
2 eggs
1 teaspoon vinegar

Mix ingredients as for pastry. Divide into separate small pieces. Roll out each piece separately very thin.

Fry in hot fat, bending one end, until golden brown. Drain.

While "pig ears" are still hot, pour 1 tablespoon syrup over each.

SYRUP:

1½ cups cane syrup
½ cup sugar
Pinch salt

Mix ingredients and cook to soft crack stage (about 275°).

YIELD: ABOUT 2 DOZEN "EARS"

Talk About Good!
THE JUNIOR LEAGUE OF LAFAYETTE, LOUISIANA

. . . .

Pecan Balls

1 stick butter
1 cup flour
2 tablespoons sugar
1 teaspoon vanilla
⅛ teaspoon salt
1 cup chopped pecans
Confectioners' sugar

Combine all ingredients except confectioners' sugar. Mix with hands and roll into bite-size balls. Place on ungreased cookie sheet and bake at 375° for 20 minutes. Remove from pan and roll each ball in confectioners' sugar.

YIELD: ABOUT 3 DOZEN BALLS

A Cook's Tour of Shreveport
THE JUNIOR LEAGUE OF SHREVEPORT, LOUISIANA

. . . .

Stained Glass Cookies

These cookies not only are tasty but also make attractive holiday decorations.

¾ cup shortening (part butter or margarine)
1 cup sugar
2 eggs
1 teaspoon vanilla
2½ cups flour
1 teaspoon baking powder
1 teaspoon salt
8 packages Lifesavers (red, green, butter rum, orange show up well)
Cookie cutters of two sizes (the smaller cutters should be
¼–½ inch smaller than the larger)

Mix shortening, sugar, eggs, and flavoring. Blend in flour, baking powder, and salt. Cover and chill at least 1 hour.

Roll dough ⅛ inch thick and cut out cookies with larger cutters. Place cookies on baking sheet that has been covered with foil. Then use smaller cutters to cut out a section from the cookie (small bell shape within larger bell, etc.). Crush candy into small pieces and fill in cut-out areas, making sure there is enough crushed candy to spread into corners. (When first making this recipe, it's a good idea to try just a few first to find the right amount of crushed candy. Too much will bleed over onto dough.) Make hole in top of each cookie with plastic straw.

Bake at 375° for 7–9 minutes or until dough is light brown and candy has melted. (If candy does not completely cover center of cookie, take a *metal* spatula and quickly spread candy out while still soft.) Cool completely on baking sheet and remove *gently*. String with ribbon for hanging.

When hanging on Christmas tree, place cookie in front of lights for a stained-glass effect. Different colored candies can be mixed together or only one color used for different effects. Cookies also look adorable on dowel tree for kitchen decoration. Heart-shaped cookies make cute Valentines.

YIELD: ABOUT 70 COOKIES

Southern Sideboards
THE JUNIOR LEAGUE OF JACKSON, MISSISSIPPI

* * * * * * * * * * * * * * * * *

Meringues

6 large egg whites
2 cups sugar
¾ teaspoon baking powder
2 teaspoons fresh lemon juice
Almond extract or vanilla

Beat egg whites until dry. Add sugar slowly, then baking powder and lemon juice. Then add either almond extract or vanilla.

Shape on wax paper on cookie sheet. Preheat oven to 400°. Place meringues in oven, cut off heat entirely, and leave in unopened oven overnight.

YIELD: 12 COOKIES

Spartanburg Secrets II
THE JUNIOR LEAGUE OF SPARTANBURG, SOUTH CAROLINA

* * * * * * * * * * * * * * * * *

Creole Kisses

1 cup sugar
3 egg whites, stiffly beaten
1 teaspoon vanilla
1 cup chopped walnuts or pecans

Recipe continues . . .

Fold sugar gradually into beaten egg whites. Fold in vanilla and chopped nuts. Drop by spoonfuls onto foil-covered baking sheet. Bake 20–30 minutes at 350°.

YIELD: ABOUT 3 DOZEN

Talk About Good!

THE JUNIOR LEAGUE OF LAFAYETTE, LOUISIANA

· ·

Scotch Shortbread

2 sticks butter
½ cup confectioners' sugar
2 cups flour
⅛ teaspoon salt
¼ teaspoon baking powder
Additional confectioners' sugar

Cream butter and sugar. Sift together flour, salt, and baking powder. Mix all together into soft dough. Put in flat shortbread tube or cookie press and press out onto baking sheet. Or roll out ½ inch thick on floured board and cut out with cookie cutters. Bake at 325° for about 20 minutes, or until golden brown. Watch carefully, as they burn easily. While hot, remove from baking sheet and sprinkle with powdered sugar. Store in air-tight container.

YIELD: 6 DOZEN

Nashville Seasons

THE JUNIOR LEAGUE OF NASHVILLE, TENNESSEE

· ·

Oatmeal Lace Cookies

2¼ cups rolled oats
2¼ cups light brown sugar
3 tablespoons flour
½ teaspoon salt
½ pound butter
1 egg, slightly beaten
1 teaspoon vanilla

Put oats, sugar, flour, and salt into bowl and stir thoroughly. Melt butter; let it get quite hot but not bubble. Stir butter into oat mixture until sugar is melted. Add slightly beaten egg and vanilla, stir all together.

Drop very small amounts from teaspoon onto greased cookie sheet. Bake about 7 minutes at 375°.

YIELD: ABOUT 2 DOZEN

The Cotton Blossom Cookbook
THE JUNIOR LEAGUE OF ATLANTA, GEORGIA

. . . .

Sour Cream Oatmeal Cookies

1 cup butter or margarine
1½ cups sugar
2 cups uncooked old-fashioned oatmeal
1 teaspoon baking soda
1 cup sour cream
½ teaspoon baking powder
2 cups flour
2 teaspoons cinnamon
1 cup nuts, chopped
1 cup raisins, chopped

Recipe continues . . .

Mix ingredients in order given. Add a little more flour if dough is too soft. Drop onto greased cookie sheet and bake at 350° for 15–18 minutes.

YIELD: ABOUT 2 DOZEN

The Gasparilla Cookbook
THE JUNIOR LEAGUE OF TAMPA, FLORIDA

· · · · · · · · · ·

Oatmeal Molasses Cookies

1½ cups flour
1 teaspoon baking soda
½ teaspoon salt
½ teaspoon cloves
½ teaspoon ginger
1 cup sugar
¾ cup butter
1 egg
¼ cup dark molasses or pancake syrup
¾ cup quick-cooking oats

Sift together flour, soda, salt, cloves, ginger, and sugar. Add butter, egg, and molasses or syrup; beat until smooth, about 2 minutes. Stir in oats.

Drop by level tablespoonfuls, 2 inches apart, on ungreased cookie sheets. Bake in preheated 375° oven until browned, approximately 8–10 minutes. Let stand a minute or so before removing to wire racks to cool.

YIELD: 3 DOZEN

Cooking Through Rose Colored Glasses
THE JUNIOR LEAGUE OF TYLER, TEXAS

Stuffed Date Drops

1 pound dates
1 13-ounce can English walnut halves
¼ cup shortening
¾ cup brown sugar
1 egg
1¼ cups flour, sifted
½ teaspoon baking soda
½ teaspoon baking powder
¼ teaspoon salt
½ cup sour cream

Stuff dates with nut halves. Cream shortening. Beat with sugar until light. Add egg and beat again. Sift dry ingredients; add alternately with sour cream to creamed mixture. Stir in dates. Drop on greased cookie sheet (one date per cookie). Bake at 400° for 8–10 minutes. Cool and spread each cookie with icing.

YIELD: ABOUT 3 DOZEN

ICING:
¼ pound butter
3 cups confectioners' sugar, sifted
¾ teaspoon vanilla
3 tablespoons milk

Lightly brown butter. Remove from heat; gradually beat in sugar and vanilla. Slowly add about 3 tablespoons milk until icing is of spreading consistency.

Of Pots and Pipkins
THE JUNIOR LEAGUE OF ROANOKE VALLEY, VIRGINIA

. . . .

Mama's Pralines

3 cups sugar
1 cup buttermilk
1 teaspoon baking soda
½ stick butter
1 teaspoon vanilla
3 cups pecans

Put all ingredients except vanilla and pecans into a big pot and boil until mixture turns brown and forms soft ball in cold water.

Add vanilla and beat a little until creamy. Stir in pecans and drop by tablespoons on waxed paper.

YIELD: ABOUT 3 DOZEN

A Cook's Tour of Shreveport
THE JUNIOR LEAGUE OF SHREVEPORT, LOUISIANA

· · · · · · · · · · · · · · ·

Caramel Candy

2 cups sugar
2 cups heavy cream
2 cups chopped pecans
1¾ cups white corn syrup
1 stick butter
Pinch salt
1 teaspoon vanilla

Mix all ingredients together except salt and vanilla and cook in 4-quart boiler (or pot large enough to keep from boiling over) to firm ball stage (238° on candy thermometer). Add salt and vanilla.

Pour in buttered 9 × 12-inch pan and let cool. This will take a couple of hours.

When cool, cut into squares and wrap in wax paper. Will keep for several weeks.

YIELD: ABOUT 6 DOZEN

Southern Sideboards
THE JUNIOR LEAGUE OF JACKSON, MISSISSIPPI

.   .   .   .

Caramel Fudge

3 cups sugar
1 cup light cream
Scant ¼ stick butter or margarine
1 cup chopped pecans

In heavy saucepan, melt 1 cup of sugar to a light brown. At the same time, mix 2 cups sugar with cream and bring to a boil.

Pour cream mixture into caramelized sugar and cook to soft ball stage (238°). Remove from fire and add butter or margarine. Let stand without stirring about 15 minutes or until cool. Then stir until thick and creamy. Add nuts and pour onto buttered pan. When cool, cut into squares.

YIELD: 3–4 DOZEN

Recipe Jubilee
THE JUNIOR LEAGUE OF MOBILE, ALABAMA

.   .   .   .

Whiskey Pralines

2½ cups sugar
Lump of butter (approximately 1 ounce)
¼ cup white corn syrup
½ cup milk
Pinch baking soda
2 tablespoons whiskey
2 cups chopped pecans

Recipe continues . . .

Cook sugar, butter, syrup, milk, and soda very slowly until soft ball is formed. Add whiskey. Stir, but do not beat, until thick. Stir in pecans.

Drop by teaspoonfuls onto wax paper. Do not let mixture become too thick before dropping.

YIELD: 50

300 Years of Carolina Cooking
THE JUNIOR LEAGUE OF GREENVILLE, SOUTH CAROLINA

. . . .

Peanut Brittle

2 cups sugar
½ cup white corn syrup
½ cup warm water
2 cups raw peanuts
1 tablespoon butter
¼ teaspoon salt
1 teaspoon vanilla
1 tablespoon baking soda

Cook sugar, corn syrup, and water until syrup spins a thread. Stir in peanuts and cook until rich caramel in color. Add butter, salt, and vanilla. Stir and remove from fire. Add soda. Stir well and pour out onto buttered marble slab. When cool, break into pieces.

YIELD: ABOUT 2 POUNDS

That Something Special
THE JUNIOR LEAGUE OF DURHAM, NORTH CAROLINA

. . . .

Beverages

Hot Vegetable Punch

2 10½-ounce cans condensed beef consommé
2 cans water
5 cups tomato juice
6–8 stalks celery, chopped
2 small onions, sliced
1 small bay leaf
7–8 whole black peppercorns
Few carrot slices
Sprinkling of parsley
¼ lemon
Cinnamon sticks

Simmer condensed consommé, an equal amount of water, and tomato juice with celery, onions, bay leaf, peppercorns, carrot slices, and parsley. When vegetables are thoroughly cooked, squeeze ¼ lemon into pot.

Strain and serve in cups with cinnamon stick muddlers.

YIELD: 8 SERVINGS

That Something Special
THE JUNIOR LEAGUE OF DURHAM, NORTH CAROLINA

. . . .

Spiced Hot Cider

½ gallon cider
10 cloves
1 teaspoon whole allspice
1 stick cinnamon
1 teaspoon orange juice
¼ cup lemon juice

Heat together cider and spices. Strain.

Before serving, reheat and add orange and lemon juices.

YIELD: 2 QUARTS

Fun Foods
THE JUNIOR LEAGUE OF GREATER LAKELAND, FLORIDA

· · · · · · · · · · · · · ·

Cajun Coffee

3 cups strong black coffee
6 tablespoons molasses
1 cup heavy cream
Grated nutmeg
Dark rum (optional)

Mix coffee and molasses, stirring to dissolve. Heat to very hot, but not boiling.

Divide mixture among 6 cups or heat-proof glasses.

Whip cream and top each cup with a swirl. Sprinkle with nutmeg.

Sip coffee mixture through the cream. Do not stir coffee and cream together before drinking.

If desired, 1 tablespoon dark rum can be placed in each cup before filling with hot coffee mixture. To make coffee quickly, use 2 tablespoons freeze-dried coffee mix with 3 cups boiling water.

YIELD: 6 SERVINGS

Southern Accent
THE JUNIOR LEAGUE OF PINE BLUFF, ARKANSAS

· · · · · · · · · · · · ·

Russian Tea

1 quart water
4 tea bags
1 stick cinnamon
1 tablespoon whole cloves

Boil the above ingredients for four minutes. Strain into the following ingredients:

2 quarts water
1 6-ounce can frozen lemonade concentrate
1 6-ounce can frozen orange juice concentrate
1 16-ounce can pineapple juice
1½ cups sugar

Stir all together and heat again.

YIELD: 25 SERVINGS

Furniture City Feasts
THE JUNIOR LEAGUE OF HIGH POINT, NORTH CAROLINA

. . . .

Hot Spiced Percolator Punch

3 cups pineapple juice
3 cups water
1 tablespoon whole cloves
½ tablespoon whole allspice
3 sticks cinnamon, broken
¼ teaspoon salt
½ cup brown sugar, lightly packed

Put pineapple juice and water in bottom of an 8-cup percolator. Put the rest of the ingredients in the top. Perk for 10 minutes. Serve hot in mugs.

YIELD: 6 SERVINGS

Fiesta: Favorite Recipes of South Texas
THE JUNIOR LEAGUE OF CORPUS CHRISTI, TEXAS

· · · · · · · · · · · ·

Banana Punch

8 cups water
4 cups sugar
2 quarts pineapple juice
4 6-ounce cans frozen orange juice concentrate, diluted with
12 cans water
½ cup lemon juice
5 large bananas, puréed in blender
2 quarts ginger ale

Combine water and sugar. Boil 15 minutes and let cool. Add all other ingredients except ginger ale, mix thoroughly, and freeze.

Take out of freezer 2 hours before serving. Add ginger ale at serving time. No extra ice needed.

YIELD: 50 SERVINGS

The Blue Denim Gourmet
THE JUNIOR LEAGUE OF ODESSA, TEXAS

· · · · · · · · · · · ·

Orange Blossom Punch

3 cups sugar
3 cups water
6 cups grapefruit juice
6 cups orange juice
1½ cups lime juice
1½ quarts ginger ale

Combine sugar and water; stir until sugar is dissolved. Bring to a boil, let boil 5 minutes without stirring. Chill. Add juices and ginger ale and pour over ice.

YIELD: 50 SERVINGS

Fun Foods
THE JUNIOR LEAGUE OF GREATER LAKELAND, FLORIDA

. . . .

Coffee Frappé

1 gallon triple-strength coffee (3-ounce jar instant coffee)
5 gallons vanilla ice cream
1 quart heavy cream
2 cups sugar
Cinnamon

Make coffee and allow to cool.

Crush ice cream slightly with potato masher. Mix all ingredients except cinnamon and store in the refrigerator (not freezer) about 30 minutes before serving.

Serve in large punch bowl. Sprinkle with cinnamon.

YIELD: 100–150 SERVINGS

Fun Foods
THE JUNIOR LEAGUE OF GREATER LAKELAND, FLORIDA

. . . .

Delicious Iced Tea

3 pints water
3 teaspoons loose tea
Handful of mint
1¼ cups sugar
Juice of 3 lemons
Juice of 3 oranges

Combine water, tea, mint, and sugar; boil 1 minute. Remove from heat and leave covered 10 minutes. Strain.

Add lemon juice and orange juice. Serve over ice.

YIELD: 10–12 SERVINGS

Cooking Through Rose Colored Glasses
THE JUNIOR LEAGUE OF TYLER, TEXAS

. . . .

Iced Tea Punch

12 tea bags
2 quarts water
1 cup sugar
2 trays ice
1 6-ounce can frozen lemonade concentrate
1 6-ounce can frozen limeade concentrate

Steep tea in water for 4 minutes. Discard bags and stir in sugar. Add ice to chill quickly. Add lemonade and limeade. Chill until serving.

YIELD: 4 QUARTS

The Charlotte Cookbook
THE JUNIOR LEAGUE OF CHARLOTTE, NORTH CAROLINA

. . . .

Spiced Tomato Juice

1 quart tomato juice
1 teaspoon onion juice
1 teaspoon salt
½ teaspoon minced marjoram
½ teaspoon sweet basil
¼ teaspoon celery seed
¼ teaspoon freshly ground black pepper
1 clove garlic, crushed

Mix all ingredients together, shake well, and chill at least 4 hours, preferably overnight. Strain before serving.

YIELD: 1 QUART

Recipe Jubilee
THE JUNIOR LEAGUE OF MOBILE, ALABAMA

· · · · · · · · · · · · · · · · ·

Ping's Special—Peach Slush

½ overripe peach
1 heaping teaspoon sugar
2 jiggers whiskey (3 ounces)
Crushed ice

Mash together peach and sugar, add whiskey, and stir well. Fill glass with crushed ice.

YIELD: 1 LARGE DRINK (12–14 OUNCES)

The Gasparilla Cookbook
THE JUNIOR LEAGUE OF TAMPA, FLORIDA

· · · · · · · · · · · · · · · · ·

Margarita

1 slice lime
Coarse kosher salt
½ ounce fresh lime juice
1½ ounces tequila
½ ounce Triple Sec
3 or 4 ice cubes

Rub the inside rim of a chilled 4-ounce cocktail glass with the slice of lime. Pour salt into a saucer and dip the glass until a thin layer of salt adheres to the moistened rim. Combine the lime juice, tequila, Triple Sec, and ice cubes in a cocktail shaker. Shake well and strain into the salt-rimmed glass.

YIELD: 1 DRINK

Seasoned with Sun: Recipes from the Southwest
THE JUNIOR LEAGUE OF EL PASO, TEXAS

. . . .

Mary Ellen's Whiskey Sours

1 6-ounce can frozen lemonade concentrate
2 cans bourbon
2 cans soda water

Blend in blender undiluted lemonade with bourbon measured in the lemonade can. Use same can to measure soda water. Add soda water, stirring in by hand—otherwise you will have whiskey sour all over the kitchen. This is a good quick method and easy to fix at the last minute. Serve over crushed ice.

YIELD: 6 SERVINGS

300 Years of Carolina Cooking
THE JUNIOR LEAGUE OF GREENVILLE, SOUTH CAROLINA

. . . .

Frozen Lime Daiquiris

1 quart dry ginger ale
1 12-ounce can frozen lemonade concentrate
1 6-ounce can frozen limeade concentrate
12 ounces white rum
2 tablespoons grenadine syrup

Put all ingredients in freezer container. Stir well and freeze overnight. Daiquiris will be "slushy," not frozen solid, and can be kept in freezer indefinitely. No need to thaw before serving.

YIELD: 2 QUARTS

Winston-Salem's Heritage of Hospitality
THE JUNIOR LEAGUE OF WINSTON-SALEM, NORTH CAROLINA

Frozen Pink Daiquiris

3 boxes frozen strawberries
1 6-ounce can frozen limeade concentrate
2 6-ounce cans frozen lemonade concentrate
½ cup grenadine
⅘ quart light rum
Water

Whirl berries in blender, then add limeade and lemonade. Add grenadine and rum and enough water to make 1 gallon. Freeze. Freezes and keeps a limited time.

YIELD: 1 GALLON

Cooking Through Rose Colored Glasses
THE JUNIOR LEAGUE OF TYLER, TEXAS

"Skip and Go Barefoot"

1 tablespoon sugar syrup or grenadine
Juice of 1 lemon
2 jiggers gin or vodka (3 ounces)
Beer

Mix sugar syrup, lemon juice, and gin. Pour into Collins glass. Stir. Add ice and fill with beer.

YIELD: 1 DRINK

Of Pots and Pipkins
THE JUNIOR LEAGUE OF ROANOKE VALLEY, VIRGINIA

· · · · · · · · · · · ·

Mint Julep

Simple syrup or granulated sugar
12 or more tender mint leaves
Bourbon
Crushed ice
Water

For each julep place 1 tablespoon simple syrup (or sugar and water) in bottom of pitcher or punch bowl.

Add the tender mint leaves. Bruise the mint gently with a muddler and blend the ingredients by stirring and pressing gently for several minutes. (Do *not* crush the leaves, for this releases the bitter, inner juices.)

Pack the pitcher or punch bowl with crushed ice and add bourbon to cover. Stir with a long bar spoon and churn the contents up and down for a few minutes. Add more bourbon if necessary.

Pour mixture into individual silver julep cups or hi-ball glasses and place in refrigerator for 5–10 minutes to frost the glass.

To serve, insert long straws or silver sippers and garnish with a sprig

Recipe continues . . .

of mint. Always serve with a cocktail napkin around bottom of glass, as touching the glass with the hand will disturb the frost.

300 Years of Carolina Cooking
THE JUNIOR LEAGUE OF GREENVILLE, SOUTH CAROLINA

. . . .

Pink Lemonade Sauterne Cocktail

A watermelon-pink drink that is very refreshing in hot weather.

*2 6-ounce cans frozen pink lemonade concentrate (barely melted—
as frozen as possible)
1 can Sauterne
Crushed ice*

Pour lemonade and wine into electric blender, add crushed ice, and mix at high speed until the consistency of "slush." Pour into champagne glasses. You may vary the proportions according to how much wine you wish to use.

YIELD: **4–6** GLASSES

Furniture City Feasts
THE JUNIOR LEAGUE OF HIGH POINT, NORTH CAROLINA

. . . .

Sangrita

*1 46-ounce can tomato juice
2 cups orange juice
6 tablespoons lime juice
6 tablespoons Worcestershire sauce
Tabasco
2 teaspoons onion juice
Salt
Pepper
1 cup tequila*

Mix all ingredients and pour over a block of ice in a punch bowl. Serve as a before-lunch drink or with light brunch.

YIELD: 10 CUPS

Fiesta: Favorite Recipes of South Texas
THE JUNIOR LEAGUE OF CORPUS CHRISTI, TEXAS

·   ·   ·   ·   ·   ·   ·   ·   ·   ·   ·   ·   ·   ·   ·   ·   ·

Charleston Light Dragoon Punch

6 dozen oranges
6 dozen lemons
1 quart grenadine syrup
1 bottle curaçao syrup
1 quart raspberry syrup
¼ pound green tea leaves
1 quart bottle red cherries
1 quart can white cherries
1 quart can sliced pineapple
3 gallons rye whiskey
2 quarts light rum
Carbonated water

First secure an 8-gallon crock. Put in the juice of the oranges and lemons and stir thoroughly, reserving the rinds. Continue to stir and slowly pour in the grenadine, curaçao, and raspberry syrups, then the green tea, which is made as described below. Add red cherries, white cherries, and pineapple and their juices. Stir thoroughly and slowly add the rye whiskey and light rum. Bear in mind the necessity of constantly stirring, as this is the only way to blend the punch properly.

To make the tea: Boil the orange and lemon rinds in 2 quarts water, then steep the tea in the orange- and lemon-flavored water. Cool before using.

This punch stock (6¼ gallons) should be made at least 4 days before using and stirred from time to time. First serving should be 2 parts of punch

Recipe continues . . .

stock to 1 part carbonated water poured over ice. Then 1 part punch stock to 1 part carbonated water can be served.

YIELD: 300–350 SERVINGS

Charleston Receipts
THE JUNIOR LEAGUE OF CHARLESTON, SOUTH CAROLINA

·   ·   ·   ·   ·   ·   ·   ·   ·   ·   ·   ·   ·   ·   ·   ·   ·   ·

Clarence Moody's Holiday Punch

3 pieces fresh ginger root
1 3-inch stick cinnamon
8 whole cloves
3–4 cardamom seeds
6 lemons
6 small oranges
1 gallon apple cider
1 quart pineapple juice
½ teaspoon salt
Rum

Tie spices in a bag of fine cheesecloth.

Peel and cut the lemons and oranges into thin slices and add to the combined cider and pineapple juice.

To this mixture add the spice bag and bring to a very low simmering boil. Stir as it simmers for 15 minutes; then add the salt and stir vigorously.

Just before serving, add as much rum as desired. This is similar to the old English wassail-type punch.

YIELD: 40–50 SERVINGS

Party Potpourri
THE JUNIOR LEAGUE OF MEMPHIS, TENNESSEE

·   ·   ·   ·   ·   ·   ·   ·   ·   ·   ·   ·   ·   ·   ·   ·   ·   ·

Wassail

6 sticks cinnamon
16 whole cloves
1 teaspoon ground allspice
1 12-ounce or 2 6-ounce cans frozen apple juice concentrate,
diluted (6 cups)
2 cups cranberry juice
¼ cup sugar
1 teaspoon bitters
¼ cup rum (optional)

Tie spices together in cloth bag. Combine juices, sugar, and bitters. Simmer together 10 minutes and remove spice bag. Serve hot. May add rum before serving.

This can be made for a large group in a 30-cup electric percolator with the spices placed in the basket. Use the same amount of spices and multiply the recipe times four.

YIELD: 8 SERVINGS

Southern Sideboards
THE JUNIOR LEAGUE OF JACKSON, MISSISSIPPI

.   .   .   .

Tennessee Eggnog

6 eggs, separated
1 pound confectioners' sugar
1 pint bourbon whiskey
2 pints heavy cream
¼ pint dark rum

Separate eggs. Put egg whites in tightly sealed jar in refrigerator.

Beat egg yolks very lightly. Add to egg yolks alternate amounts of

Recipe continues . . .

sugar and whiskey, *very* slowly, and in very small quantity. Can use electric mixer at low speed.

Put this mixture in quart jar in refrigerator for 24 hours. When ready to serve, whip cream and add egg-yolk-and-whiskey mixture. Beat egg whites until stiff and add last.

The "trick" is to add the egg yolks very, very slowly . . . just a trickle. This keeps for some time, but at least 24 hours is required for whiskey to slowly "cook" egg yolks.

YIELD: 12 SERVINGS

Nashville Seasons
THE JUNIOR LEAGUE OF NASHVILLE, TENNESSEE

·　·　·　·　·　·　·　·　·　·　·　·　·　·　·

Virginia Eggnog

12 eggs, separated
1½ cups sugar, divided
⅘ quart whiskey
1 quart light cream
Jamaica rum to taste (about 6 ounces)
1 pint heavy cream

Use electric mixer or a very strong arm. Beat egg yolks until lemon-yellow. Beat in 1 cup sugar. Pour whiskey over egg yolks slowly with beater at slowest speed. Add light cream. Fold in egg whites that have been beaten stiff with ½ cup sugar. Add rum. Whip cream and add before serving.

This mixture will keep for quite a long time refrigerated but loses some of its volume.

YIELD: 1 GALLON

Of Pots and Pipkins
THE JUNIOR LEAGUE OF ROANOKE VALLEY, VIRGINIA

·　·　·　·　·　·　·　·　·　·　·　·　·　·

Kahlua

2 ounces instant coffee
4 cups sugar
2 cups water
1 vanilla bean, coarsely chopped
1 fifth brandy
1 fifth vodka

Bring all ingredients except liquor to a boil slowly, stirring occasionally. Remove from heat and cool. Add liquor.

YIELD: 2½ QUARTS

The Blue Denim Gourmet
THE JUNIOR LEAGUE OF ODESSA, TEXAS

Order Information

The recipes for *The Southern Junior League Cookbook* have been selected from the cookbooks published by the individual Junior Leagues. To obtain a particular League's own book of recipes, send a check or money order plus a complete return address to the appropriate address listed below. (Prices of all cookbooks subject to change.)

All proceeds from the sale of cookbooks will be used for charitable purposes.

The Cotton Blossom Cookbook, published by The Junior League of Atlanta, Inc., is out of print and not available for sale.

Charleston Receipts
The Junior League of Charleston
P.O. Box 177
Charleston, South Carolina 29402
Price per copy: $5.00
Postage per copy: 50¢
South Carolina residents add 20¢ sales tax per copy.
Make checks payable to: Charleston Receipts.

Mountain Measures
The Junior League of Charleston, West Virginia, Inc.
P.O. Box 1924
Charleston, West Virginia 25327
Price per copy: $4.95
Postage per copy: 50¢
West Virginia residents add 15¢ sales tax per book.
Make checks payable to: Mountain Measures.

The Charlotte Cookbook
The Junior League of Charlotte
1332 Maryland Avenue
Charlotte, North Carolina 28209
Price per copy (postage included): $5.00
North Carolina residents add 18¢ sales tax per book.
Make checks payable to: The Charlotte Cookbook.

Fiesta: Favorite Recipes of South Texas
The Junior League of Corpus Christi, Inc.
P.O. Box 837
Corpus Christi, Texas 78403
Price per copy: $7.95
Postage per copy: 60¢
Texas residents add 40¢ sales tax per book.
Make checks payable to: Fiesta Cookbook.

The Dallas Jr. League Cookbook
The Junior League of Dallas, Inc.
5500 Greenville Avenue, Suite 803
Dallas, Texas 75206

Price per copy: $8.95
Postage per copy: 75¢
Texas residents add 45¢ sales tax per copy.
Make checks payable to: Dallas Junior League Cookbook.

That Something Special
The Junior League of Durham, Inc.
900 South Duke Street
Durham, North Carolina 27707
Price per copy: $4.50
Postage per copy: 50¢
North Carolina residents add 18¢ sales tax per book.
Make checks payable to: The Junior League of Durham, Inc.

Seasoned with Sun: Recipes from the Southwest
The Junior League of El Paso, Inc.
520 Thunderbird
El Paso, Texas 79912
Price per copy: $6.00
Postage per copy: $1.00
Texas residents add 30¢ sales tax per book.
Make checks payable to: The Junior League of El Paso, Inc.

Gator Country Cooks
The Junior League of Gainesville, Florida, Inc.
P.O. Box 422
Gainesville, Florida 32602
Price per copy: $6.00
Postage per copy: 75¢
Florida residents add 24¢ sales tax per book.
Make checks payable to: Gator Country Cooks.

300 Years of Carolina Cooking
The Junior League of Greenville, Inc.
Box 8703, Station A
Greenville, South Carolina 29604
Price per copy: $5.95
Postage per copy: 50¢
South Carolina residents add 24¢ sales tax per book.
Make checks payable to: 300 Years of Carolina Cooking.

Furniture City Feasts
The Junior League of High Point, Inc.
P.O. Box 5217
High Point, North Carolina 27262
Price per copy: $5.95
Postage per copy: 50¢
Make checks payable to: Furniture City Feasts.

Huntsville Heritage Cookbook
The Junior League of Huntsville
P.O. Box 816
Huntsville, Alabama 35804
Price per copy: $6.00
Postage per copy: 55¢
Alabama residents add 36¢ sales tax per book.
Make checks payable to: Huntsville Heritage Cookbook.

Southern Sideboards
The Junior League of Jackson, Mississippi
P.O. Box 4805
Jackson, Mississippi 39216
Price per copy: $7.00
Postage per copy: 95¢
Make checks payable to: Junior League of Jackson, Mississippi.

Talk About Good!
The Junior League of Lafayette, Inc.
P.O. Box 52387
Lafayette, Louisiana 70505
Price per copy: $6.00
Postage per copy: 75¢ ($1.75 outside the U.S., Canada, and Mexico)
Make checks payable to: Junior League of Lafayette, Inc.

Fun Foods, published by The Junior League of Greater Lakeland, Inc., is out of print and not available for sale.

Little Rock Cooks
The Junior League of Little Rock, Inc.
P.O. Box 7421
Little Rock, Arkansas 72217
Price per copy: $5.00
Postage per copy: 50¢
Make checks payable to: Little Rock Cooks.

The Memphis Cook Book and *Party Potpourri*
The Junior League of Memphis, Inc.
2711 Union Avenue, Extended
Memphis, Tennessee 38112
Price per copy (postpaid):
    The Memphis Cook Book: $4.00
    Party Potpourri: $5.50
Tennessee residents add the following sales tax per book:
    The Memphis Cook Book: 23¢
    Party Potpourri: 30¢
Make checks payable to: The Memphis Cook Book and/or Party Potpourri.

Recipe Jubilee
The Junior League of Mobile, Inc.
350 Church Street
Mobile, Alabama 36602
Price per copy (postpaid): $7.00
Mobile County residents add 42¢ sales tax per book; other Alabama residents include 28¢ sales tax per book.
Make checks payable to: Recipe Jubilee.

Nashville Seasons and *Nashville Seasons Encore*
The Junior League of Nashville, Inc.
3850 Green Hills Village Drive
Nashville, Tennessee 37215
Price per copy:
    Nashville Seasons: $5.30
    Nashville Seasons Encore: $8.95
Postage per copy:
    Nashville Seasons: 35¢
    Nashville Seasons Encore: 75¢
Tennessee residents add 6% sales tax per book.
Make checks payable to: The Junior League of Nashville, Inc.

The Blue Denim Gourmet
The Junior League of Odessa, Inc.
P.O. Box 7273
Odessa, Texas 79760
Price per copy: $6.00
Postage per copy: 75¢
Texas residents add 30¢ sales tax per book.
Make checks payable to: The Junior League of Odessa, Inc.

Southern Accent
The Junior League of Pine Bluff, Inc.
P.O. Box 1693
Pine Bluff, Arkansas 71613
Price per copy: $7.95
Postage per copy: 75¢
Make checks payable to: Southern Accent.

Of Pots and Pipkins
The Junior League of Roanoke Valley, Virginia, Inc.
P.O. Box 8182
Roanoke, Virginia 24014
Price per copy: $4.95
Postage per copy: 30¢
Virginia residents add 20¢ sales tax per book.
Make checks payable to: The Junior League of Roanoke Valley, Virginia, Inc.

A Cook's Tour of Shreveport
The Junior League of Shreveport, Inc.
P.O. Box 5271
Shreveport, Louisiana 71105
Price per copy: $5.75
Postage per copy: 75¢
Louisiana residents add 29¢ sales tax per book.
Make checks payable to: A Cook's Tour of Shreveport.

Spartanburg Secrets II
The Junior League of Spartanburg, Inc.
Box 2764
Spartanburg, South Carolina 29302
Price per copy: $4.00
Postage per copy: 50¢
South Carolina residents add 16¢ sales tax per book.
Make checks payable to: Spartanburg Secrets.

The Gasparilla Cookbook and *A Taste of Tampa*
The Junior League of Tampa, Inc.
P.O. Box 10223
Tampa, Florida 33679
Price per copy:
   The Gasparilla Cookbook: $6.50
   A Taste of Tampa: $4.95
Postage per copy:
   * *The Gasparilla Cookbook*: 50¢
   A Taste of Tampa: 50¢
Florida residents add 4% sales tax per book.
Make checks payable to: The Gasparilla Cookbook and/or A Taste of Tampa.

Cooking Through Rose Colored Glasses
The Junior League of Tyler, Inc.
113 West Ferguson
Tyler, Texas 75702
Price per copy: $7.95
Postage per copy: $1.00
Texas residents add 40¢ sales tax per book.
Make checks payable to: The Junior League of Tyler, Inc.

Home Cookin'
The Junior League of Wichita Falls
#2 Eureka Circle
Wichita Falls, Texas 76308
Price per copy: $6.00
Postage per copy: $1.00
Texas residents add 30¢ sales tax per book.
Make checks payable to: Home Cookin'

Seafood Sorcery
The Junior League of Wilmington, North Carolina, Inc.
The Carriage House Cottage Lane
Wilmington, North Carolina 28401
Price per copy: $2.00
Postage per copy: 25¢
Make checks payable to: The Junior League of Wilmington, North Carolina, Inc.

Winston-Salem's Heritage of Hospitality
The Junior League of Winston-Salem
909 South Main Street
Winston-Salem, North Carolina 27101
Price per copy: $6.00
Postage per copy: 60¢
Make checks payable to: The Junior League of Winston-Salem.

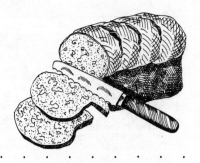

Index